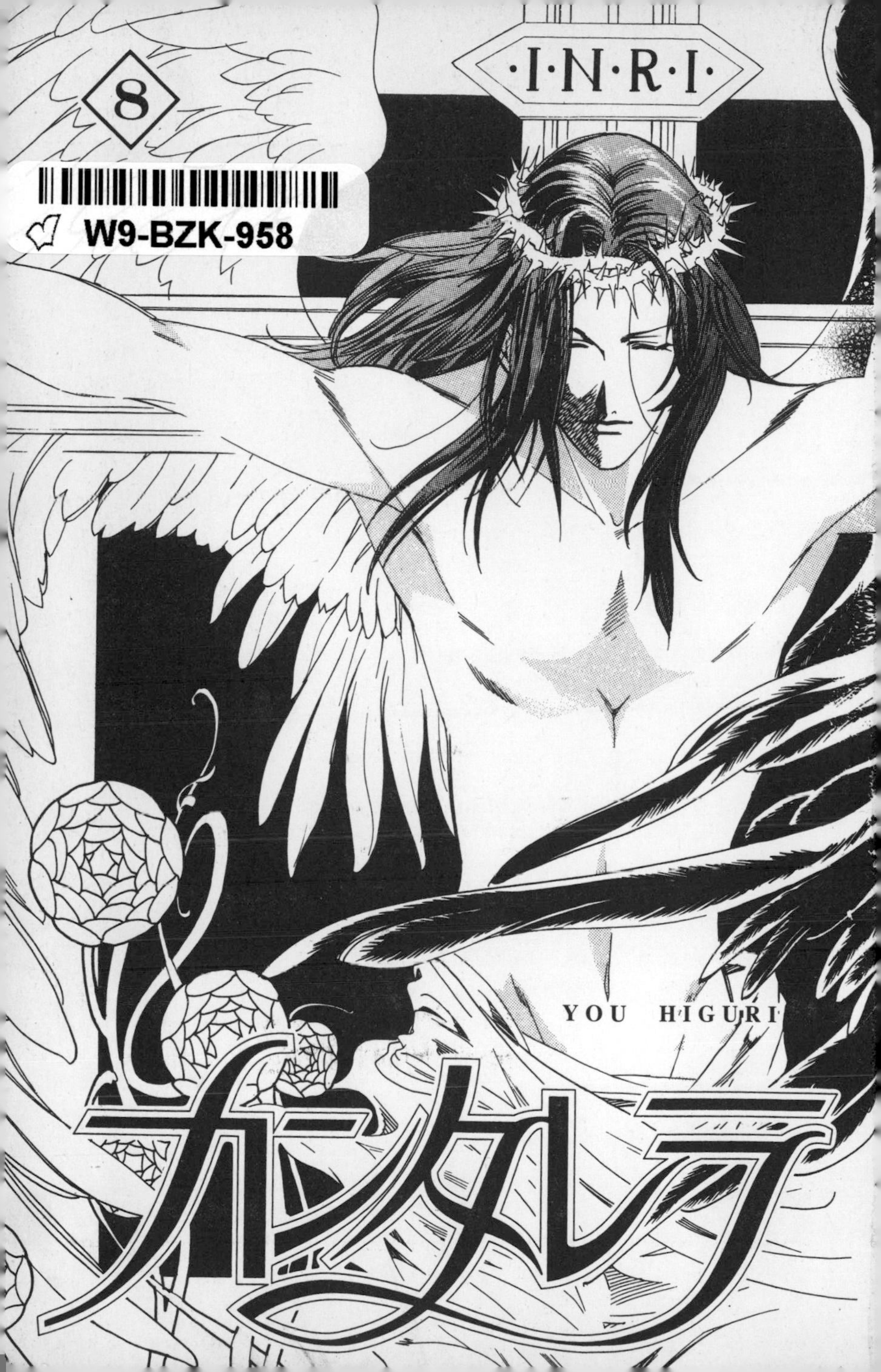
8
·I·N·R·I·
YOU HIGURI

Translation – Christine Schilling
Adaptation – Brynne Chandler
Editorial Assistant – Mallory Reaves
Lettering & Design– Fawn Lau
Production Manager – James Dashiell
Editor – Brynne Chandler

A Go! Comi manga

Published by Go! Media Entertainment, LLC

Cantarella Volume 8
© YOU HIGURI 2004
Originally published in Japan in 2004 by Akita Publishing Co., Ltd., Tokyo.
English translation rights arranged with Akita Publishing Co., Ltd.
through TOHAN CORPORATION, Tokyo.

Visit us online at www.gocomi.com
e-mail: info@gocomi.com

ISBN 978-1-933617-30-5

First printed in September 2007

1 2 3 4 5 6 7 8 9

Manufactured in the United States of America

Cantarella

STORY AND ART BY
YOU HIGURI

VOLUME 8

go!comi

Cantarella 8

OUR STORY SO FAR AND INTRODUCTION OF CHARACTERS

Chiaro suffers over betraying Cesare by secretly loving his sister, Lucrezia. When Cesare discovers their love, Lucrezia is put under house arrest and Chiaro is commanded to return to Rome. When Il Perotto, under the influence of the evil forces, attacks Lucrezia, Chiaro shows up for a farewell visit only to be saved by her in the nick of time. Unable to bear being parted, the two flee to Rome. Betrayed and abandoned by Chiaro and Lucrezia – the two people he loves most – Cesare is helpless as the demon within him grows even stronger...

TABLE OF CONTENTS

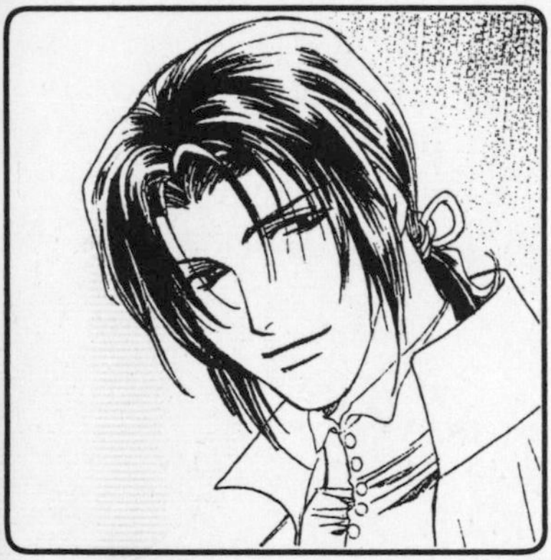

CESARE BORGIA

The hero of our story. His soul was sold to the devil, and though he lives a harsh fate, he is a driven man with an unstoppable will to follow his dream of unifying Italy.

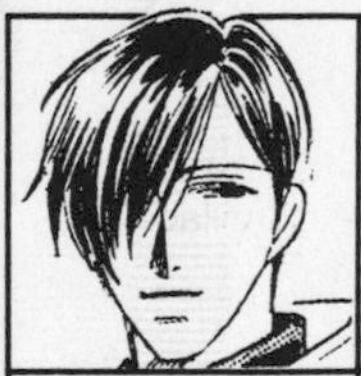	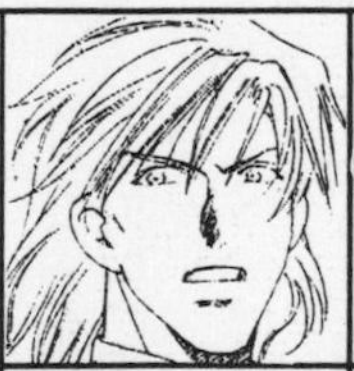	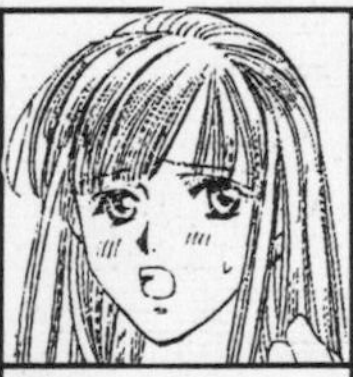	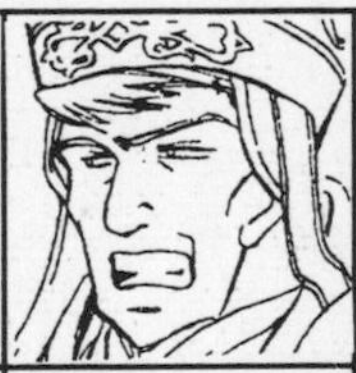	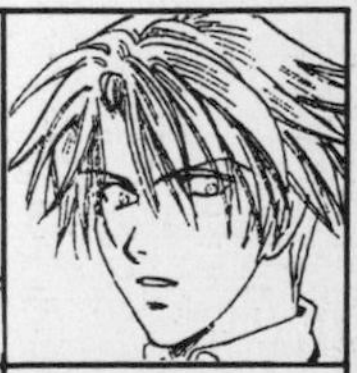
ALFONSO D'ARAGON	DELLA VOLPE	LUCREZIA BORGIA	POPE ALEXANDER VI	MICHELOTTO (CHIARO)
The younger brother of Sancia, who was wed to the youngest son of the Borgia family. He's been chosen to be Lucrezia's next husband.	Cesare's loyal retainer, who looks up to Cesare for his tyrannical nature. He is antagonistic toward Chiaro...	She used to suffer from her forbidden love for her own brother, Cesare, but now is bound heart, body and soul to Chiaro...	An ambitious man who sold his own son Cesare's soul to the devil in exchange for the Papal throne.	A legendary assassin who wears the mask of "Michelotto". His passionate affair with Lucrezia has estranged him from Cesare.

Various cities and territories of Italy during *Cantarella* period

(end of the 15th century)

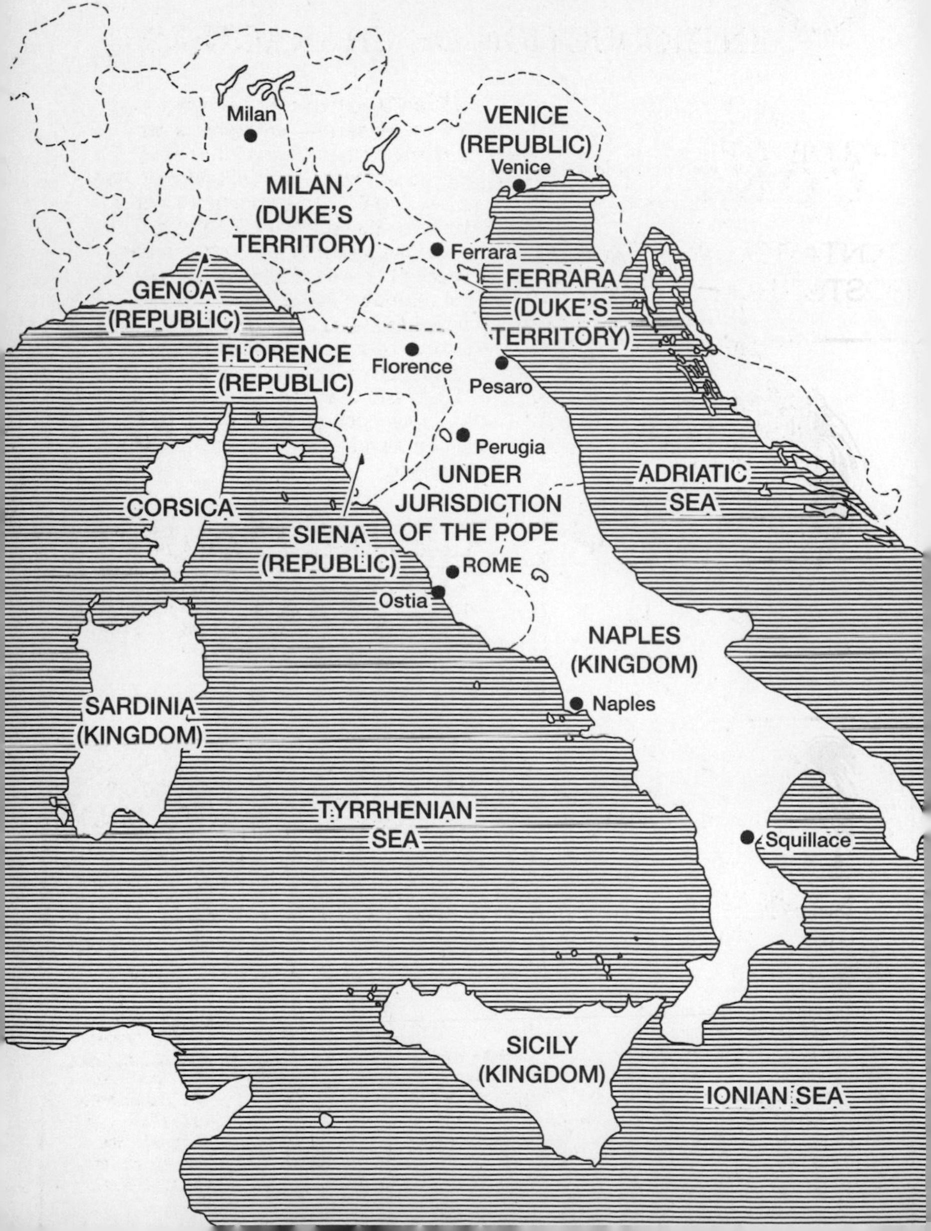

Milan
VENICE (REPUBLIC)
Venice
MILAN (DUKE'S TERRITORY)
Ferrara
GENOA (REPUBLIC)
FERRARA (DUKE'S TERRITORY)
FLORENCE (REPUBLIC)
Florence
Pesaro
Perugia
UNDER JURISDICTION OF THE POPE
ADRIATIC SEA
CORSICA
SIENA (REPUBLIC)
ROME
Ostia
NAPLES (KINGDOM)
Naples
SARDINIA (KINGDOM)
TYRRHENIAN SEA
Squillace
SICILY (KINGDOM)
IONIAN SEA

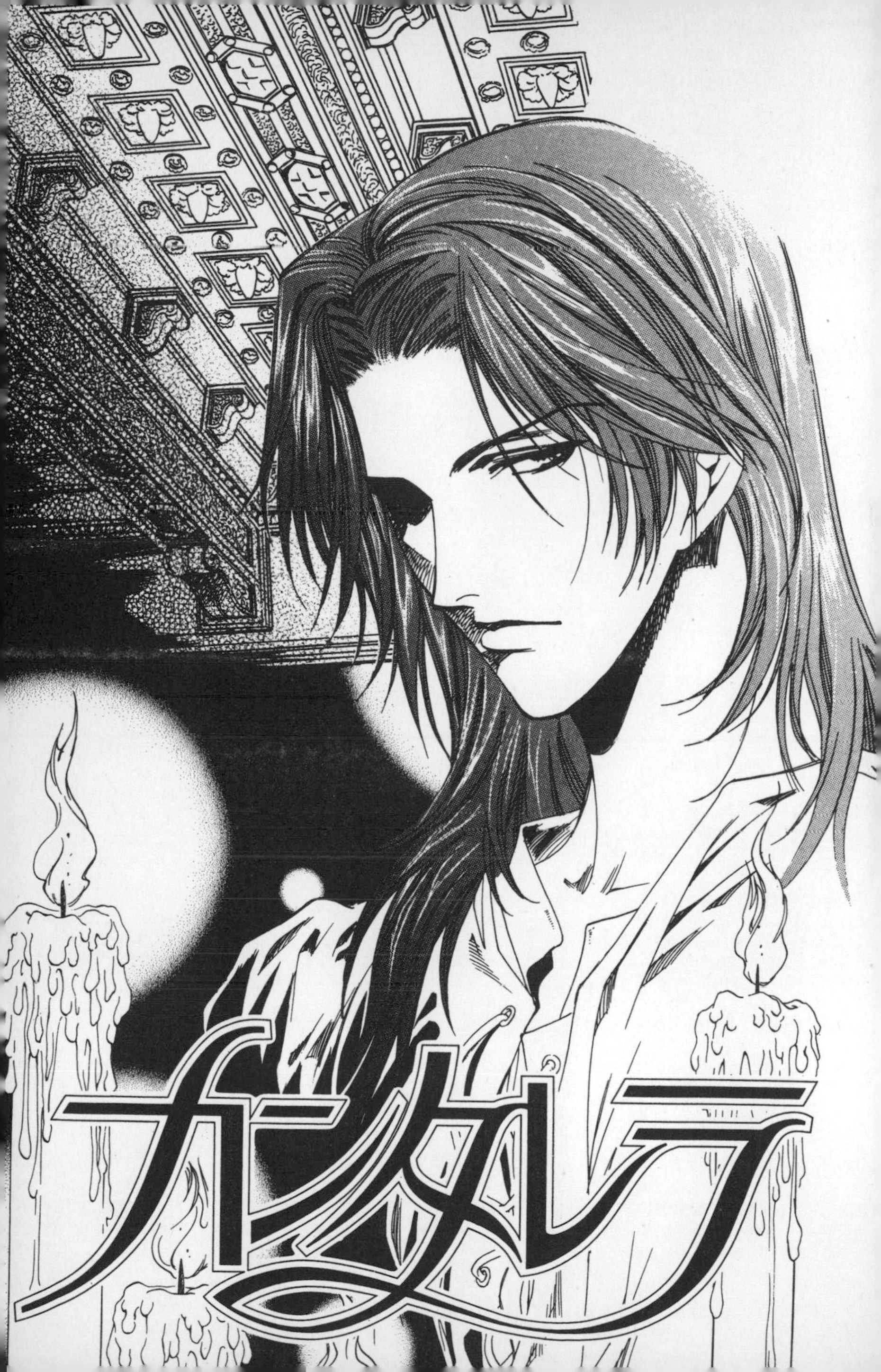

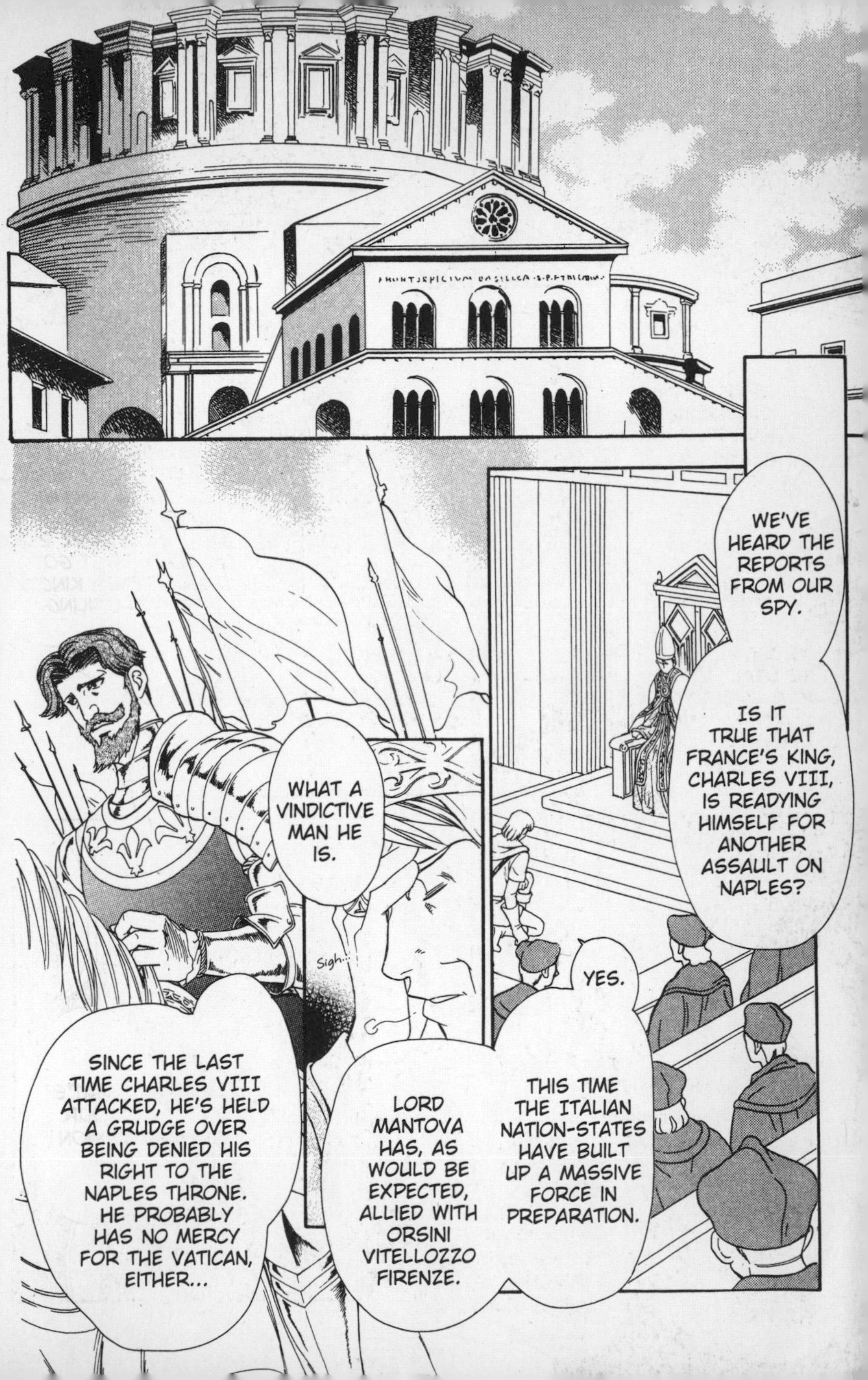
WE'VE HEARD THE REPORTS FROM OUR SPY.
IS IT TRUE THAT FRANCE'S KING, CHARLES VIII, IS READYING HIMSELF FOR ANOTHER ASSAULT ON NAPLES?
YES.
THIS TIME THE ITALIAN NATION-STATES HAVE BUILT UP A MASSIVE FORCE IN PREPARATION.
WHAT A VINDICTIVE MAN HE IS.
Sigh...
LORD MANTOVA HAS, AS WOULD BE EXPECTED, ALLIED WITH ORSINI VITELLOZZO FIRENZE.
SINCE THE LAST TIME CHARLES VIII ATTACKED, HE'S HELD A GRUDGE OVER BEING DENIED HIS RIGHT TO THE NAPLES THRONE. HE PROBABLY HAS NO MERCY FOR THE VATICAN, EITHER...

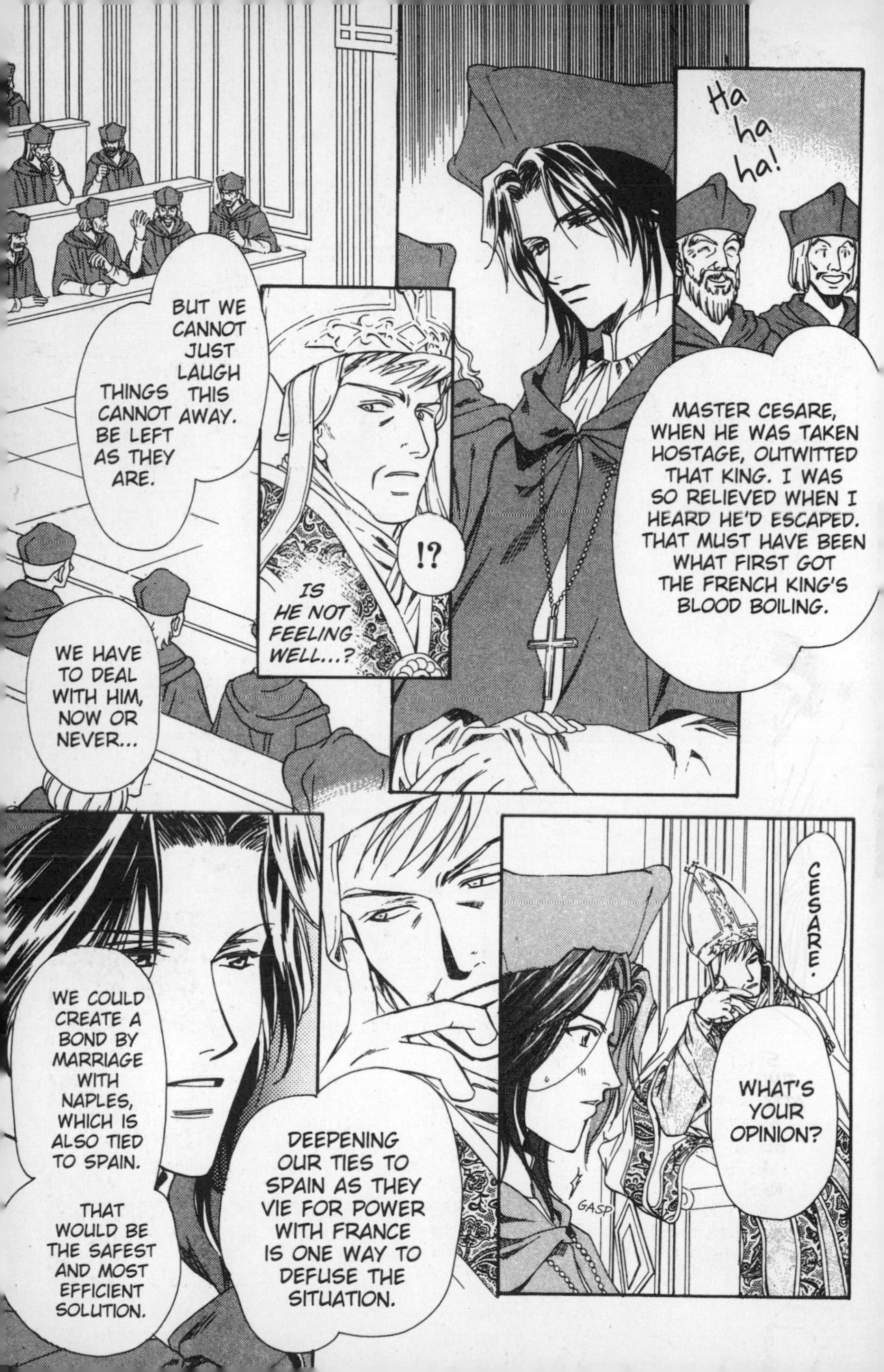
Ha ha ha!
MASTER CESARE, WHEN HE WAS TAKEN HOSTAGE, OUTWITTED THAT KING. I WAS SO RELIEVED WHEN I HEARD HE'D ESCAPED. THAT MUST HAVE BEEN WHAT FIRST GOT THE FRENCH KING'S BLOOD BOILING.
!?
IS HE NOT FEELING WELL...?
BUT WE CANNOT JUST LAUGH THIS AWAY.
THINGS CANNOT BE LEFT AS THEY ARE.
WE HAVE TO DEAL WITH HIM, NOW OR NEVER...
CESARE.
WHAT'S YOUR OPINION?
GASP
DEEPENING OUR TIES TO SPAIN AS THEY VIE FOR POWER WITH FRANCE IS ONE WAY TO DEFUSE THE SITUATION.
WE COULD CREATE A BOND BY MARRIAGE WITH NAPLES, WHICH IS ALSO TIED TO SPAIN.
THAT WOULD BE THE SAFEST AND MOST EFFICIENT SOLUTION.

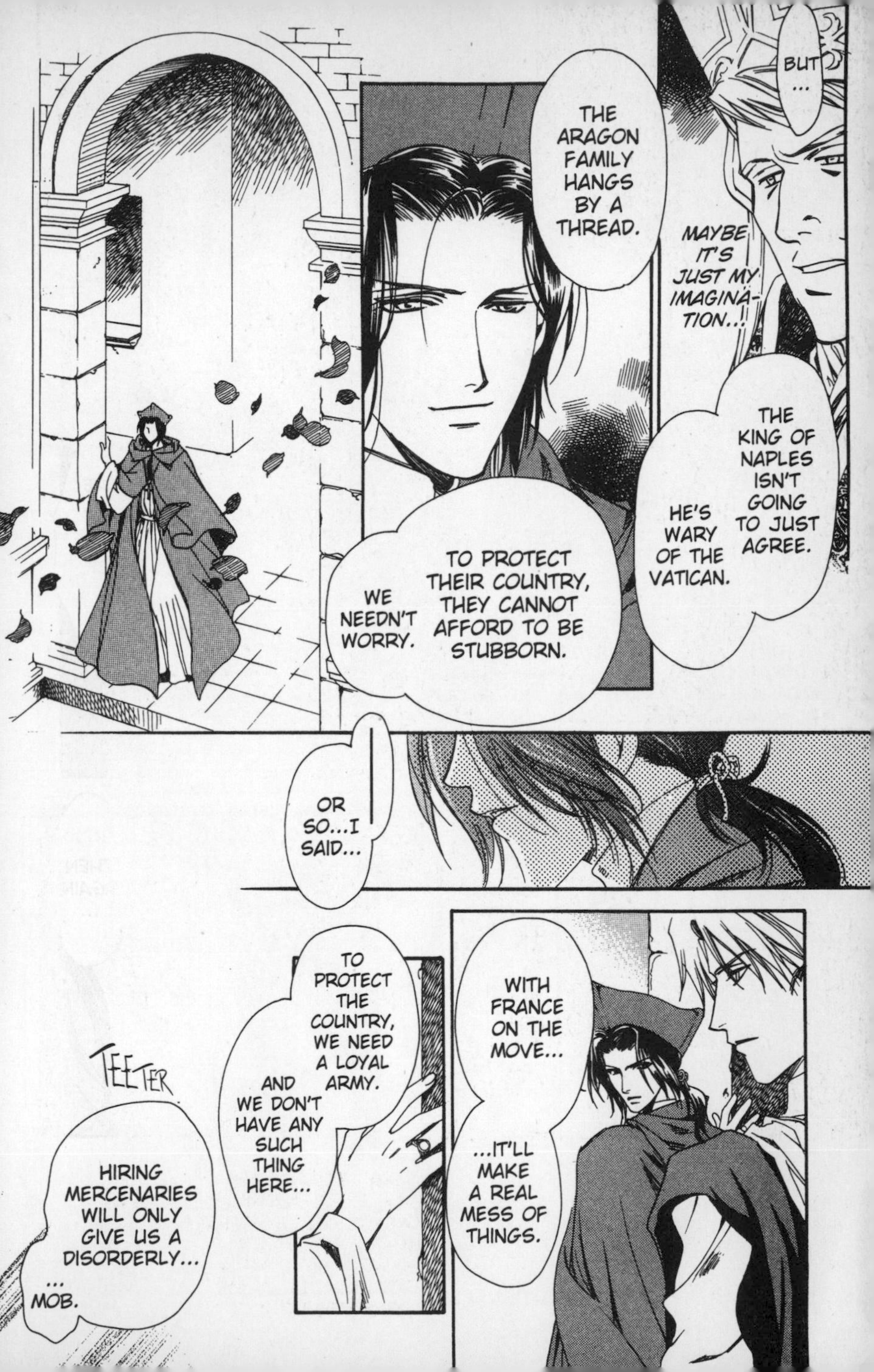
BUT ...
MAYBE IT'S JUST MY IMAGINATION...!
THE ARAGON FAMILY HANGS BY A THREAD.
THE KING OF NAPLES ISN'T GOING TO JUST AGREE.
HE'S WARY OF THE VATICAN.
TO PROTECT THEIR COUNTRY, THEY CANNOT AFFORD TO BE STUBBORN.
WE NEEDN'T WORRY.
OR SO...I SAID...
WITH FRANCE ON THE MOVE...
...IT'LL MAKE A REAL MESS OF THINGS.
TO PROTECT THE COUNTRY, WE NEED A LOYAL ARMY.
AND WE DON'T HAVE ANY SUCH THING HERE...
TEETER
HIRING MERCENARIES WILL ONLY GIVE US A DISORDERLY...
... MOB.

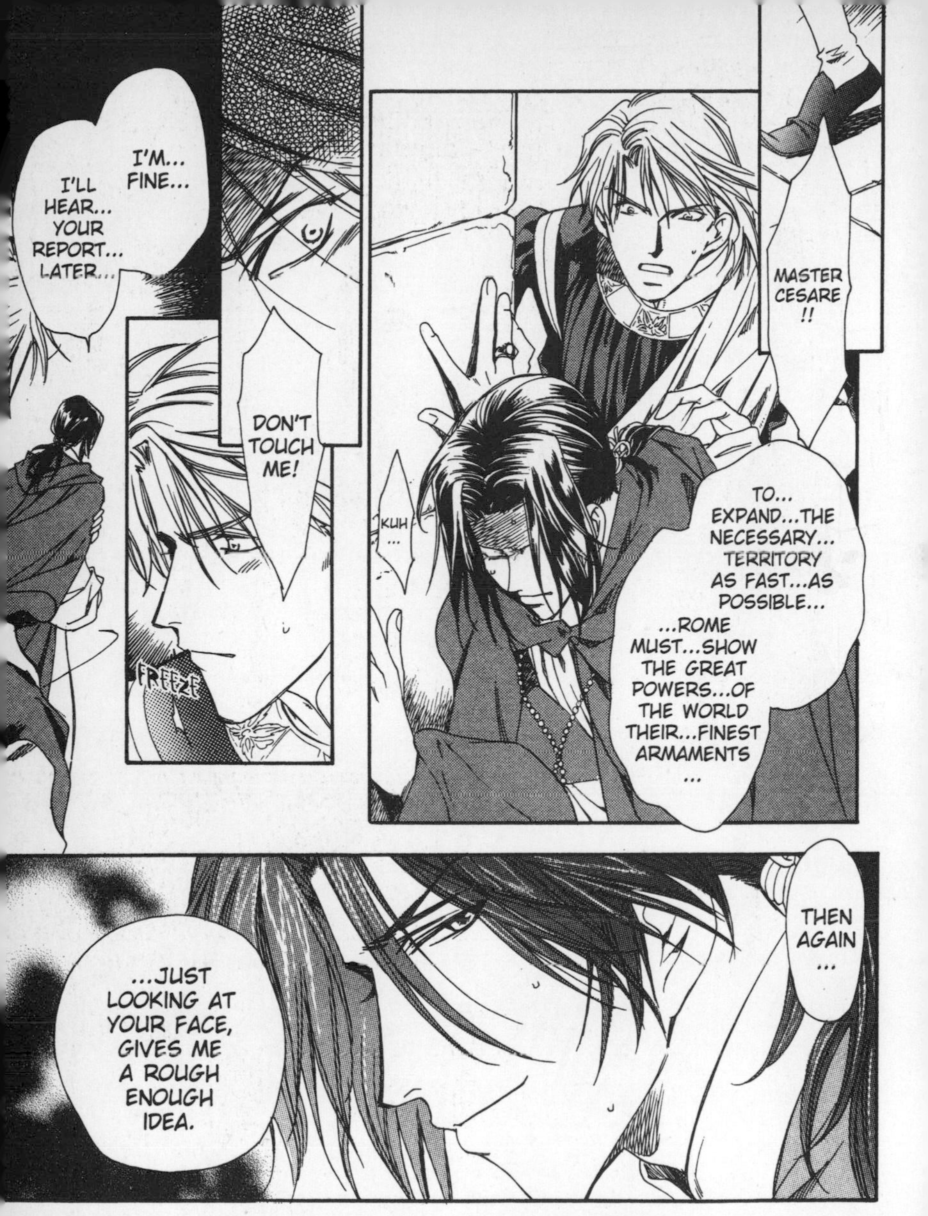
MASTER CESARE !!
TO... EXPAND...THE NECESSARY... TERRITORY AS FAST...AS POSSIBLE...
...ROME MUST...SHOW THE GREAT POWERS...OF THE WORLD THEIR...FINEST ARMAMENTS ...
KUH ...
DON'T TOUCH ME!
I'M... FINE...
I'LL HEAR... YOUR REPORT... LATER...
FREEZE
THEN AGAIN ...
...JUST LOOKING AT YOUR FACE, GIVES ME A ROUGH ENOUGH IDEA.

THAT COOL AND CONFIDENT FACE YOU WEAR BEFORE OTHERS IS A MASK. ONLY I, WHO HAVE SEEN YOUR SUFFERING ALL ALONG, SEE BEHIND IT.

IN REALITY, YOU CANNOT EVEN STAND ON YOUR OWN!

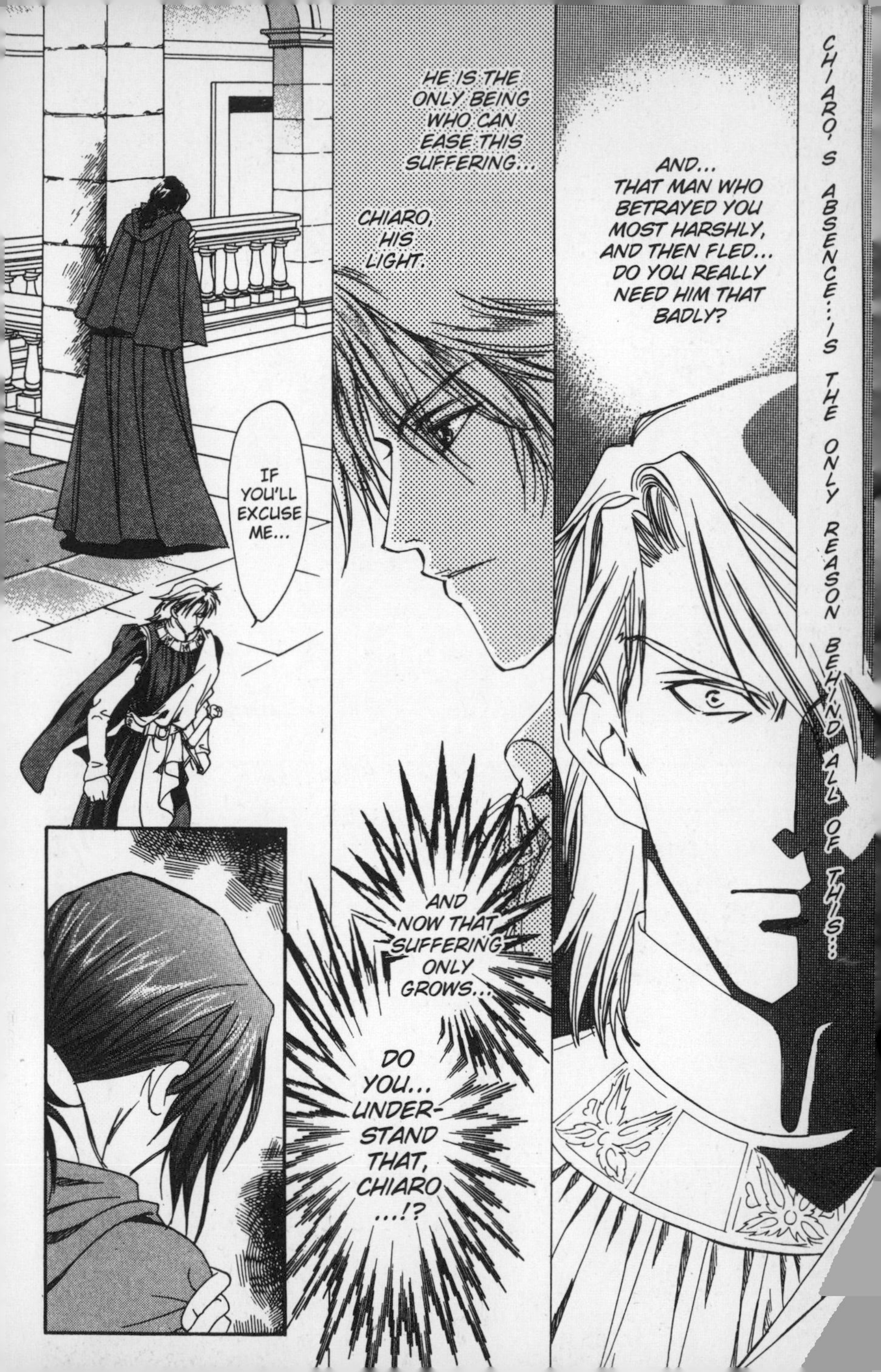
CHIARO'S ABSENCE...IS THE ONLY REASON BEHIND ALL OF THIS...
AND... THAT MAN WHO BETRAYED YOU MOST HARSHLY, AND THEN FLED... DO YOU REALLY NEED HIM THAT BADLY?
HE IS THE ONLY BEING WHO CAN EASE THIS SUFFERING...
CHIARO, HIS LIGHT.
AND NOW THAT SUFFERING ONLY GROWS...
DO YOU... UNDER-STAND THAT, CHIARO ...!?
IF YOU'LL EXCUSE ME...

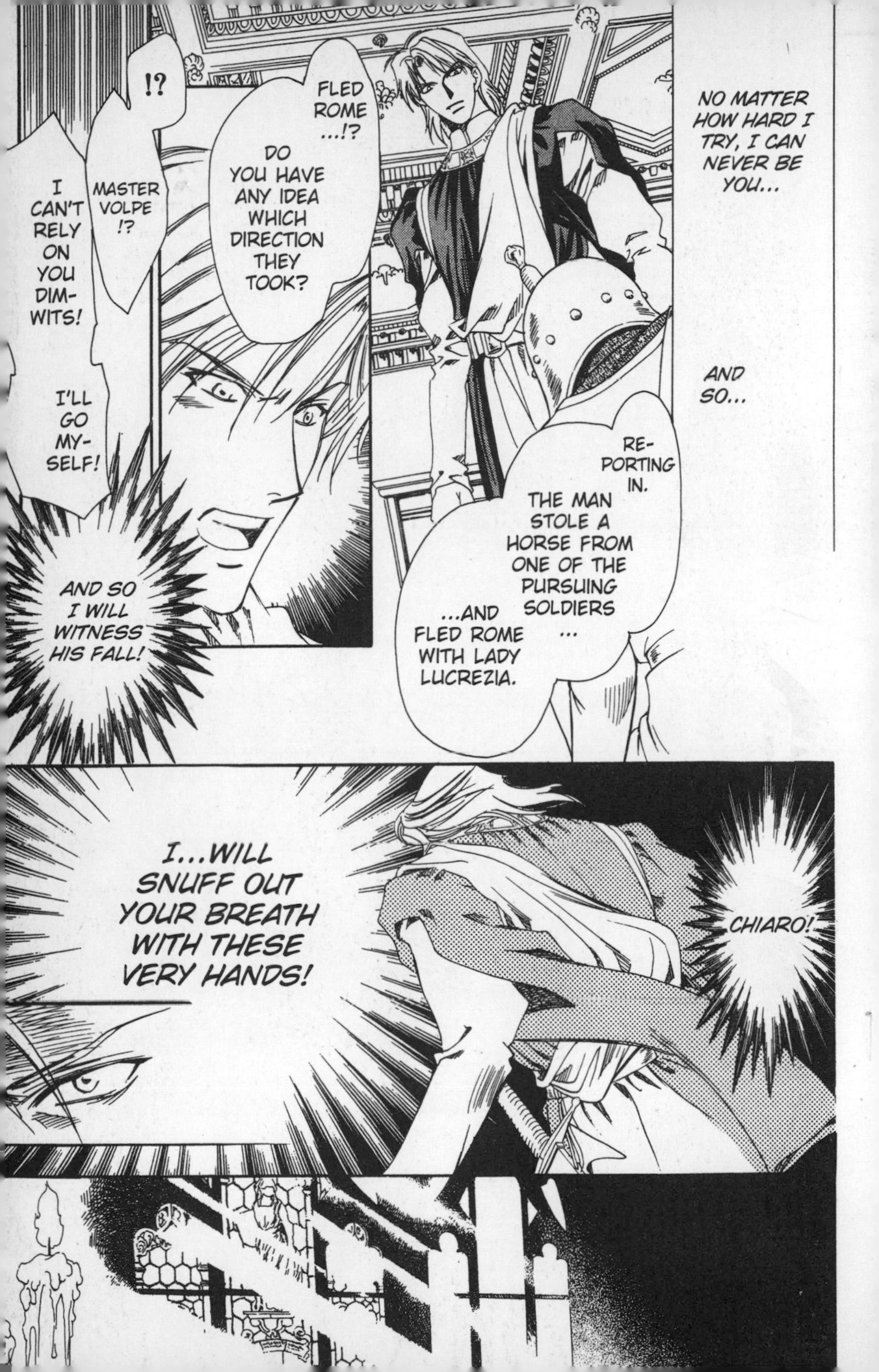
NO MATTER HOW HARD I TRY, I CAN NEVER BE YOU...
AND SO...
REPORTING IN.
THE MAN STOLE A HORSE FROM ONE OF THE PURSUING SOLDIERS...
...AND FLED ROME WITH LADY LUCREZIA.
FLED ROME ...!?
DO YOU HAVE ANY IDEA WHICH DIRECTION THEY TOOK?
!?
MASTER VOLPE !?
I CAN'T RELY ON YOU DIM-WITS!
I'LL GO MY-SELF!
AND SO I WILL WITNESS HIS FALL!
CHIARO!
I...WILL SNUFF OUT YOUR BREATH WITH THESE VERY HANDS!

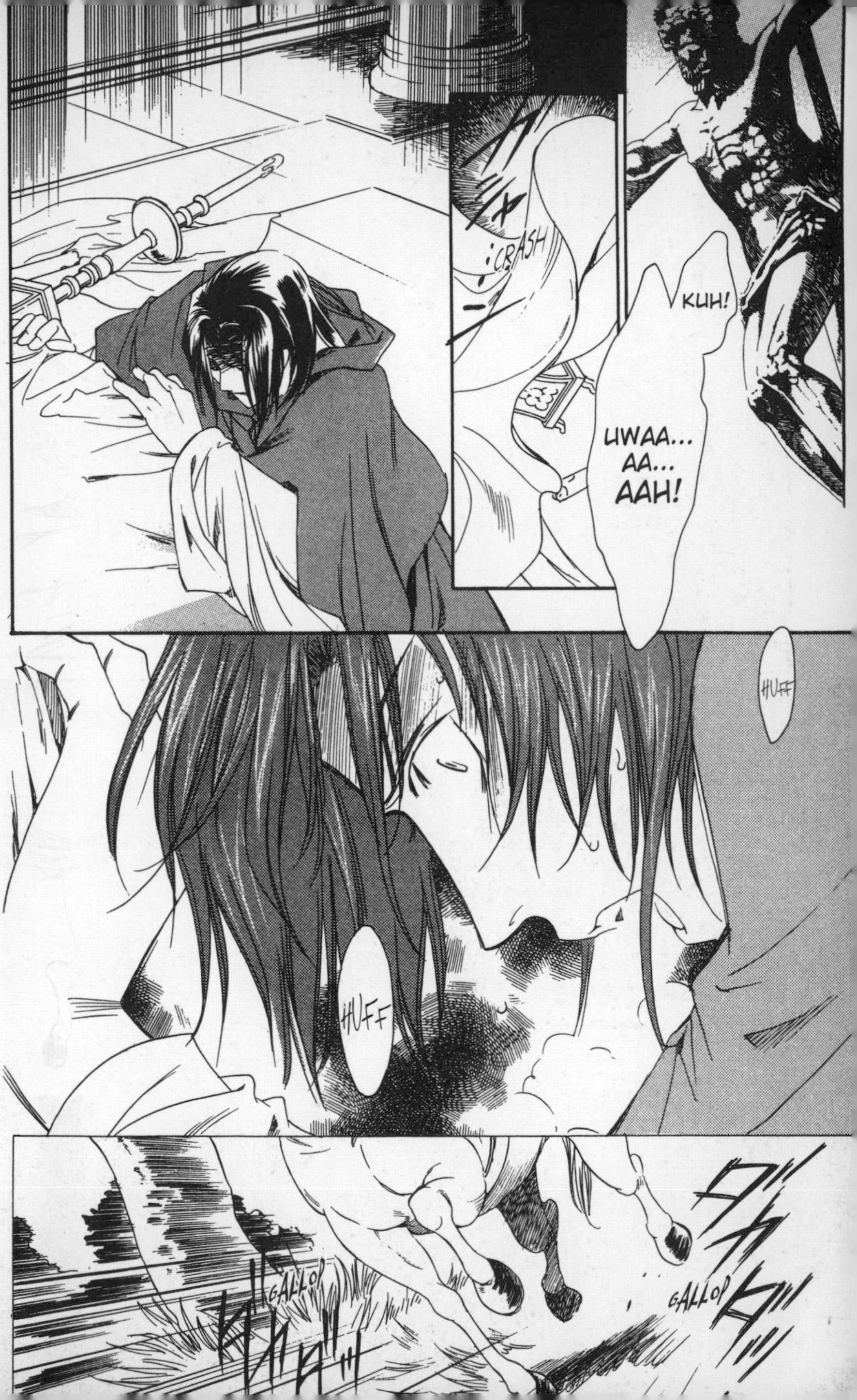
KUH!
UWAA... AA... AAH!
CRASH
HUFF
HUFF
GALLOP
GALLOP

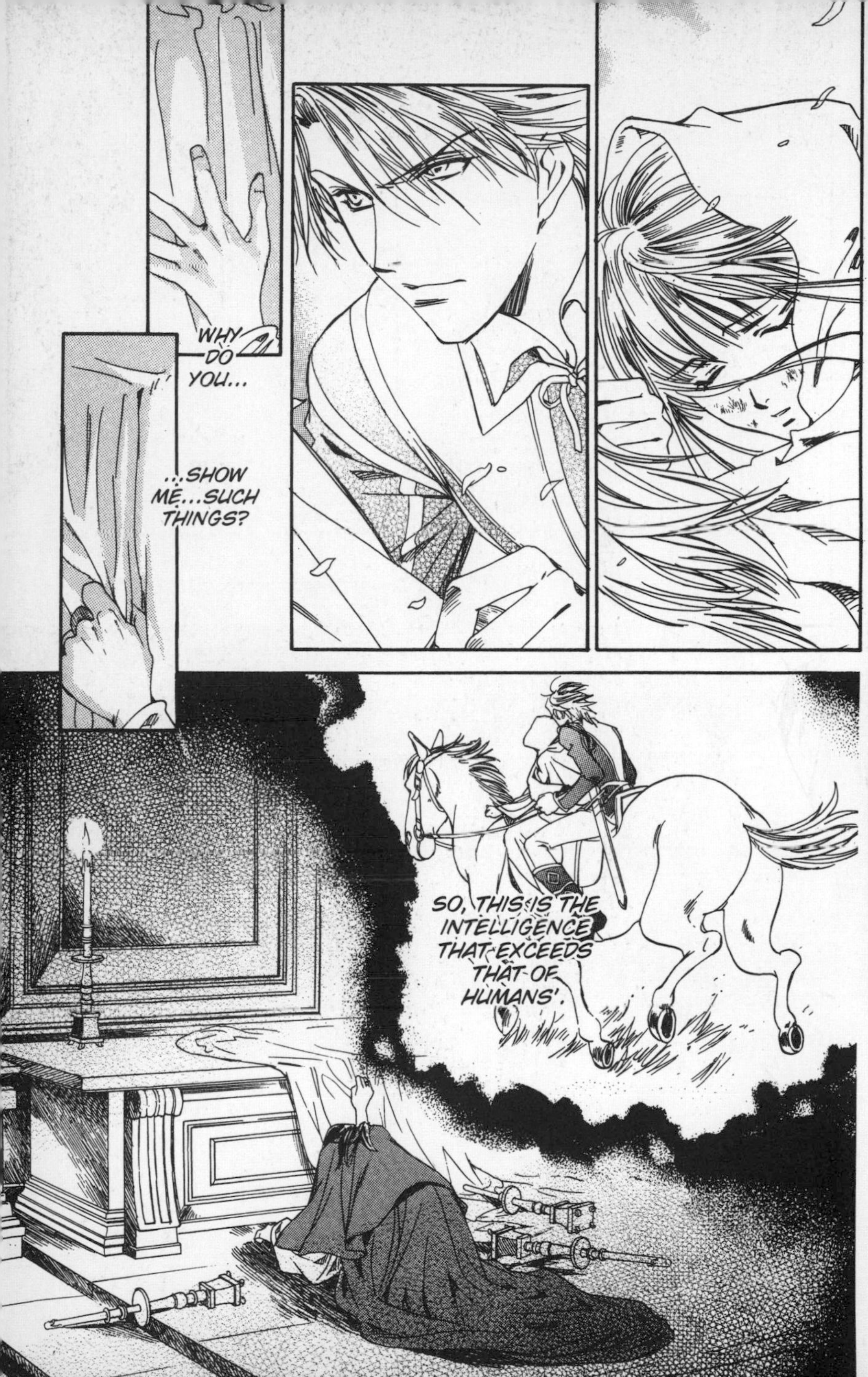
WHY DO YOU...
...SHOW ME...SUCH THINGS?
SO, THIS IS THE INTELLIGENCE THAT EXCEEDS THAT OF HUMANS'.

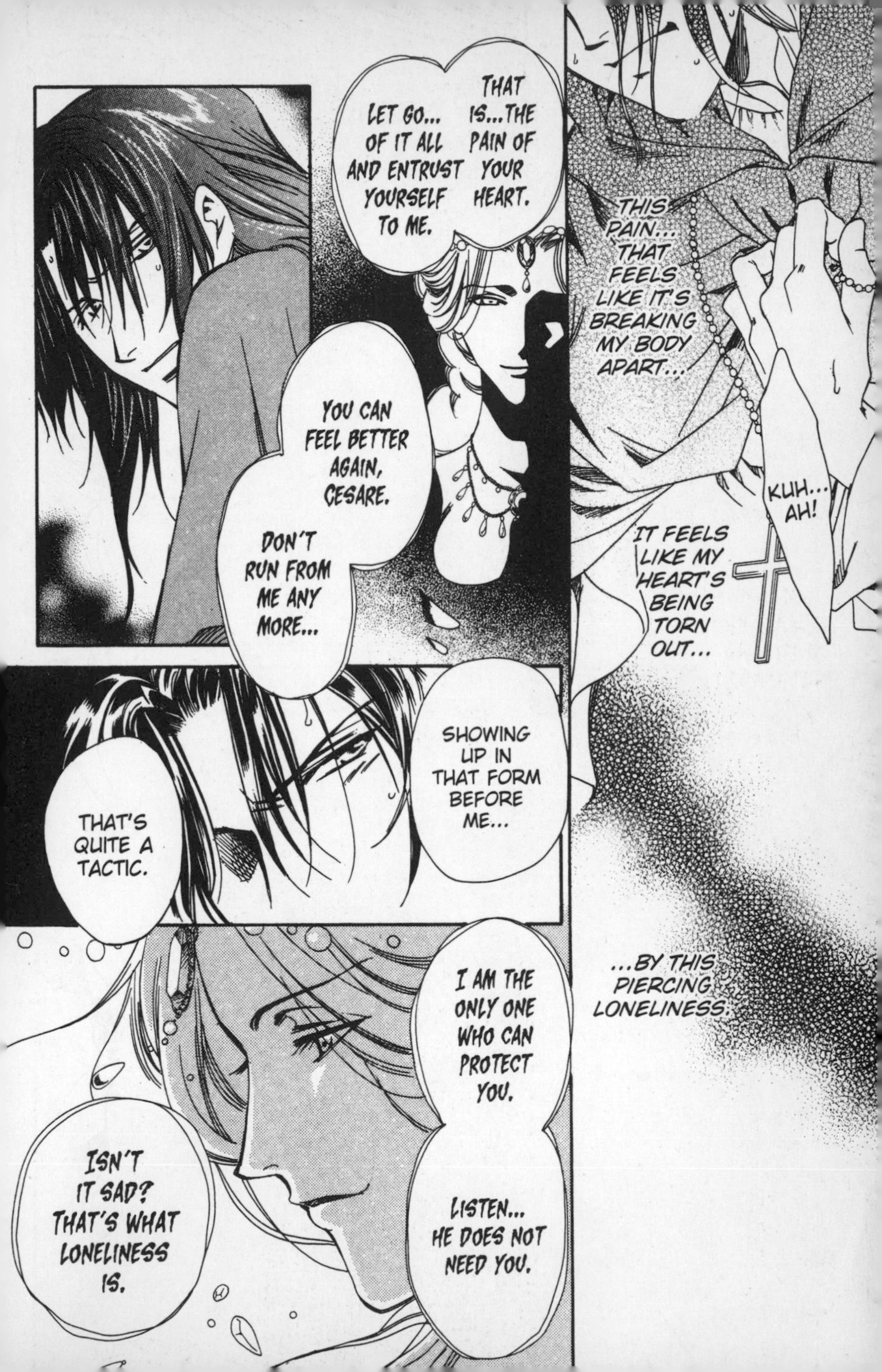
THIS PAIN... THAT FEELS LIKE IT'S BREAKING MY BODY APART...
KUH... AH!
IT FEELS LIKE MY HEART'S BEING TORN OUT...
...BY THIS PIERCING LONELINESS.
THAT IS...THE PAIN OF YOUR HEART.
LET GO... OF IT ALL AND ENTRUST YOURSELF TO ME.
YOU CAN FEEL BETTER AGAIN, CESARE.
DON'T RUN FROM ME ANY MORE...
SHOWING UP IN THAT FORM BEFORE ME...
THAT'S QUITE A TACTIC.
I AM THE ONLY ONE WHO CAN PROTECT YOU.
LISTEN... HE DOES NOT NEED YOU.
ISN'T IT SAD? THAT'S WHAT LONELINESS IS.

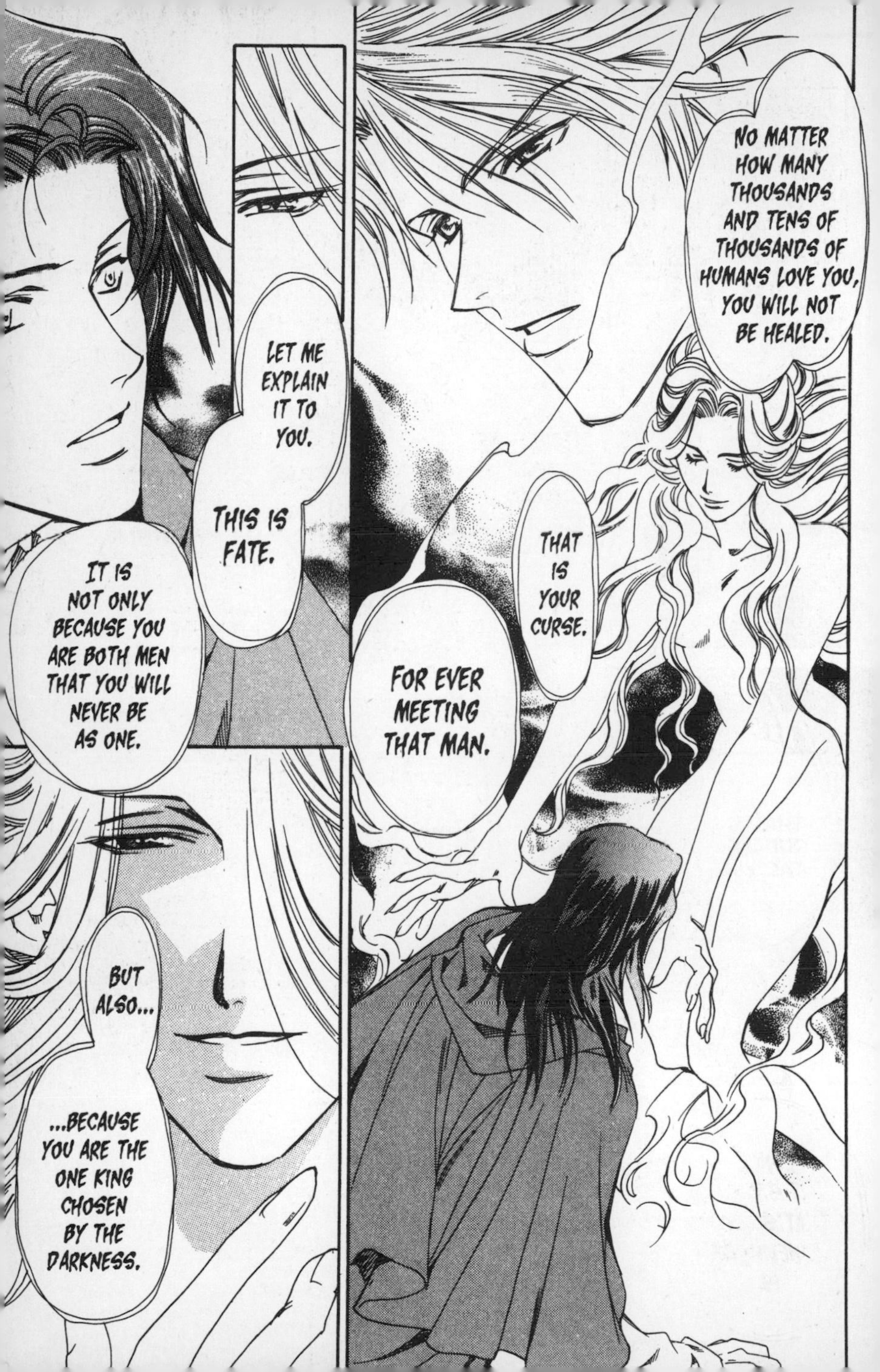
NO MATTER HOW MANY THOUSANDS AND TENS OF THOUSANDS OF HUMANS LOVE YOU, YOU WILL NOT BE HEALED.
THAT IS YOUR CURSE.
FOR EVER MEETING THAT MAN.
LET ME EXPLAIN IT TO YOU.
THIS IS FATE.
IT IS NOT ONLY BECAUSE YOU ARE BOTH MEN THAT YOU WILL NEVER BE AS ONE.
BUT ALSO...
...BECAUSE YOU ARE THE ONE KING CHOSEN BY THE DARKNESS.

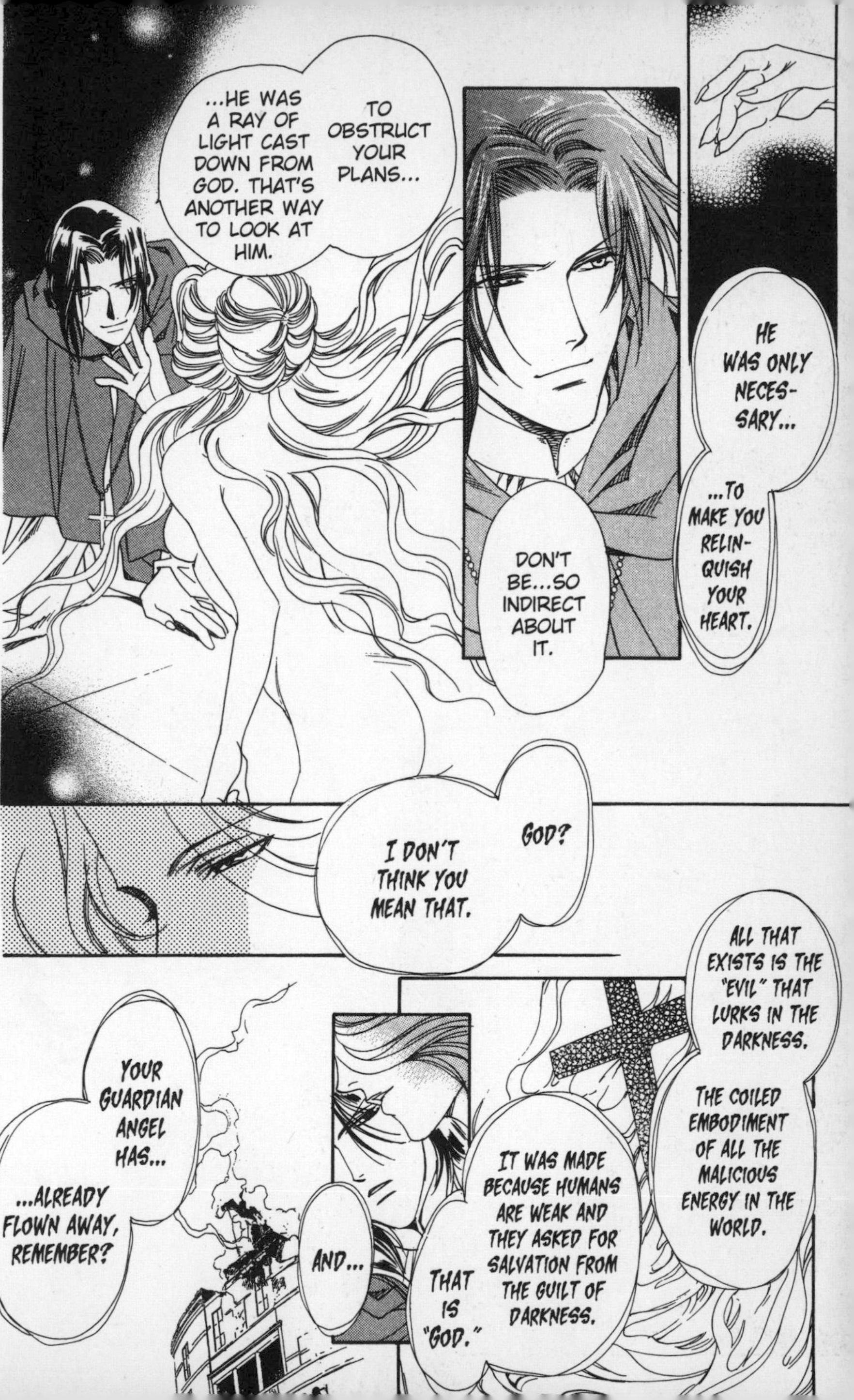
HE WAS ONLY NECESSARY...
...TO MAKE YOU RELINQUISH YOUR HEART.
DON'T BE...SO INDIRECT ABOUT IT.
TO OBSTRUCT YOUR PLANS...
...HE WAS A RAY OF LIGHT CAST DOWN FROM GOD. THAT'S ANOTHER WAY TO LOOK AT HIM.
GOD?
I DON'T THINK YOU MEAN THAT.
ALL THAT EXISTS IS THE "EVIL" THAT LURKS IN THE DARKNESS.
THE COILED EMBODIMENT OF ALL THE MALICIOUS ENERGY IN THE WORLD.
IT WAS MADE BECAUSE HUMANS ARE WEAK AND THEY ASKED FOR SALVATION FROM THE GUILT OF DARKNESS.
THAT IS "GOD."
AND...
YOUR GUARDIAN ANGEL HAS...
...ALREADY FLOWN AWAY, REMEMBER?

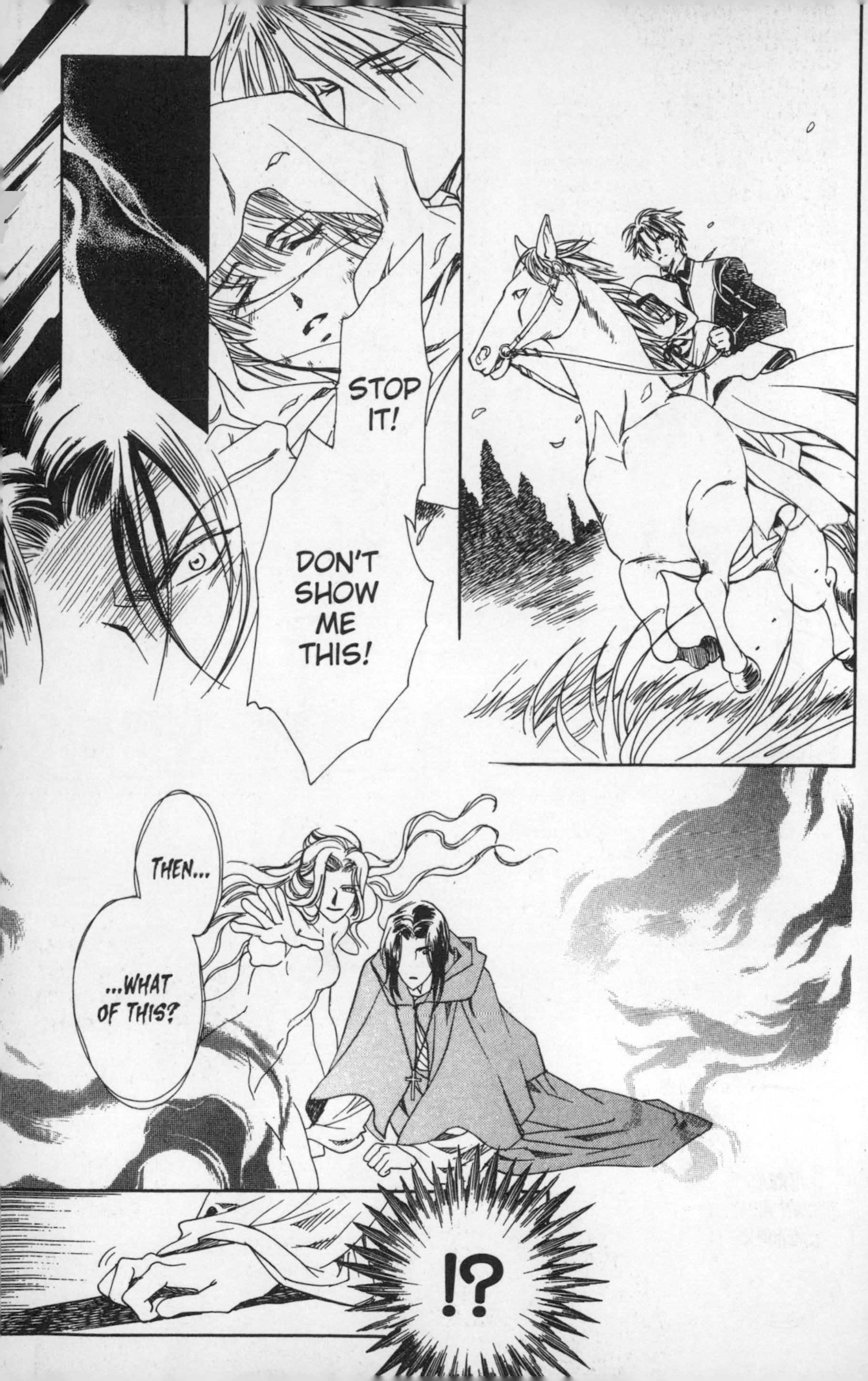
STOP IT!
DON'T SHOW ME THIS!
THEN...
...WHAT OF THIS?
!?

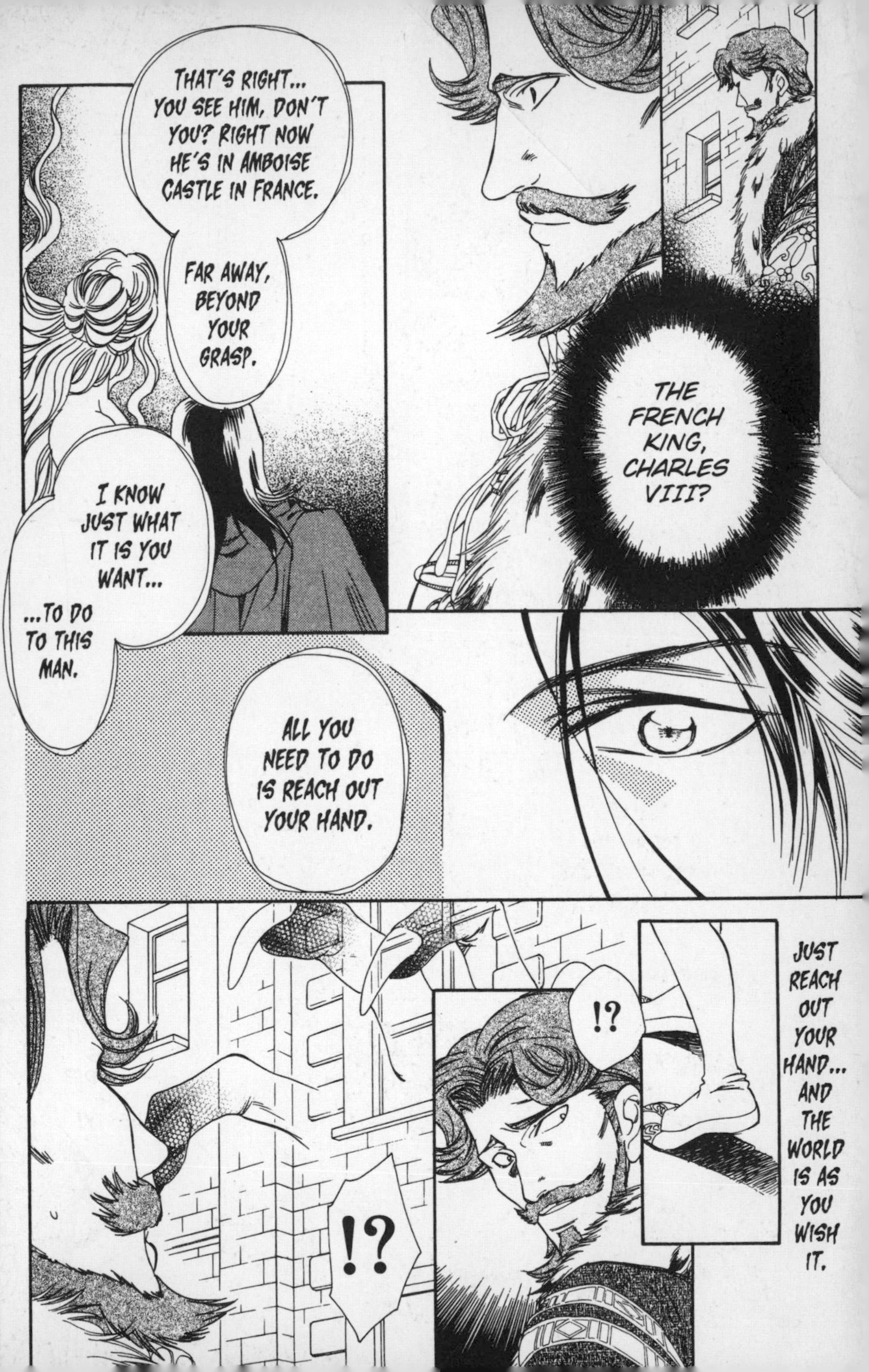
THE FRENCH KING, CHARLES VIII?
THAT'S RIGHT... YOU SEE HIM, DON'T YOU? RIGHT NOW HE'S IN AMBOISE CASTLE IN FRANCE.
FAR AWAY, BEYOND YOUR GRASP.
I KNOW JUST WHAT IT IS YOU WANT...
...TO DO TO THIS MAN.
ALL YOU NEED TO DO IS REACH OUT YOUR HAND.
JUST REACH OUT YOUR HAND... AND THE WORLD IS AS YOU WISH IT.
!?
!?

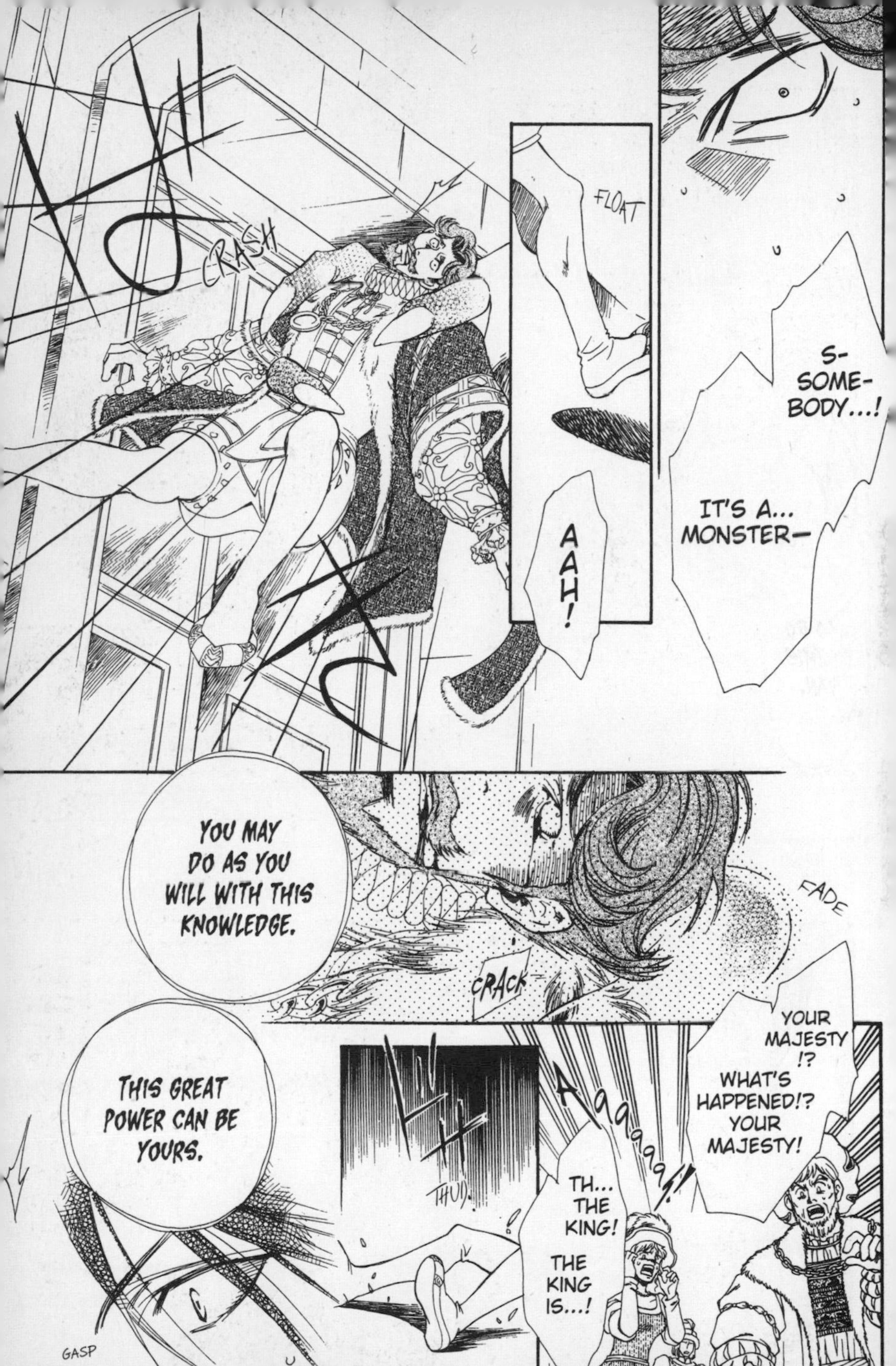
S-SOME-BODY...!
IT'S A... MONSTER—
FLOAT
AAH!
CRASH
YOU MAY DO AS YOU WILL WITH THIS KNOWLEDGE.
FADE
CRACK
YOUR MAJESTY!? WHAT'S HAPPENED!? YOUR MAJESTY!
Aaggggg!!
TH... THE KING!
THE KING IS...!
THUD
THIS GREAT POWER CAN BE YOURS.
GASP

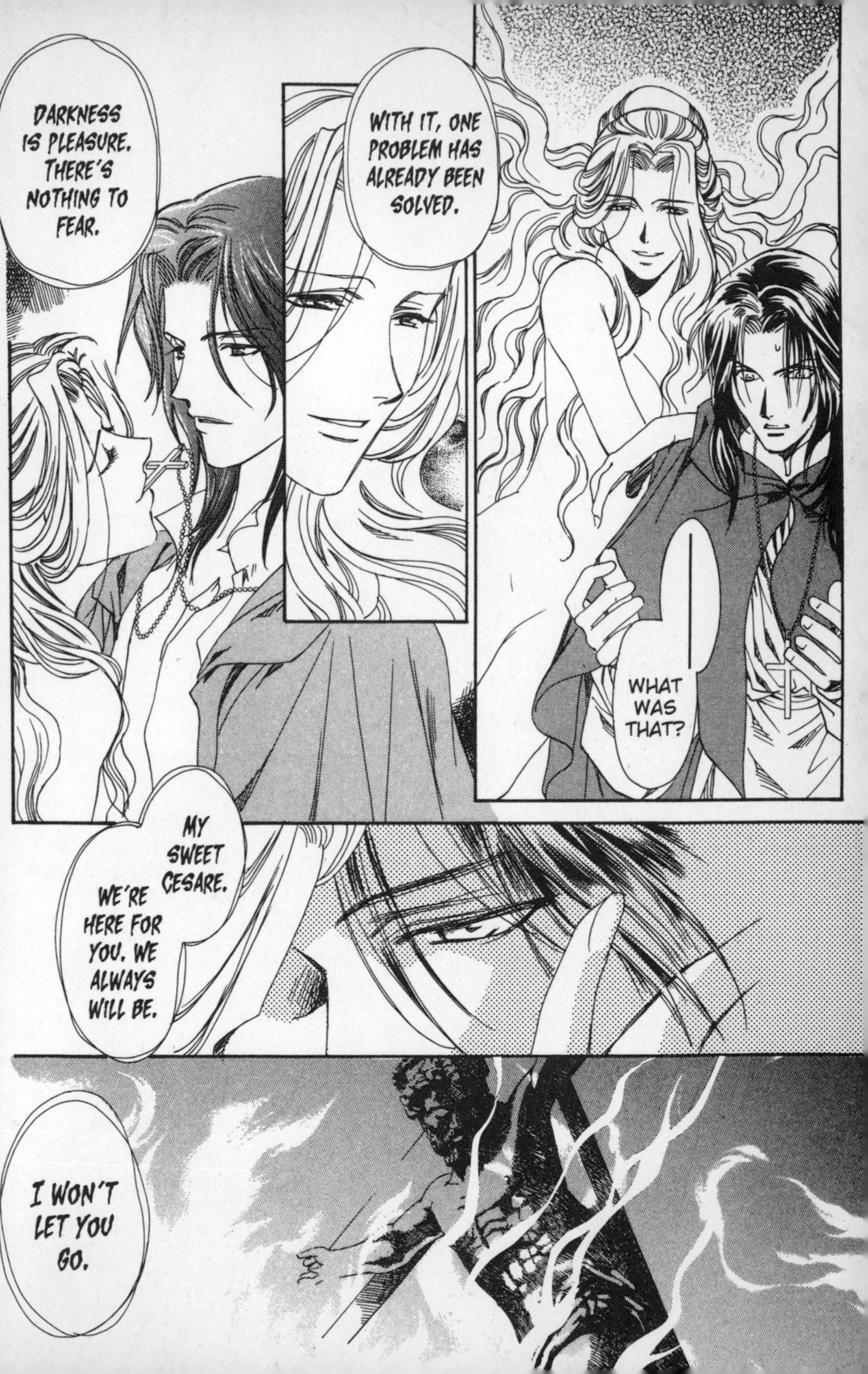
WHAT WAS THAT?
WITH IT, ONE PROBLEM HAS ALREADY BEEN SOLVED.
DARKNESS IS PLEASURE. THERE'S NOTHING TO FEAR.
MY SWEET CESARE.
WE'RE HERE FOR YOU. WE ALWAYS WILL BE.
I WON'T LET YOU GO.

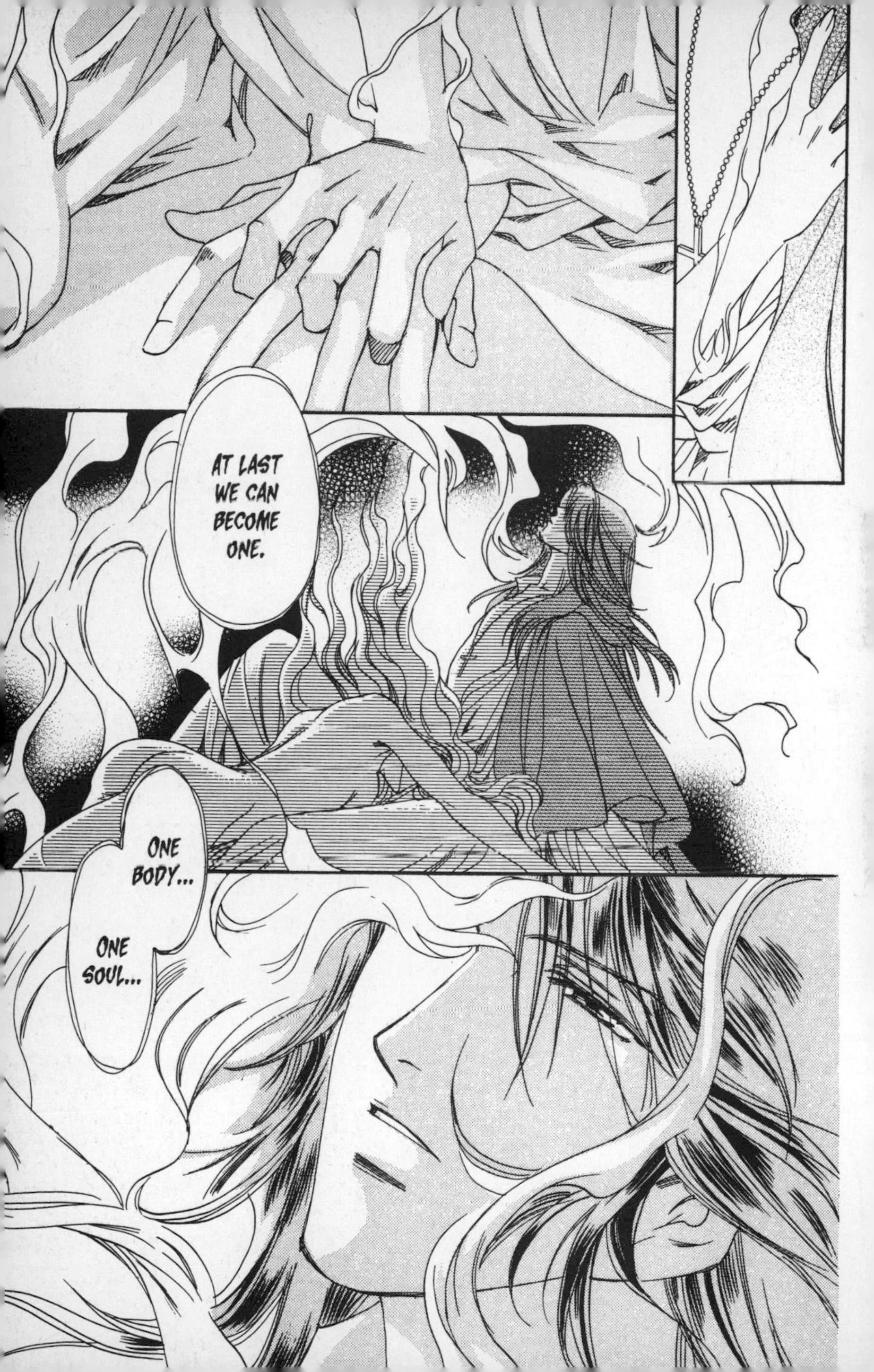
AT LAST WE CAN BECOME ONE.
ONE BODY...
ONE SOUL...

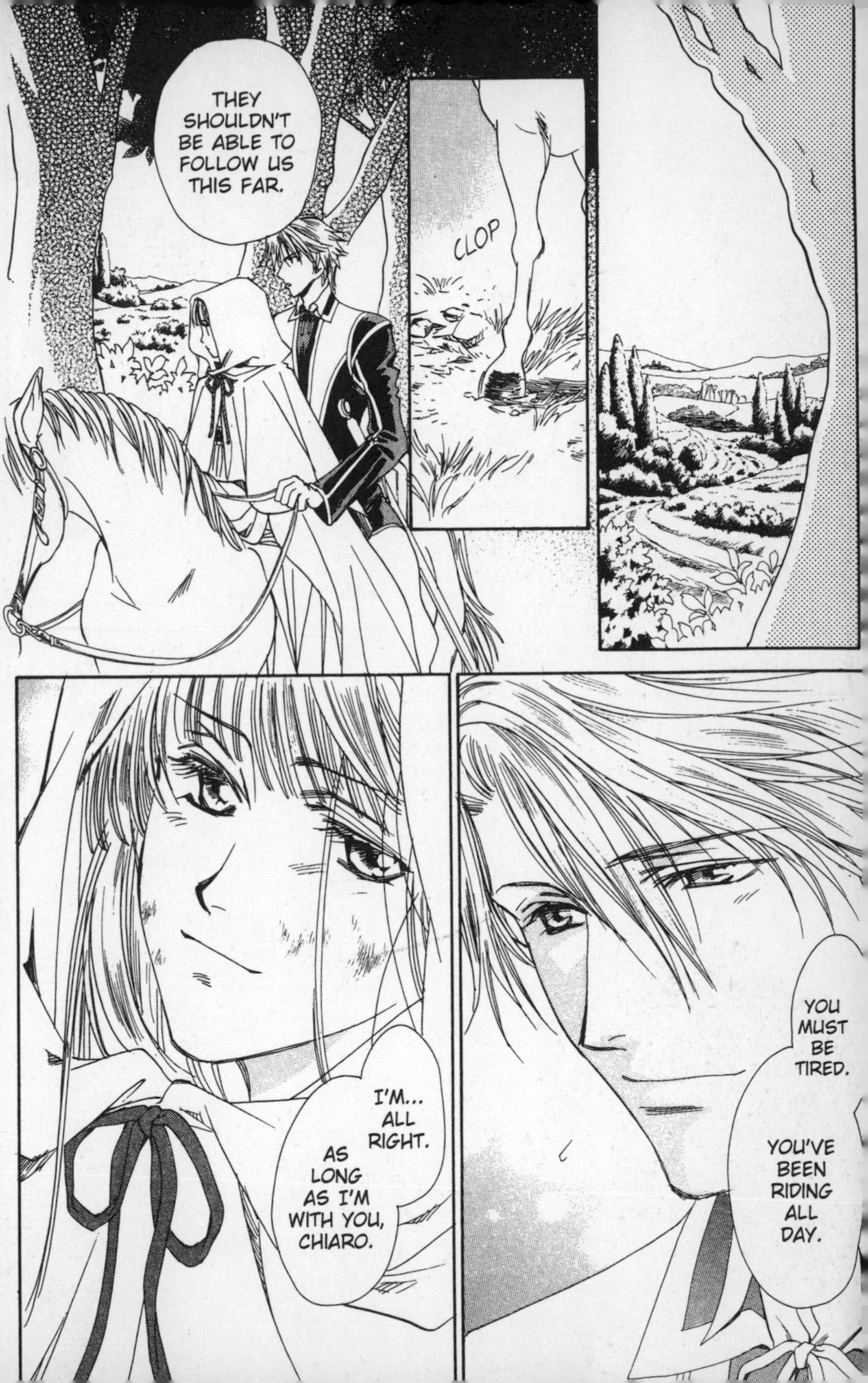
CLOP
THEY SHOULDN'T BE ABLE TO FOLLOW US THIS FAR.
YOU MUST BE TIRED.
YOU'VE BEEN RIDING ALL DAY.
I'M... ALL RIGHT.
AS LONG AS I'M WITH YOU, CHIARO.

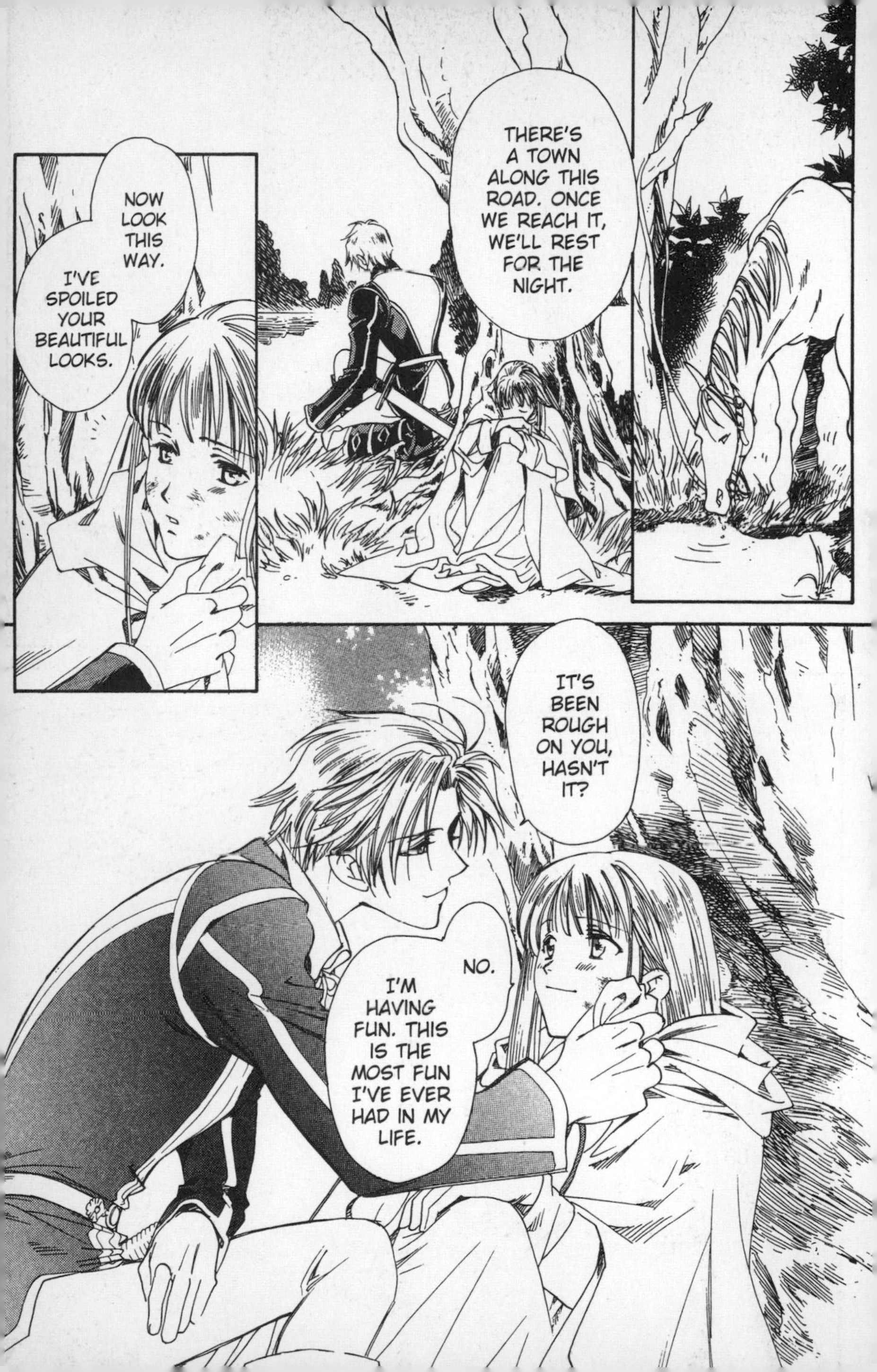
THERE'S A TOWN ALONG THIS ROAD. ONCE WE REACH IT, WE'LL REST FOR THE NIGHT.
NOW LOOK THIS WAY.
I'VE SPOILED YOUR BEAUTIFUL LOOKS.
IT'S BEEN ROUGH ON YOU, HASN'T IT?
NO.
I'M HAVING FUN. THIS IS THE MOST FUN I'VE EVER HAD IN MY LIFE.

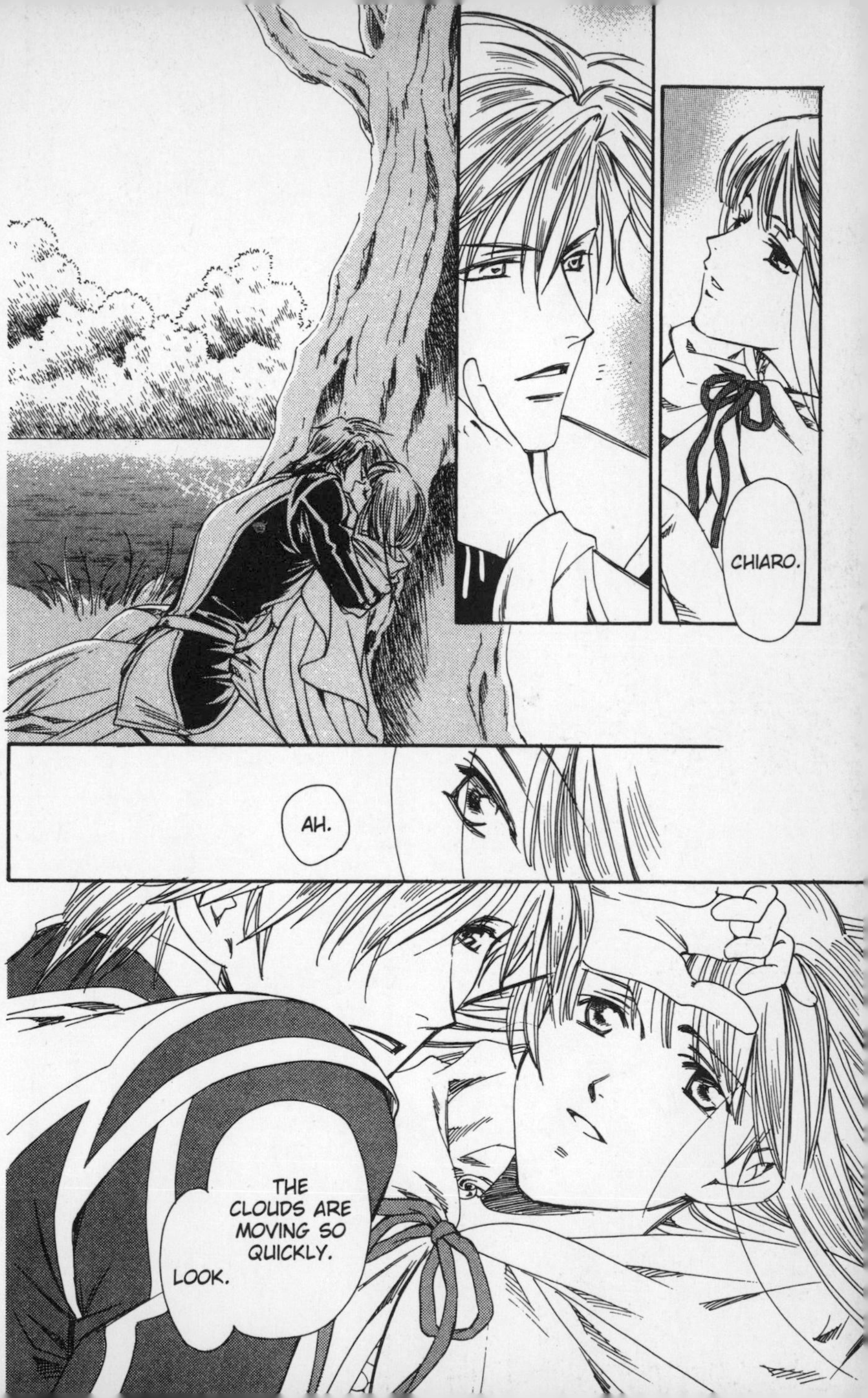
CHIARO.
AH.
THE CLOUDS ARE MOVING SO QUICKLY.
LOOK.

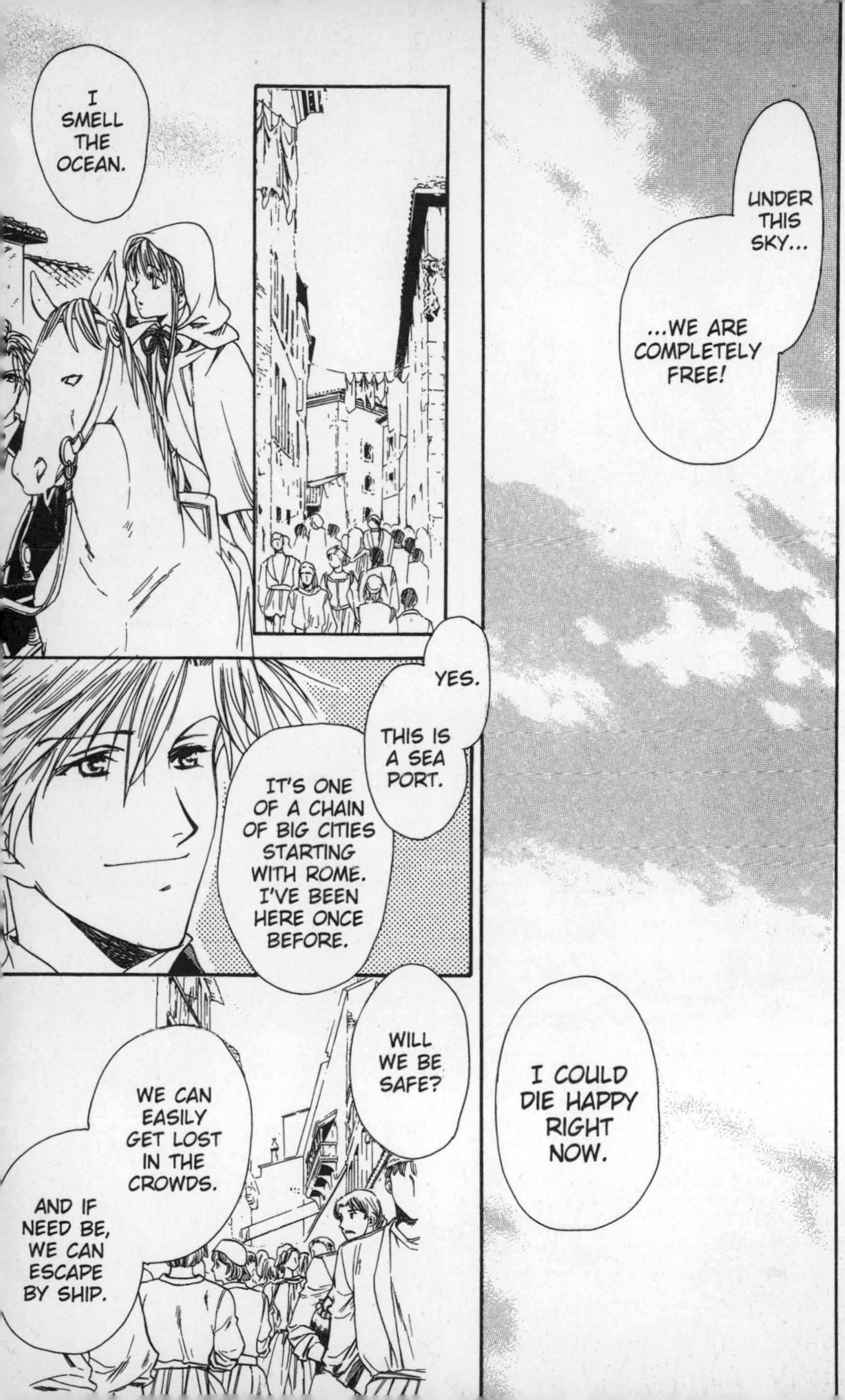
UNDER THIS SKY...
...WE ARE COMPLETELY FREE!
I COULD DIE HAPPY RIGHT NOW.
I SMELL THE OCEAN.
YES.
THIS IS A SEA PORT.
IT'S ONE OF A CHAIN OF BIG CITIES STARTING WITH ROME. I'VE BEEN HERE ONCE BEFORE.
WILL WE BE SAFE?
WE CAN EASILY GET LOST IN THE CROWDS.
AND IF NEED BE, WE CAN ESCAPE BY SHIP.

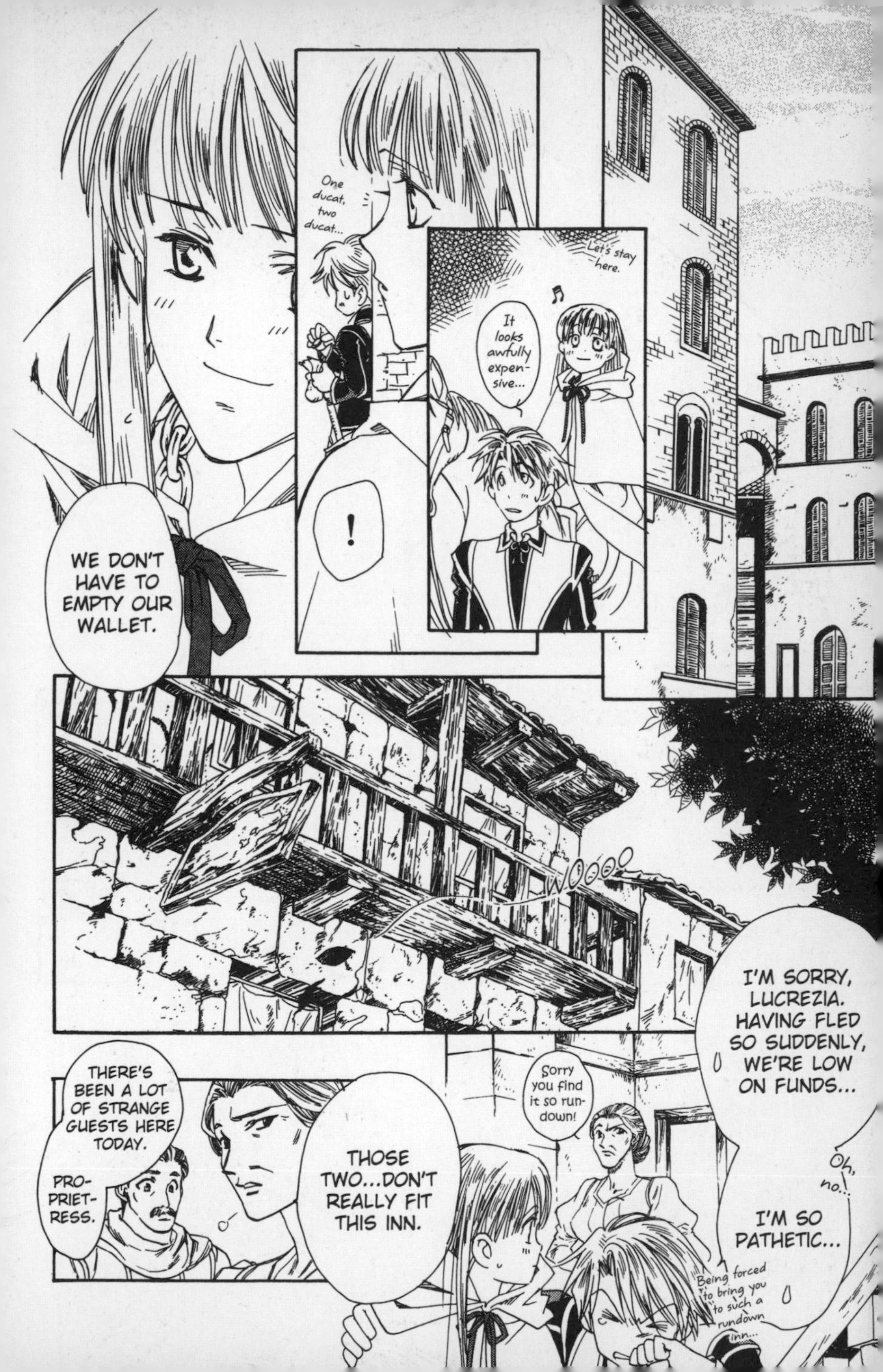
Let's stay here.
It looks awfully expensive...
One ducat, two ducat...
!
WE DON'T HAVE TO EMPTY OUR WALLET.
WOOO
I'M SORRY, LUCREZIA. HAVING FLED SO SUDDENLY, WE'RE LOW ON FUNDS...
Oh, no...
I'M SO PATHETIC...
Being forced to bring you to such a rundown inn...
Sorry you find it so run-down!
THOSE TWO...DON'T REALLY FIT THIS INN.
THERE'S BEEN A LOT OF STRANGE GUESTS HERE TODAY.
PRO-PRIET-RESS.

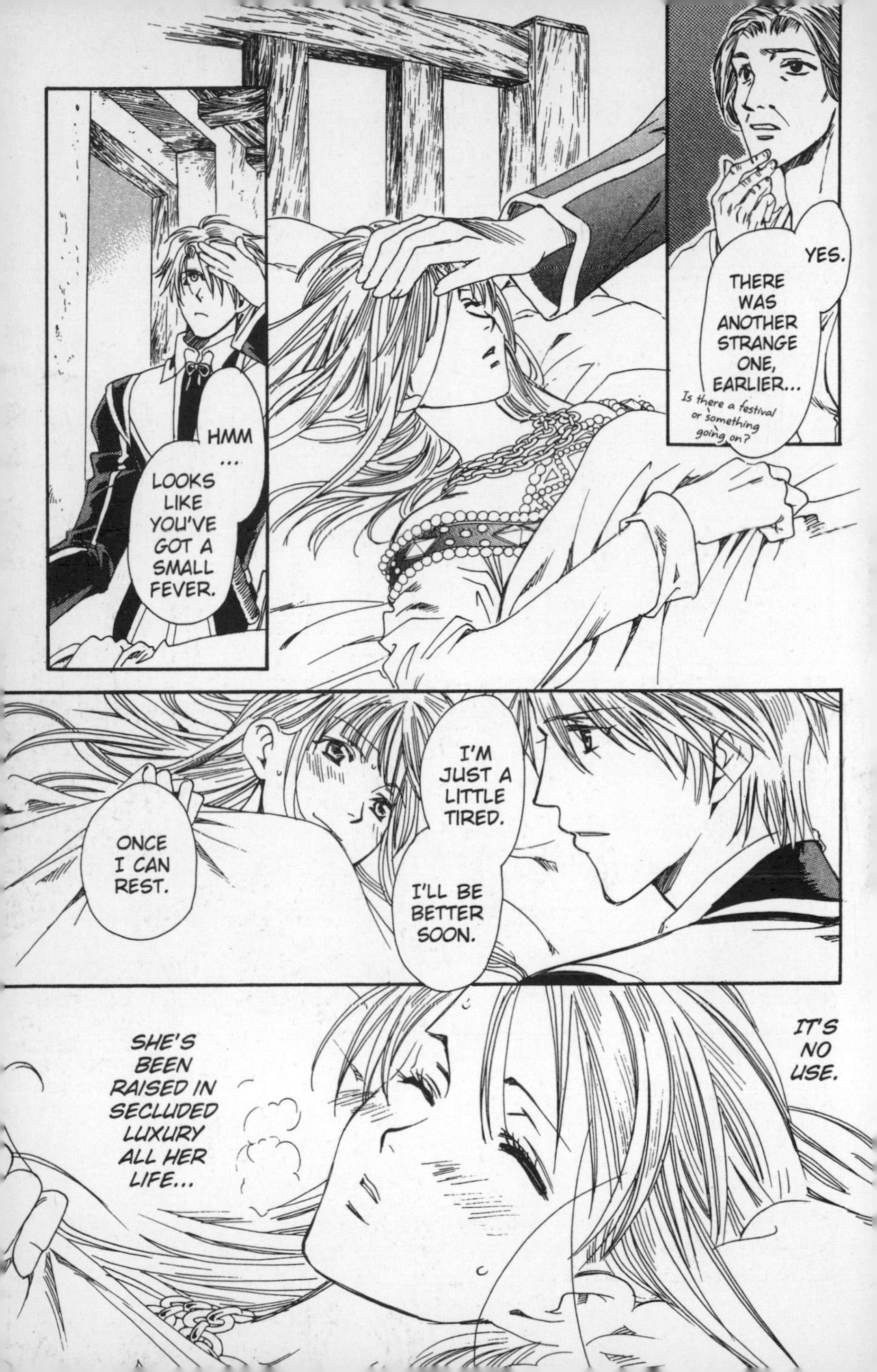
YES.
THERE WAS ANOTHER STRANGE ONE, EARLIER...
Is there a festival or something going on?
HMM... LOOKS LIKE YOU'VE GOT A SMALL FEVER.
I'M JUST A LITTLE TIRED.
ONCE I CAN REST.
I'LL BE BETTER SOON.
IT'S NO USE.
SHE'S BEEN RAISED IN SECLUDED LUXURY ALL HER LIFE...

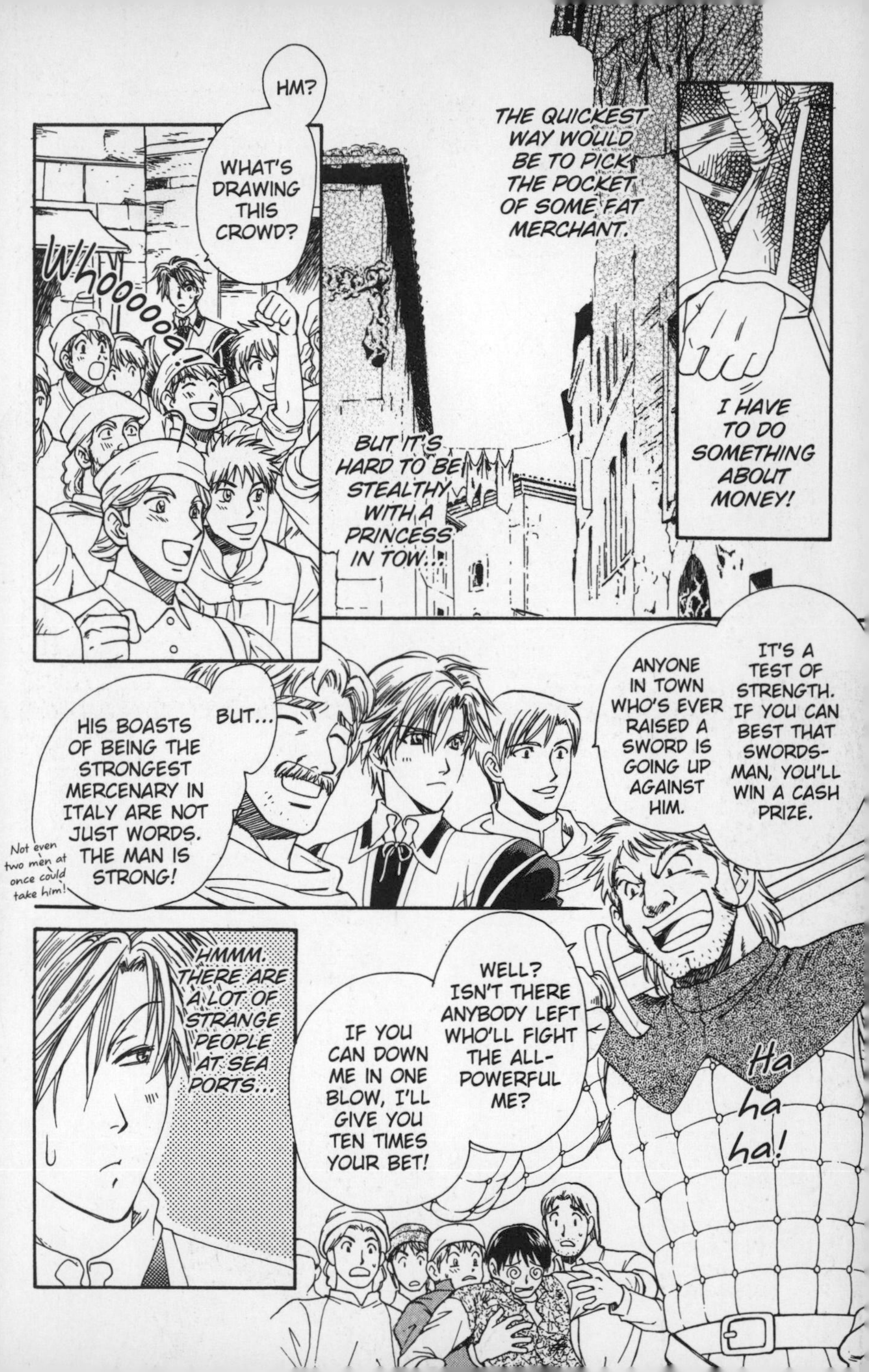

I HAVE TO DO SOMETHING ABOUT MONEY!
THE QUICKEST WAY WOULD BE TO PICK THE POCKET OF SOME FAT MERCHANT.
BUT IT'S HARD TO BE STEALTHY WITH A PRINCESS IN TOW...
HM?
WHAT'S DRAWING THIS CROWD?
Whoooooooo!
IT'S A TEST OF STRENGTH. IF YOU CAN BEST THAT SWORDSMAN, YOU'LL WIN A CASH PRIZE.
ANYONE IN TOWN WHO'S EVER RAISED A SWORD IS GOING UP AGAINST HIM.
BUT...
HIS BOASTS OF BEING THE STRONGEST MERCENARY IN ITALY ARE NOT JUST WORDS. THE MAN IS STRONG!
Not even two men at once could take him!
Ha ha ha!
WELL? ISN'T THERE ANYBODY LEFT WHO'LL FIGHT THE ALL-POWERFUL ME?
IF YOU CAN DOWN ME IN ONE BLOW, I'LL GIVE YOU TEN TIMES YOUR BET!
HMMM. THERE ARE A LOT OF STRANGE PEOPLE AT SEA PORTS...

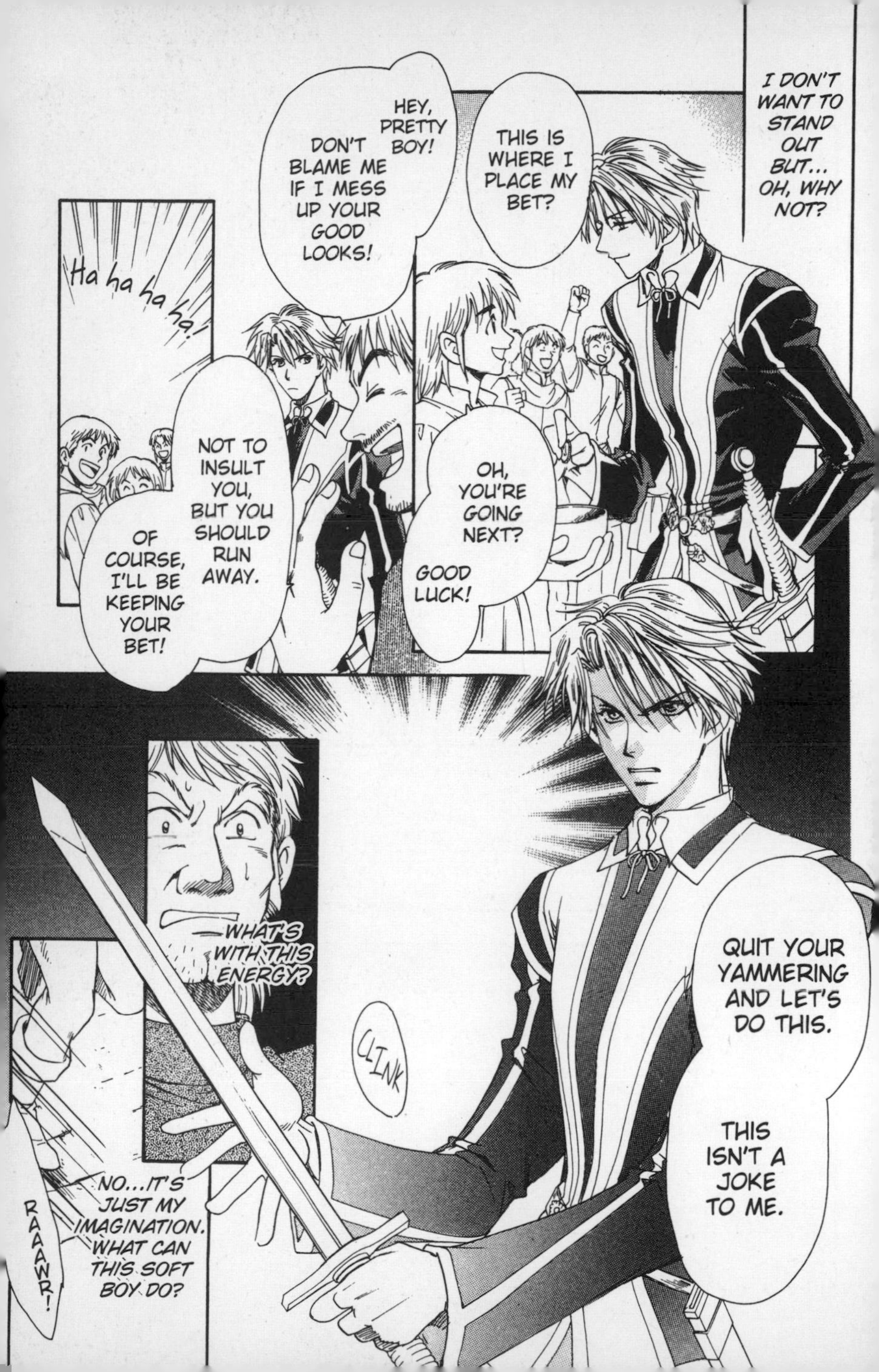
I DON'T WANT TO STAND OUT BUT... OH, WHY NOT?
THIS IS WHERE I PLACE MY BET?
HEY, PRETTY BOY!
DON'T BLAME ME IF I MESS UP YOUR GOOD LOOKS!
OH, YOU'RE GOING NEXT?
GOOD LUCK!
Ha ha ha ha!
NOT TO INSULT YOU, BUT YOU SHOULD RUN AWAY.
OF COURSE, I'LL BE KEEPING YOUR BET!
QUIT YOUR YAMMERING AND LET'S DO THIS.
THIS ISN'T A JOKE TO ME.
CLINK
WHAT'S WITH THIS ENERGY?
NO...IT'S JUST MY IMAGINATION. WHAT CAN THIS SOFT BOY DO?
RAAAWR!

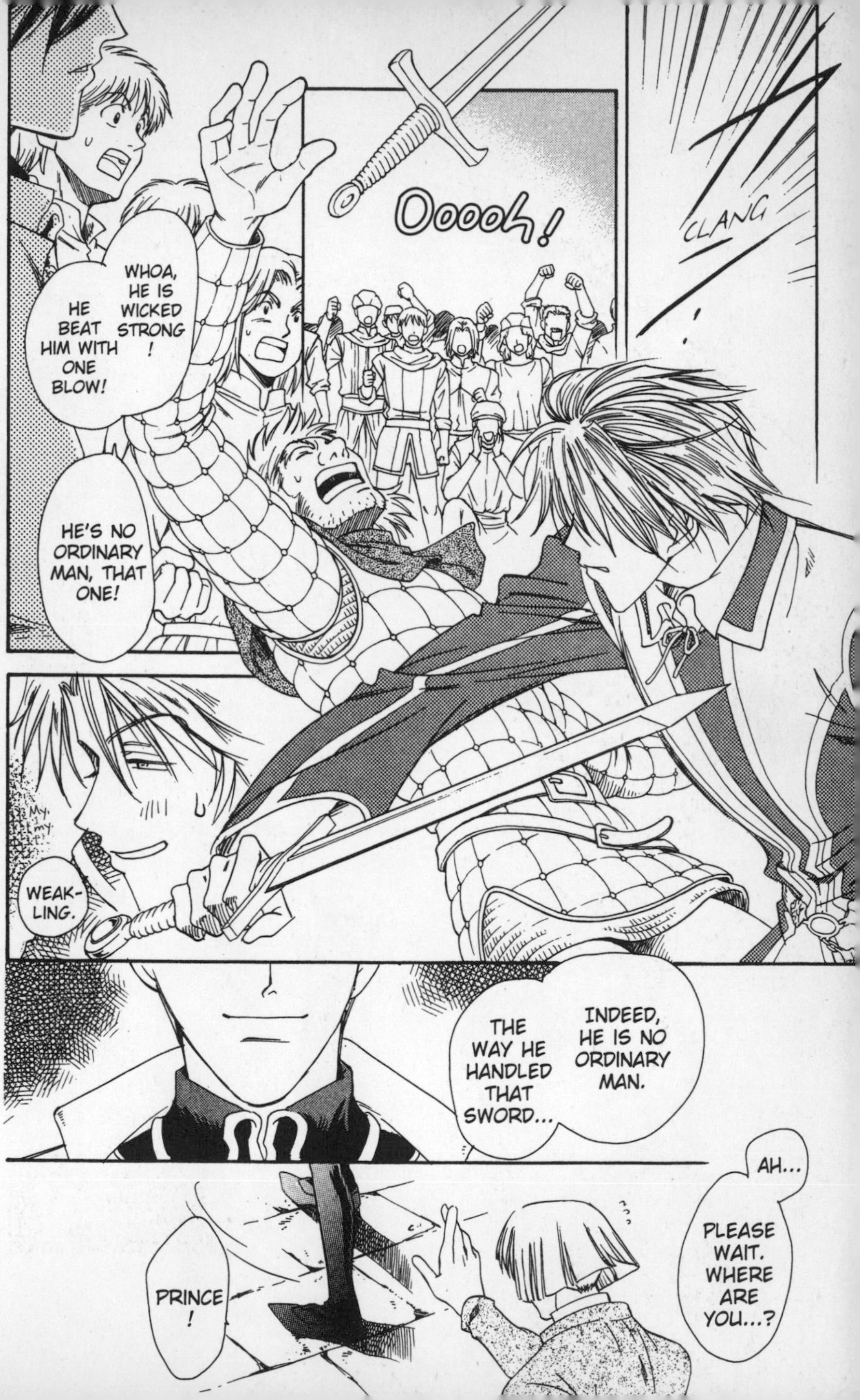
CLANG
Ooooh!
WHOA, HE IS WICKED STRONG!
HE BEAT HIM WITH ONE BLOW!
HE'S NO ORDINARY MAN, THAT ONE!
My, my.
WEAK-LING.
INDEED, HE IS NO ORDINARY MAN.
THE WAY HE HANDLED THAT SWORD...
AH...
PLEASE WAIT. WHERE ARE YOU...?
PRINCE!

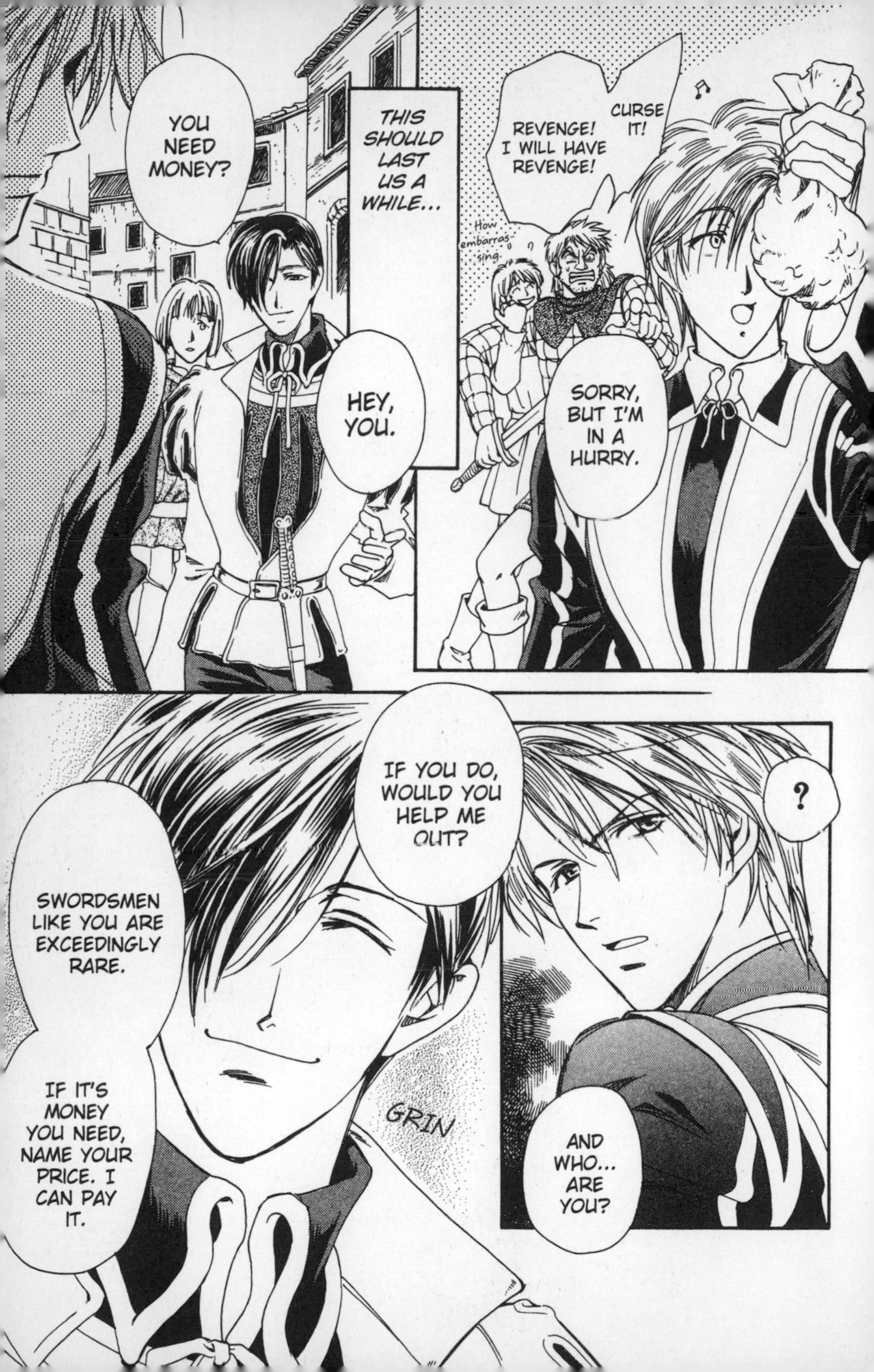
CURSE IT!
REVENGE! I WILL HAVE REVENGE!
How embarrassing.
SORRY, BUT I'M IN A HURRY.
THIS SHOULD LAST US A WHILE...
HEY, YOU.
YOU NEED MONEY?
IF YOU DO, WOULD YOU HELP ME OUT?
SWORDSMEN LIKE YOU ARE EXCEEDINGLY RARE.
IF IT'S MONEY YOU NEED, NAME YOUR PRICE. I CAN PAY IT.
GRIN
?
AND WHO... ARE YOU?

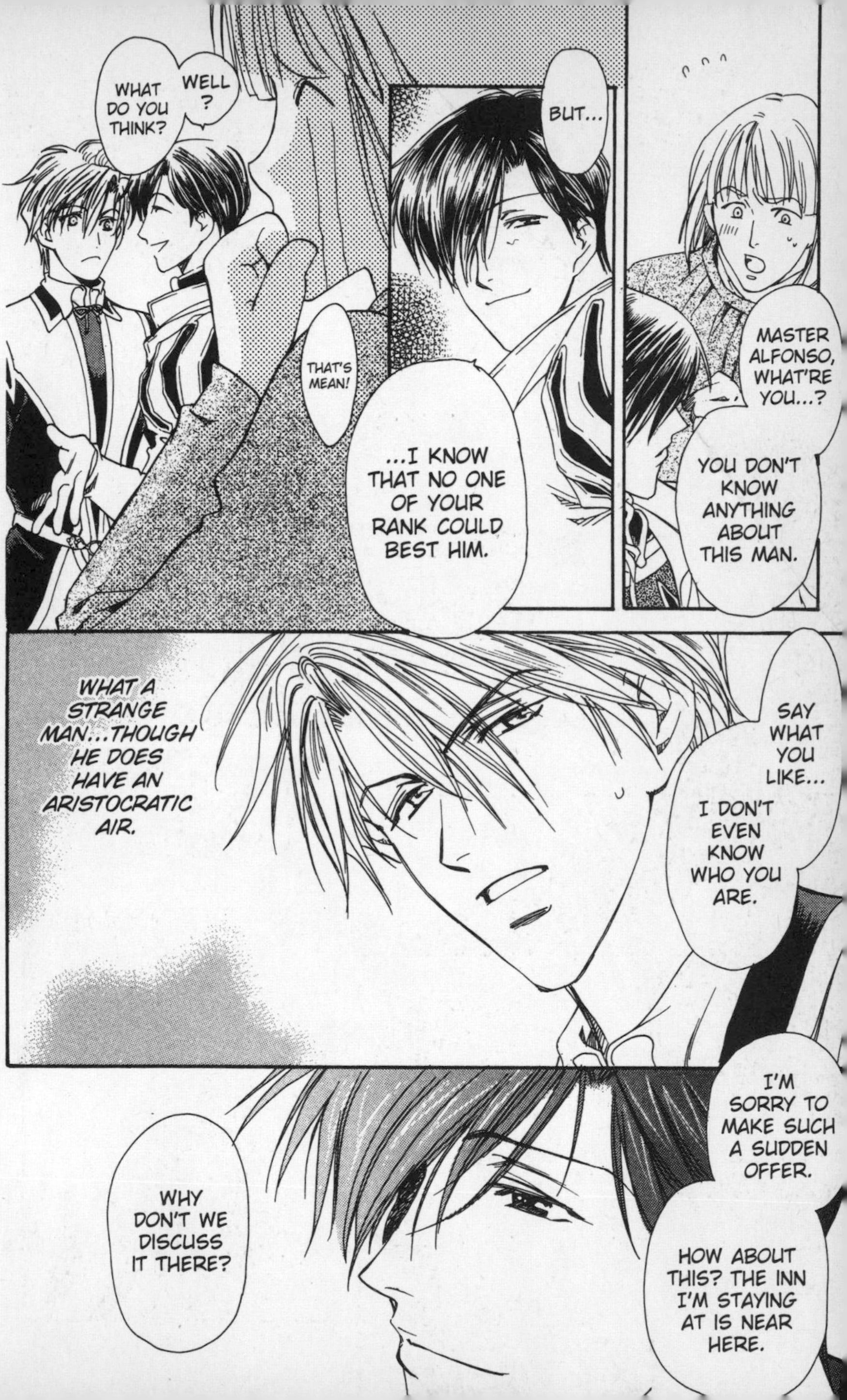
MASTER ALFONSO, WHAT'RE YOU...?
YOU DON'T KNOW ANYTHING ABOUT THIS MAN.
BUT...
...I KNOW THAT NO ONE OF YOUR RANK COULD BEST HIM.
WELL ?
WHAT DO YOU THINK?
THAT'S MEAN!
SAY WHAT YOU LIKE...
I DON'T EVEN KNOW WHO YOU ARE.
WHAT A STRANGE MAN...THOUGH HE DOES HAVE AN ARISTOCRATIC AIR.
I'M SORRY TO MAKE SUCH A SUDDEN OFFER.
HOW ABOUT THIS? THE INN I'M STAYING AT IS NEAR HERE.
WHY DON'T WE DISCUSS IT THERE?

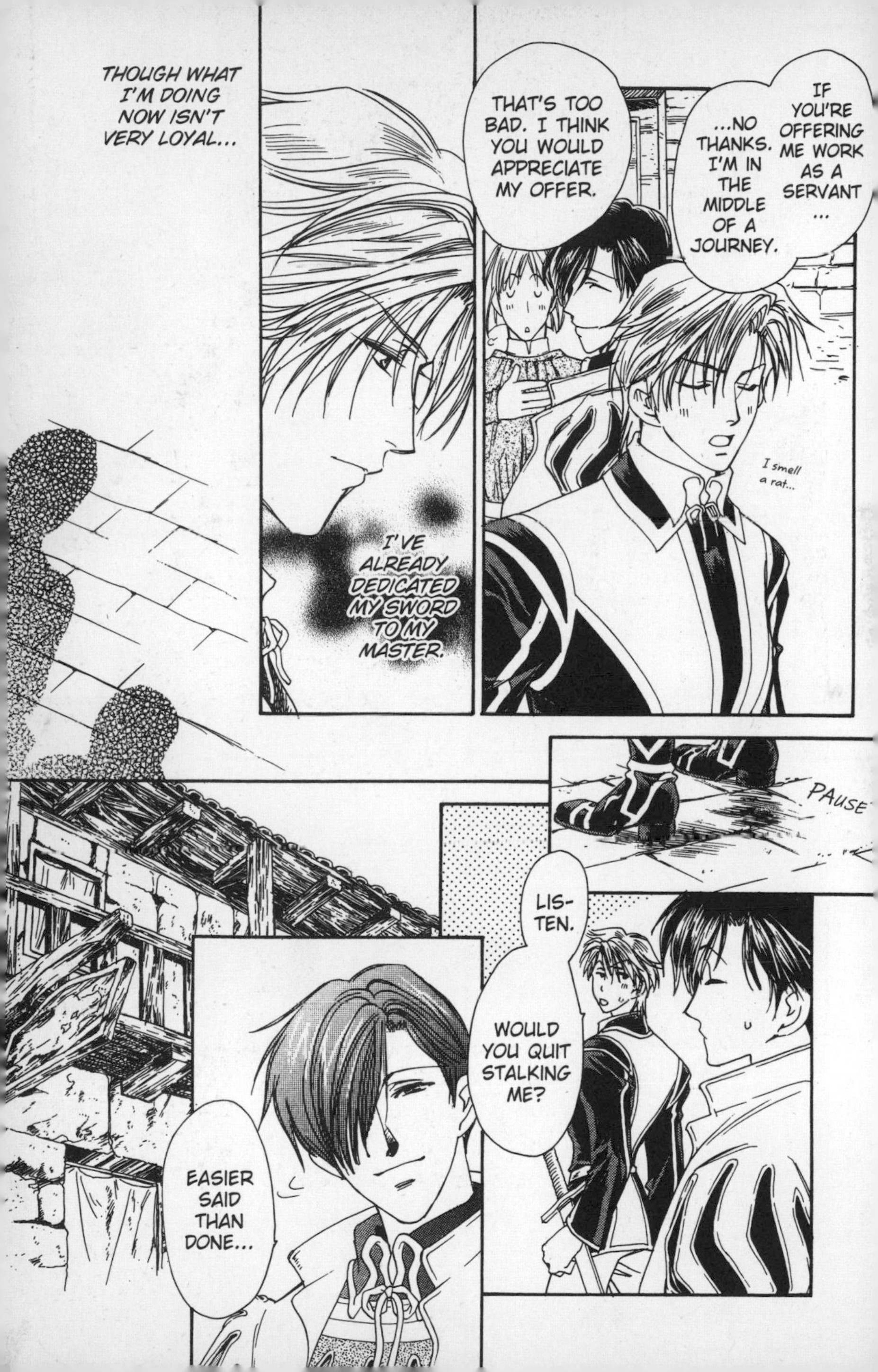
IF YOU'RE OFFERING ME WORK AS A SERVANT ...
...NO THANKS. I'M IN THE MIDDLE OF A JOURNEY.
THAT'S TOO BAD. I THINK YOU WOULD APPRECIATE MY OFFER.
I smell a rat...
I'VE ALREADY DEDICATED MY SWORD TO MY MASTER.
THOUGH WHAT I'M DOING NOW ISN'T VERY LOYAL...
PAUSE
LIS-TEN.
WOULD YOU QUIT STALKING ME?
EASIER SAID THAN DONE...

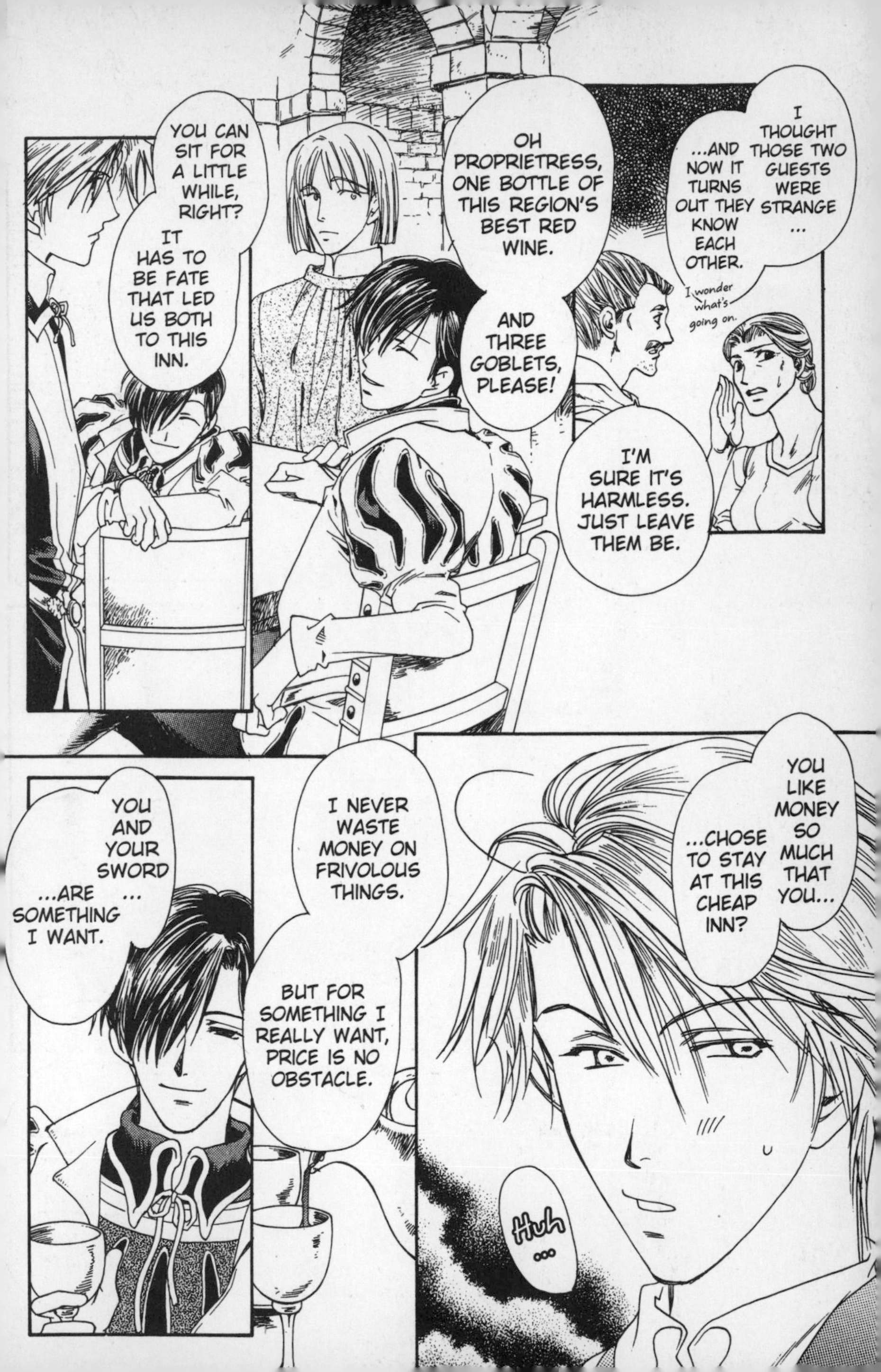
I THOUGHT THOSE TWO GUESTS WERE STRANGE...
...AND NOW IT TURNS OUT THEY KNOW EACH OTHER.
I wonder what's going on.
I'M SURE IT'S HARMLESS. JUST LEAVE THEM BE.
OH PROPRIETRESS, ONE BOTTLE OF THIS REGION'S BEST RED WINE.
AND THREE GOBLETS, PLEASE!
YOU CAN SIT FOR A LITTLE WHILE, RIGHT?
IT HAS TO BE FATE THAT LED US BOTH TO THIS INN.
YOU LIKE MONEY SO MUCH THAT YOU...
...CHOSE TO STAY AT THIS CHEAP INN?
Huh...
I NEVER WASTE MONEY ON FRIVOLOUS THINGS.
BUT FOR SOMETHING I REALLY WANT, PRICE IS NO OBSTACLE.
YOU AND YOUR SWORD...
...ARE SOMETHING I WANT.

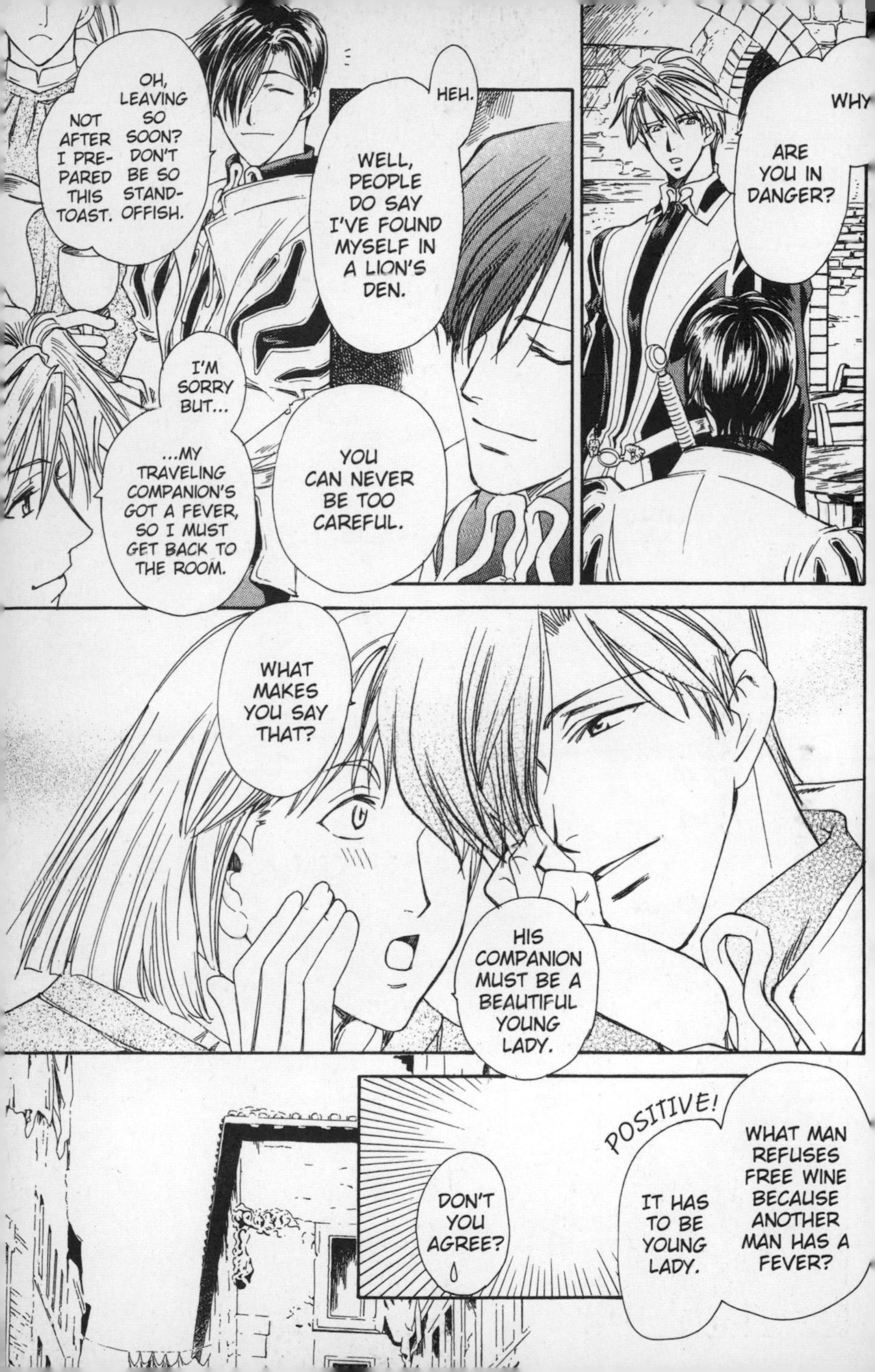
WHY
ARE YOU IN DANGER?
HEH.
WELL, PEOPLE DO SAY I'VE FOUND MYSELF IN A LION'S DEN.
YOU CAN NEVER BE TOO CAREFUL.
OH, LEAVING SO SOON? DON'T BE SO STAND-OFFISH.
NOT AFTER I PRE-PARED THIS TOAST.
I'M SORRY BUT...
...MY TRAVELING COMPANION'S GOT A FEVER, SO I MUST GET BACK TO THE ROOM.
WHAT MAKES YOU SAY THAT?
HIS COMPANION MUST BE A BEAUTIFUL YOUNG LADY.
WHAT MAN REFUSES FREE WINE BECAUSE ANOTHER MAN HAS A FEVER?
POSITIVE!
IT HAS TO BE YOUNG LADY.
DON'T YOU AGREE?

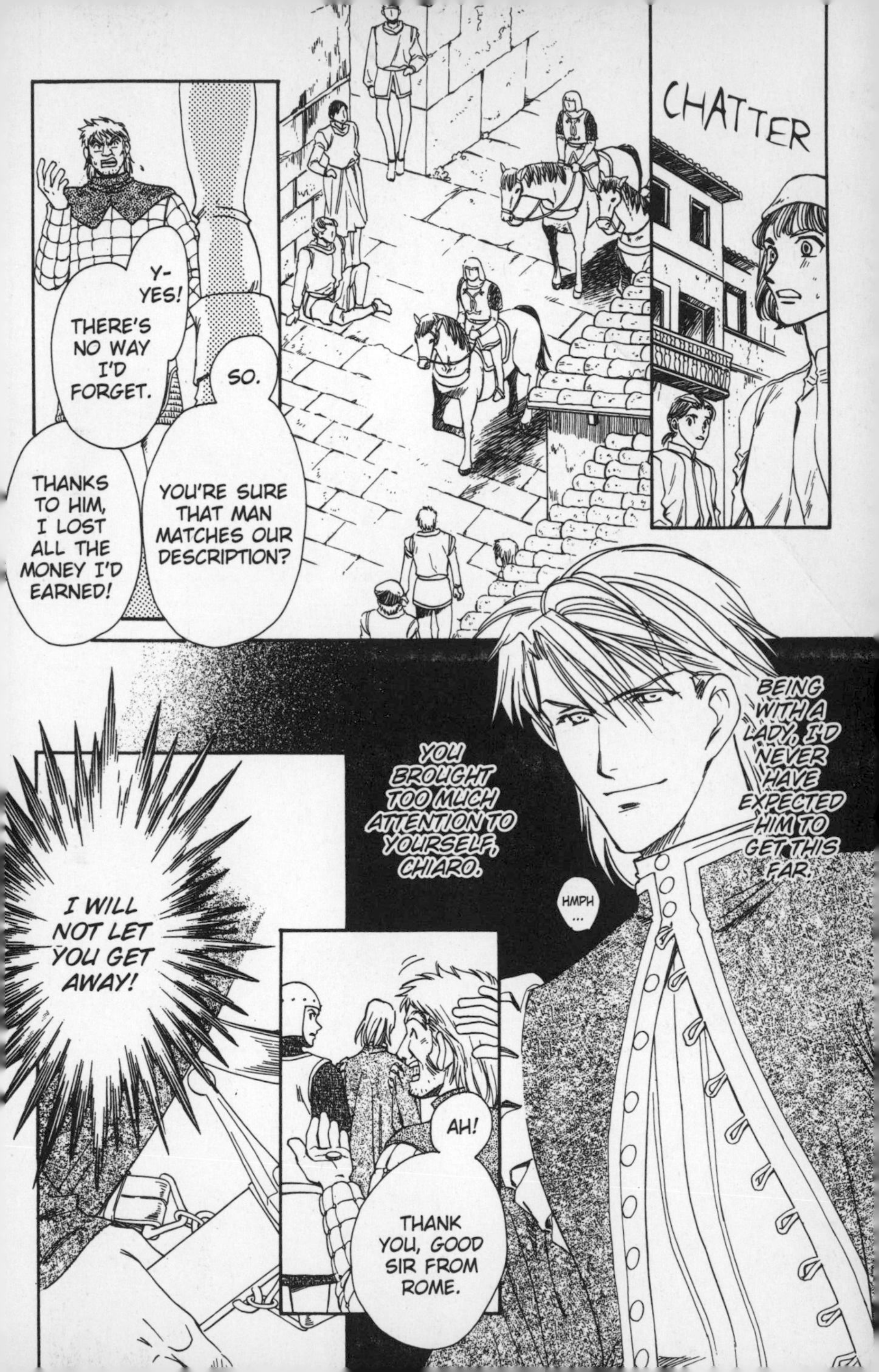
CHATTER
SO.
YOU'RE SURE THAT MAN MATCHES OUR DESCRIPTION?
Y- YES! THERE'S NO WAY I'D FORGET.
THANKS TO HIM, I LOST ALL THE MONEY I'D EARNED!
BEING WITH A LADY, I'D NEVER HAVE EXPECTED HIM TO GET THIS FAR.
YOU BROUGHT TOO MUCH ATTENTION TO YOURSELF, CHIARO.
HMPH ...
AH!
THANK YOU, GOOD SIR FROM ROME.
I WILL NOT LET YOU GET AWAY!

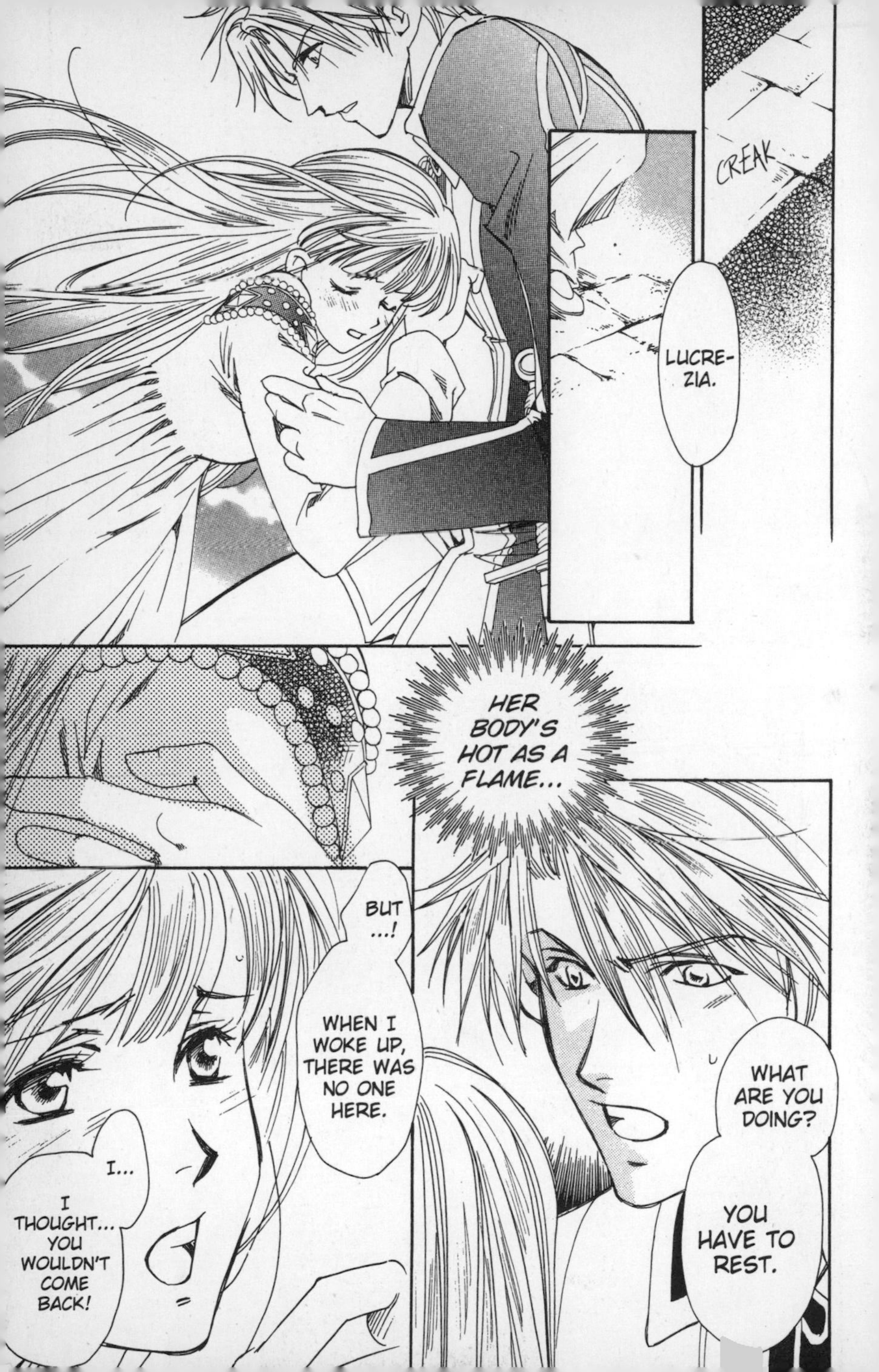
CREAK
LUCREZIA.
HER BODY'S HOT AS A FLAME...
WHAT ARE YOU DOING?
YOU HAVE TO REST.
BUT ...!
WHEN I WOKE UP, THERE WAS NO ONE HERE.
I...
I THOUGHT... YOU WOULDN'T COME BACK!

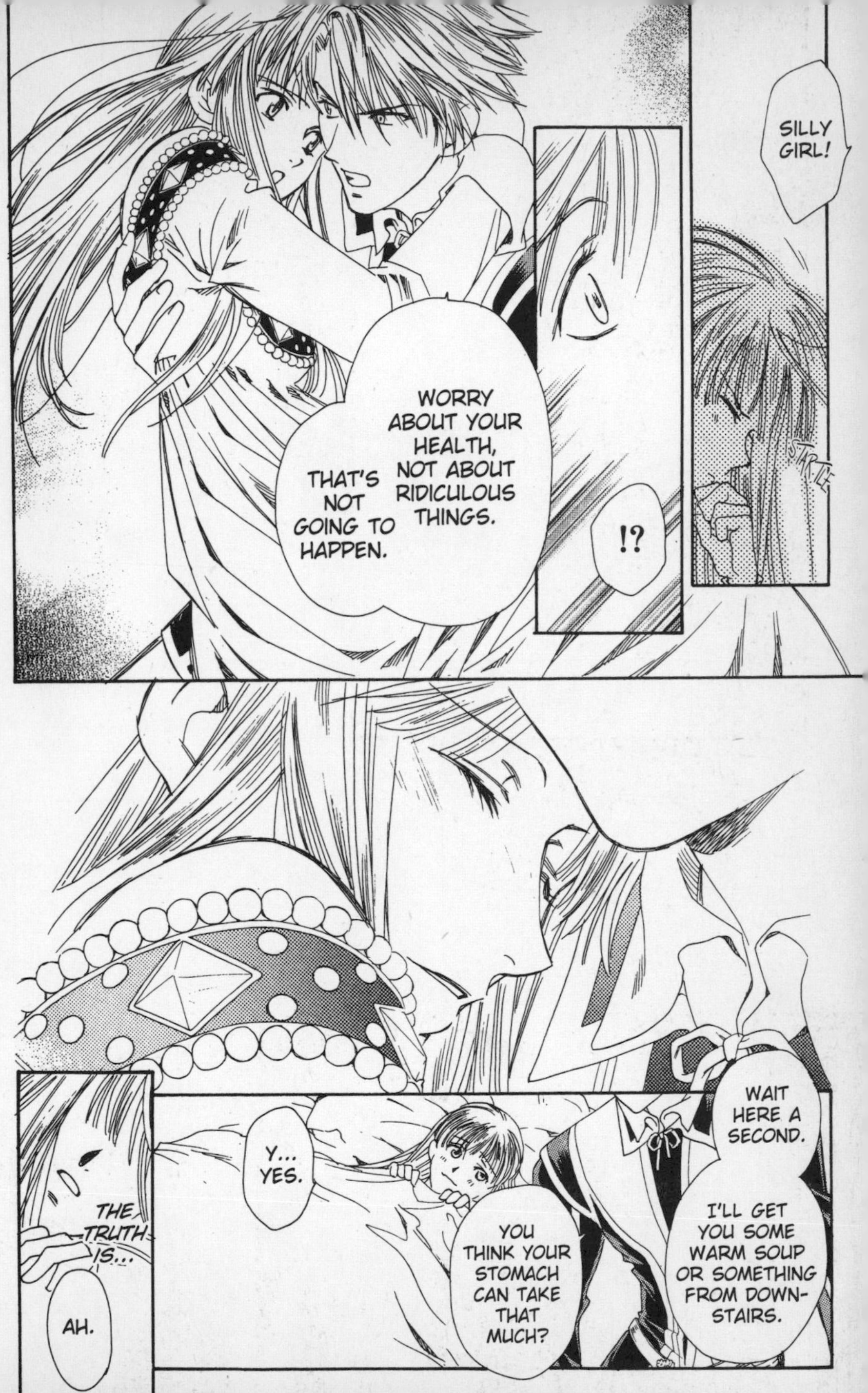
SILLY GIRL!
STARTLE
!?
WORRY ABOUT YOUR HEALTH, NOT ABOUT RIDICULOUS THINGS.
THAT'S NOT GOING TO HAPPEN.
WAIT HERE A SECOND.
I'LL GET YOU SOME WARM SOUP OR SOMETHING FROM DOWN-STAIRS.
YOU THINK YOUR STOMACH CAN TAKE THAT MUCH?
Y... YES.
THE TRUTH IS...
AH.

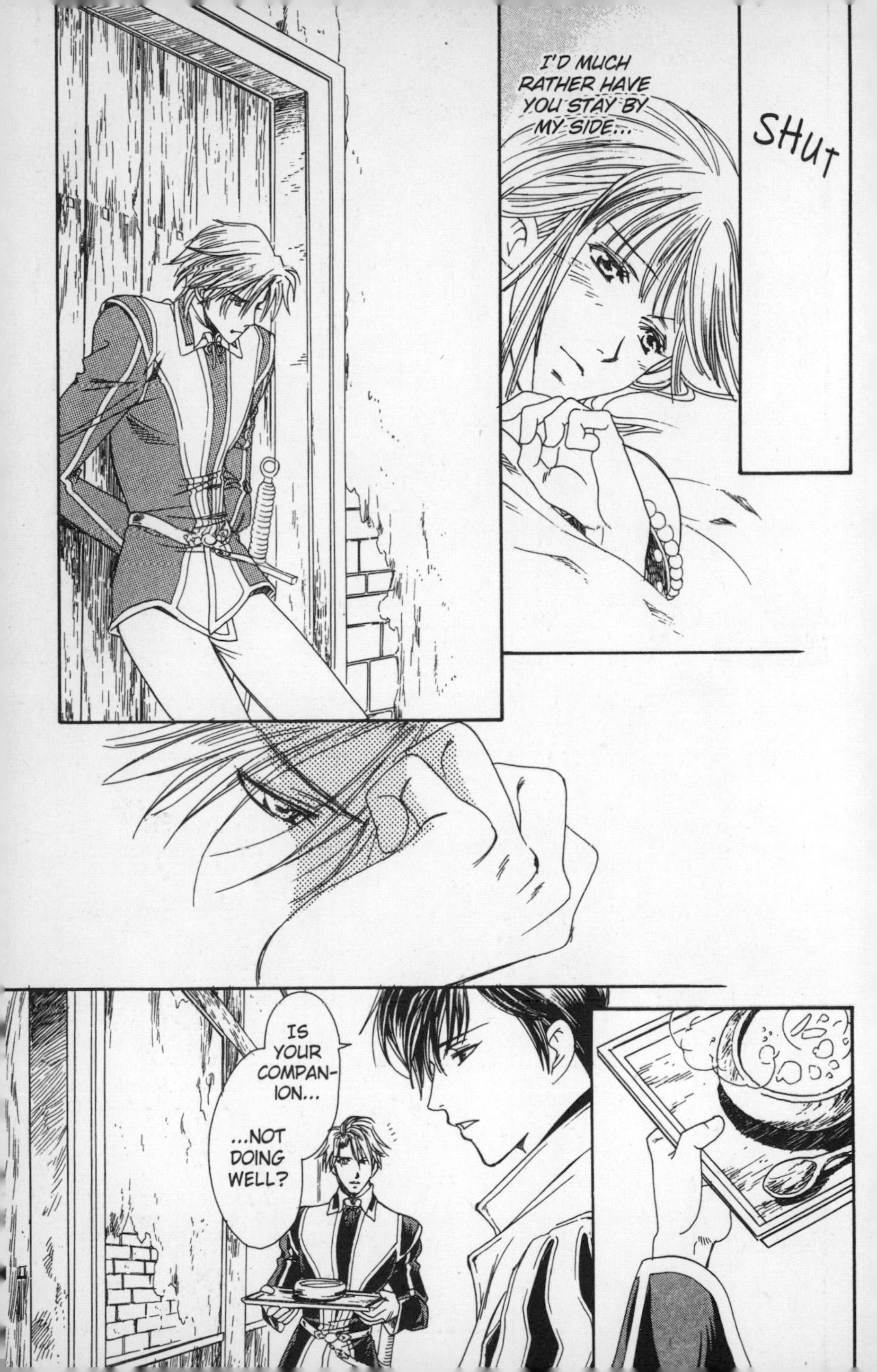
SHUT
I'D MUCH RATHER HAVE YOU STAY BY MY SIDE...
IS YOUR COMPANION...
...NOT DOING WELL?

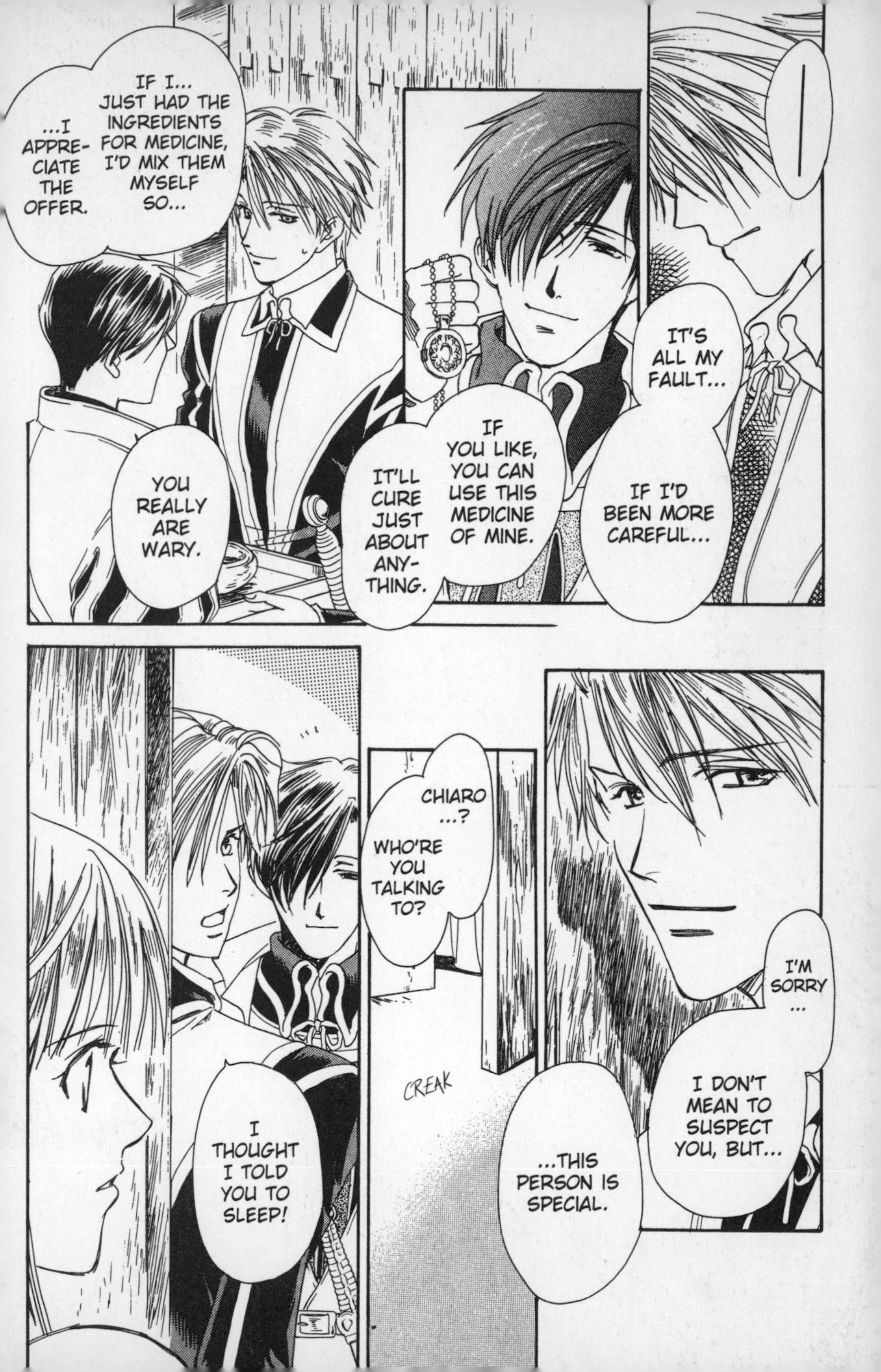
—
IT'S ALL MY FAULT...
IF I'D BEEN MORE CAREFUL...
IF YOU LIKE, YOU CAN USE THIS MEDICINE OF MINE.
IT'LL CURE JUST ABOUT ANYTHING.
IF I... JUST HAD THE INGREDIENTS FOR MEDICINE, I'D MIX THEM MYSELF SO...
...I APPRECIATE THE OFFER.
YOU REALLY ARE WARY.
I'M SORRY...
I DON'T MEAN TO SUSPECT YOU, BUT...
...THIS PERSON IS SPECIAL.
CHIARO...?
WHO'RE YOU TALKING TO?
CREAK
...
I THOUGHT I TOLD YOU TO SLEEP!

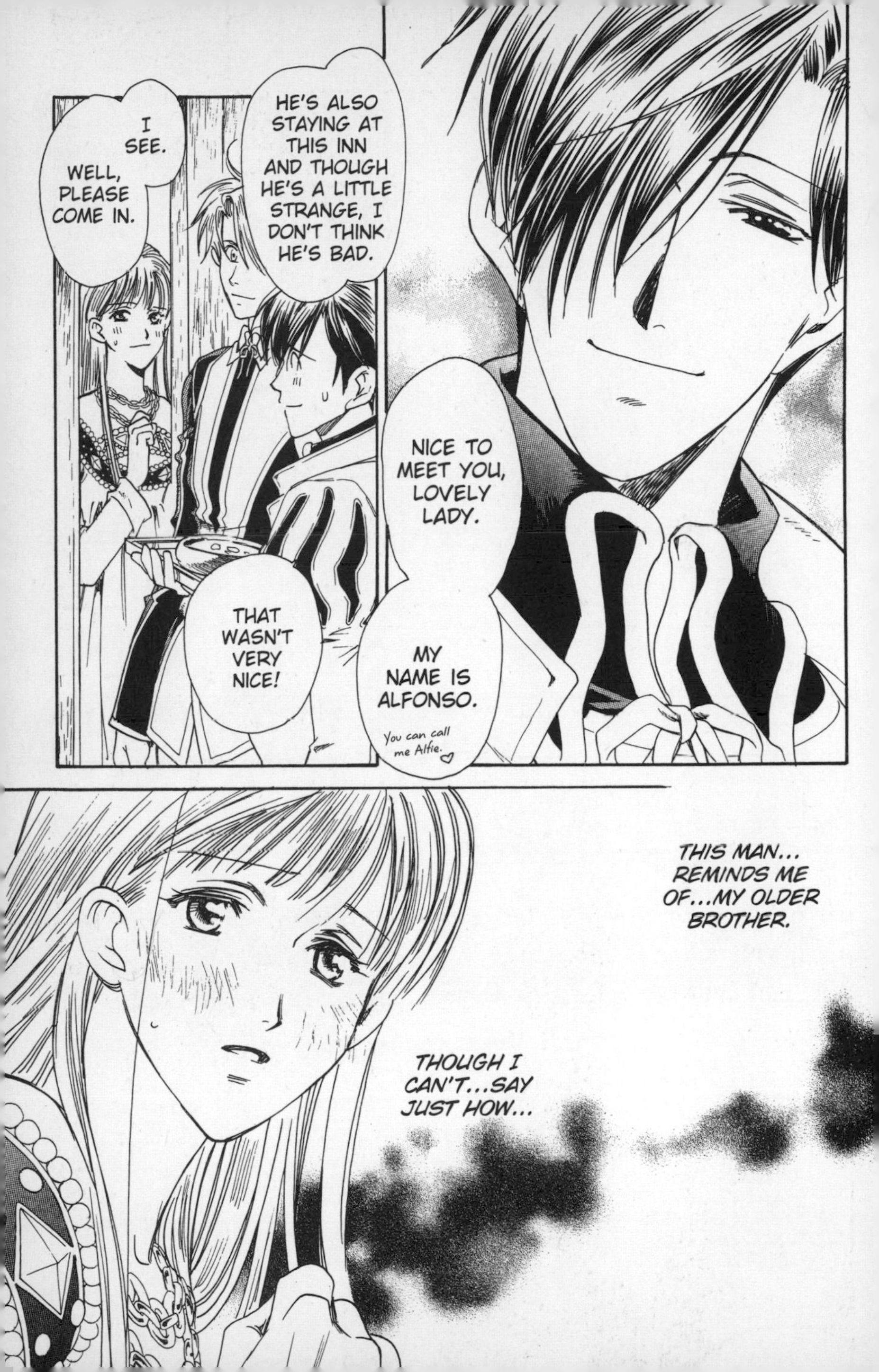
NICE TO MEET YOU, LOVELY LADY.
MY NAME IS ALFONSO.
You can call me Alfie.♡
HE'S ALSO STAYING AT THIS INN AND THOUGH HE'S A LITTLE STRANGE, I DON'T THINK HE'S BAD.
I SEE.
WELL, PLEASE COME IN.
THAT WASN'T VERY NICE!
THIS MAN... REMINDS ME OF...MY OLDER BROTHER.
THOUGH I CAN'T...SAY JUST HOW...

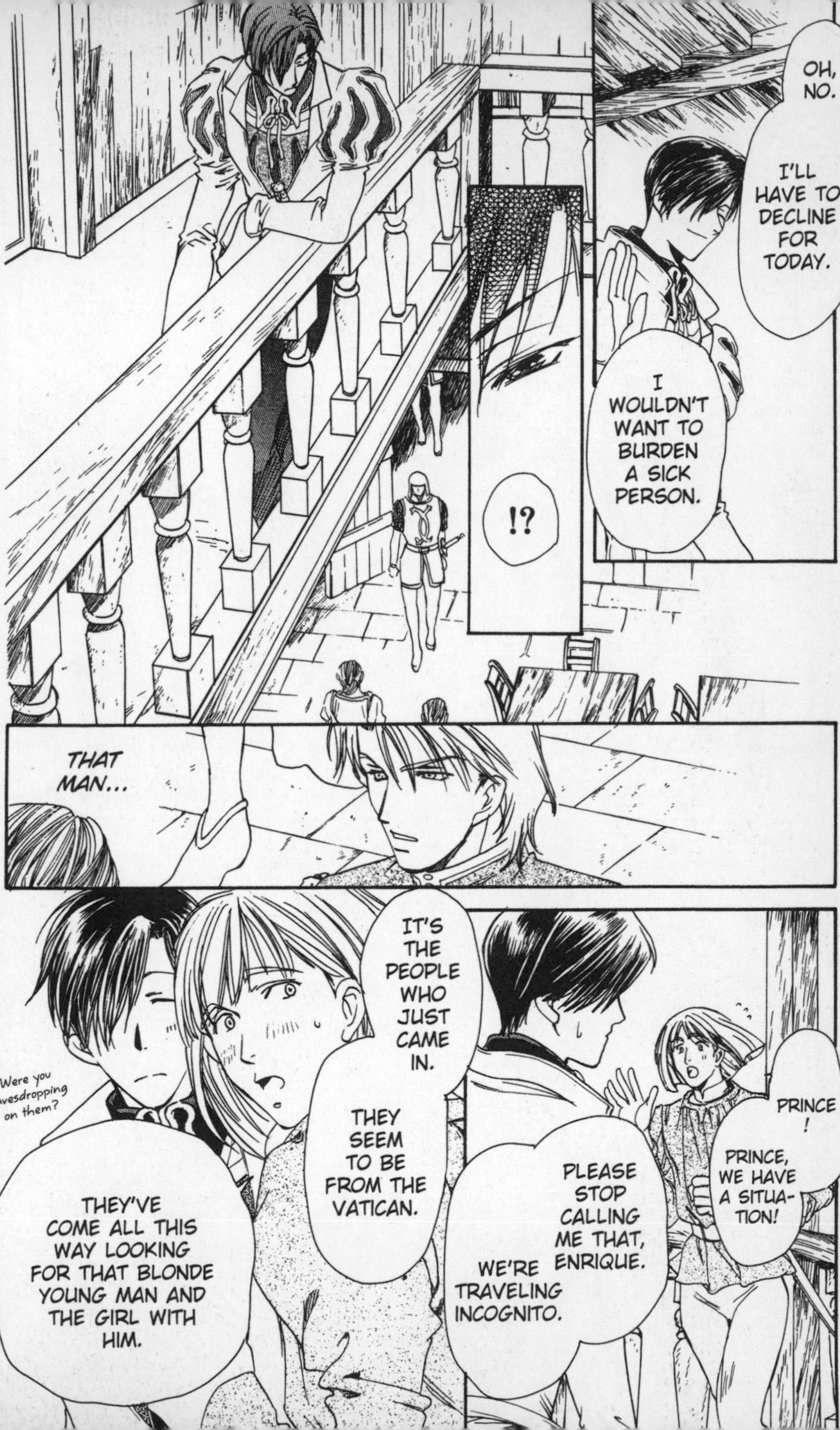
OH, NO.
I'LL HAVE TO DECLINE FOR TODAY.
I WOULDN'T WANT TO BURDEN A SICK PERSON.
!?
THAT MAN...
PRINCE!
PRINCE, WE HAVE A SITUA-TION!
PLEASE STOP CALLING ME THAT, ENRIQUE.
WE'RE TRAVELING INCOGNITO.
IT'S THE PEOPLE WHO JUST CAME IN.
THEY SEEM TO BE FROM THE VATICAN.
THEY'VE COME ALL THIS WAY LOOKING FOR THAT BLONDE YOUNG MAN AND THE GIRL WITH HIM.
Were you eavesdropping on them?

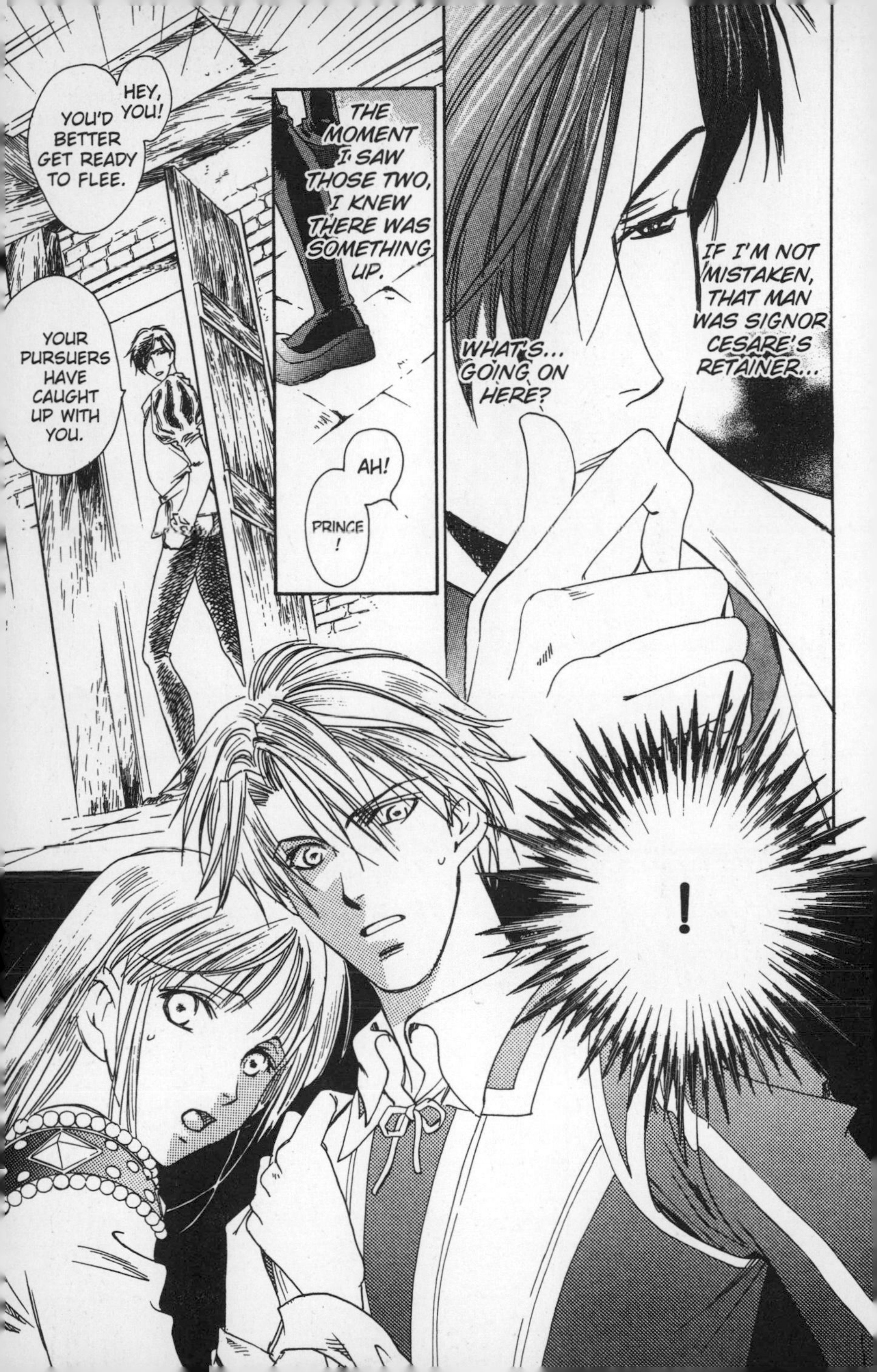
IF I'M NOT MISTAKEN, THAT MAN WAS SIGNOR CESARE'S RETAINER...
WHAT'S... GOING ON HERE?
THE MOMENT I SAW THOSE TWO, I KNEW THERE WAS SOMETHING UP.
AH!
PRINCE!
HEY, YOU!
YOU'D BETTER GET READY TO FLEE.
YOUR PURSUERS HAVE CAUGHT UP WITH YOU.
!

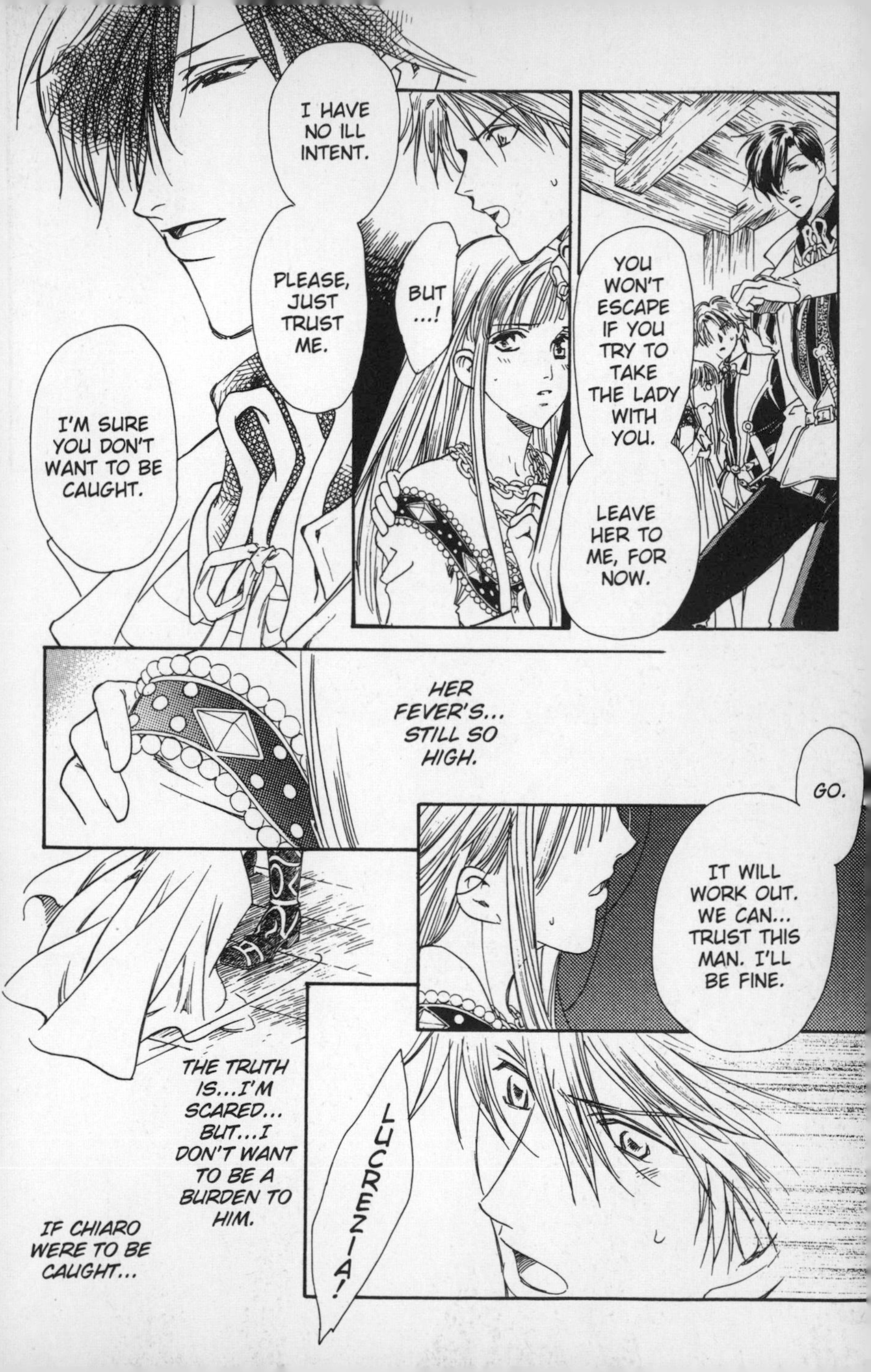
YOU WON'T ESCAPE IF YOU TRY TO TAKE THE LADY WITH YOU.
LEAVE HER TO ME, FOR NOW.
BUT ...!
I HAVE NO ILL INTENT.
PLEASE, JUST TRUST ME.
I'M SURE YOU DON'T WANT TO BE CAUGHT.
HER FEVER'S... STILL SO HIGH.
GO.
IT WILL WORK OUT. WE CAN... TRUST THIS MAN. I'LL BE FINE.
LUCREZIA!
THE TRUTH IS...I'M SCARED... BUT...I DON'T WANT TO BE A BURDEN TO HIM.
IF CHIARO WERE TO BE CAUGHT...

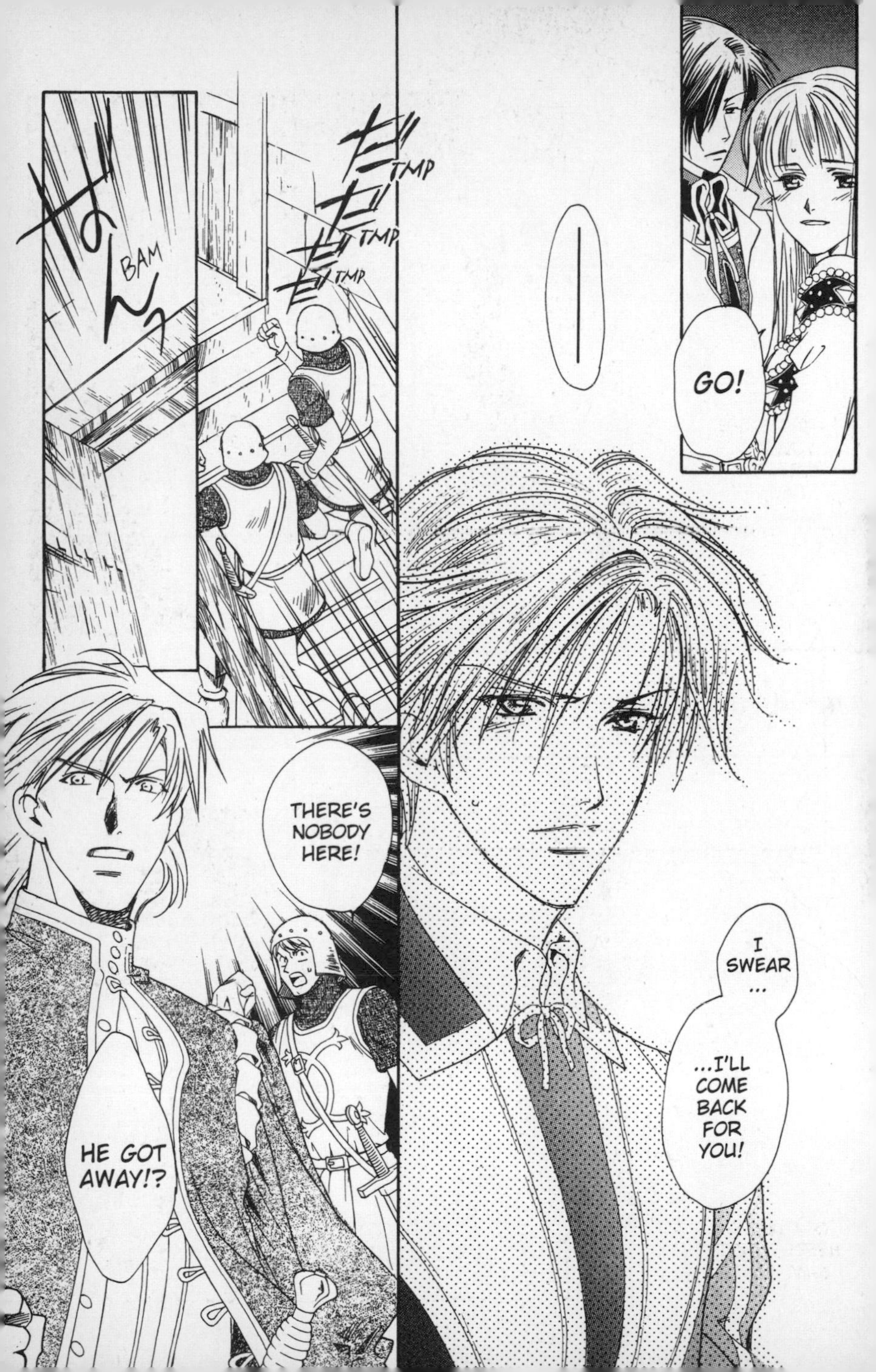
GO!
I SWEAR ...
...I'LL COME BACK FOR YOU!
BAM
TMP
TMP
TMP
THERE'S NOBODY HERE!
HE GOT AWAY!?

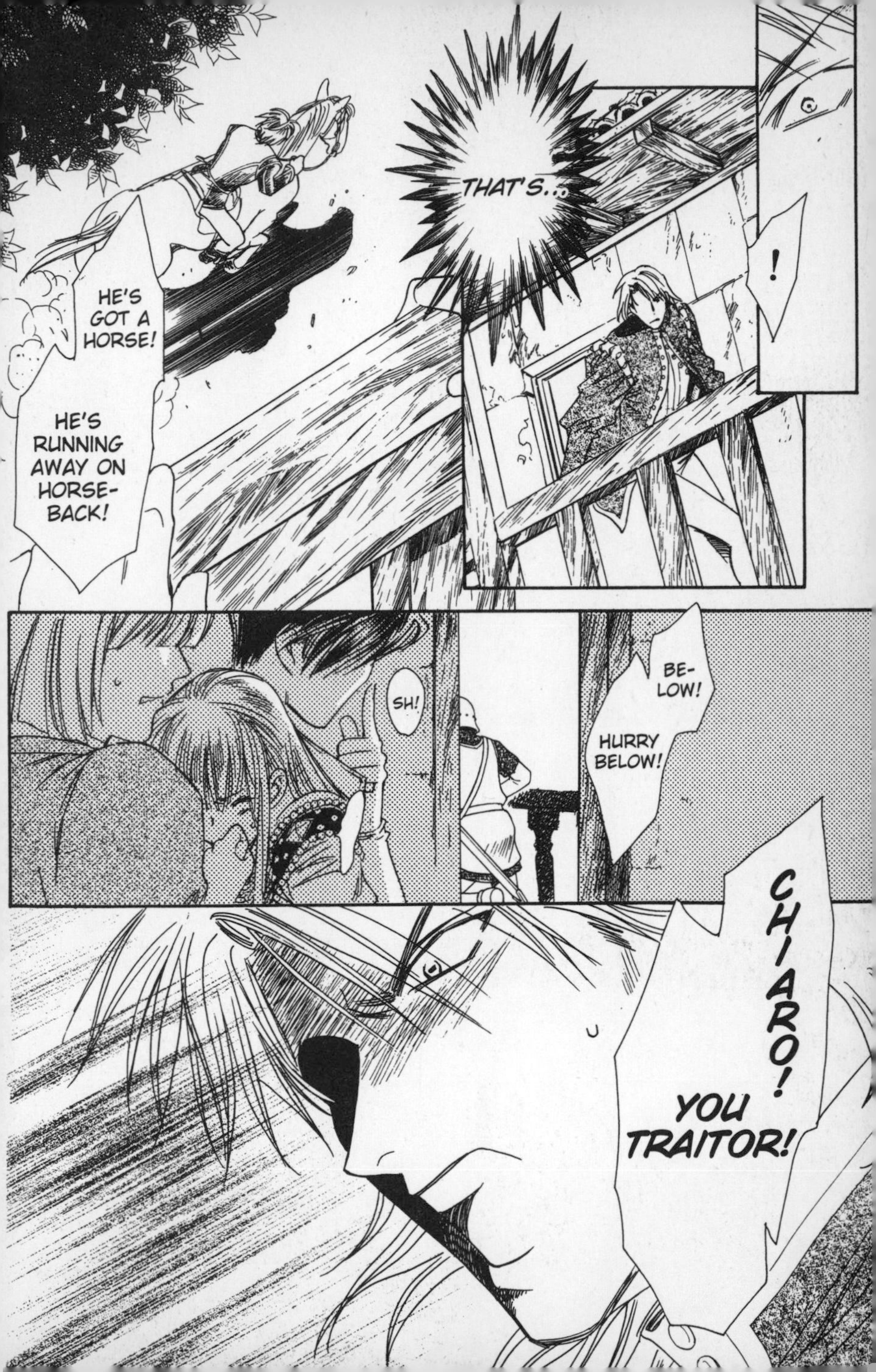
!
THAT'S...
HE'S GOT A HORSE!
HE'S RUNNING AWAY ON HORSE-BACK!
BE-LOW!
HURRY BELOW!
SH!
CHIARO!
YOU TRAITOR!

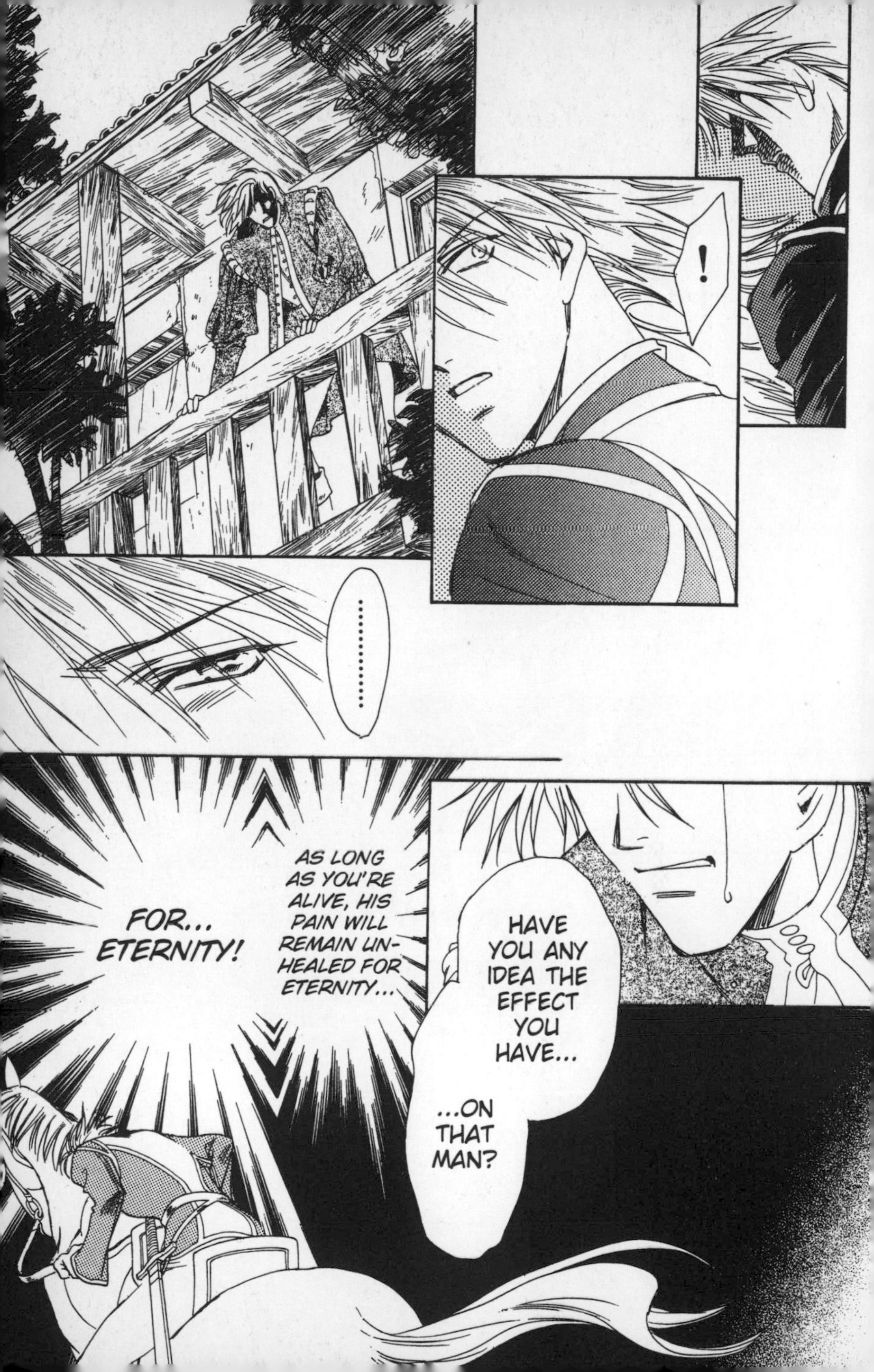
!
......
HAVE YOU ANY IDEA THE EFFECT YOU HAVE...
...ON THAT MAN?
AS LONG AS YOU'RE ALIVE, HIS PAIN WILL REMAIN UN-HEALED FOR ETERNITY...
FOR... ETERNITY!

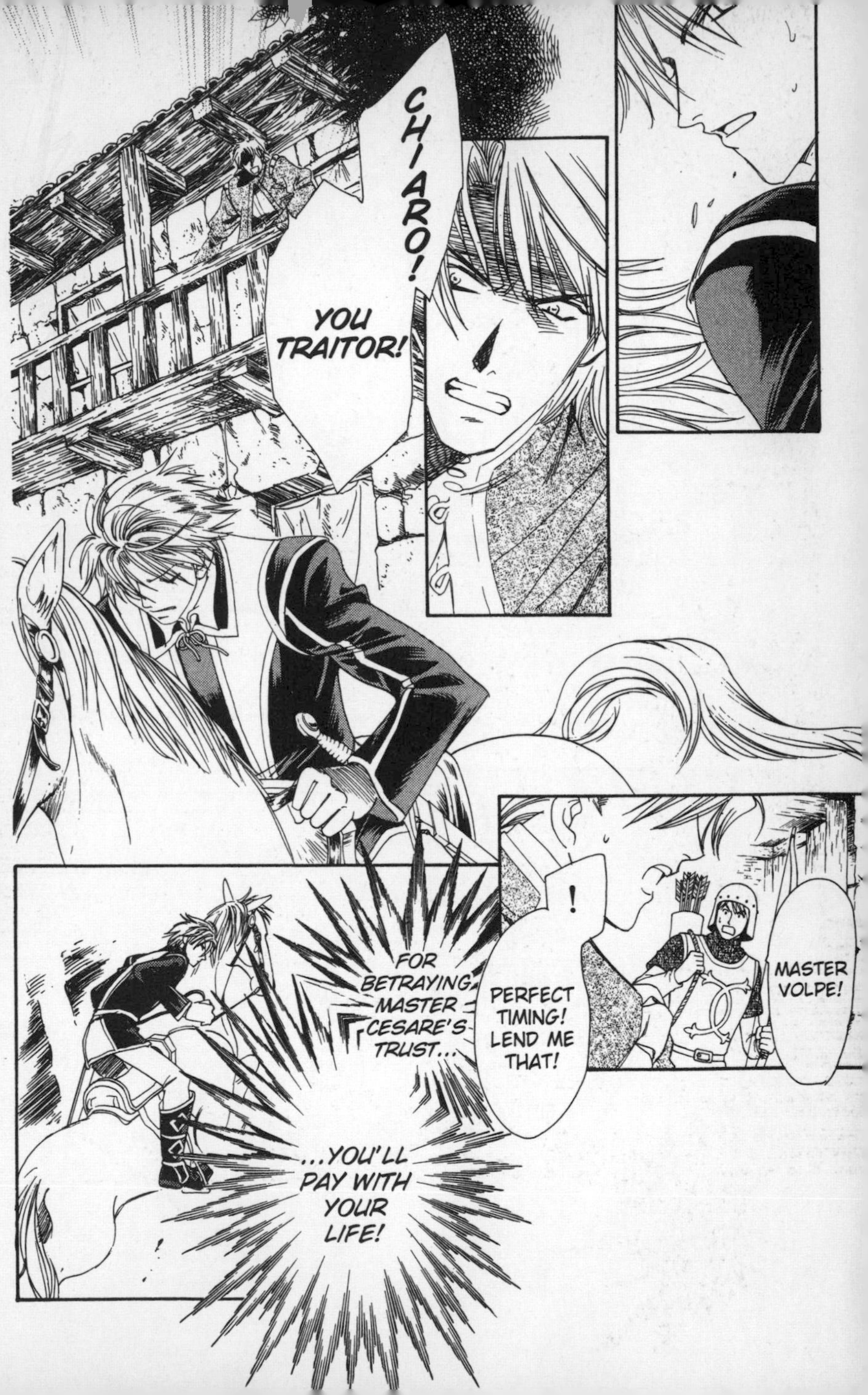
CHIARO!
YOU TRAITOR!
MASTER VOLPE!
!
PERFECT TIMING! LEND ME THAT!
FOR BETRAYING MASTER CESARE'S TRUST...
...YOU'LL PAY WITH YOUR LIFE!

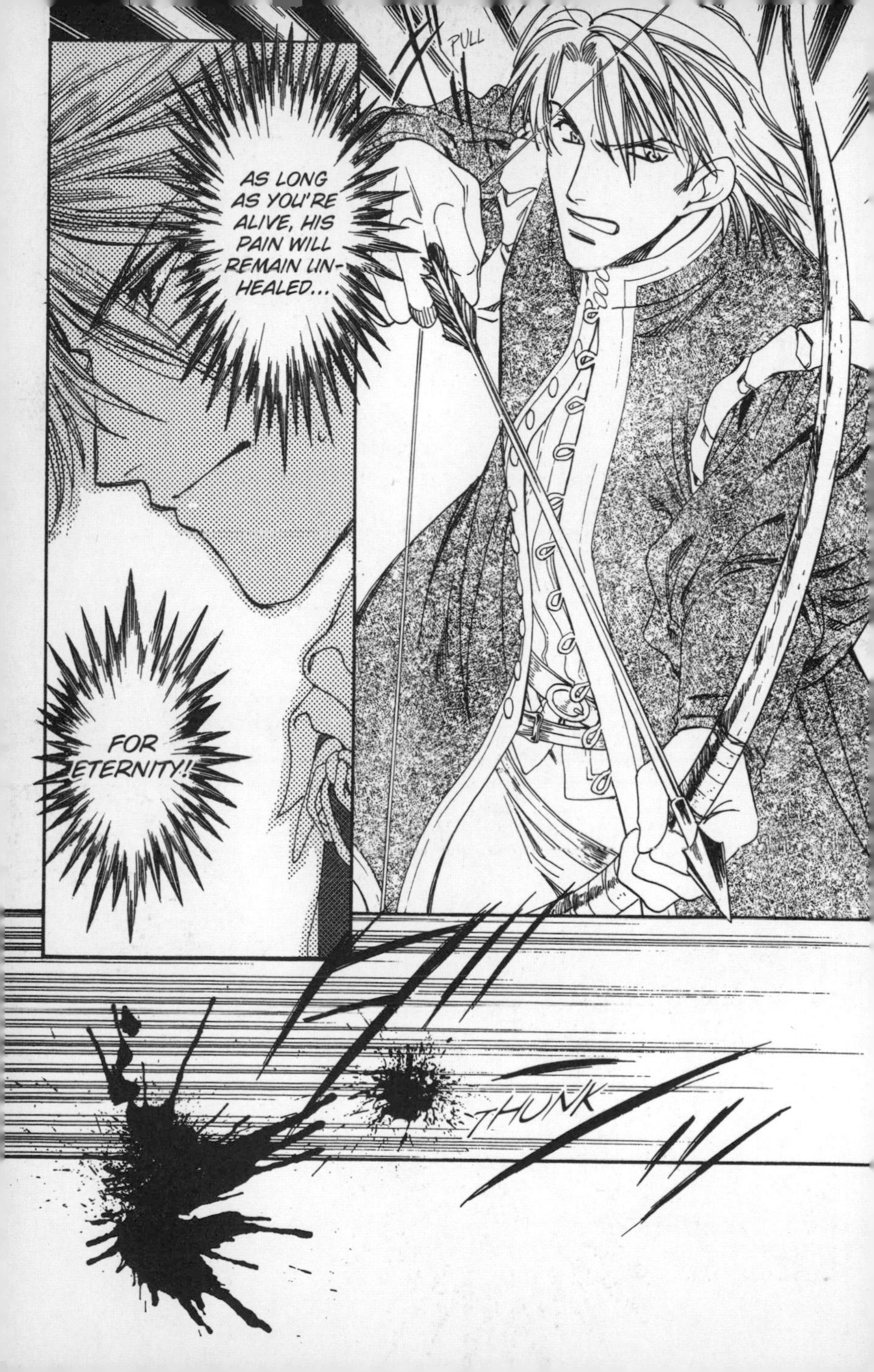
PULL
AS LONG AS YOU'RE ALIVE, HIS PAIN WILL REMAIN UN-HEALED...
FOR ETERNITY!!
THUNK

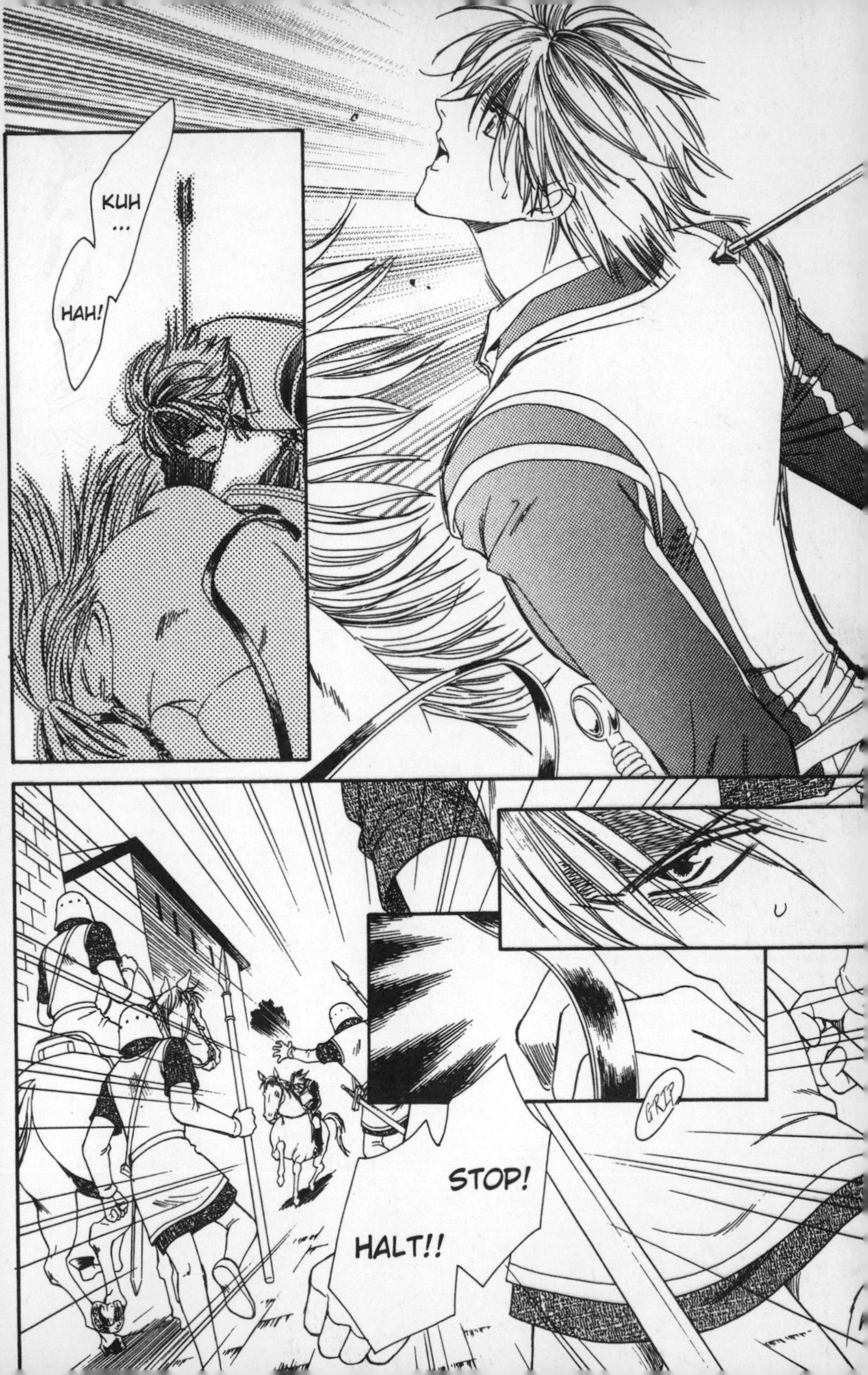
KUH ... HAH!
GRIP
STOP!
HALT!!

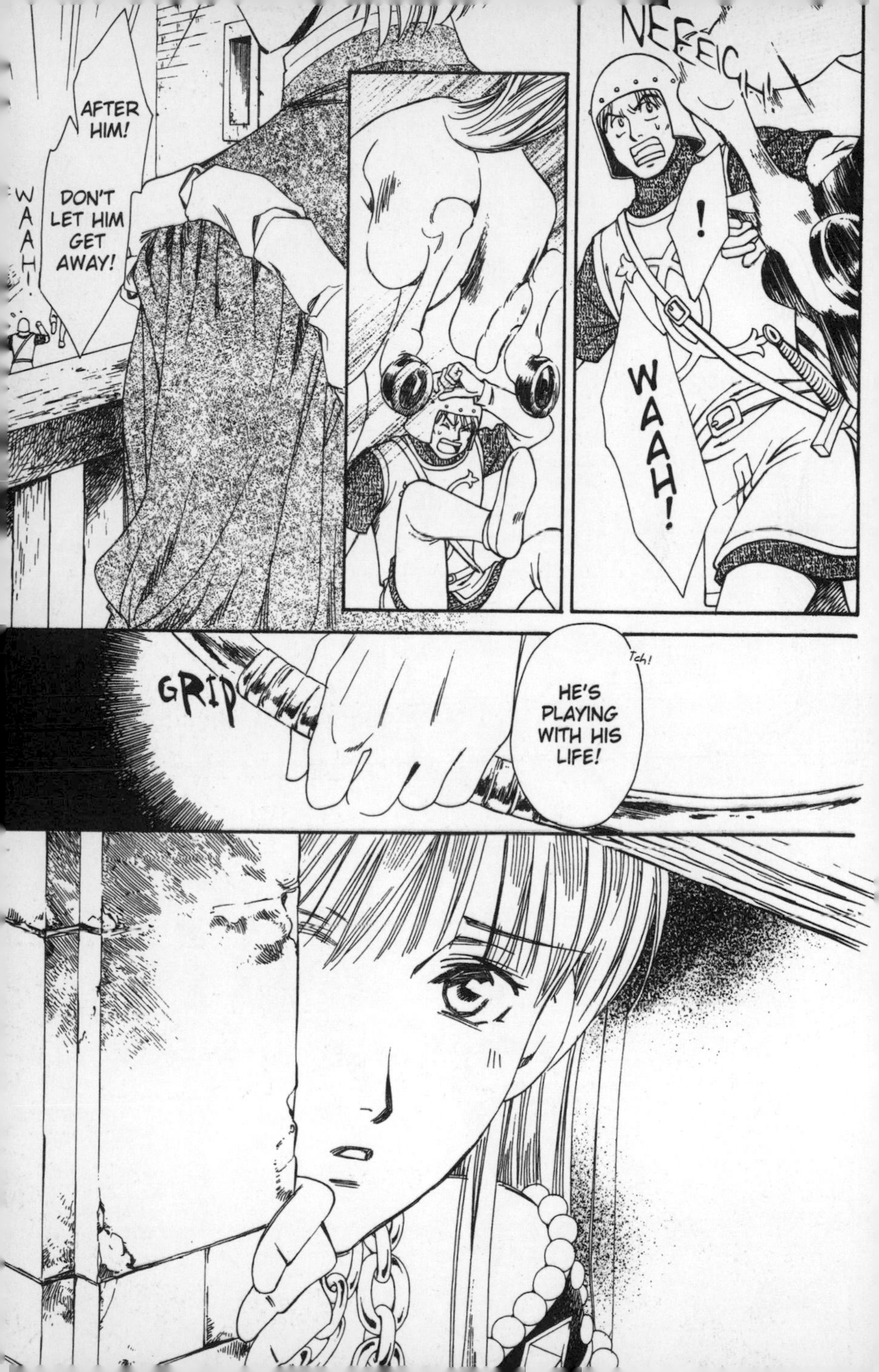
NEEEICH!
!
WAAH!
AFTER HIM!
DON'T LET HIM GET AWAY!
WAAH!
Tch!
HE'S PLAYING WITH HIS LIFE!
GRIP

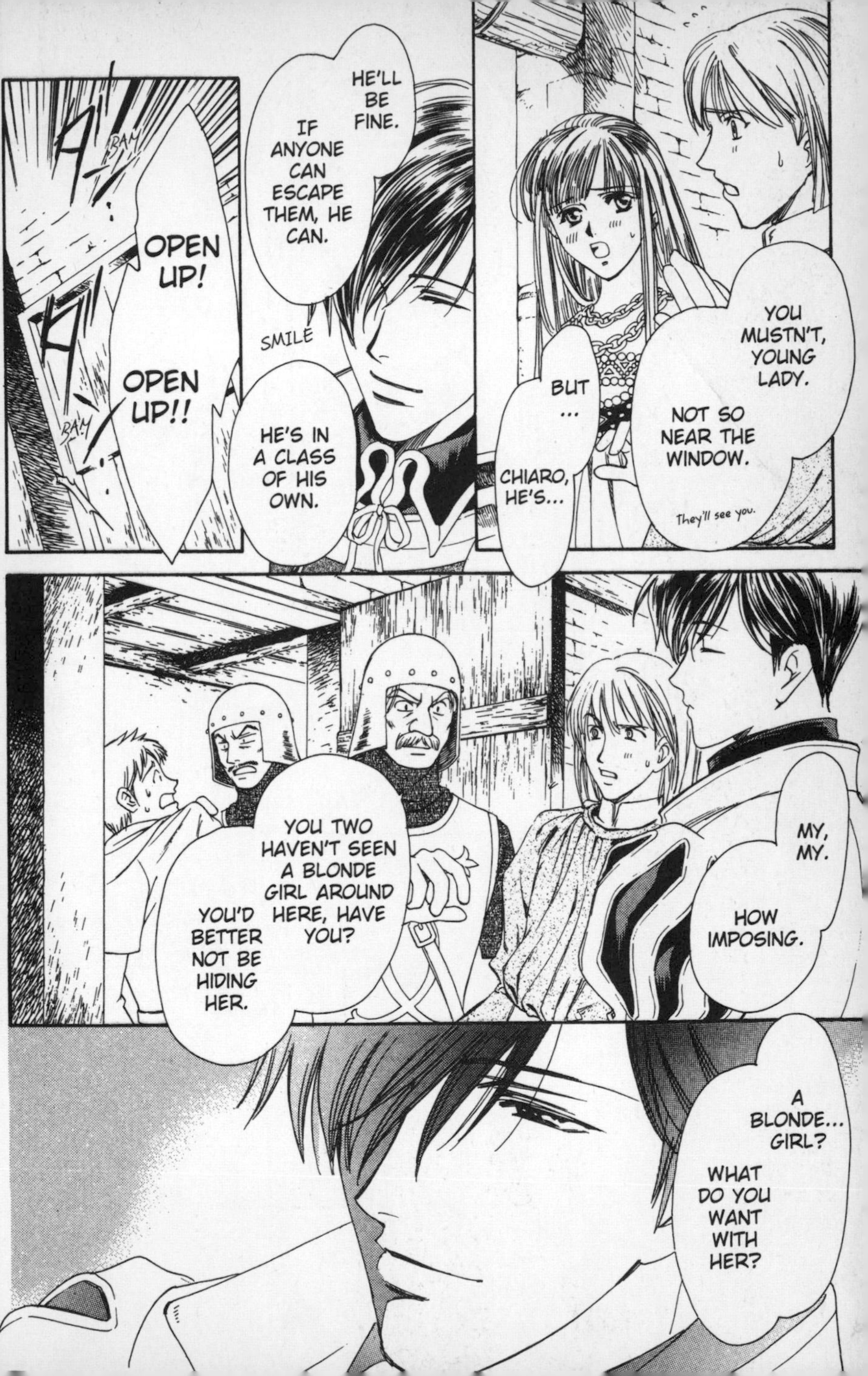

YOU MUSTN'T, YOUNG LADY.
NOT SO NEAR THE WINDOW.
They'll see you.
BUT...
CHIARO, HE'S...
HE'LL BE FINE.
IF ANYONE CAN ESCAPE THEM, HE CAN.
SMILE
HE'S IN A CLASS OF HIS OWN.
BAM
OPEN UP!
BAM
OPEN UP!!
MY, MY.
HOW IMPOSING.
YOU TWO HAVEN'T SEEN A BLONDE GIRL AROUND HERE, HAVE YOU?
YOU'D BETTER NOT BE HIDING HER.
A BLONDE... GIRL?
WHAT DO YOU WANT WITH HER?

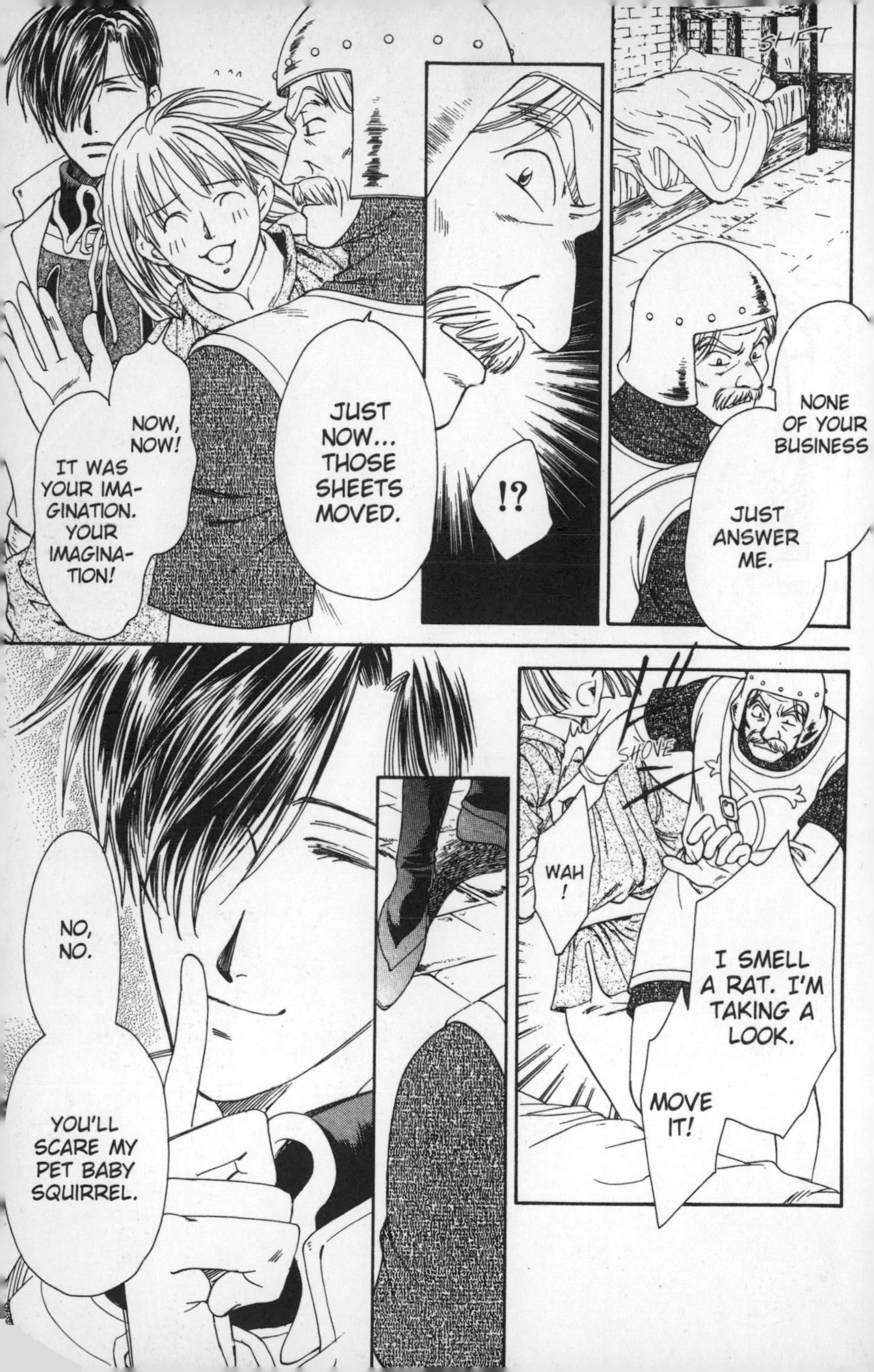
SHIFT
NONE OF YOUR BUSINESS
JUST ANSWER ME.
!?
JUST NOW... THOSE SHEETS MOVED.
NOW, NOW! IT WAS YOUR IMAGINATION. YOUR IMAGINATION!
SHOVE
WAH!
I SMELL A RAT. I'M TAKING A LOOK.
MOVE IT!
NO, NO.
YOU'LL SCARE MY PET BABY SQUIRREL.

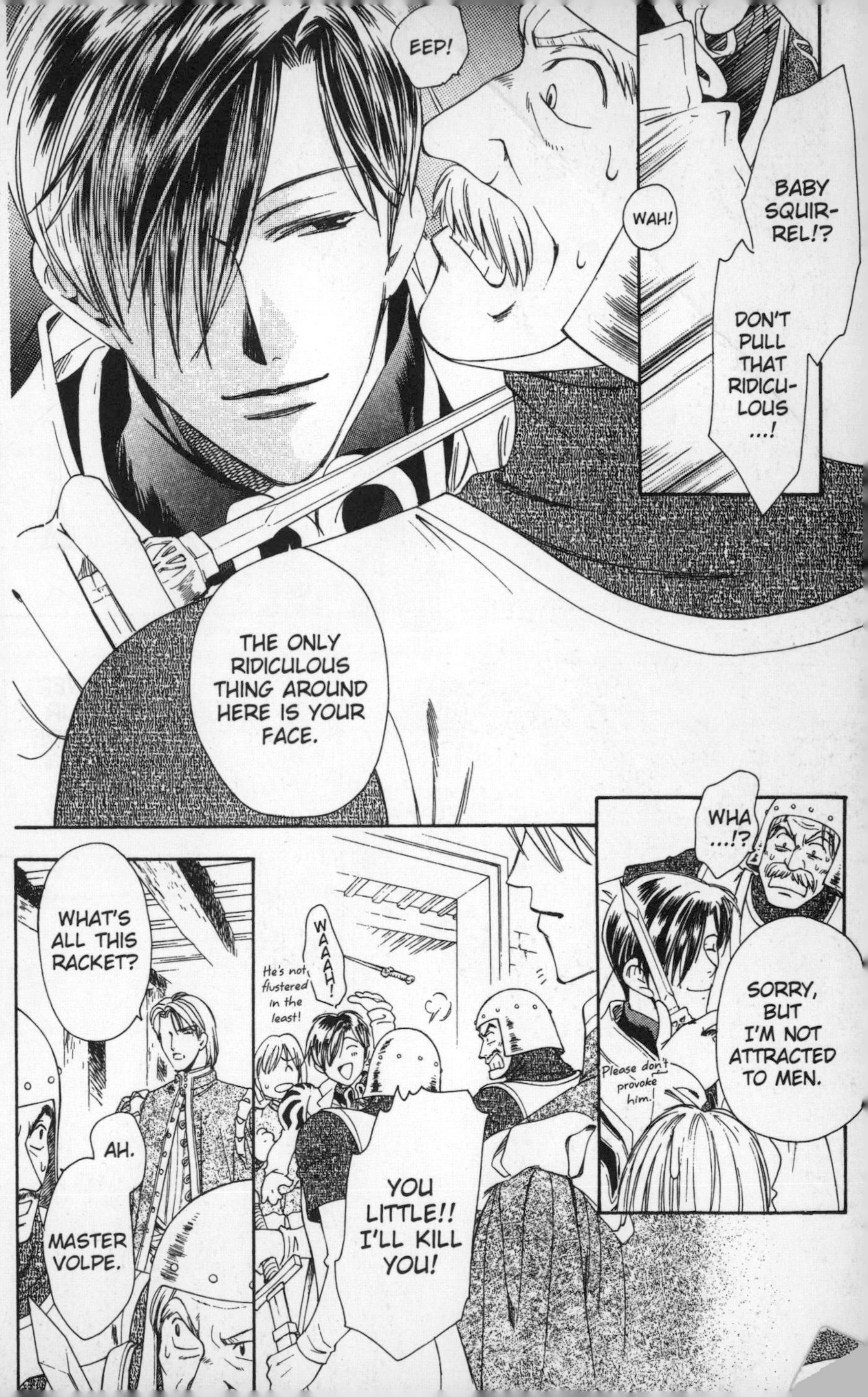
BABY SQUIRREL!?
DON'T PULL THAT RIDICULOUS ...!
EEP!
WAH!
THE ONLY RIDICULOUS THING AROUND HERE IS YOUR FACE.
WHA ...!?
SORRY, BUT I'M NOT ATTRACTED TO MEN.
Please don't provoke him.
YOU LITTLE!! I'LL KILL YOU!
WAAAH!
He's not flustered in the least!
WHAT'S ALL THIS RACKET?
AH.
MASTER VOLPE.

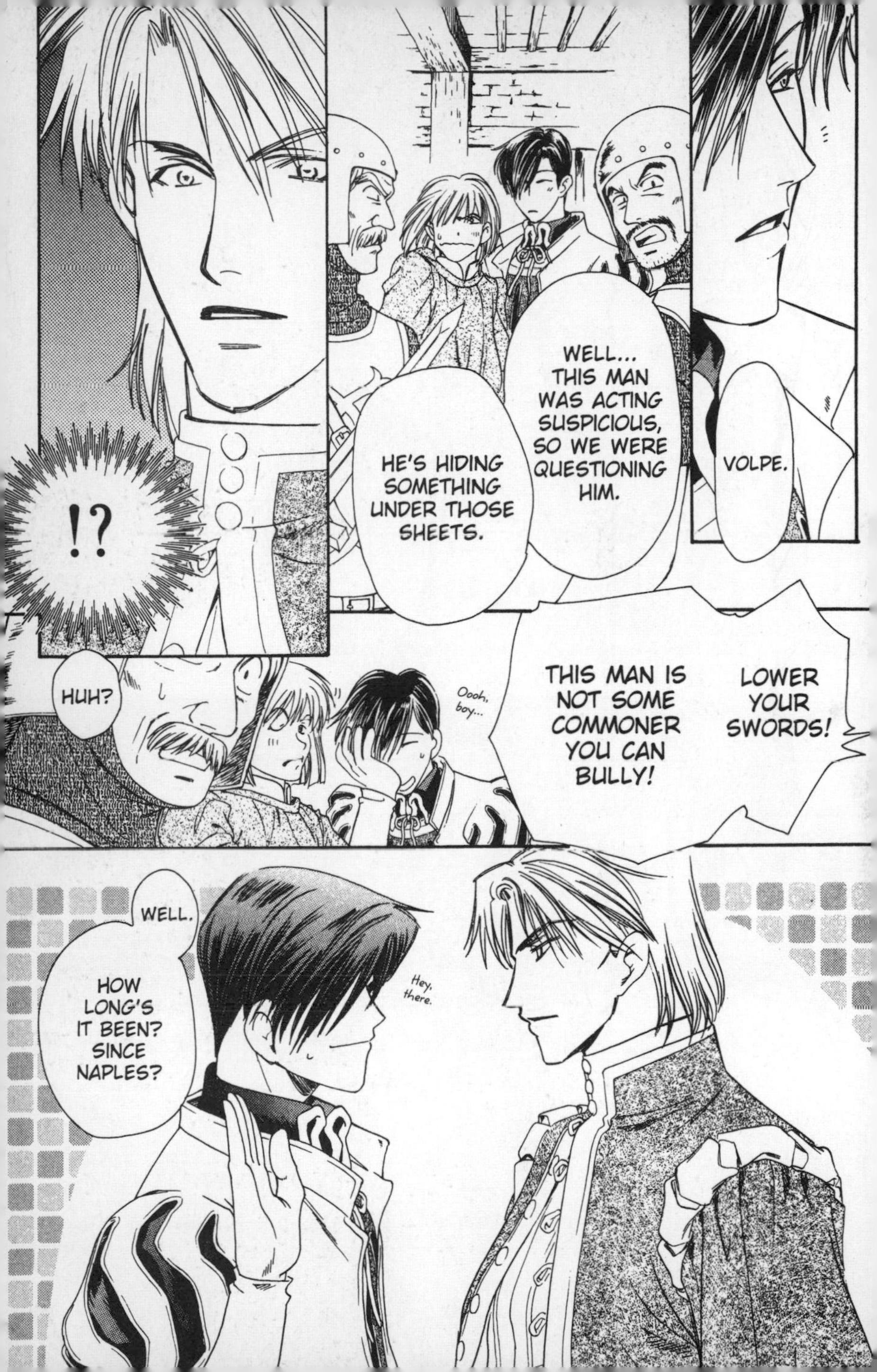
VOLPE.
WELL... THIS MAN WAS ACTING SUSPICIOUS, SO WE WERE QUESTIONING HIM.
HE'S HIDING SOMETHING UNDER THOSE SHEETS.
!?
LOWER YOUR SWORDS!
THIS MAN IS NOT SOME COMMONER YOU CAN BULLY!
Oooh, boy...
HUH?
Hey, there.
WELL.
HOW LONG'S IT BEEN? SINCE NAPLES?

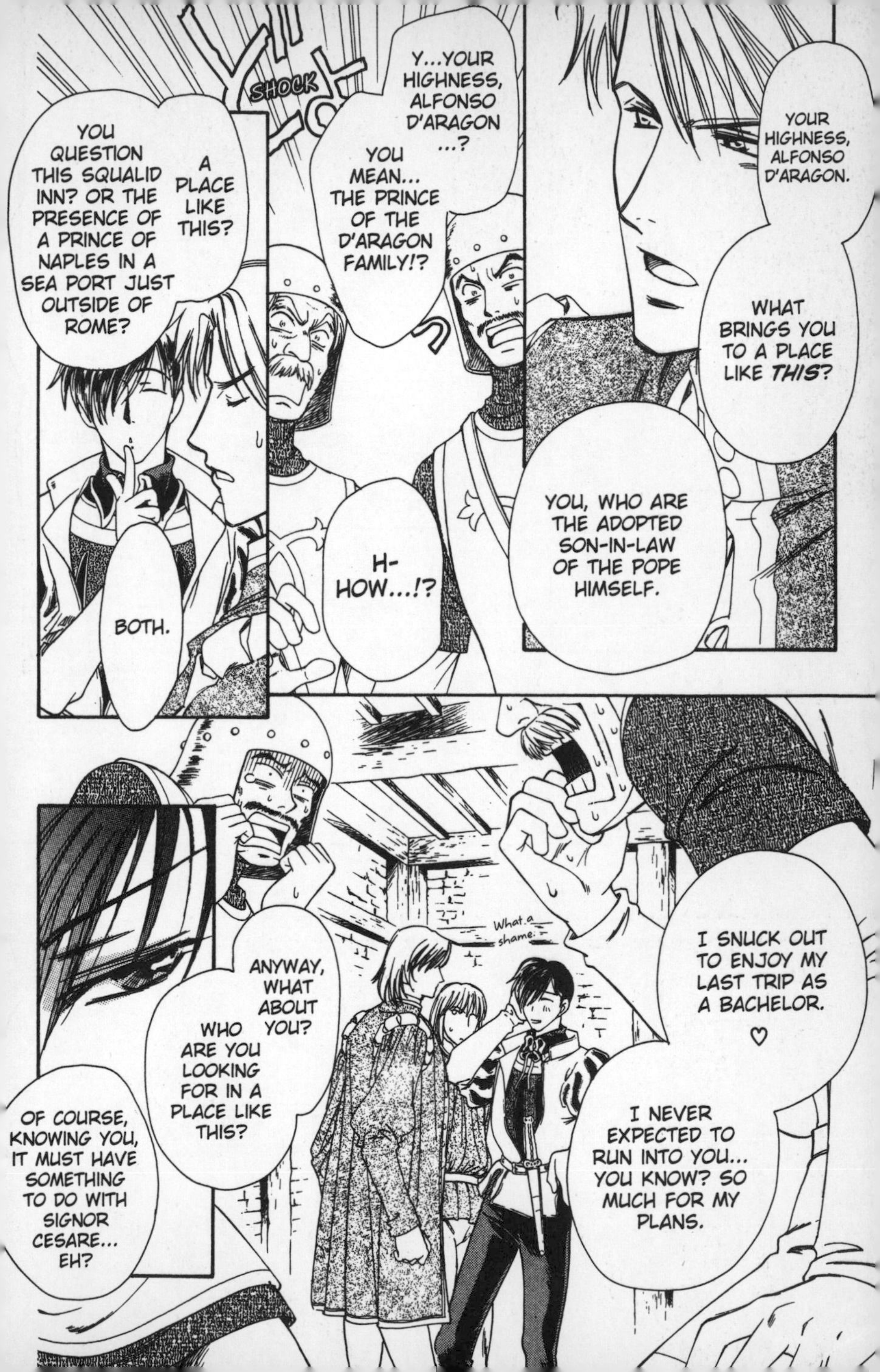
YOUR HIGHNESS, ALFONSO D'ARAGON.
WHAT BRINGS YOU TO A PLACE LIKE *THIS*?
YOU, WHO ARE THE ADOPTED SON-IN-LAW OF THE POPE HIMSELF.
Y...YOUR HIGHNESS, ALFONSO D'ARAGON ...?
YOU MEAN... THE PRINCE OF THE D'ARAGON FAMILY!?
SHOCK
H- HOW...!?
A PLACE LIKE THIS?
YOU QUESTION THIS SQUALID INN? OR THE PRESENCE OF A PRINCE OF NAPLES IN A SEA PORT JUST OUTSIDE OF ROME?
BOTH.
I SNUCK OUT TO ENJOY MY LAST TRIP AS A BACHELOR. ♡
I NEVER EXPECTED TO RUN INTO YOU... YOU KNOW? SO MUCH FOR MY PLANS.
What a shame.
ANYWAY, WHAT ABOUT YOU?
WHO ARE YOU LOOKING FOR IN A PLACE LIKE THIS?
OF COURSE, KNOWING YOU, IT MUST HAVE SOMETHING TO DO WITH SIGNOR CESARE... EH?

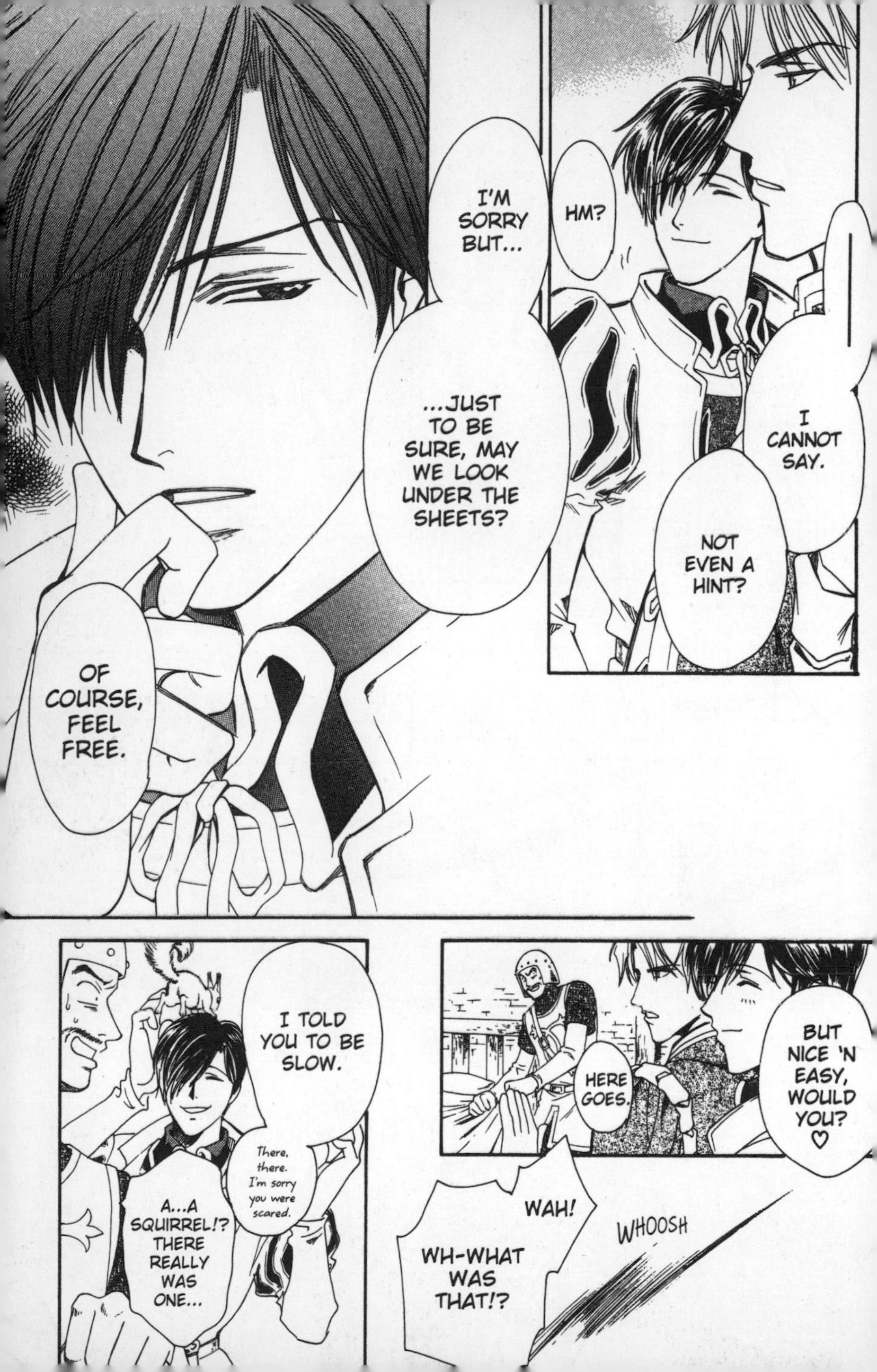
I CANNOT SAY.
NOT EVEN A HINT?
HM?
I'M SORRY BUT...
...JUST TO BE SURE, MAY WE LOOK UNDER THE SHEETS?
OF COURSE, FEEL FREE.
BUT NICE 'N EASY, WOULD YOU? ♡
HERE GOES.
WHOOSH
WAH!
WH-WHAT WAS THAT!?
I TOLD YOU TO BE SLOW.
There, there. I'm sorry you were scared.
A...A SQUIRREL!? THERE REALLY WAS ONE...

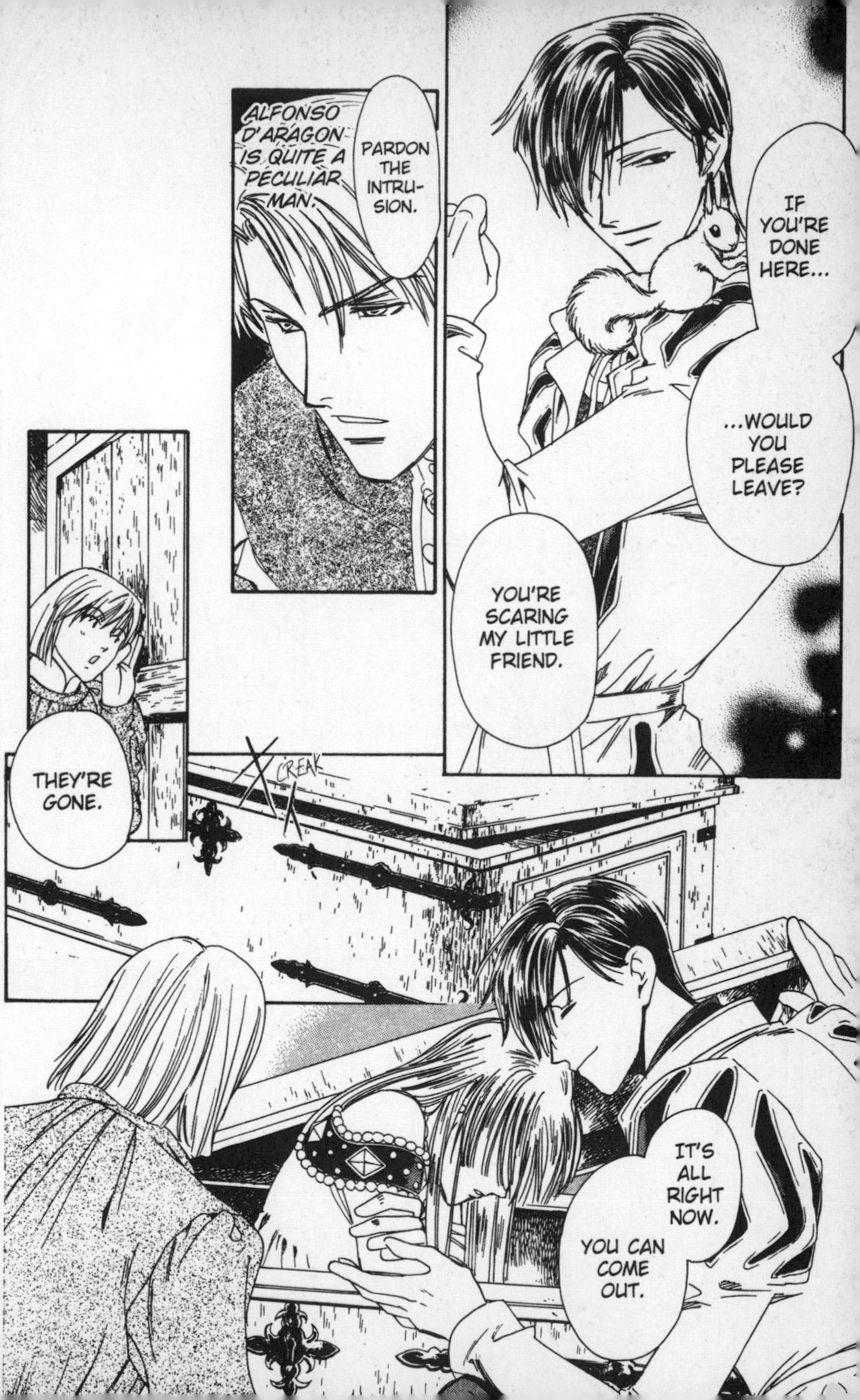
IF YOU'RE DONE HERE...
...WOULD YOU PLEASE LEAVE?
YOU'RE SCARING MY LITTLE FRIEND.
PARDON THE INTRU-SION.
ALFONSO D'ARAGON IS QUITE A PECULIAR MAN.
THEY'RE GONE.
CREAK
IT'S ALL RIGHT NOW.
YOU CAN COME OUT.

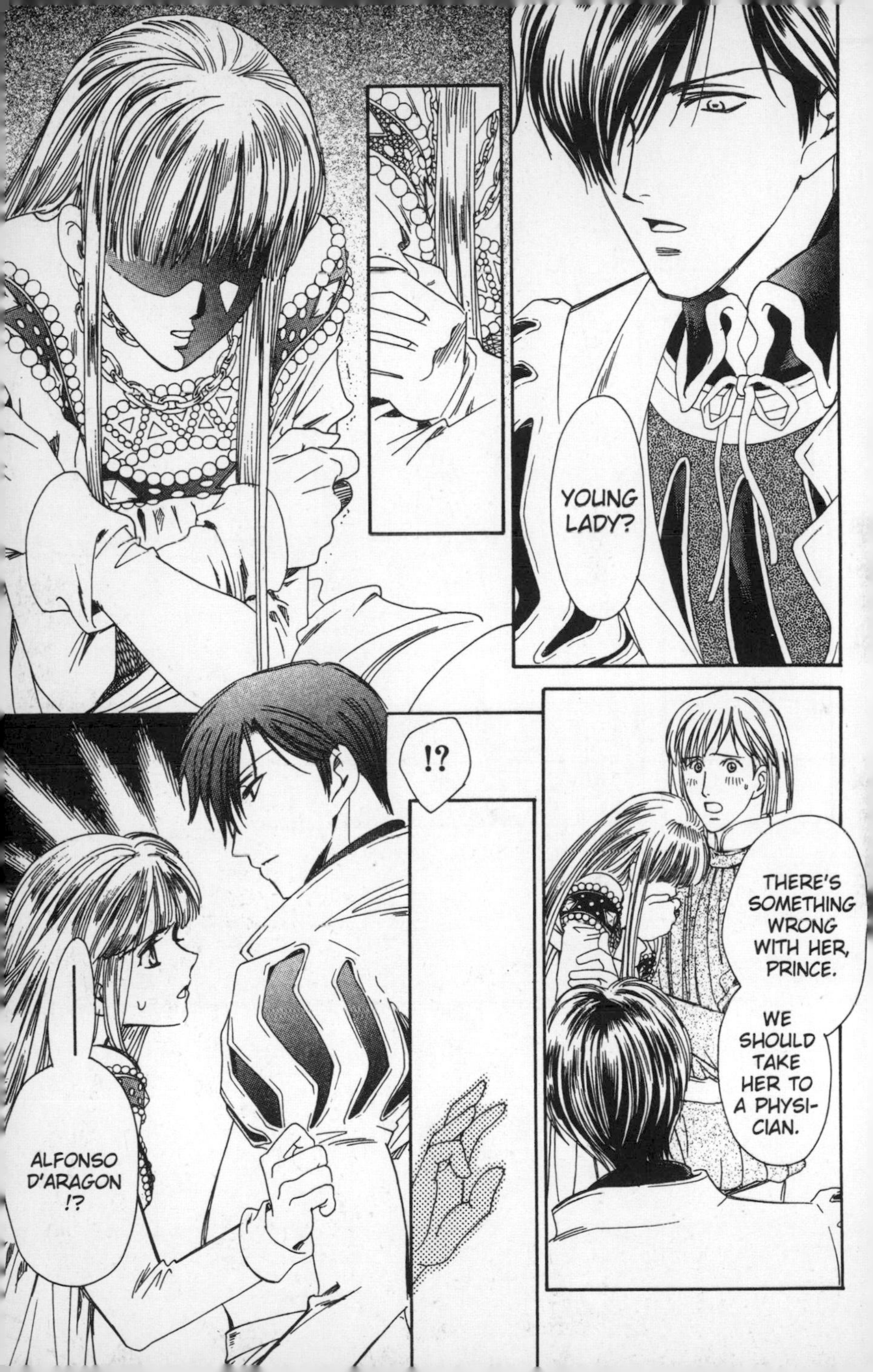
YOUNG LADY?
THERE'S SOMETHING WRONG WITH HER, PRINCE.
WE SHOULD TAKE HER TO A PHYSICIAN.
!?
ALFONSO D'ARAGON !?

YES.

THIS MAN
IS MY...!?

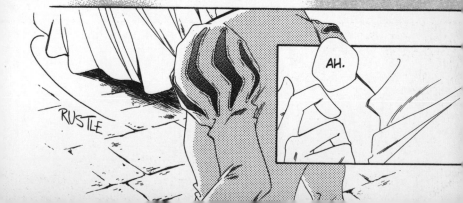

RUSTLE

AH.

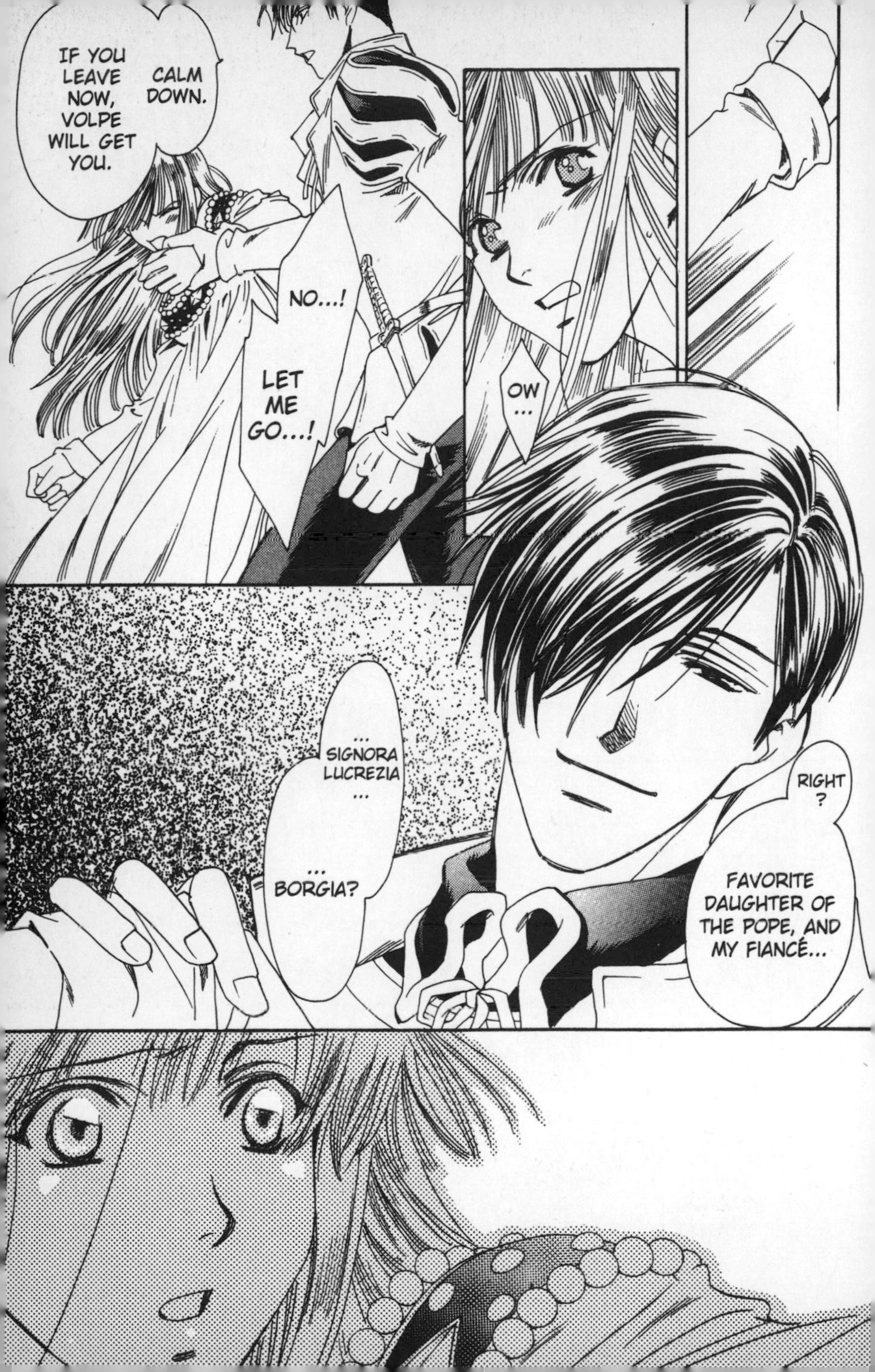
OW ...
CALM DOWN.
IF YOU LEAVE NOW, VOLPE WILL GET YOU.
NO...!
LET ME GO...!
RIGHT?
FAVORITE DAUGHTER OF THE POPE, AND MY FIANCÉ...
... SIGNORA LUCREZIA ...
... BORGIA?

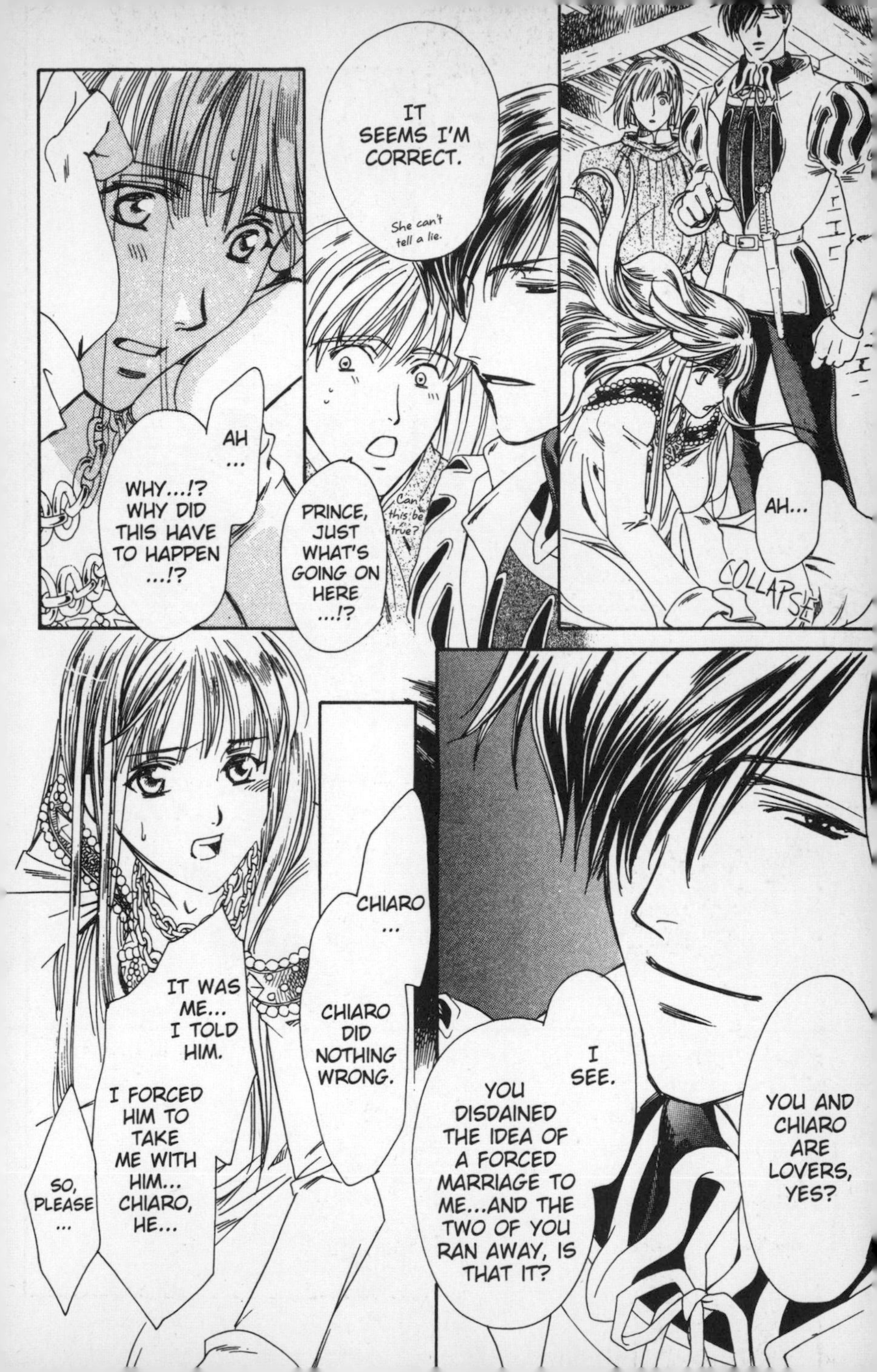
AH...
COLLAPSE
IT SEEMS I'M CORRECT.
She can't tell a lie.
PRINCE, JUST WHAT'S GOING ON HERE ...!?
Can't this be true?
AH ...
WHY...!? WHY DID THIS HAVE TO HAPPEN ...!?
YOU AND CHIARO ARE LOVERS, YES?
I SEE.
YOU DISDAINED THE IDEA OF A FORCED MARRIAGE TO ME...AND THE TWO OF YOU RAN AWAY, IS THAT IT?
CHIARO ...
CHIARO DID NOTHING WRONG.
IT WAS ME... I TOLD HIM.
I FORCED HIM TO TAKE ME WITH HIM... CHIARO, HE...
SO, PLEASE ...

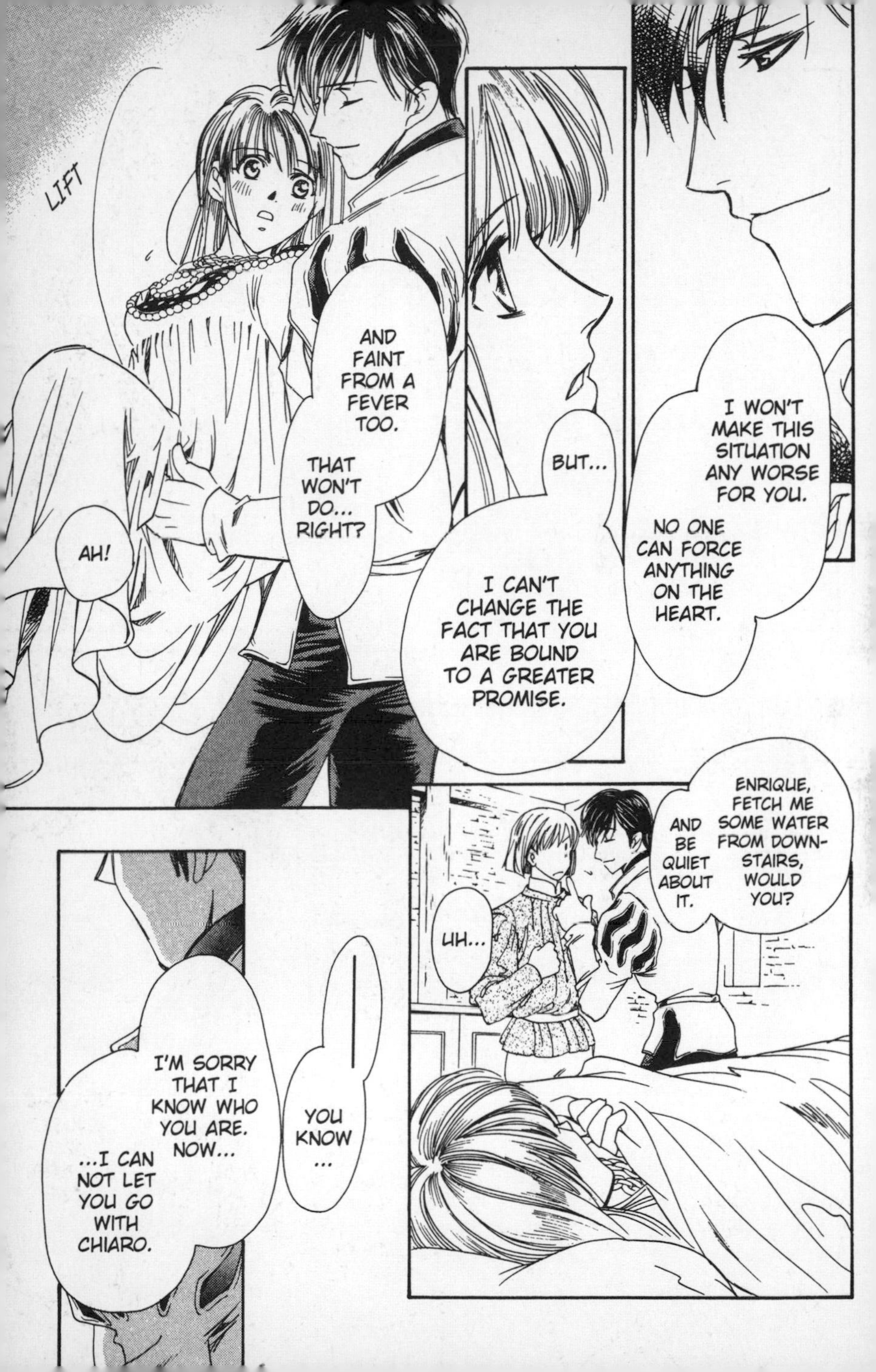
I WON'T MAKE THIS SITUATION ANY WORSE FOR YOU.
NO ONE CAN FORCE ANYTHING ON THE HEART.
BUT...
I CAN'T CHANGE THE FACT THAT YOU ARE BOUND TO A GREATER PROMISE.
LIFT
AND FAINT FROM A FEVER TOO.
THAT WON'T DO... RIGHT?
AH!
ENRIQUE, FETCH ME SOME WATER FROM DOWN-STAIRS, WOULD YOU?
AND BE QUIET ABOUT IT.
UH...
YOU KNOW ...
I'M SORRY THAT I KNOW WHO YOU ARE. NOW...
...I CAN NOT LET YOU GO WITH CHIARO.

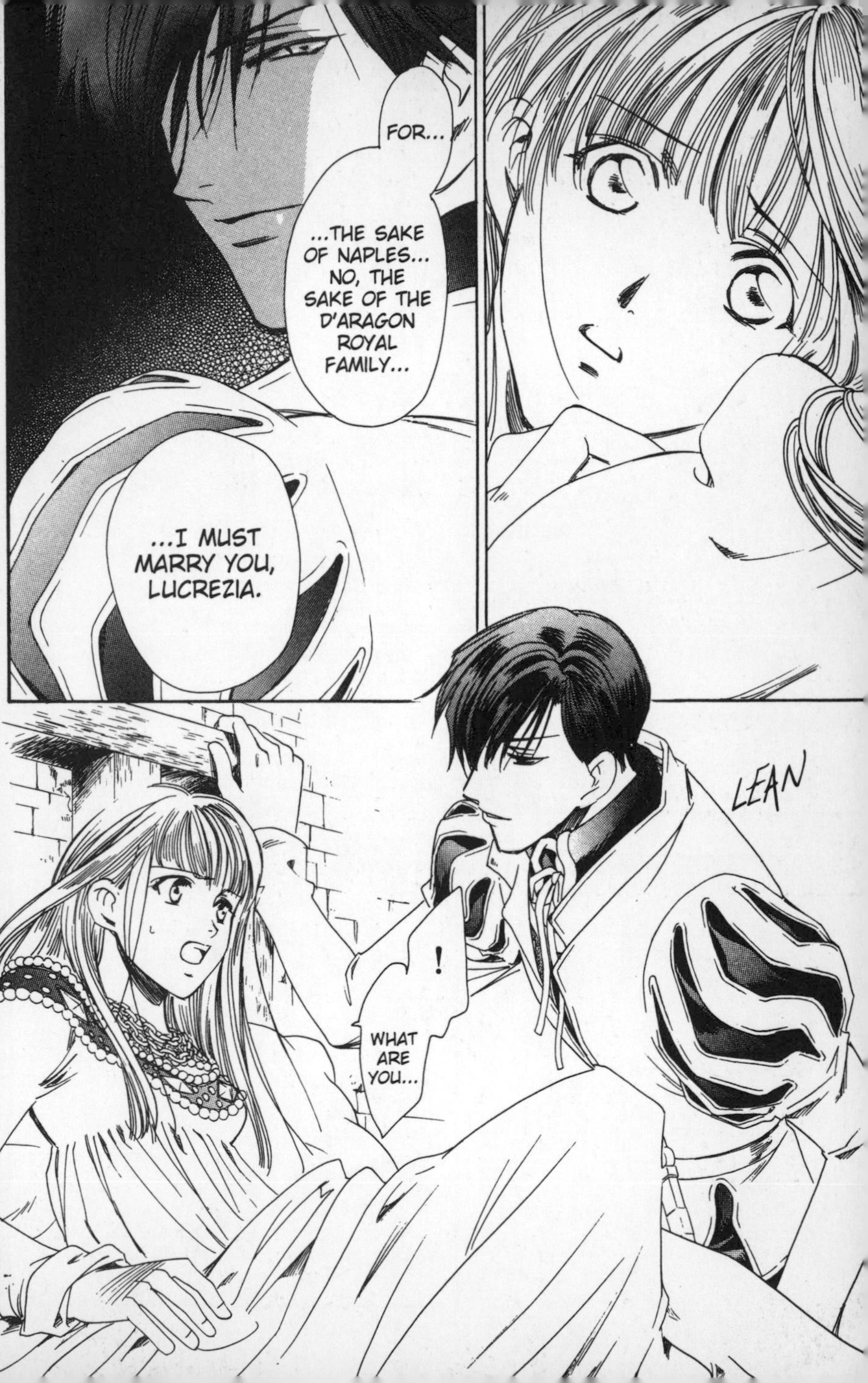
FOR...
...THE SAKE OF NAPLES... NO, THE SAKE OF THE D'ARAGON ROYAL FAMILY...
...I MUST MARRY YOU, LUCREZIA.
LEAN
!
WHAT ARE YOU...

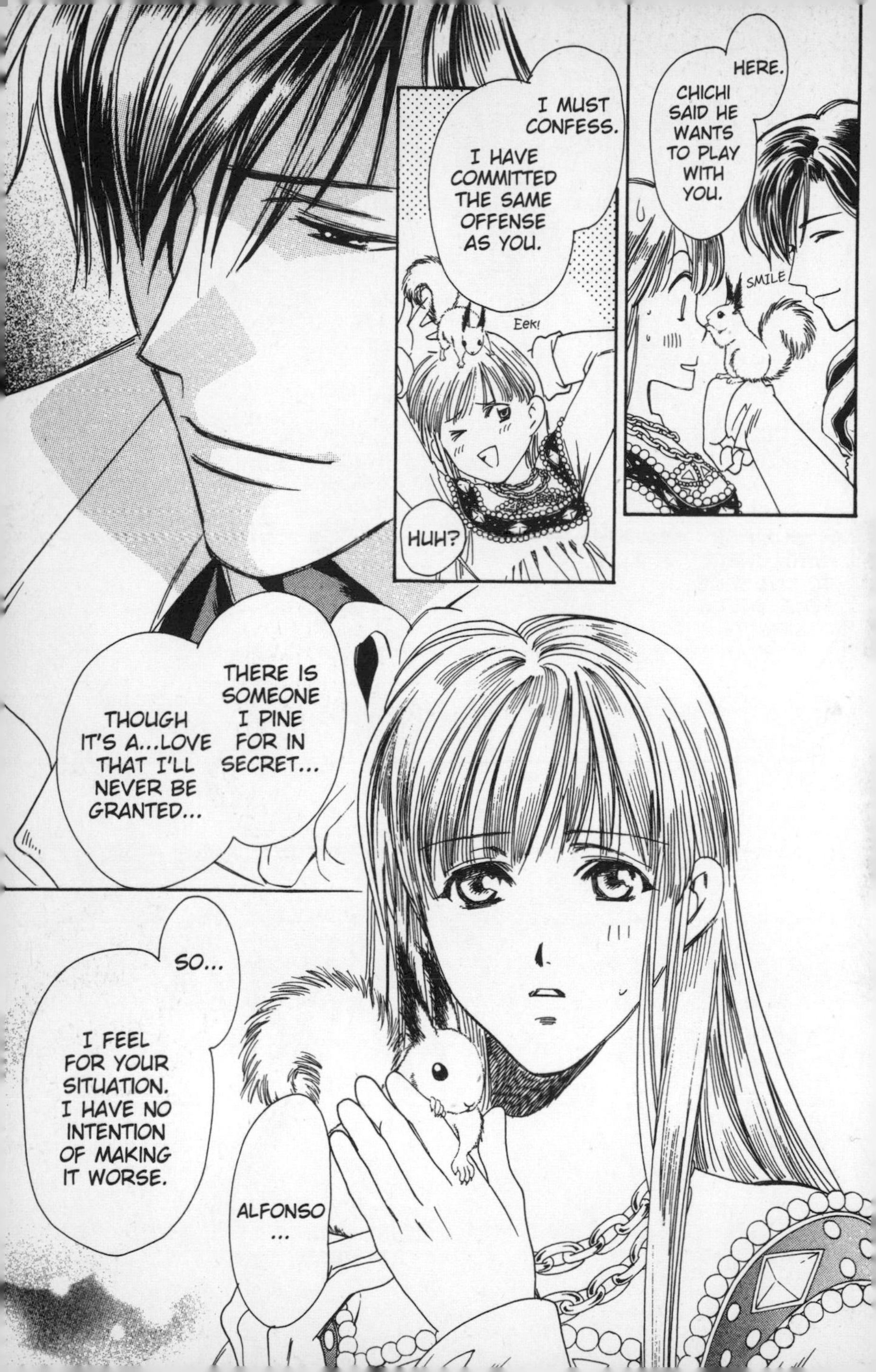
HERE.
CHICHI SAID HE WANTS TO PLAY WITH YOU.
SMILE
I MUST CONFESS.
I HAVE COMMITTED THE SAME OFFENSE AS YOU.
Eek!
HUH?
THERE IS SOMEONE I PINE FOR IN SECRET...
THOUGH IT'S A...LOVE THAT I'LL NEVER BE GRANTED...
SO...
I FEEL FOR YOUR SITUATION. I HAVE NO INTENTION OF MAKING IT WORSE.
ALFONSO ...

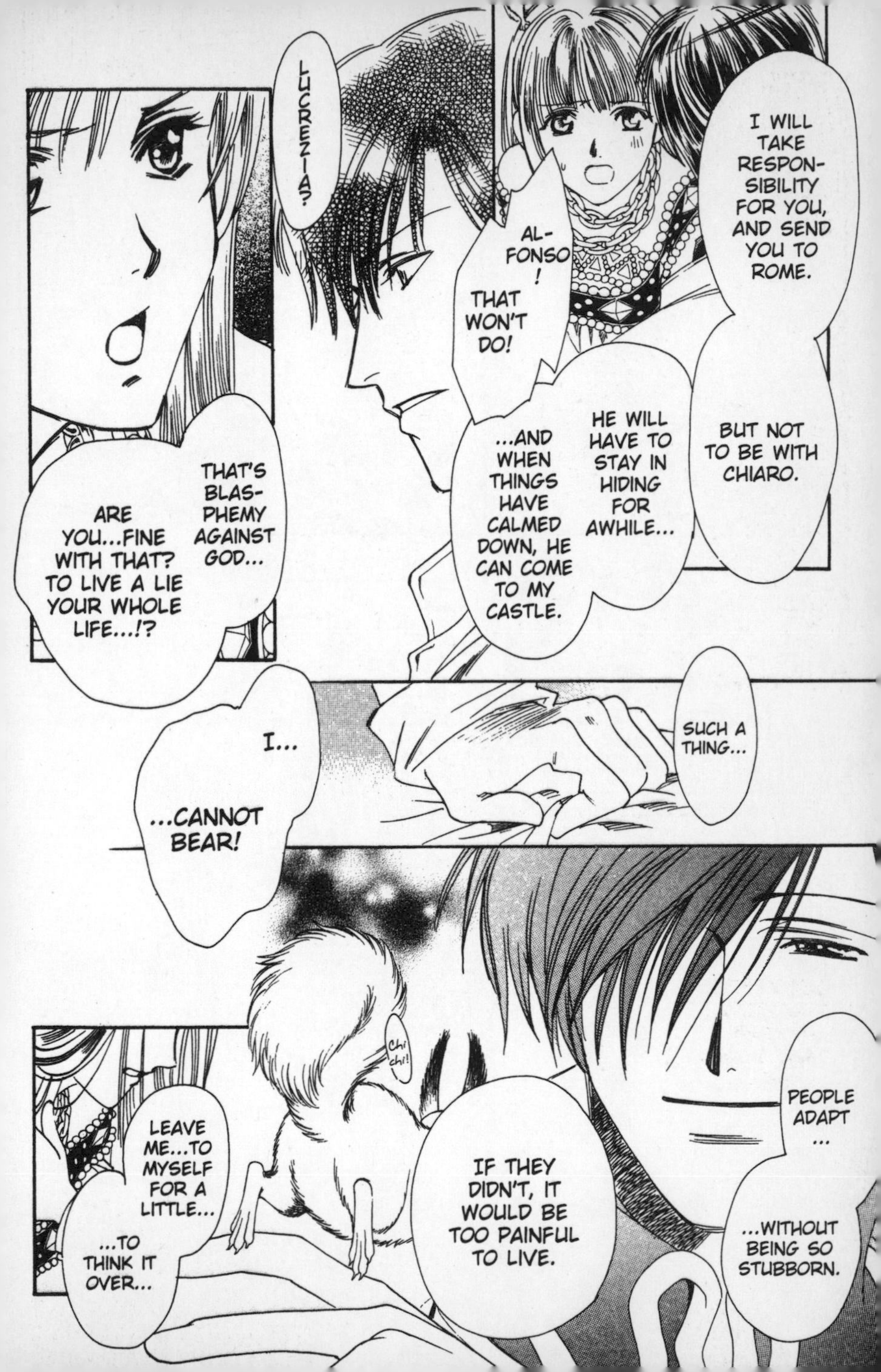
I WILL TAKE RESPONSIBILITY FOR YOU, AND SEND YOU TO ROME.
BUT NOT TO BE WITH CHIARO.
HE WILL HAVE TO STAY IN HIDING FOR AWHILE...
...AND WHEN THINGS HAVE CALMED DOWN, HE CAN COME TO MY CASTLE.
ALFONSO!
THAT WON'T DO!
LUCREZIA?
THAT'S BLASPHEMY AGAINST GOD...
ARE YOU...FINE WITH THAT? TO LIVE A LIE YOUR WHOLE LIFE...!?
SUCH A THING...
I...
...CANNOT BEAR!
PEOPLE ADAPT...
...WITHOUT BEING SO STUBBORN.
IF THEY DIDN'T, IT WOULD BE TOO PAINFUL TO LIVE.
Chi chi!
LEAVE ME...TO MYSELF FOR A LITTLE...
...TO THINK IT OVER...

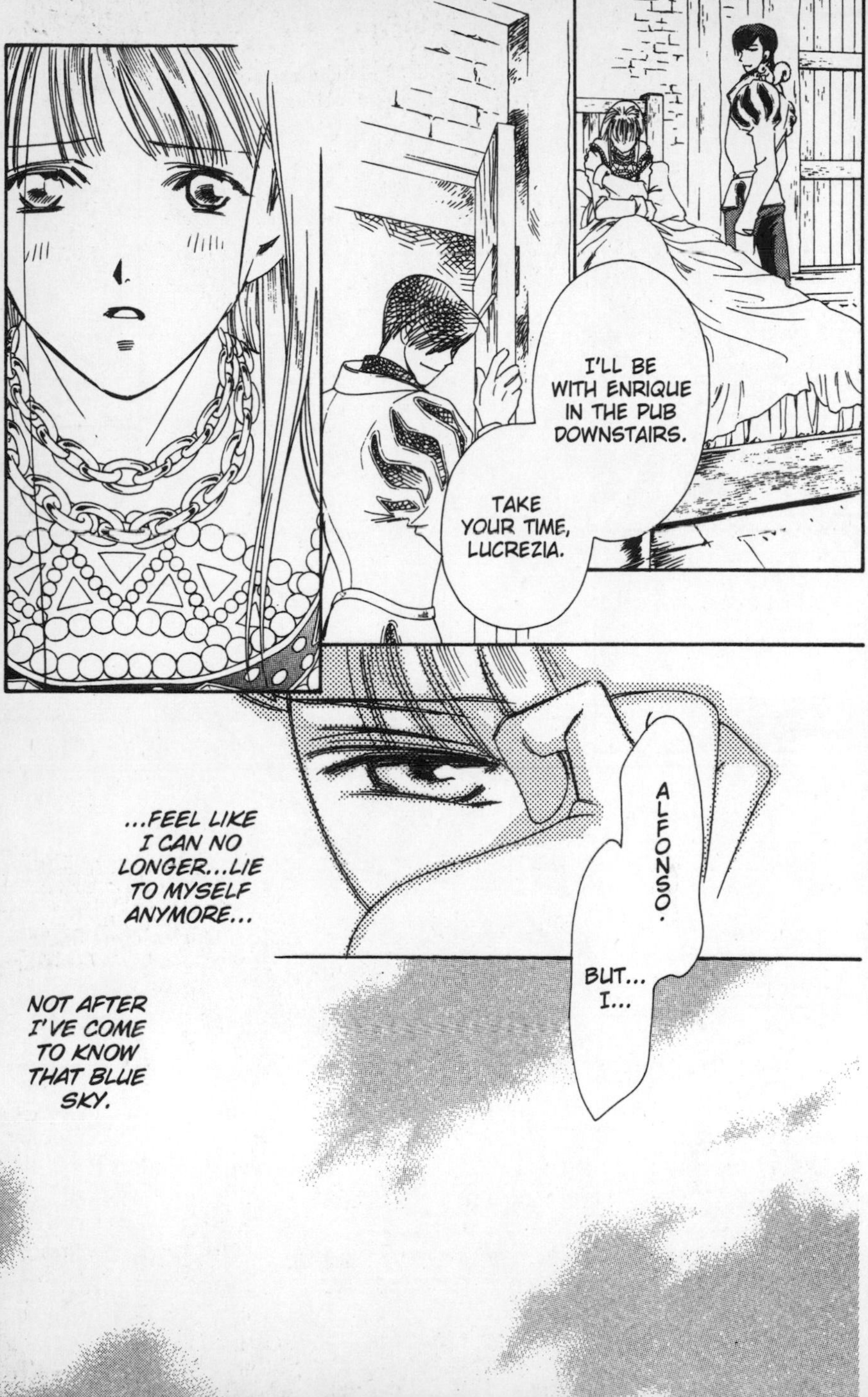
I'LL BE WITH ENRIQUE IN THE PUB DOWNSTAIRS.
TAKE YOUR TIME, LUCREZIA.
ALFONSO.
...FEEL LIKE I CAN NO LONGER...LIE TO MYSELF ANYMORE...
BUT... I...
NOT AFTER I'VE COME TO KNOW THAT BLUE SKY.

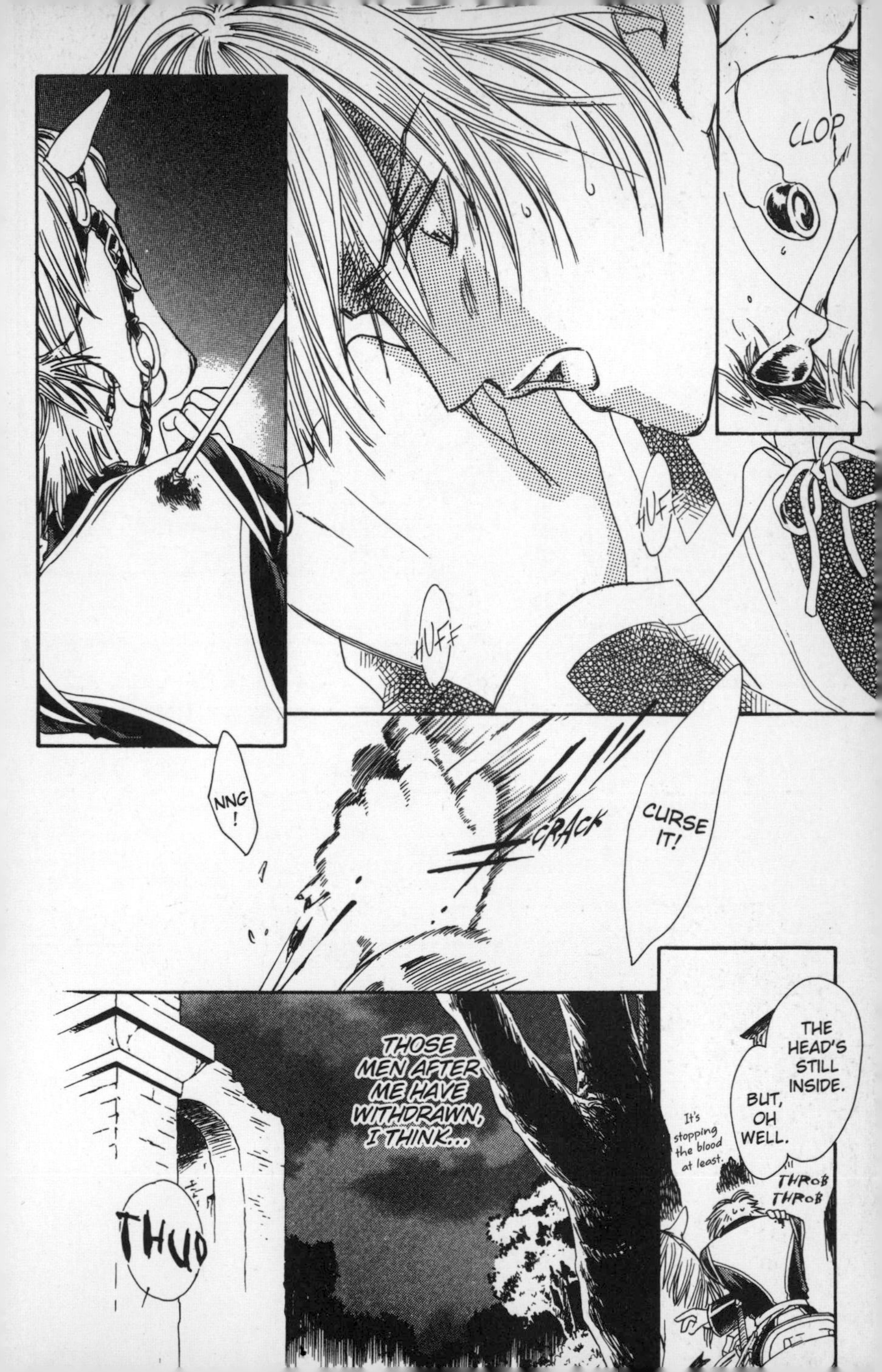
CLOP
HUFF
HUFF
CURSE IT!
CRACK
NNG!
THE HEAD'S STILL INSIDE.
BUT, OH WELL.
It's stopping the blood at least.
THROB THROB
THOSE MEN AFTER ME HAVE WITHDRAWN, I THINK...
THUD

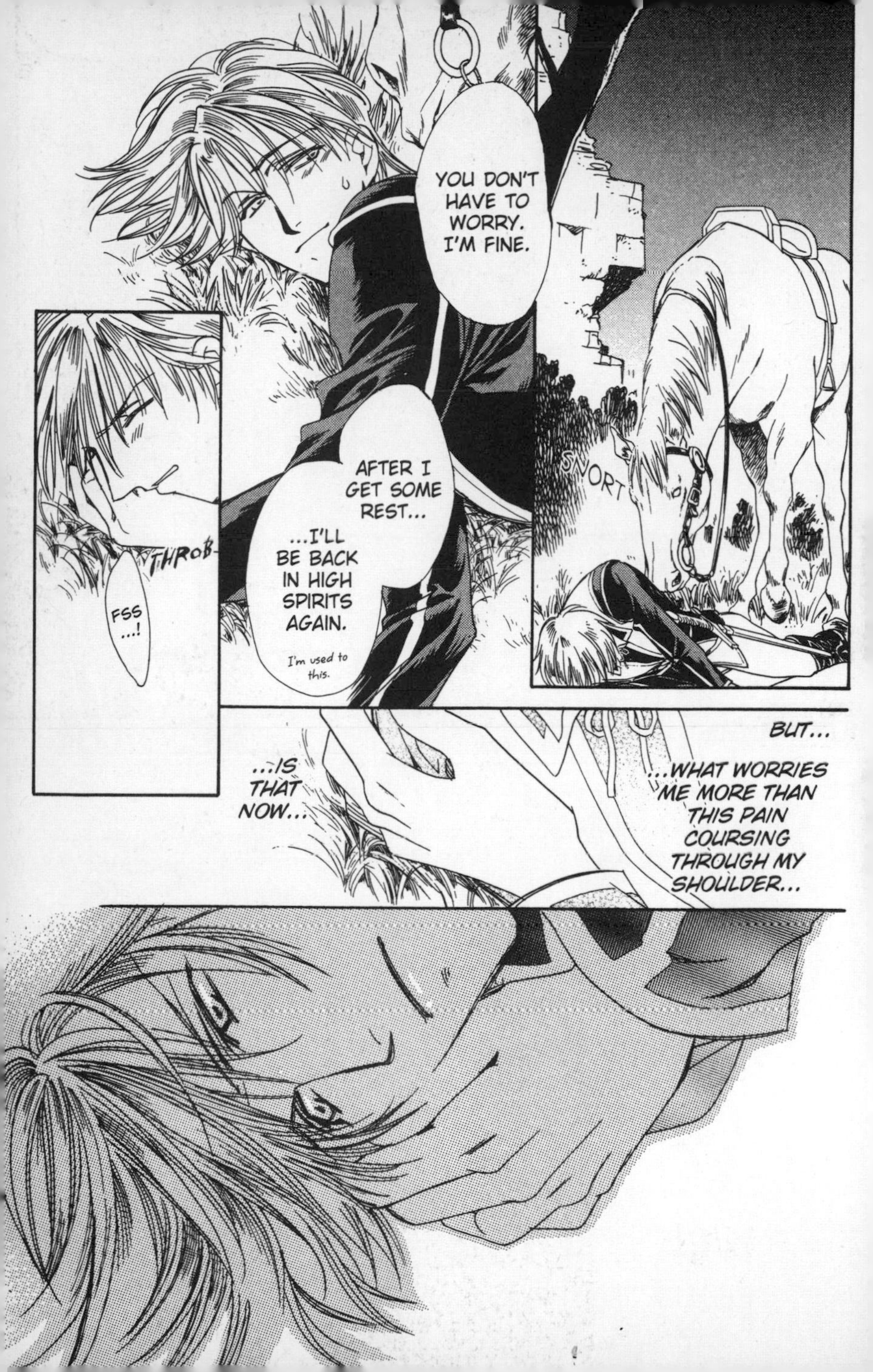
SNORT
YOU DON'T HAVE TO WORRY. I'M FINE.
AFTER I GET SOME REST...
...I'LL BE BACK IN HIGH SPIRITS AGAIN.
I'm used to this.
THROB
FSS ...!
BUT...
...WHAT WORRIES ME MORE THAN THIS PAIN COURSING THROUGH MY SHOULDER...
...IS THAT NOW...

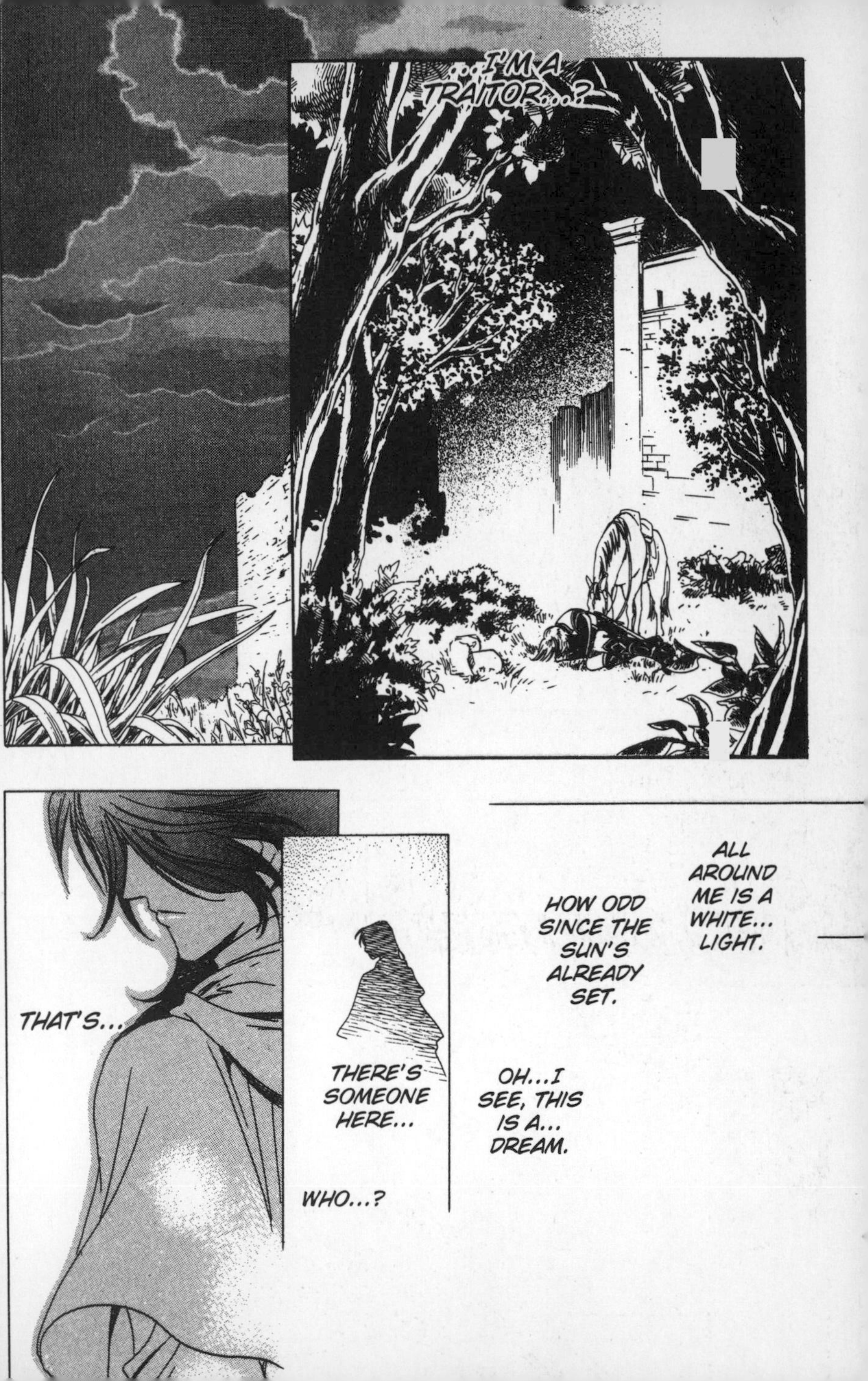
...I'M A TRAITOR...?
ALL AROUND ME IS A WHITE... LIGHT.
HOW ODD SINCE THE SUN'S ALREADY SET.
OH...I SEE, THIS IS A... DREAM.
THERE'S SOMEONE HERE...
WHO...?
THAT'S...

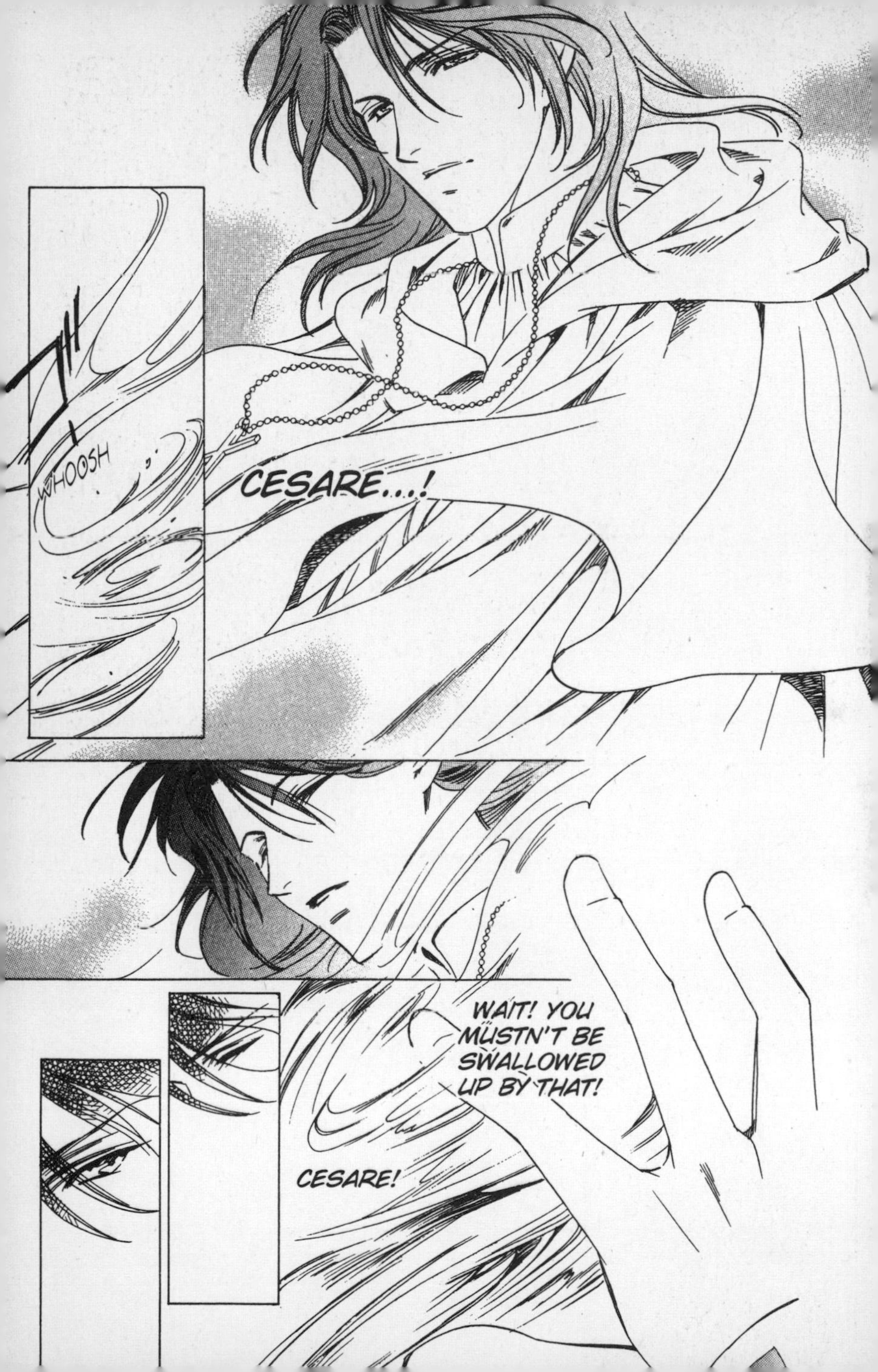
CESARE...!
WHOOSH
WAIT! YOU MUSTN'T BE SWALLOWED UP BY THAT!
CESARE!

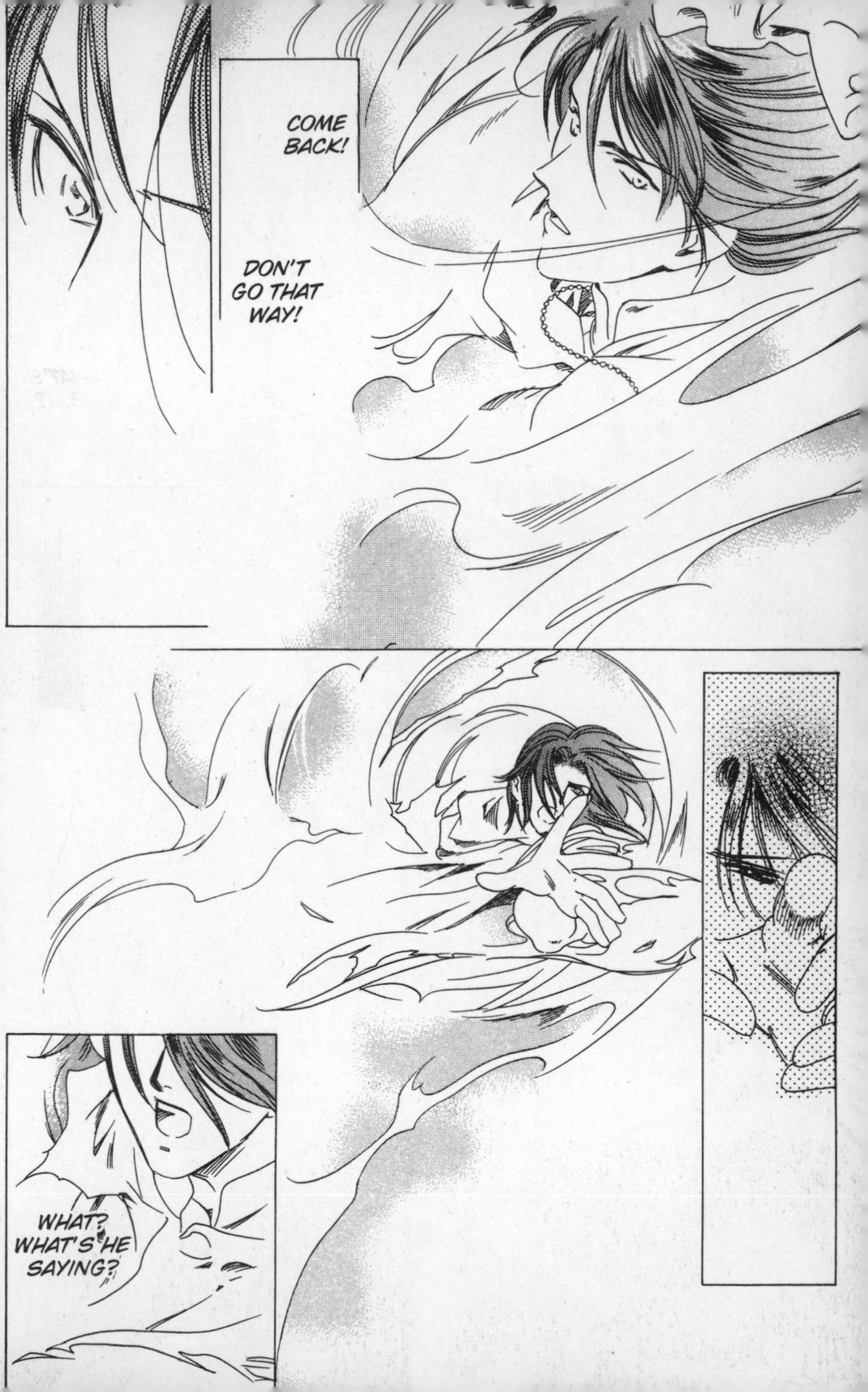
COME BACK!
DON'T GO THAT WAY!
WHAT? WHAT'S HE SAYING?

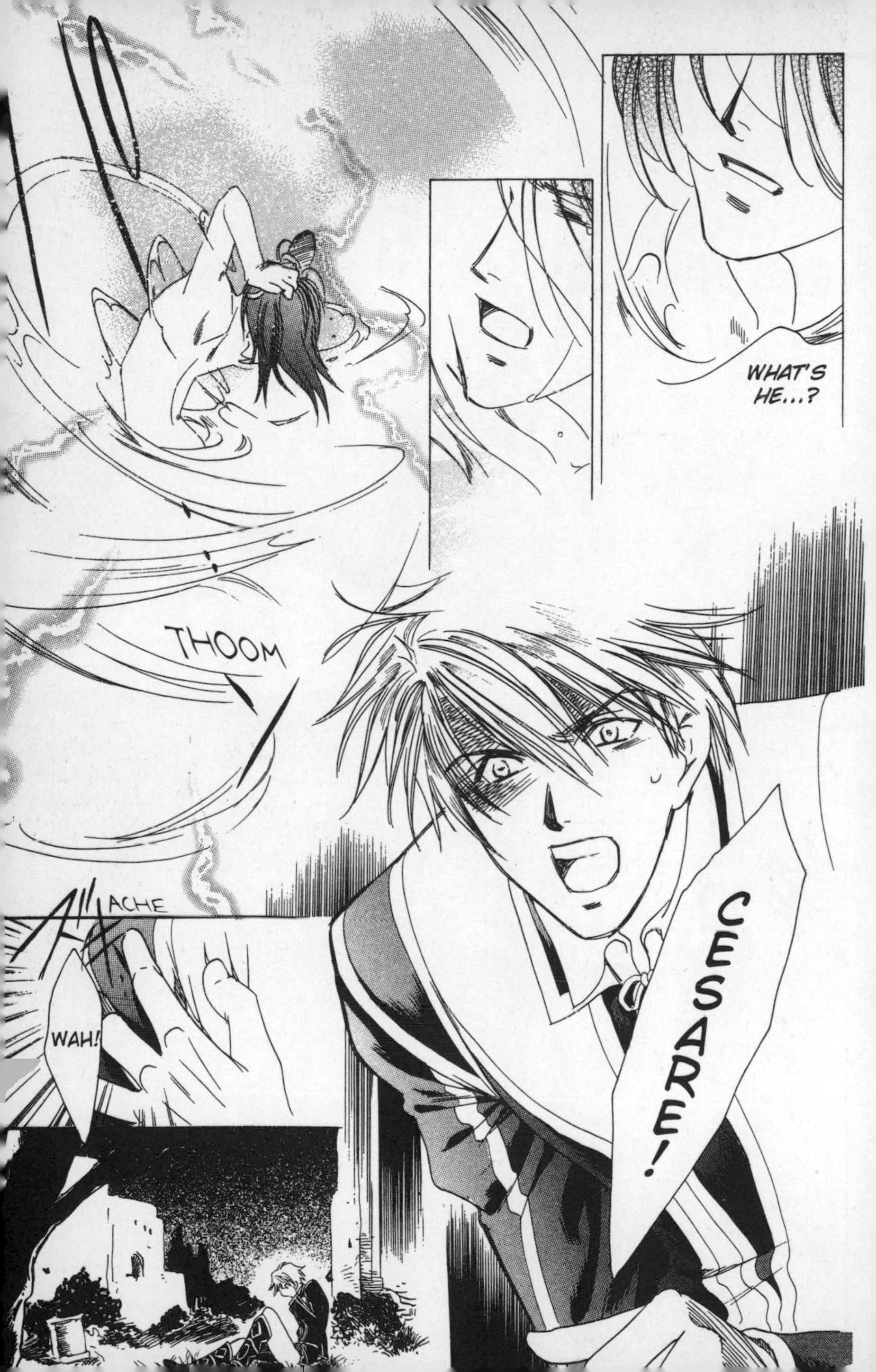
WHAT'S HE...?
THOOM
CESARE!
ACHE
WAH!

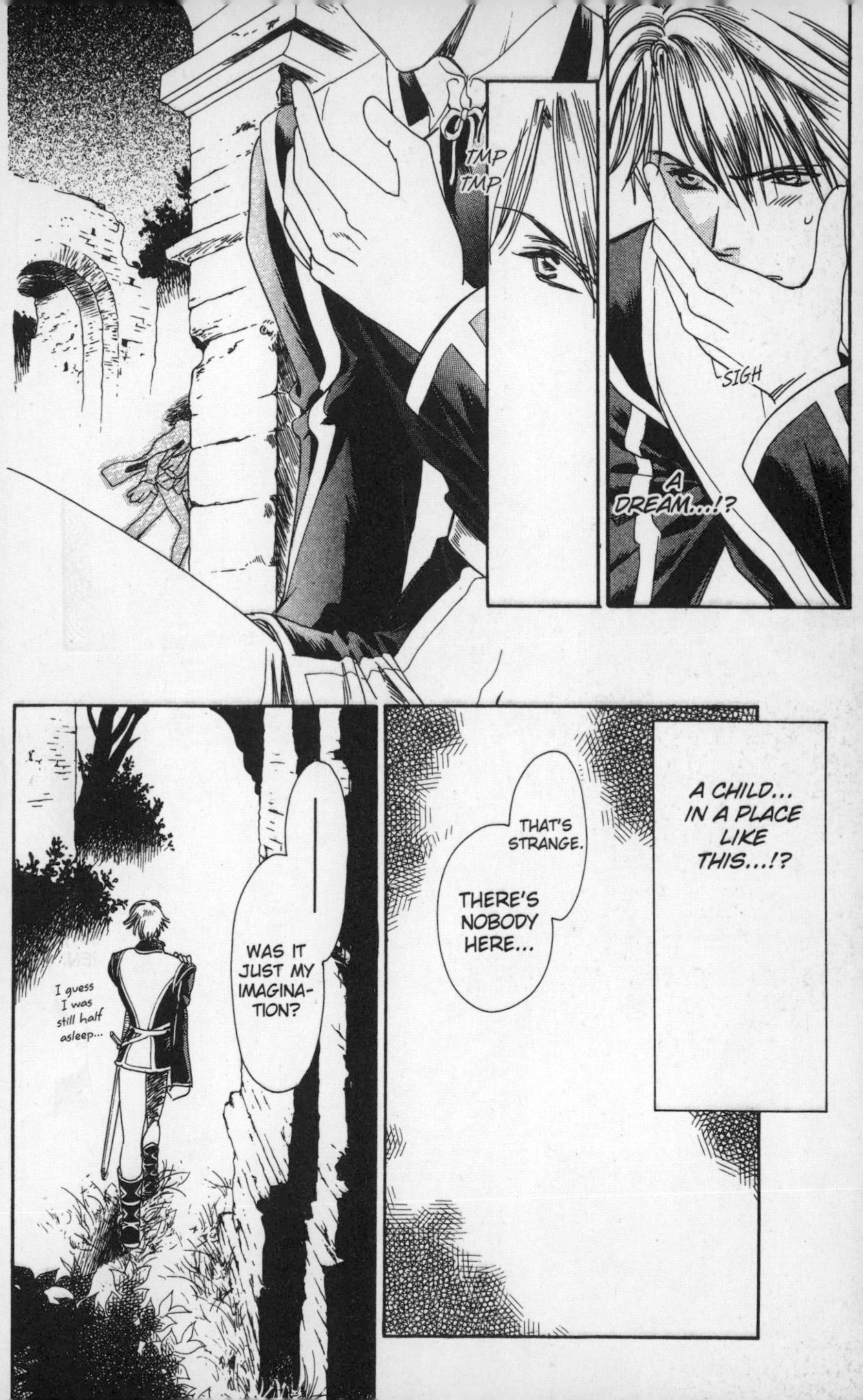
SIGH
A DREAM...!?
TMP TMP
A CHILD... IN A PLACE LIKE THIS...!?
THAT'S STRANGE.
THERE'S NOBODY HERE...
WAS IT JUST MY IMAGINA-TION?
I guess I was still half asleep...

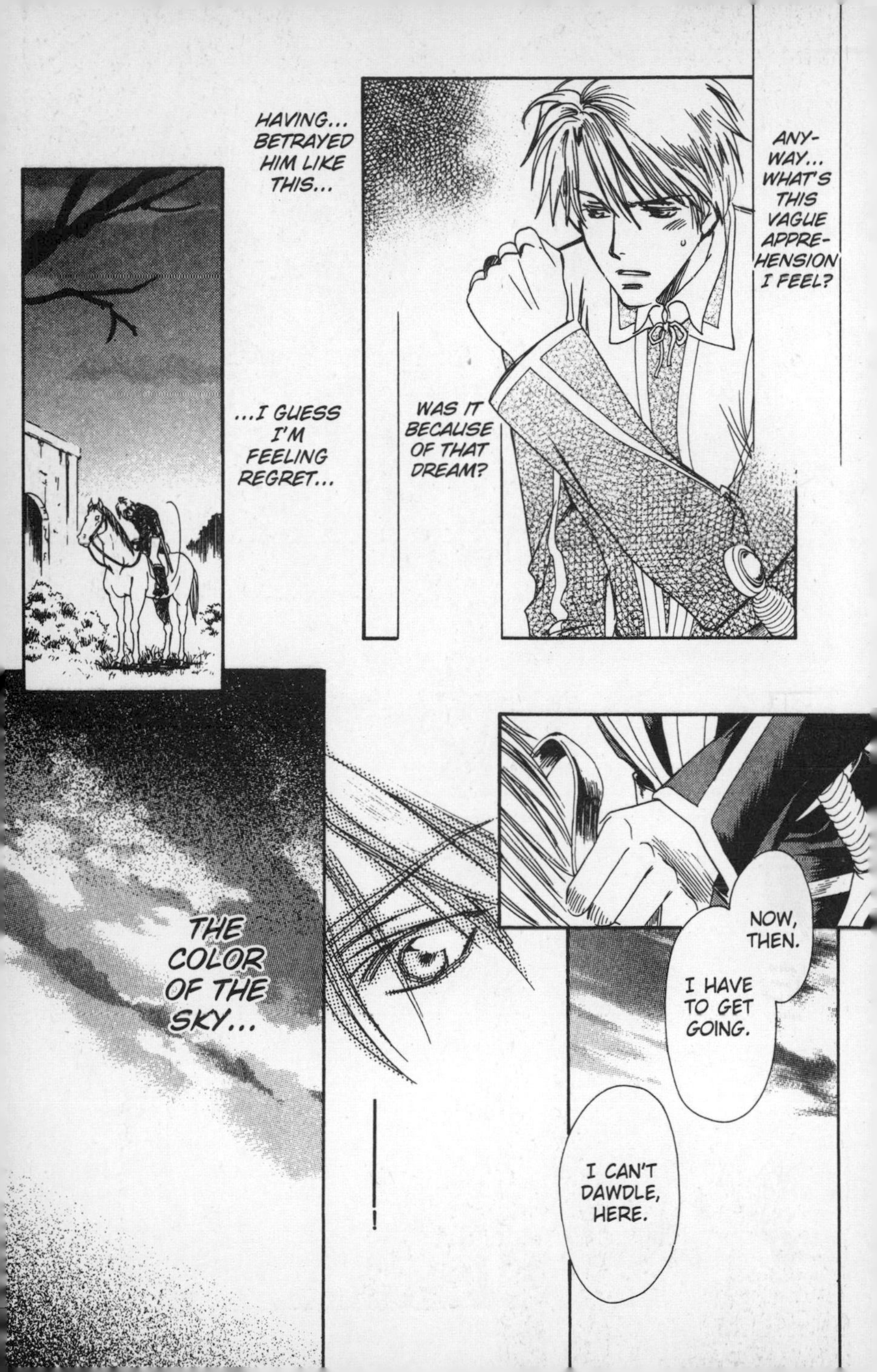
ANY-WAY... WHAT'S THIS VAGUE APPRE-HENSION I FEEL?
WAS IT BECAUSE OF THAT DREAM?
HAVING... BETRAYED HIM LIKE THIS...
...I GUESS I'M FEELING REGRET...
NOW, THEN.
I HAVE TO GET GOING.
I CAN'T DAWDLE, HERE.
THE COLOR OF THE SKY...

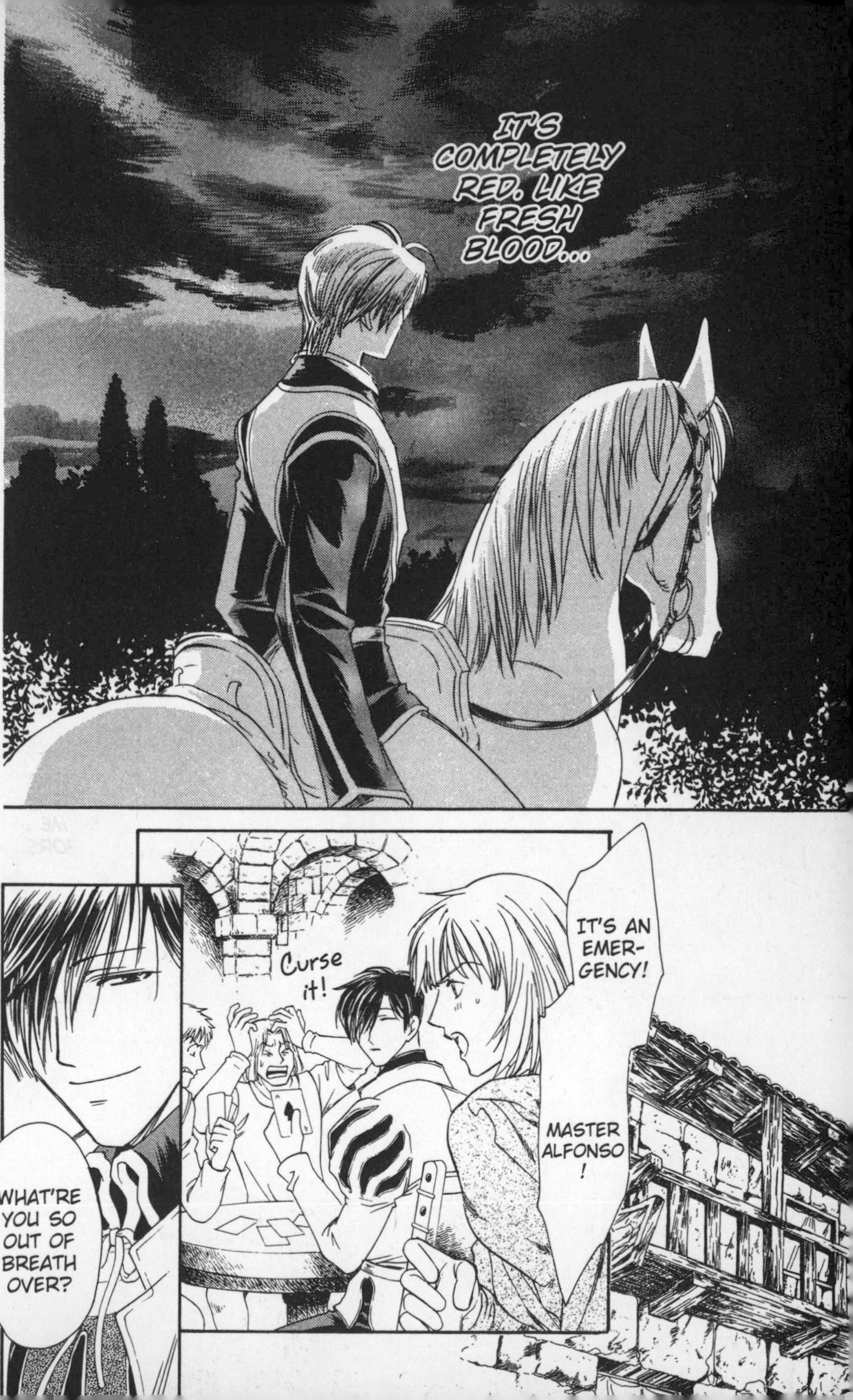
IT'S COMPLETELY RED. LIKE FRESH BLOOD...
IT'S AN EMER-GENCY!
MASTER ALFONSO!
Curse it!
WHAT'RE YOU SO OUT OF BREATH OVER?

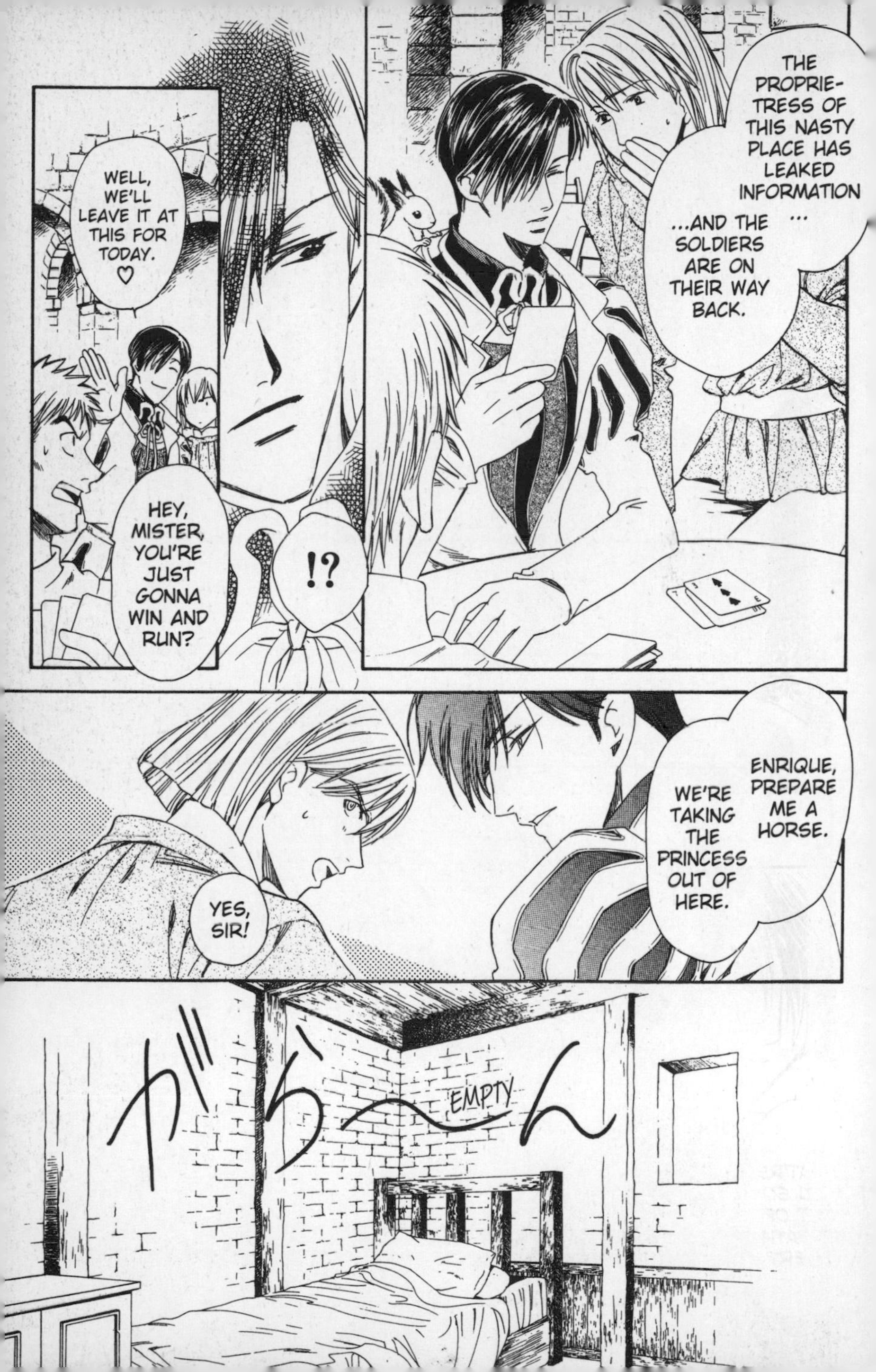
THE PROPRIETRESS OF THIS NASTY PLACE HAS LEAKED INFORMATION ...
...AND THE SOLDIERS ARE ON THEIR WAY BACK.
!?
WELL, WE'LL LEAVE IT AT THIS FOR TODAY. ♡
HEY, MISTER, YOU'RE JUST GONNA WIN AND RUN?
ENRIQUE, PREPARE ME A HORSE.
WE'RE TAKING THE PRINCESS OUT OF HERE.
YES, SIR!
がら〜ん
EMPTY

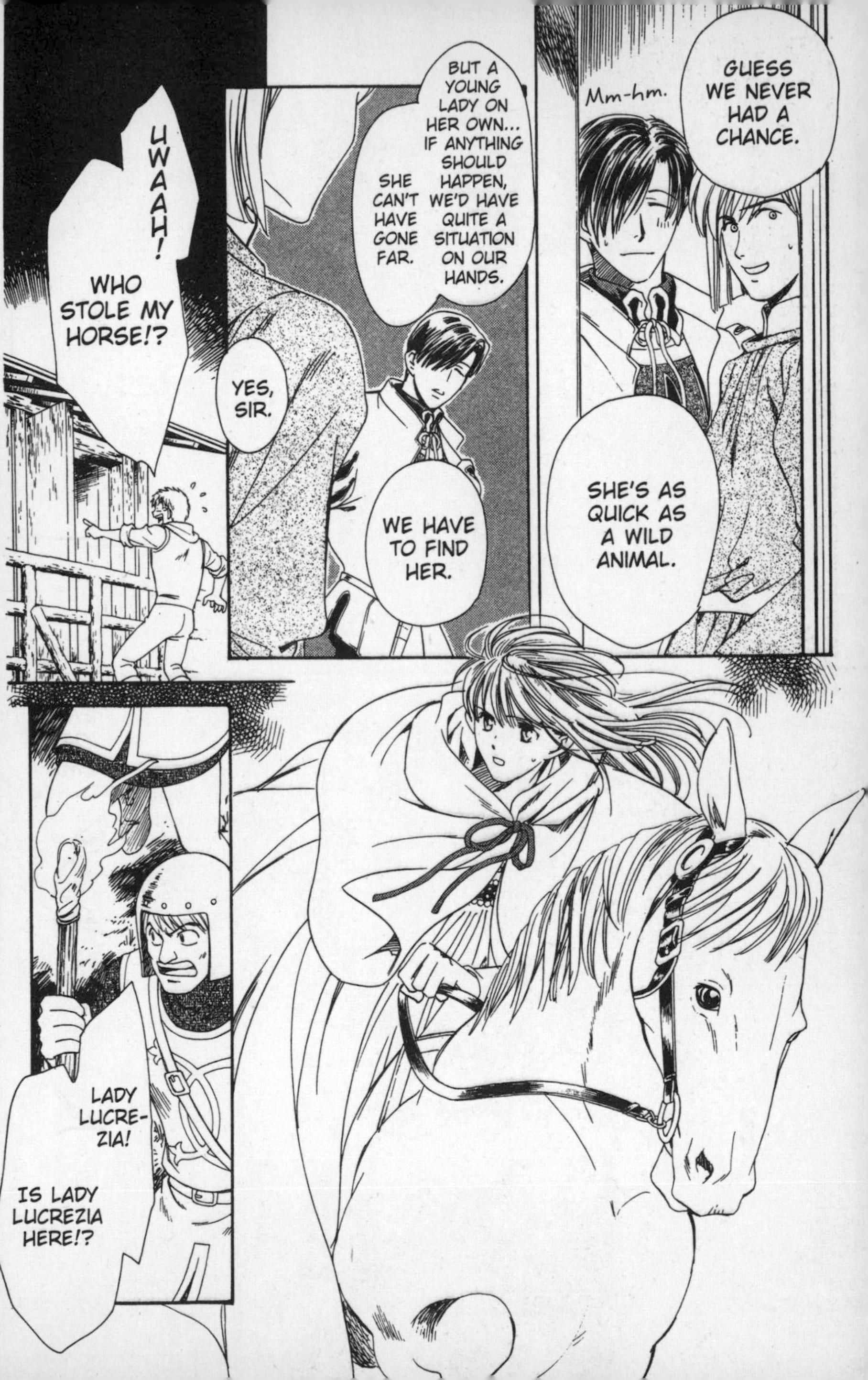
GUESS WE NEVER HAD A CHANCE.
Mm-hm.
SHE'S AS QUICK AS A WILD ANIMAL.
BUT A YOUNG LADY ON HER OWN... IF ANYTHING SHOULD HAPPEN, WE'D HAVE QUITE A SITUATION ON OUR HANDS.
SHE CAN'T HAVE GONE FAR.
YES, SIR.
WE HAVE TO FIND HER.
UWAAH!
WHO STOLE MY HORSE!?
LADY LUCREZIA!
IS LADY LUCREZIA HERE!?

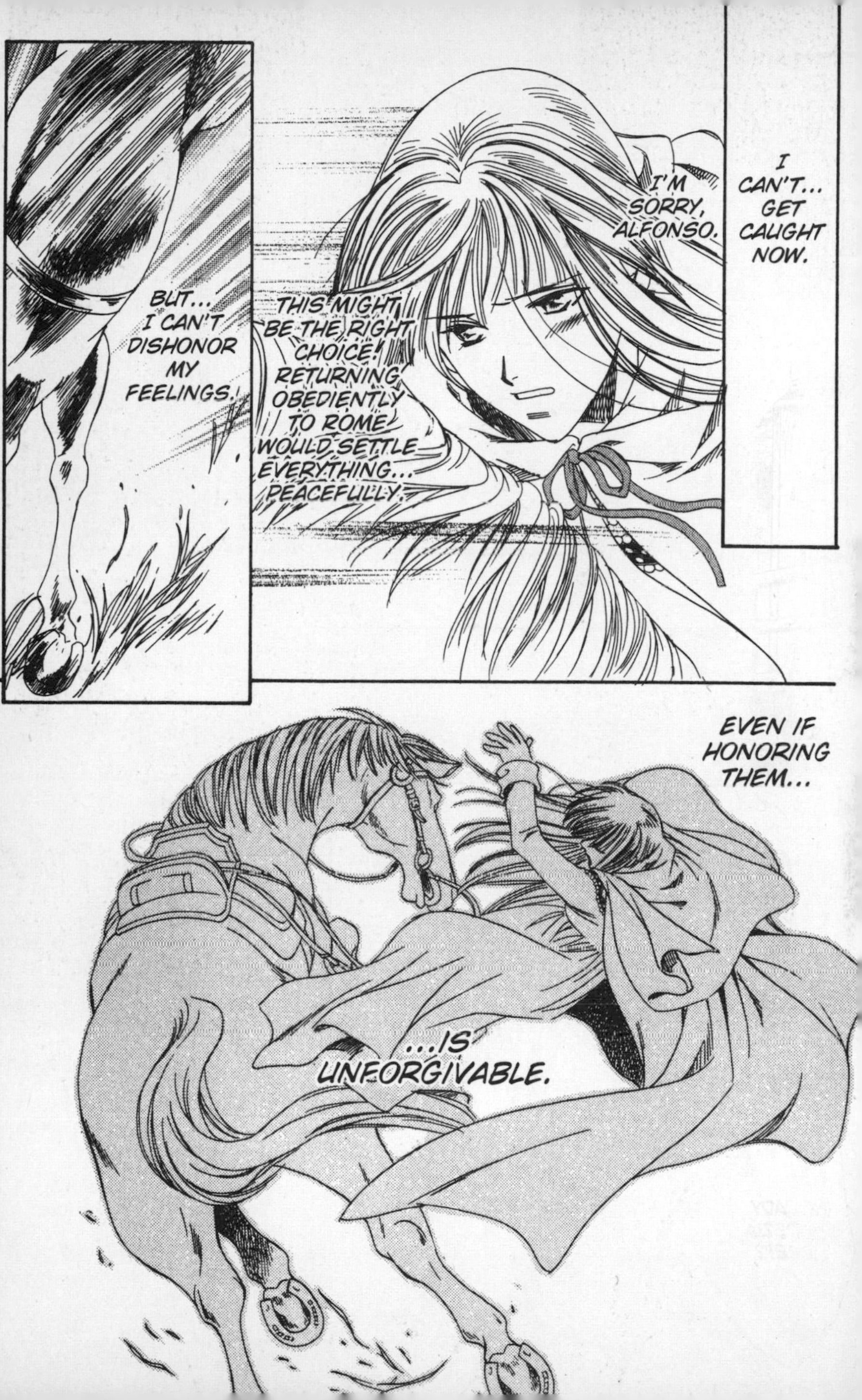
I CAN'T... GET CAUGHT NOW.
I'M SORRY, ALFONSO.
THIS MIGHT BE THE RIGHT CHOICE! RETURNING OBEDIENTLY TO ROME WOULD SETTLE EVERYTHING... PEACEFULLY.
BUT... I CAN'T DISHONOR MY FEELINGS.
EVEN IF HONORING THEM...
...IS UNFORGIVABLE.

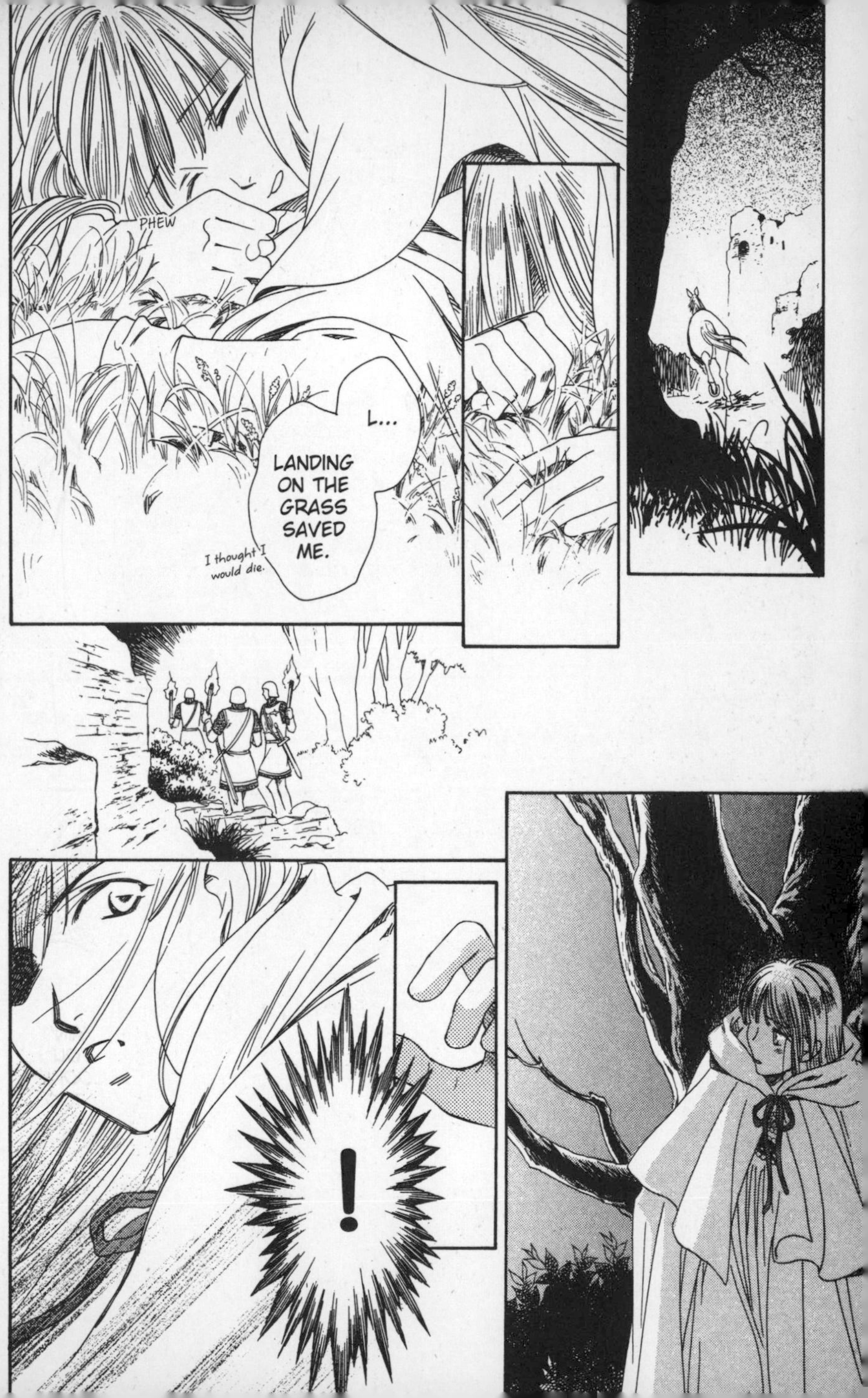
PHEW
L...
LANDING ON THE GRASS SAVED ME.
I thought I would die.
!

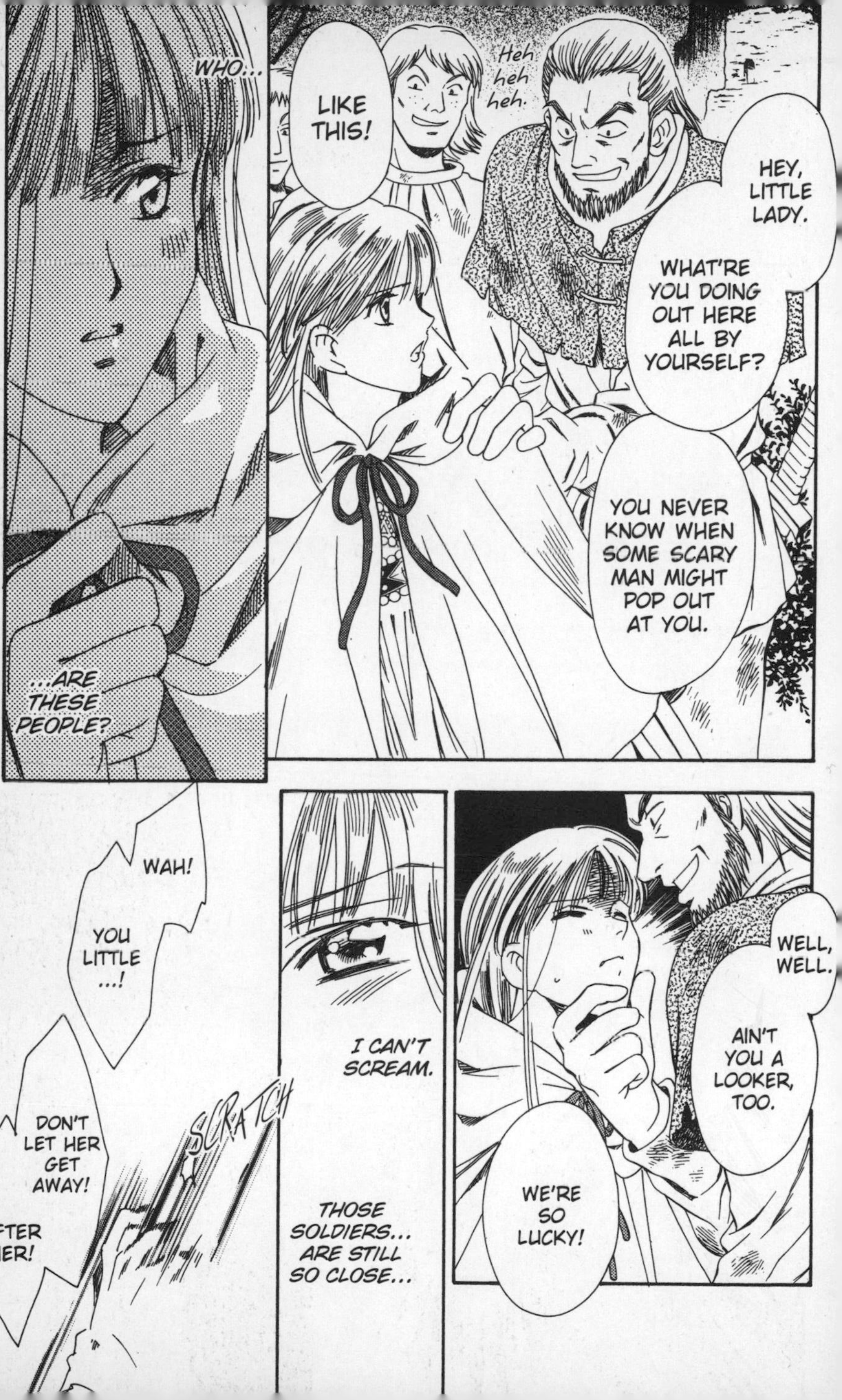
HEY, LITTLE LADY.
WHAT'RE YOU DOING OUT HERE ALL BY YOURSELF?
YOU NEVER KNOW WHEN SOME SCARY MAN MIGHT POP OUT AT YOU.
LIKE THIS!
Heh heh heh.
WHO...
...ARE THESE PEOPLE?
WELL, WELL.
AIN'T YOU A LOOKER, TOO.
WE'RE SO LUCKY!
I CAN'T SCREAM.
THOSE SOLDIERS... ARE STILL SO CLOSE...
SCRATCH
WAH!
YOU LITTLE ...!
DON'T LET HER GET AWAY!
AFTER HER!

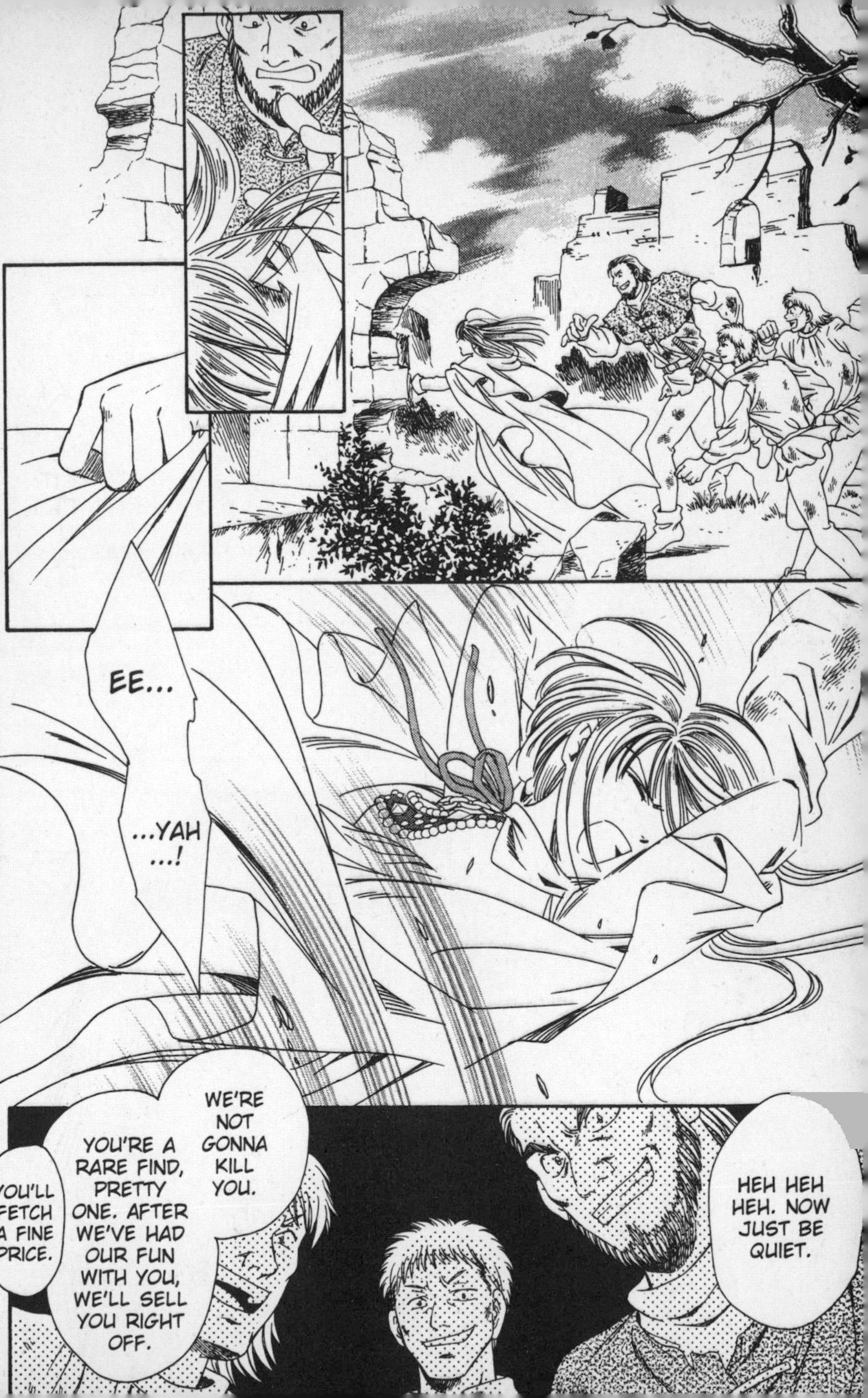
EE...
...YAH ...!
HEH HEH HEH. NOW JUST BE QUIET.
WE'RE NOT GONNA KILL YOU.
YOU'RE A RARE FIND, PRETTY ONE. AFTER WE'VE HAD OUR FUN WITH YOU, WE'LL SELL YOU RIGHT OFF.
YOU'LL FETCH A FINE PRICE.

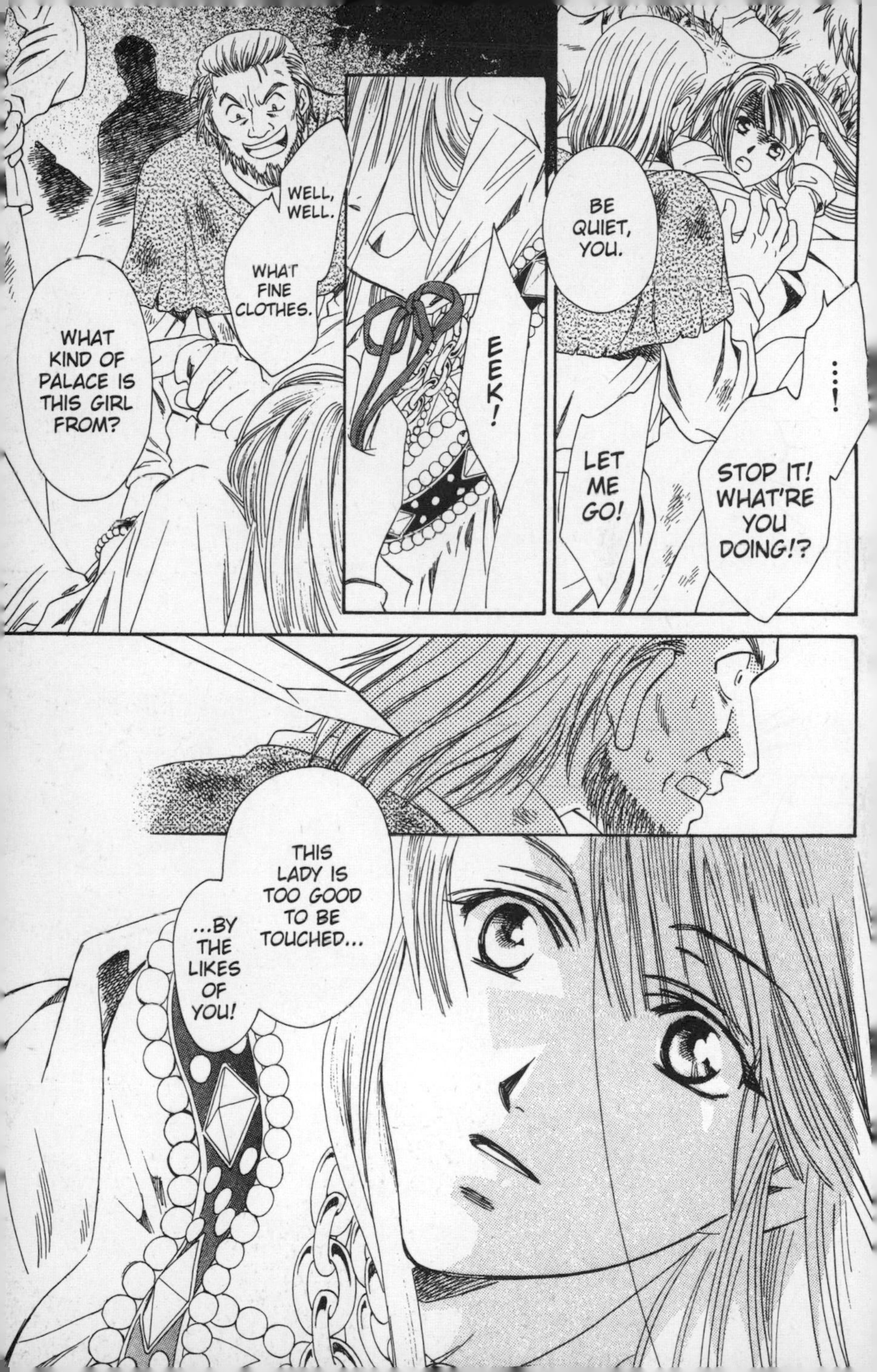
BE QUIET, YOU.
...!
STOP IT! WHAT'RE YOU DOING!?
LET ME GO!
EEK!
WELL, WELL.
WHAT FINE CLOTHES.
WHAT KIND OF PALACE IS THIS GIRL FROM?
THIS LADY IS TOO GOOD TO BE TOUCHED...
...BY THE LIKES OF YOU!

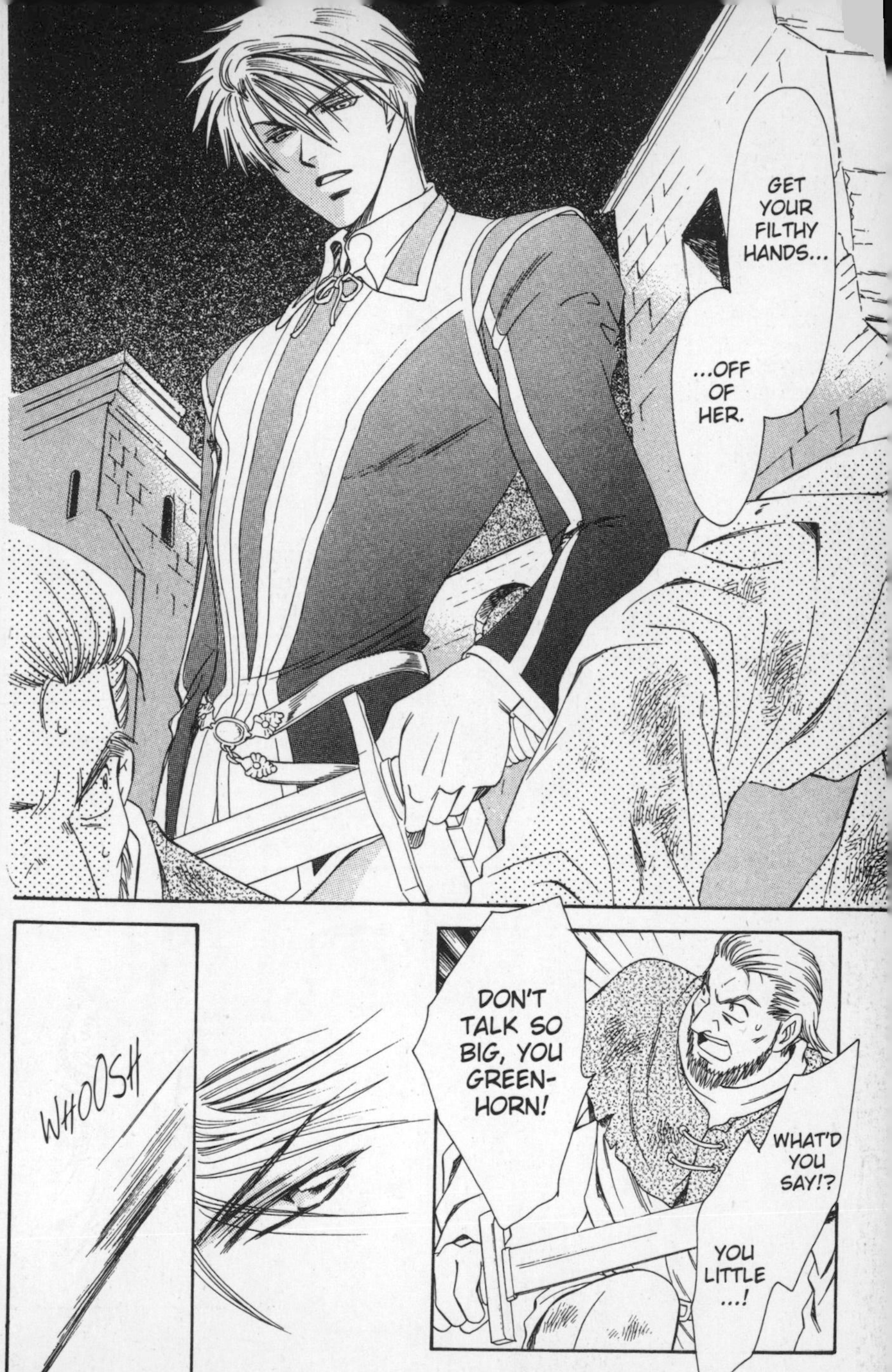
GET YOUR FILTHY HANDS...
...OFF OF HER.
DON'T TALK SO BIG, YOU GREEN-HORN!
WHAT'D YOU SAY!?
YOU LITTLE ...!
WHOOSH

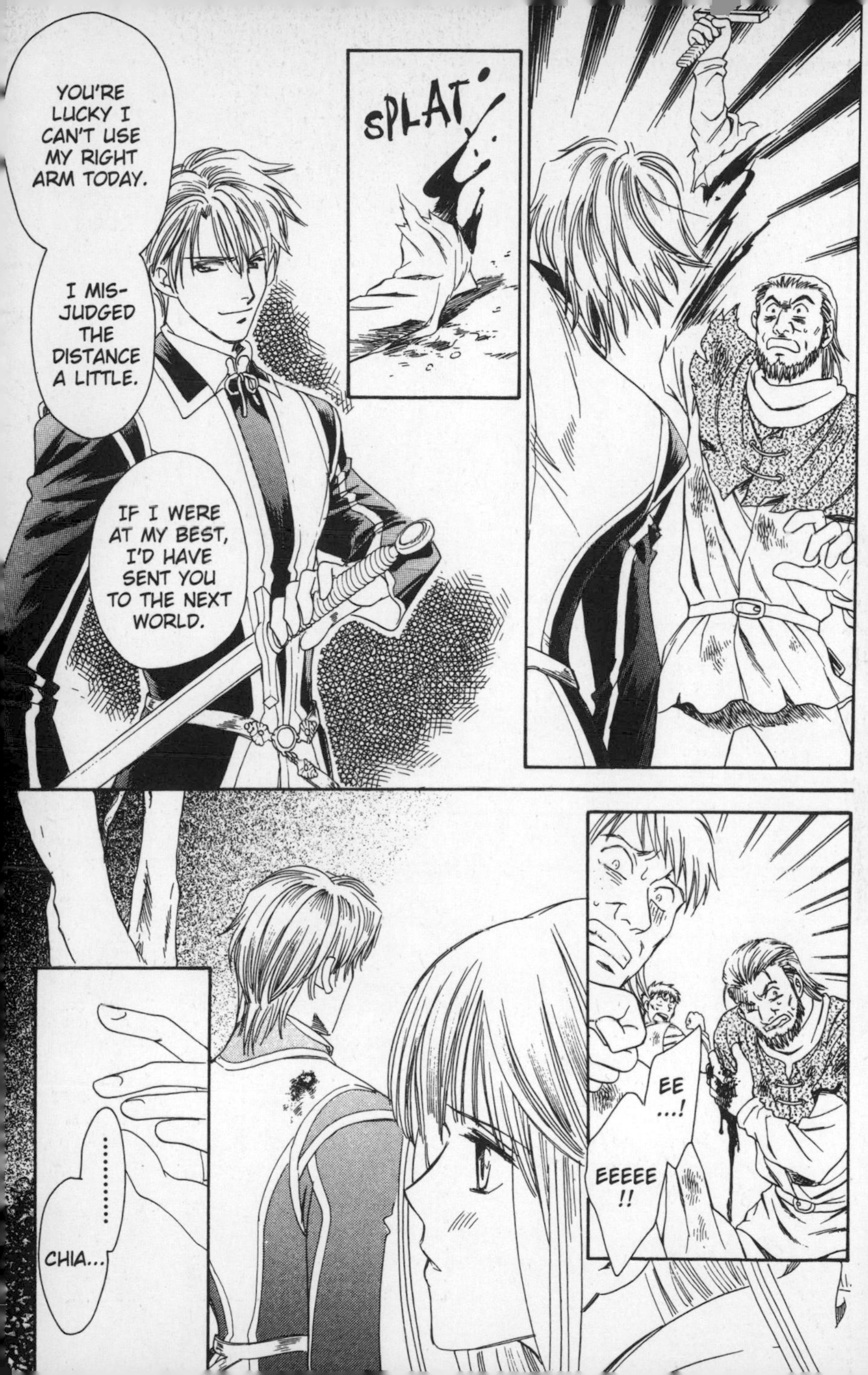
SPLAT
YOU'RE LUCKY I CAN'T USE MY RIGHT ARM TODAY.
I MIS-JUDGED THE DISTANCE A LITTLE.
IF I WERE AT MY BEST, I'D HAVE SENT YOU TO THE NEXT WORLD.
EE ...!
EEEEE !!
....
CHIA...

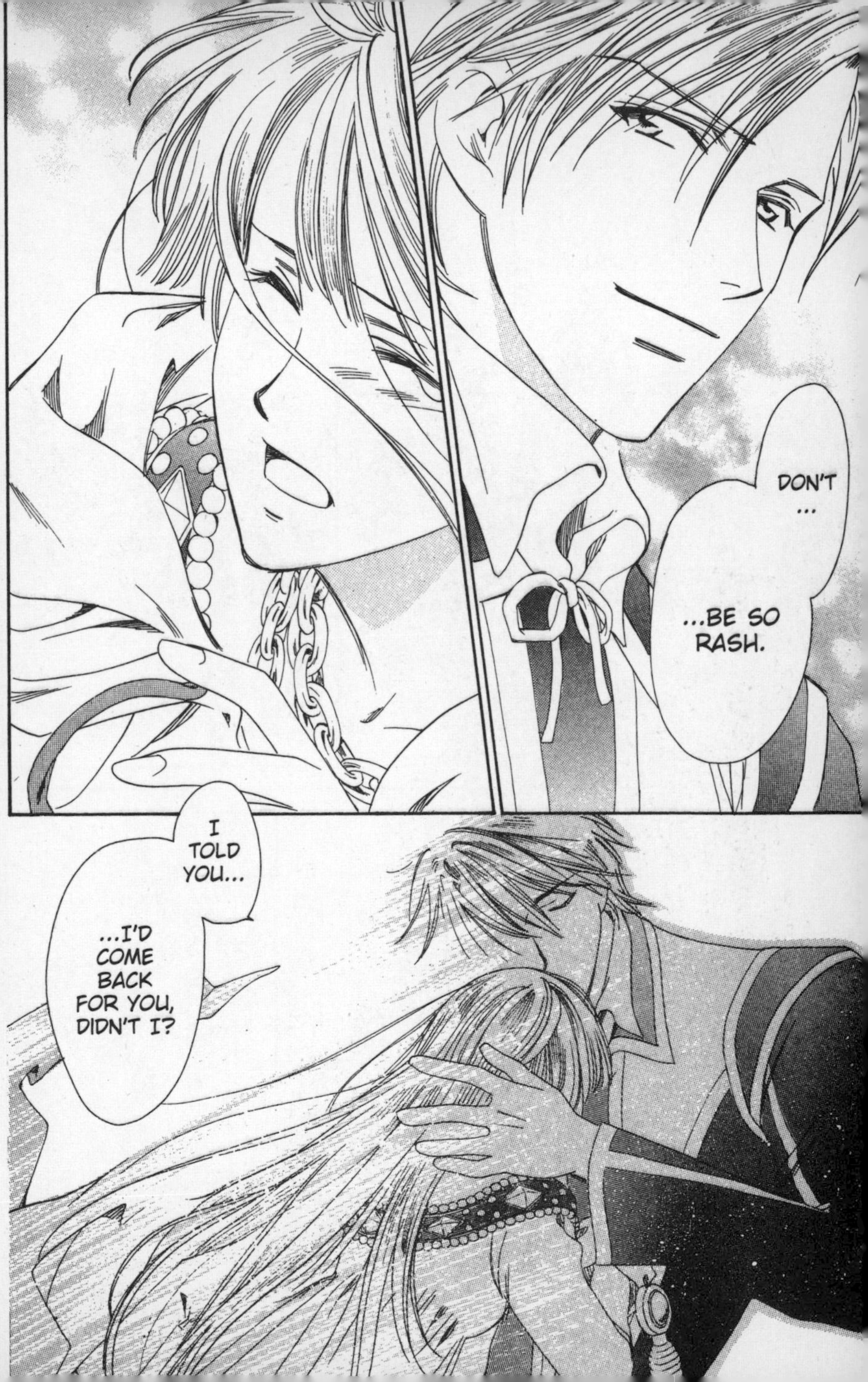
DON'T ...
...BE SO RASH.
I TOLD YOU...
...I'D COME BACK FOR YOU, DIDN'T I?

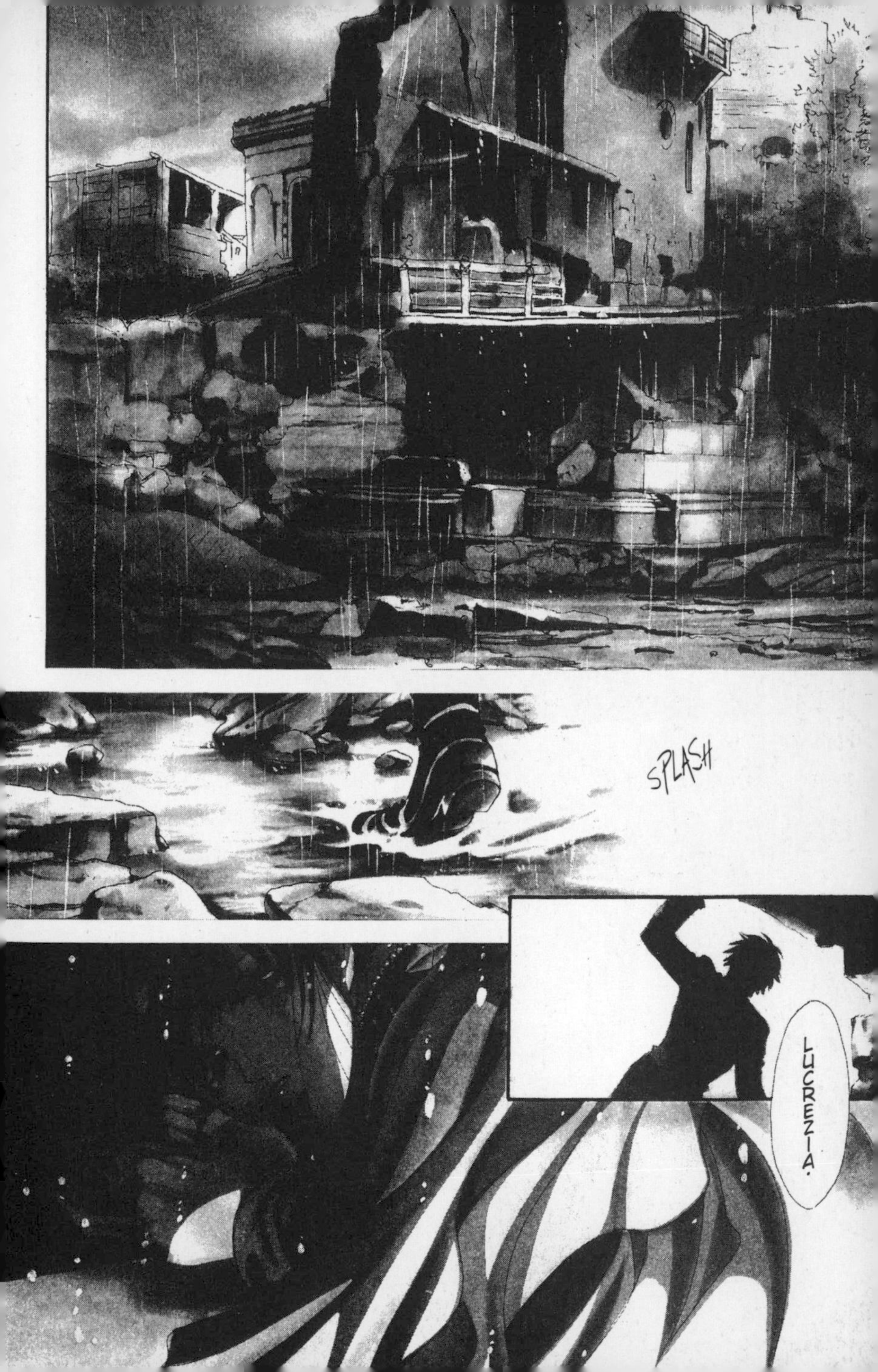
SPLASH
LUCREZIA.

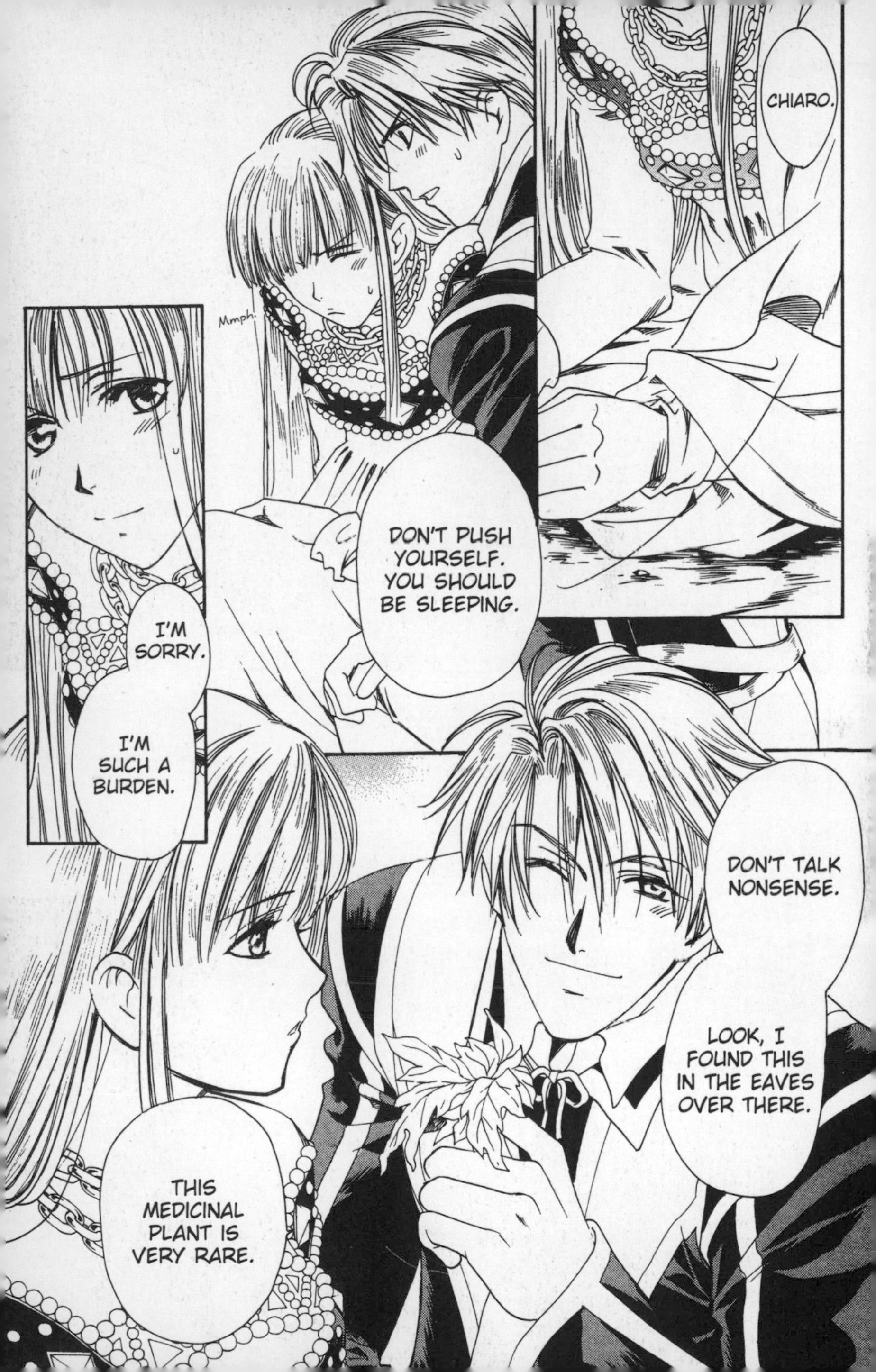
CHIARO.
Mmph.
DON'T PUSH YOURSELF. YOU SHOULD BE SLEEPING.
I'M SORRY.
I'M SUCH A BURDEN.
DON'T TALK NONSENSE.
LOOK, I FOUND THIS IN THE EAVES OVER THERE.
THIS MEDICINAL PLANT IS VERY RARE.

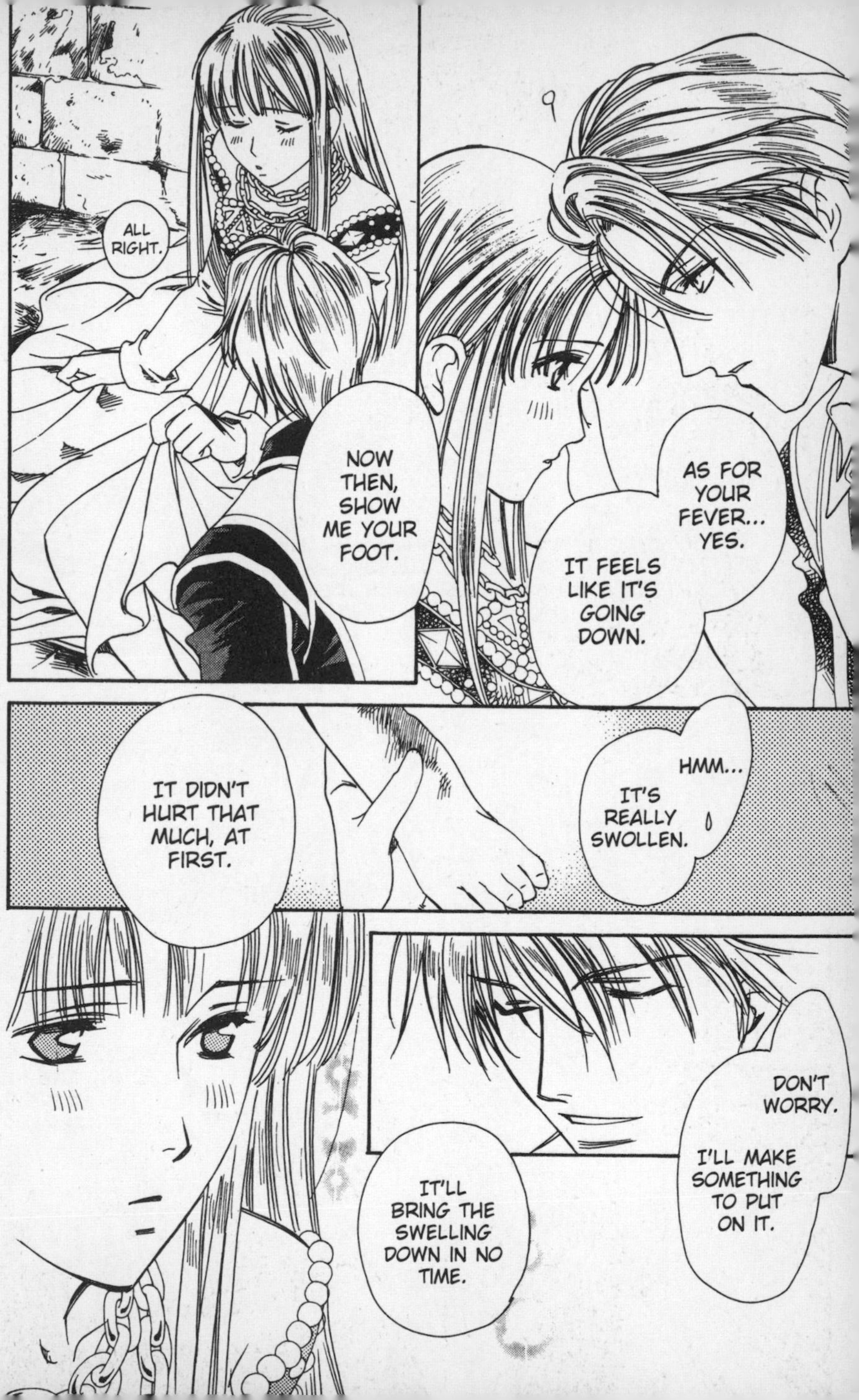
AS FOR YOUR FEVER... YES.
IT FEELS LIKE IT'S GOING DOWN.
NOW THEN, SHOW ME YOUR FOOT.
ALL RIGHT.
HMM... IT'S REALLY SWOLLEN.
IT DIDN'T HURT THAT MUCH, AT FIRST.
DON'T WORRY.
I'LL MAKE SOMETHING TO PUT ON IT.
IT'LL BRING THE SWELLING DOWN IN NO TIME.

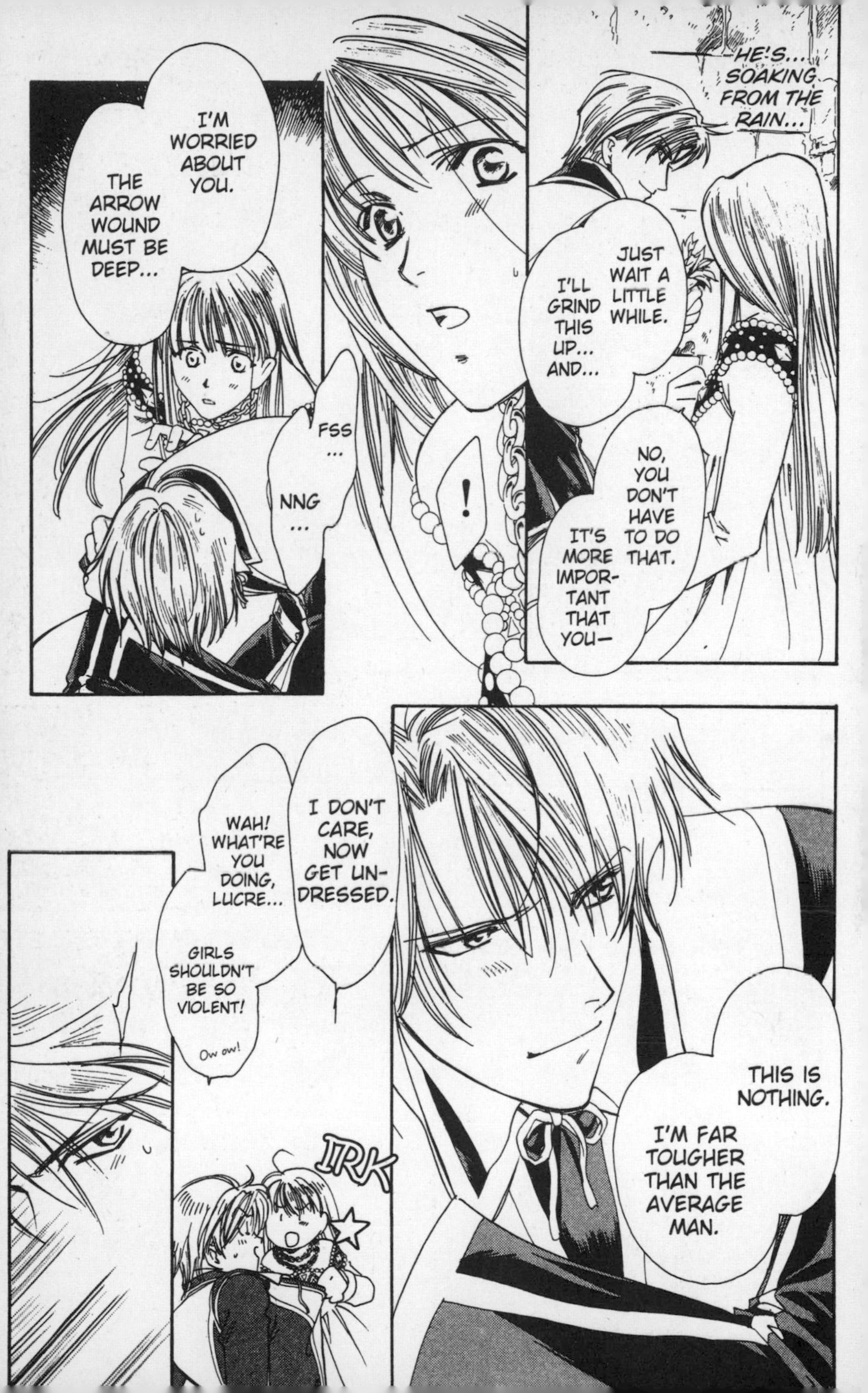
HE'S... SOAKING FROM THE RAIN...
JUST WAIT A LITTLE WHILE.
I'LL GRIND THIS UP... AND...
NO, YOU DON'T HAVE TO DO THAT.
IT'S MORE IMPORTANT THAT YOU—
!
I'M WORRIED ABOUT YOU.
THE ARROW WOUND MUST BE DEEP...
FSS...
NNG...
THIS IS NOTHING.
I'M FAR TOUGHER THAN THE AVERAGE MAN.
I DON'T CARE, NOW GET UNDRESSED.
WAH! WHAT'RE YOU DOING, LUCRE...
GIRLS SHOULDN'T BE SO VIOLENT!
Ow ow!
IRK

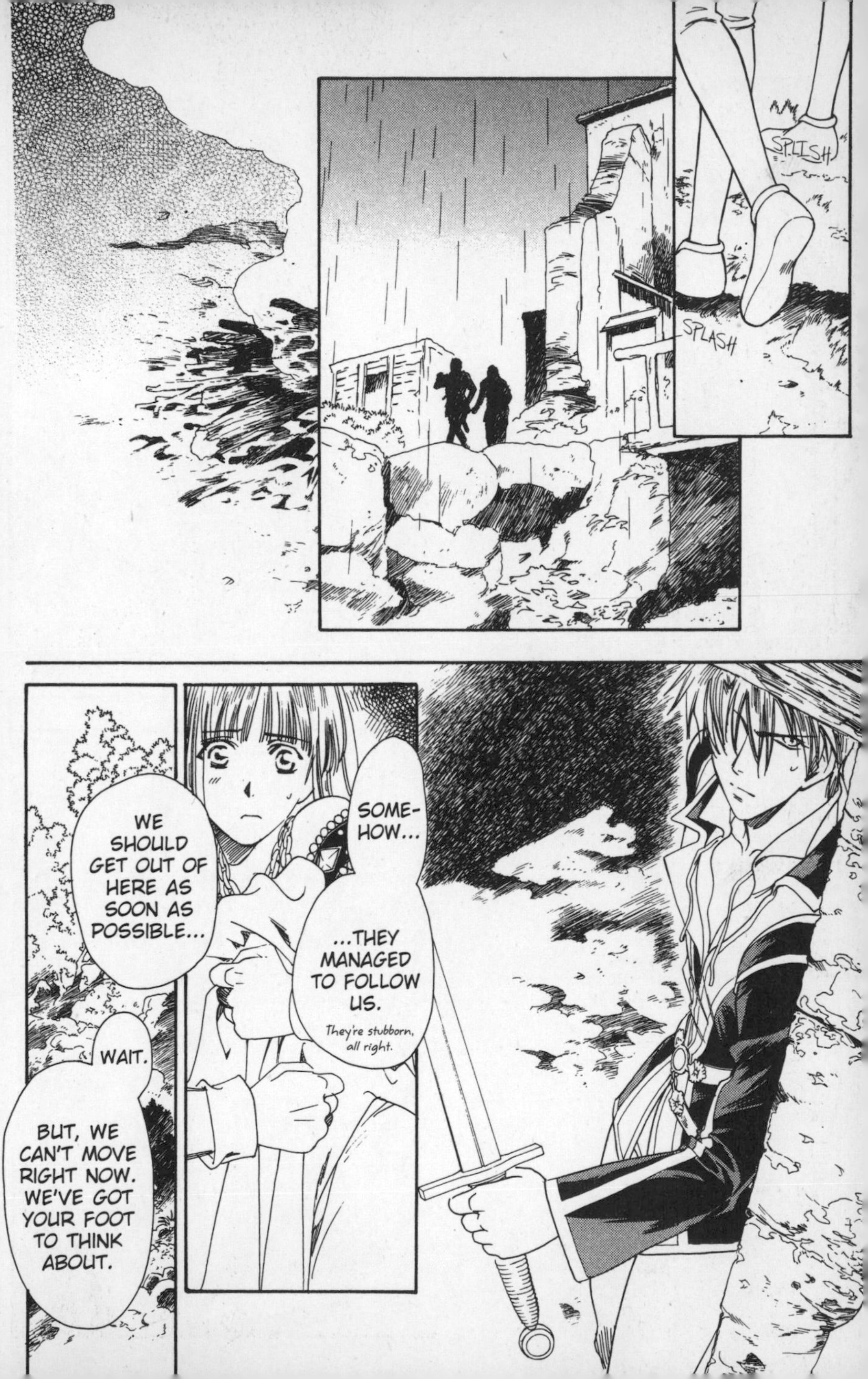
SPLISH
SPLASH
SOME-HOW...
...THEY MANAGED TO FOLLOW US.
They're stubborn, all right.
WE SHOULD GET OUT OF HERE AS SOON AS POSSIBLE...
WAIT.
BUT, WE CAN'T MOVE RIGHT NOW. WE'VE GOT YOUR FOOT TO THINK ABOUT.

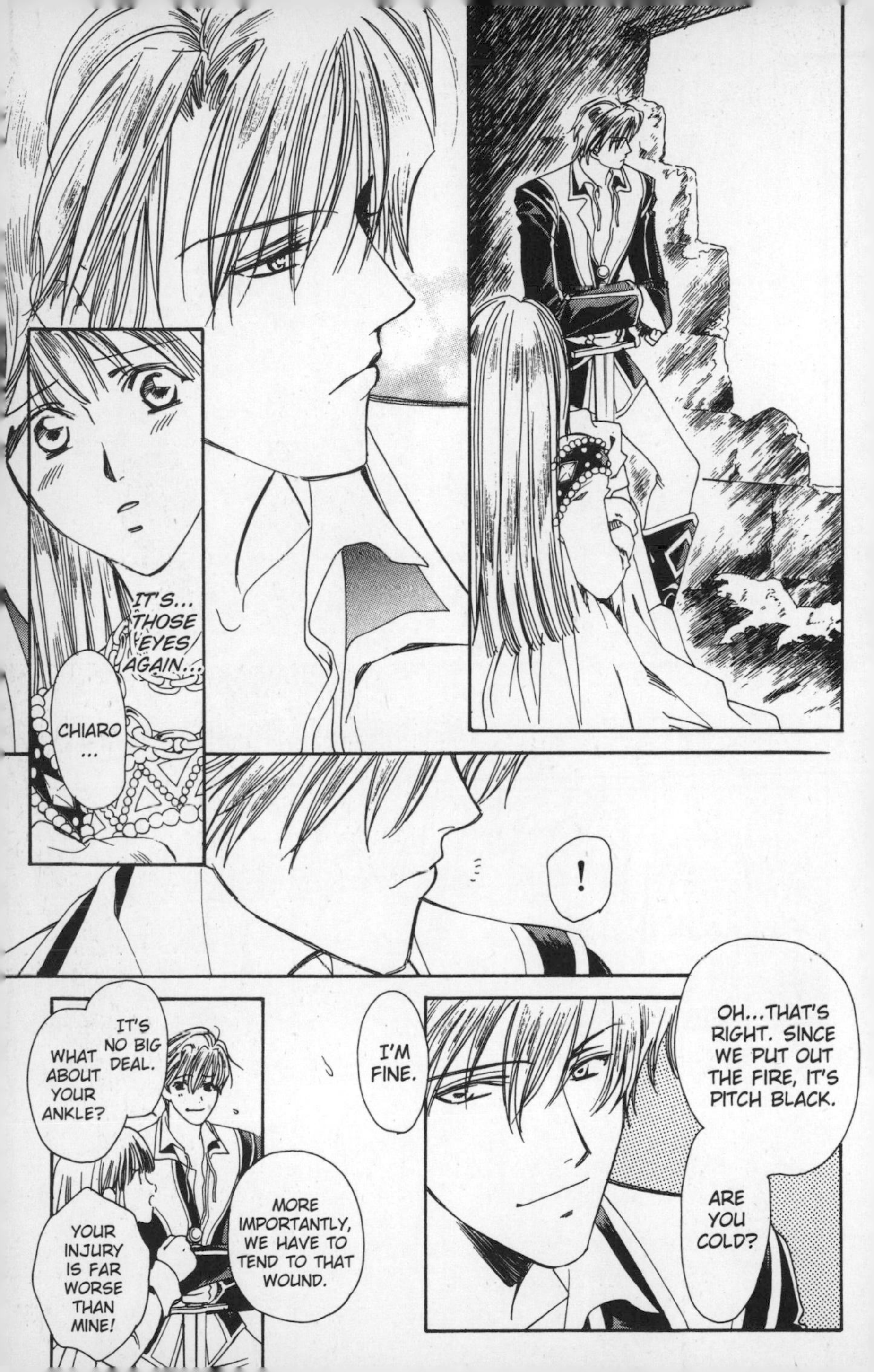
IT'S... THOSE EYES AGAIN...
CHIARO ...
!
OH...THAT'S RIGHT. SINCE WE PUT OUT THE FIRE, IT'S PITCH BLACK.
ARE YOU COLD?
I'M FINE.
WHAT ABOUT YOUR ANKLE?
IT'S NO BIG DEAL.
MORE IMPORTANTLY, WE HAVE TO TEND TO THAT WOUND.
YOUR INJURY IS FAR WORSE THAN MINE!

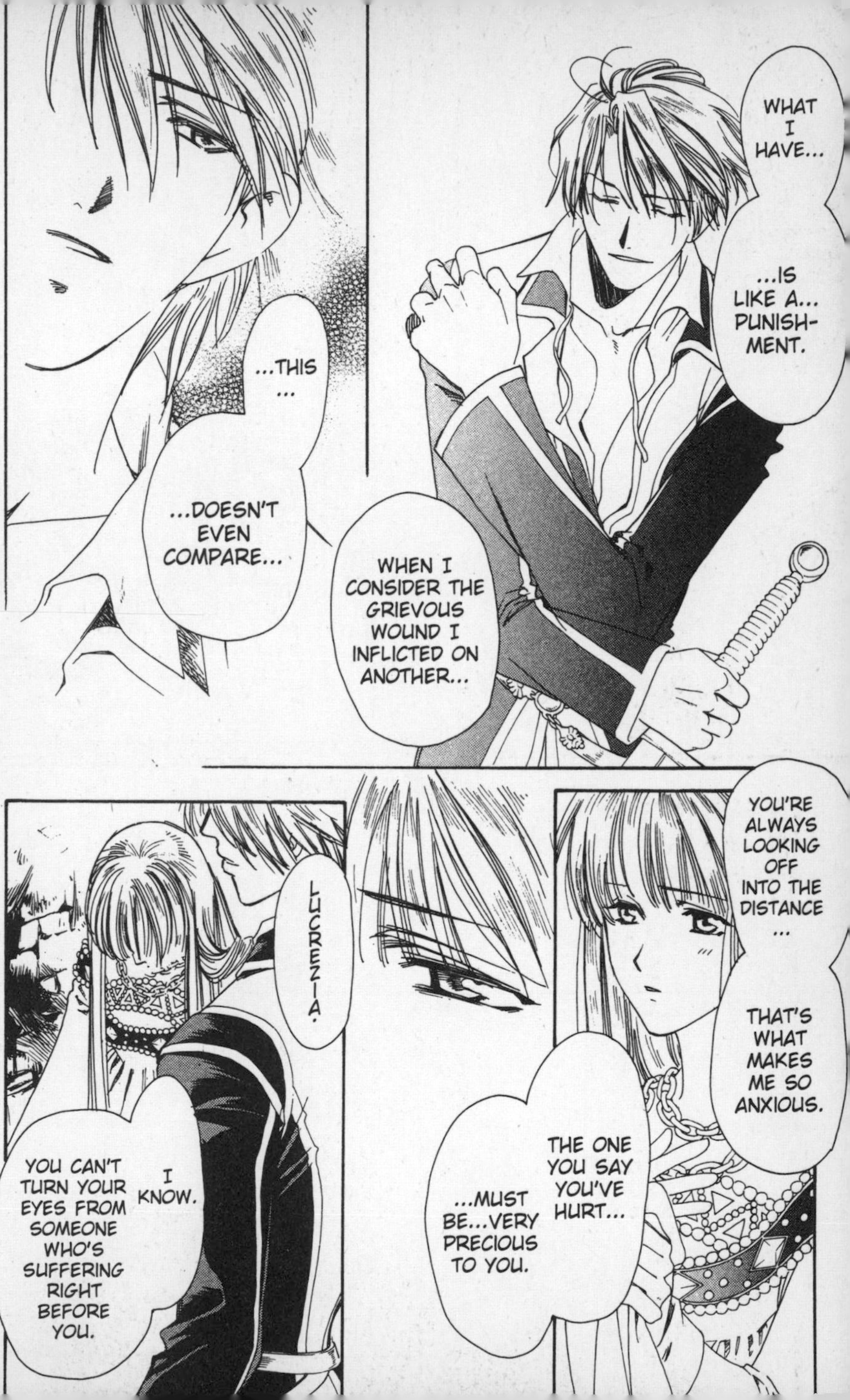

WHAT I HAVE...
...IS LIKE A... PUNISHMENT.
WHEN I CONSIDER THE GRIEVOUS WOUND I INFLICTED ON ANOTHER...
...THIS ...
...DOESN'T EVEN COMPARE...
YOU'RE ALWAYS LOOKING OFF INTO THE DISTANCE ...
THAT'S WHAT MAKES ME SO ANXIOUS.
THE ONE YOU SAY YOU'VE HURT...
...MUST BE...VERY PRECIOUS TO YOU.
LUCREZIA.
I KNOW.
YOU CAN'T TURN YOUR EYES FROM SOMEONE WHO'S SUFFERING RIGHT BEFORE YOU.

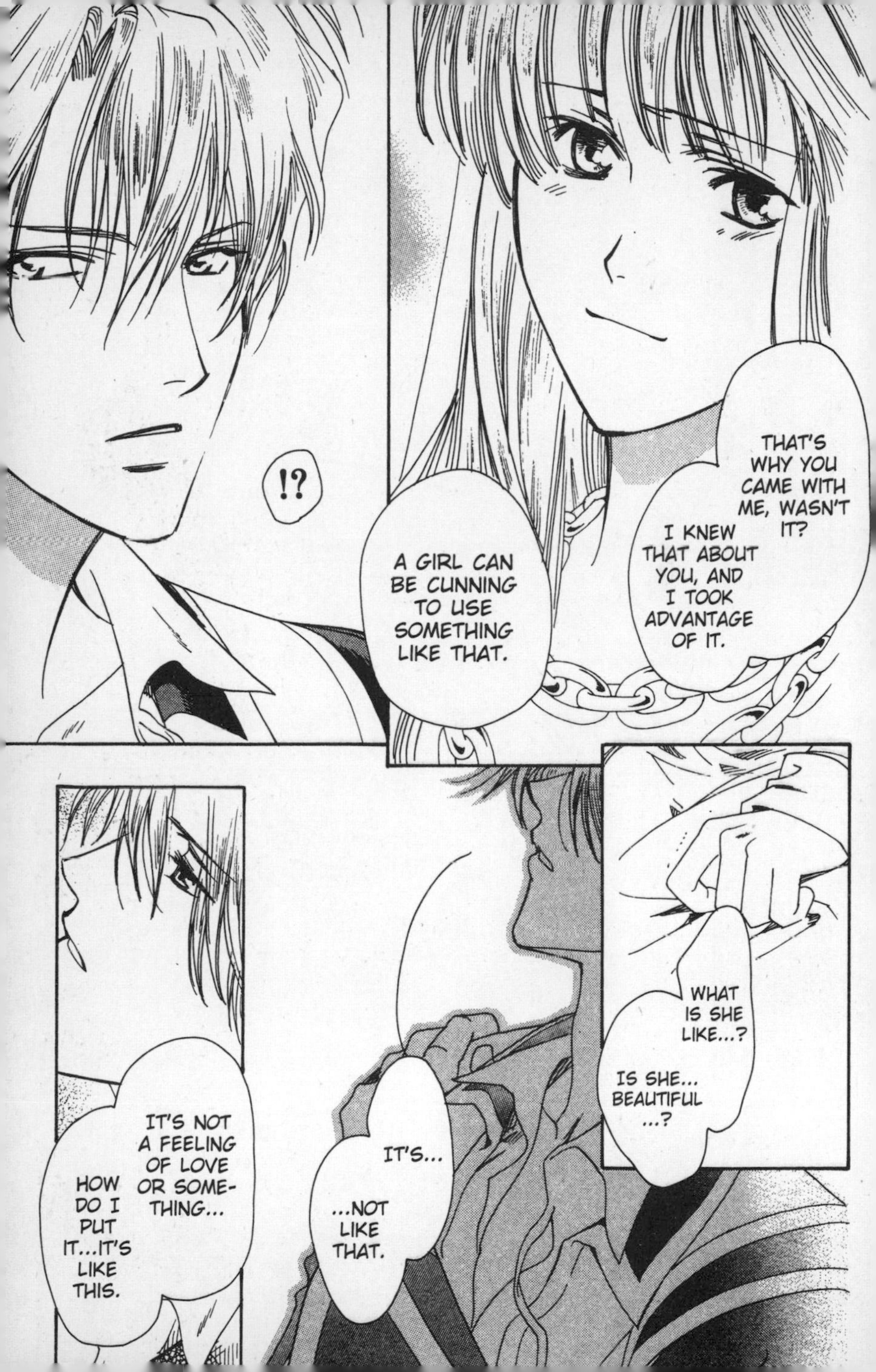
THAT'S WHY YOU CAME WITH ME, WASN'T IT?
I KNEW THAT ABOUT YOU, AND I TOOK ADVANTAGE OF IT.
A GIRL CAN BE CUNNING TO USE SOMETHING LIKE THAT.
!?
WHAT IS SHE LIKE...?
IS SHE... BEAUTIFUL ...?
IT'S...
...NOT LIKE THAT.
IT'S NOT A FEELING OF LOVE OR SOME-THING...
HOW DO I PUT IT...IT'S LIKE THIS.

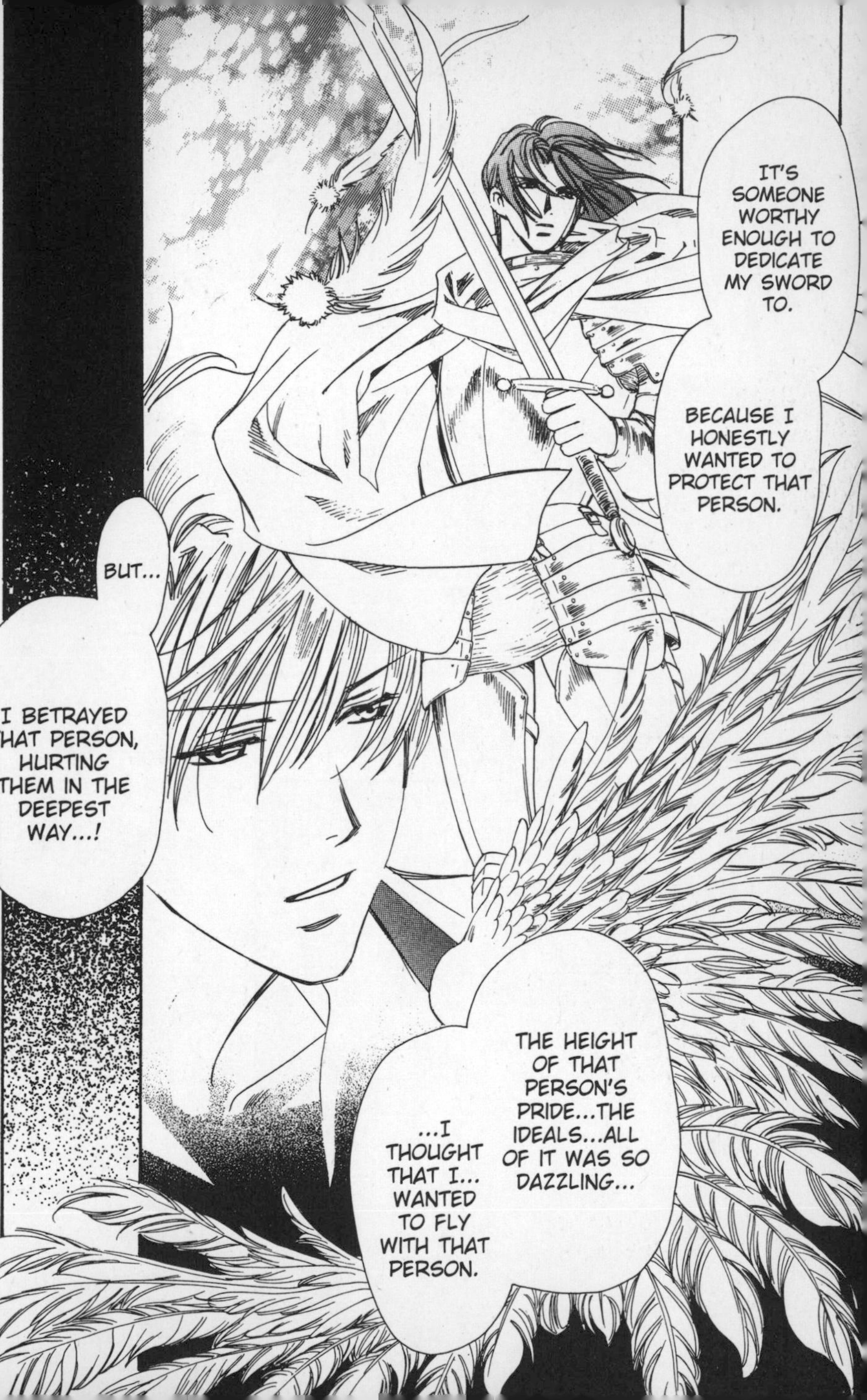
IT'S SOMEONE WORTHY ENOUGH TO DEDICATE MY SWORD TO.
BECAUSE I HONESTLY WANTED TO PROTECT THAT PERSON.
BUT...
I BETRAYED THAT PERSON, HURTING THEM IN THE DEEPEST WAY...!
THE HEIGHT OF THAT PERSON'S PRIDE...THE IDEALS...ALL OF IT WAS SO DAZZLING...
...I THOUGHT THAT I... WANTED TO FLY WITH THAT PERSON.

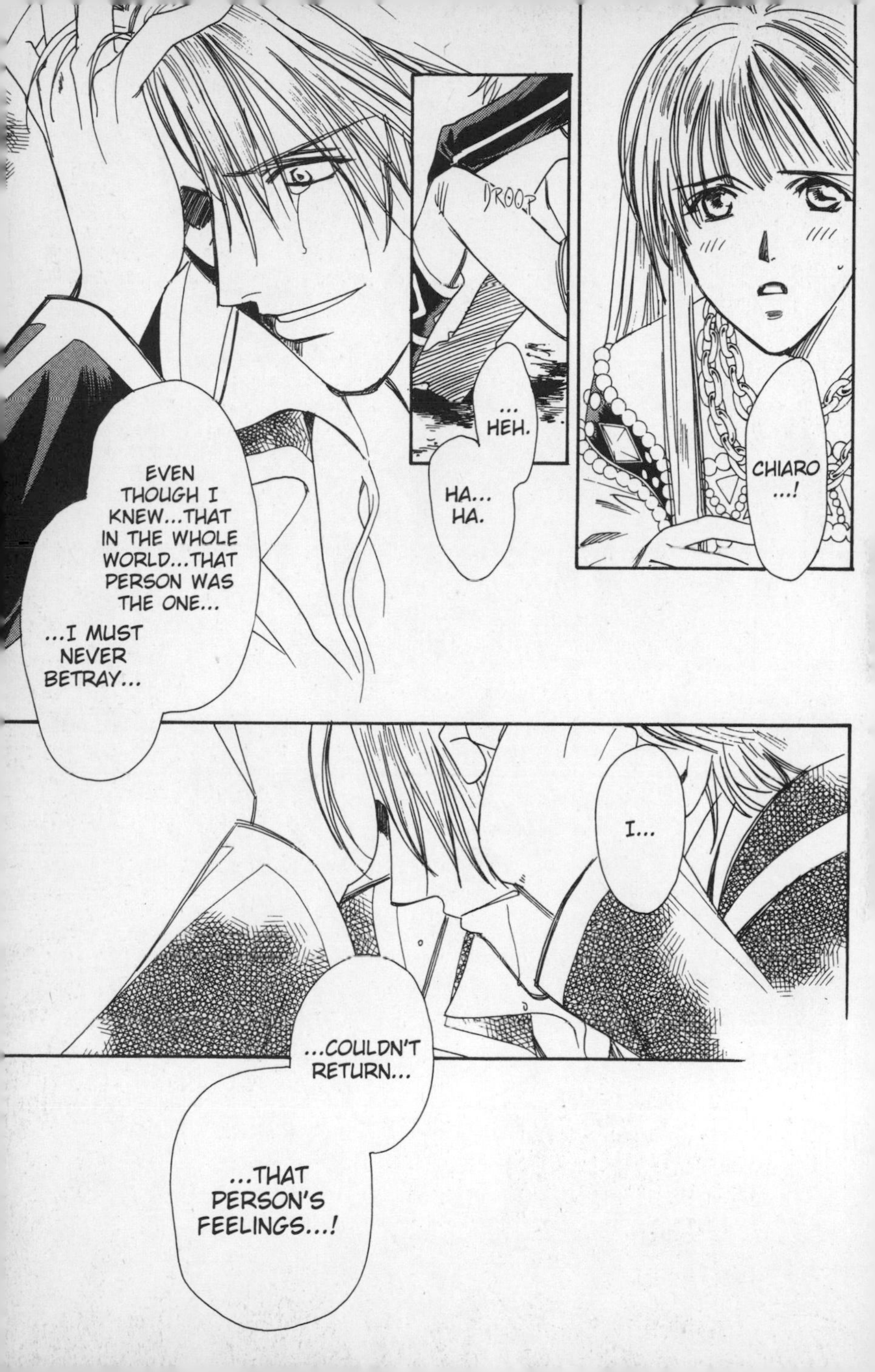
CHIARO ...!
DROOP
... HEH.
HA... HA.
EVEN THOUGH I KNEW...THAT IN THE WHOLE WORLD...THAT PERSON WAS THE ONE...
...I MUST NEVER BETRAY...
I...
...COULDN'T RETURN...
...THAT PERSON'S FEELINGS...!

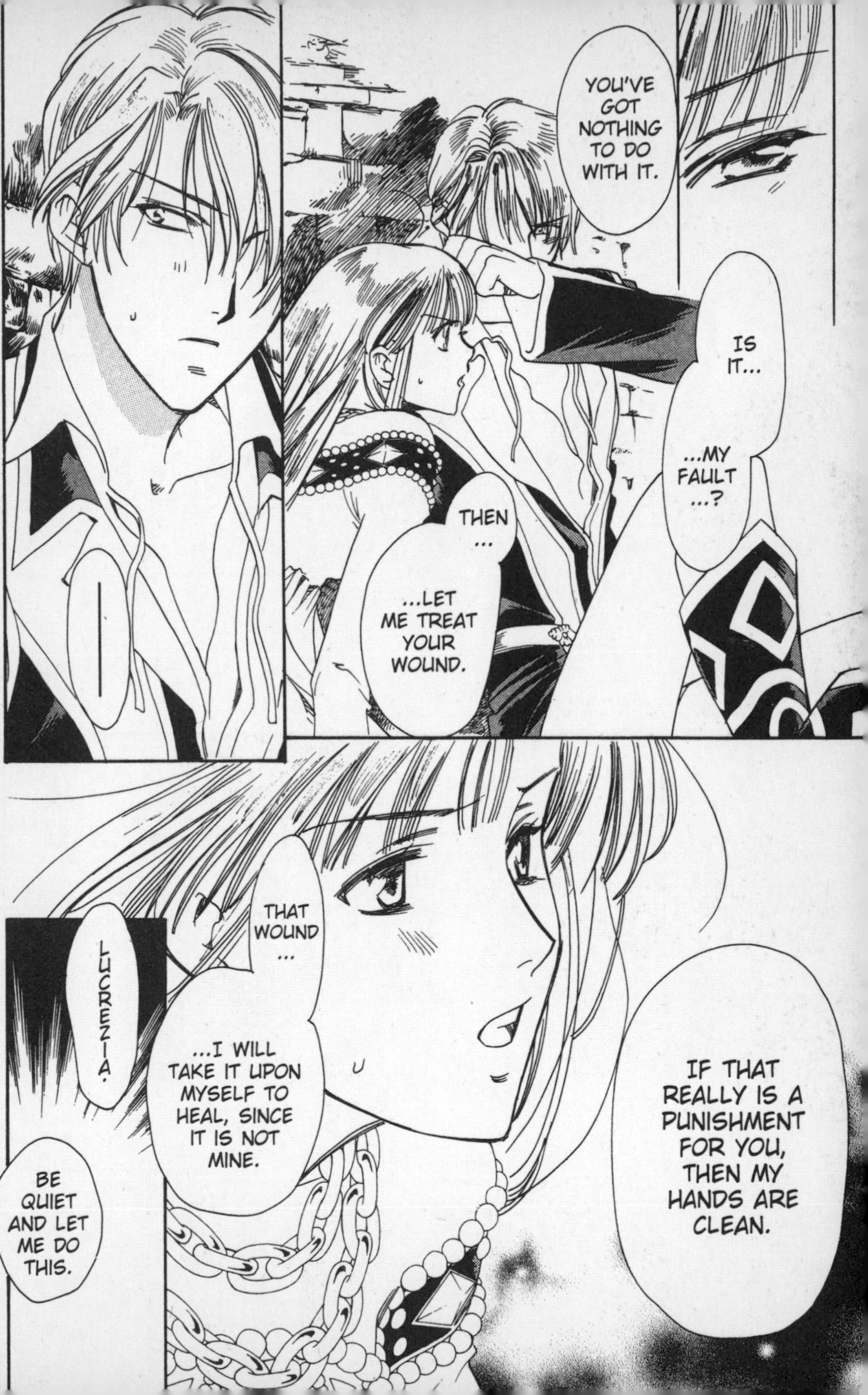
YOU'VE GOT NOTHING TO DO WITH IT.
IS IT...
...MY FAULT ...?
THEN ...
...LET ME TREAT YOUR WOUND.
—
IF THAT REALLY IS A PUNISHMENT FOR YOU, THEN MY HANDS ARE CLEAN.
THAT WOUND ...
...I WILL TAKE IT UPON MYSELF TO HEAL, SINCE IT IS NOT MINE.
LUCREZIA.
BE QUIET AND LET ME DO THIS.

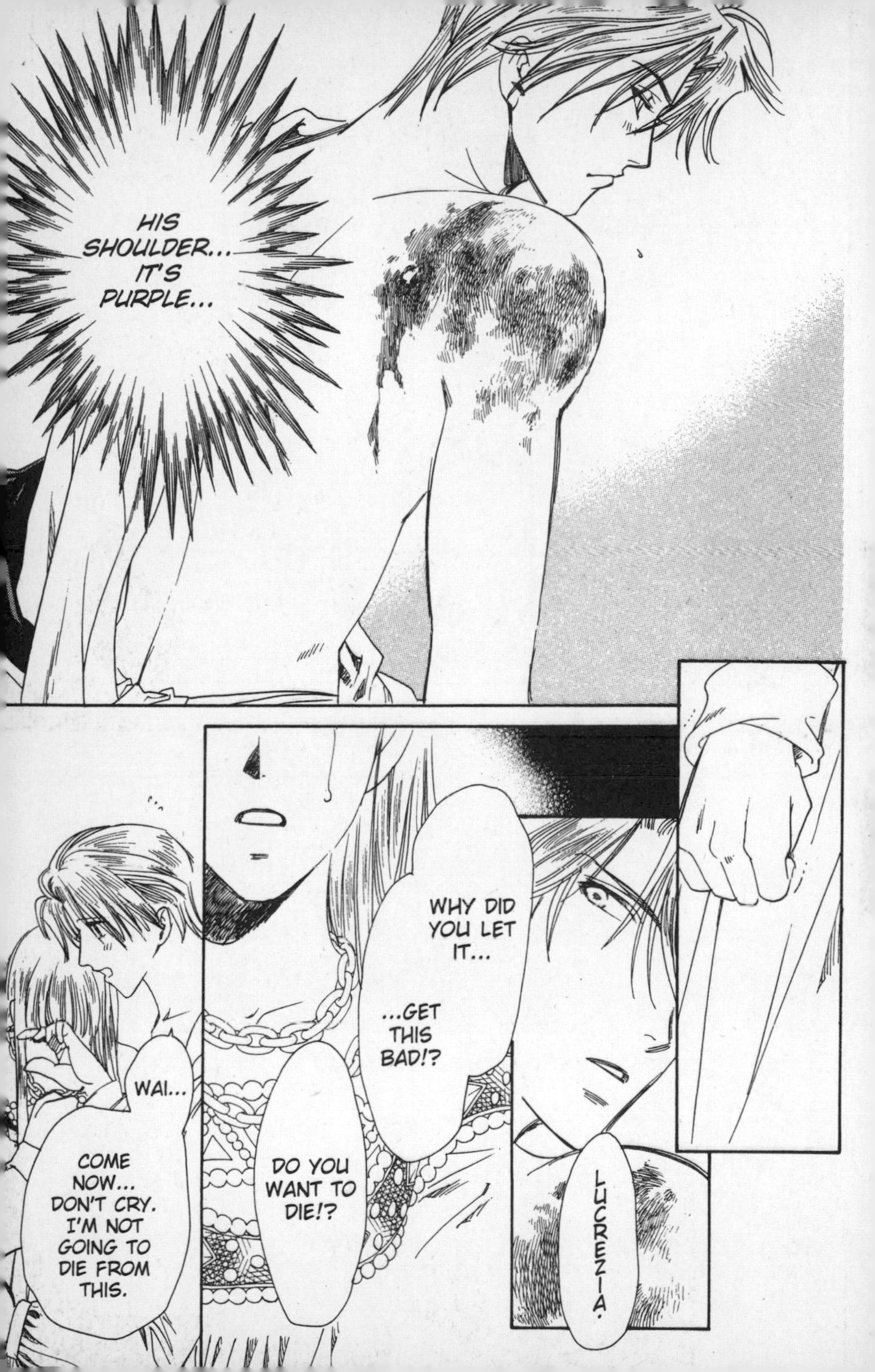
HIS SHOULDER... IT'S PURPLE...
LUCREZIA.
WHY DID YOU LET IT...
...GET THIS BAD!?
DO YOU WANT TO DIE!?
WAI...
COME NOW... DON'T CRY. I'M NOT GOING TO DIE FROM THIS.

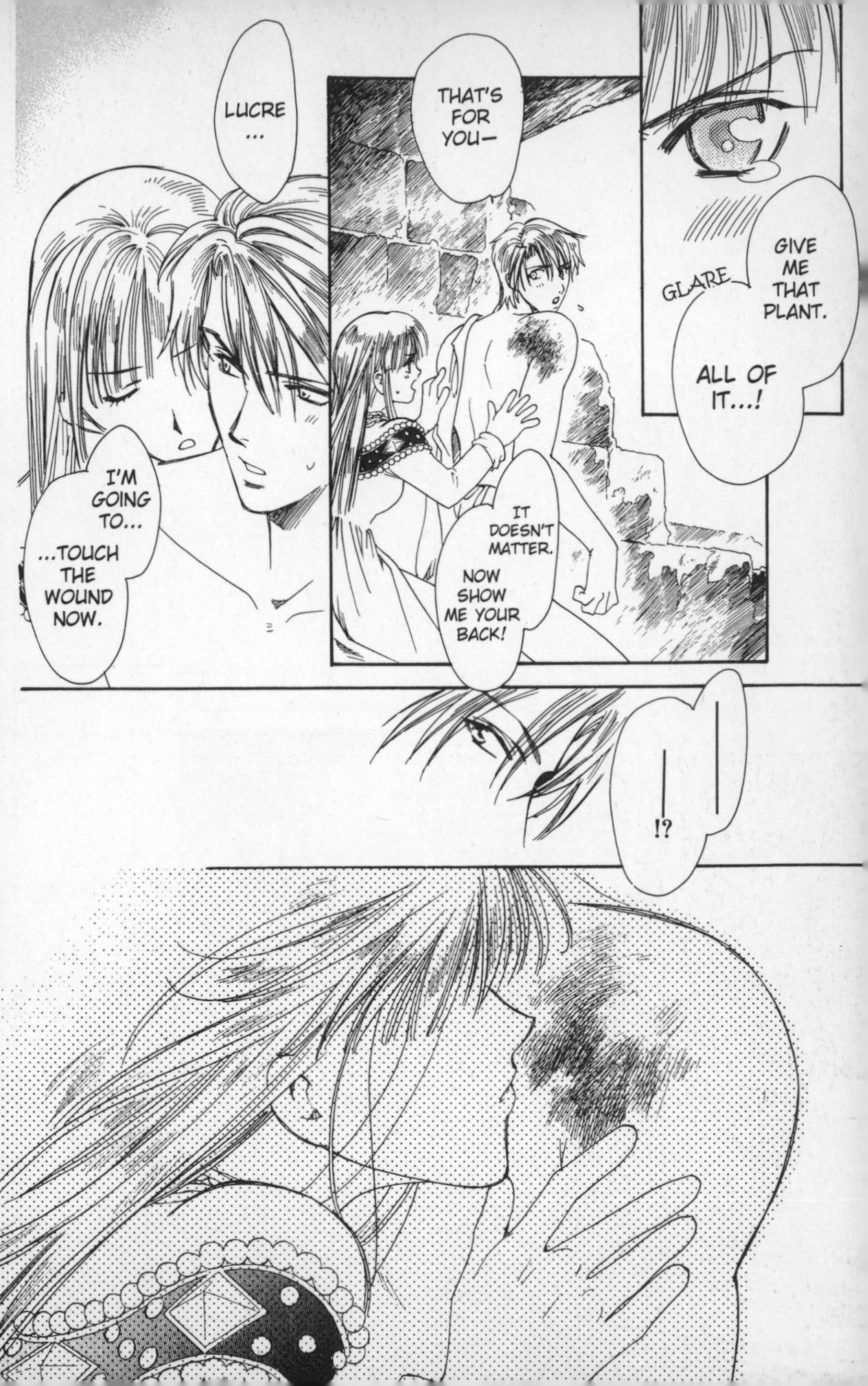
GIVE ME THAT PLANT.
GLARE
ALL OF IT...!
THAT'S FOR YOU—
IT DOESN'T MATTER. NOW SHOW ME YOUR BACK!
LUCRE ...
I'M GOING TO... ...TOUCH THE WOUND NOW.
—— —— !?

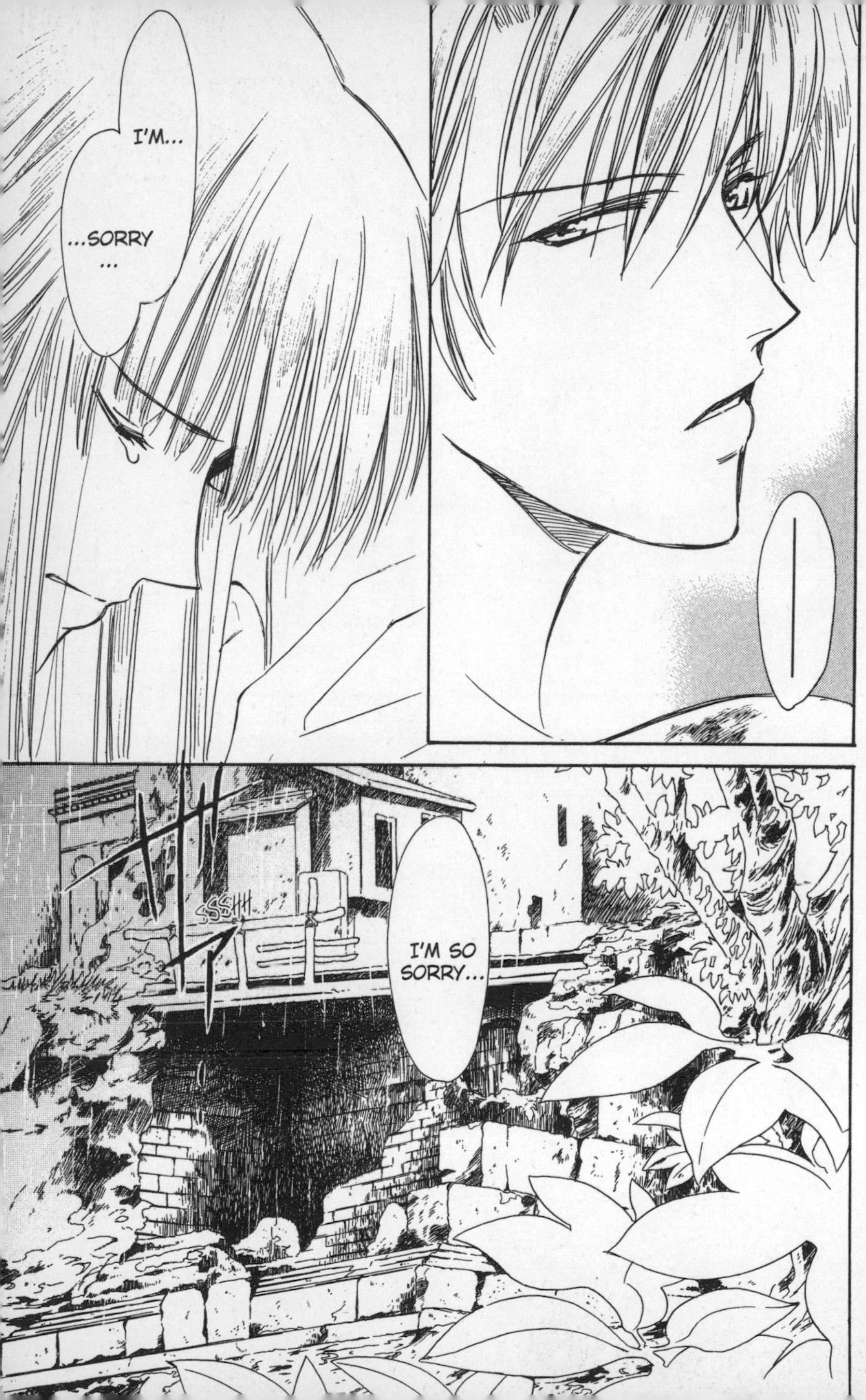
I'M...
...SORRY
...
SSSHH
I'M SO SORRY...

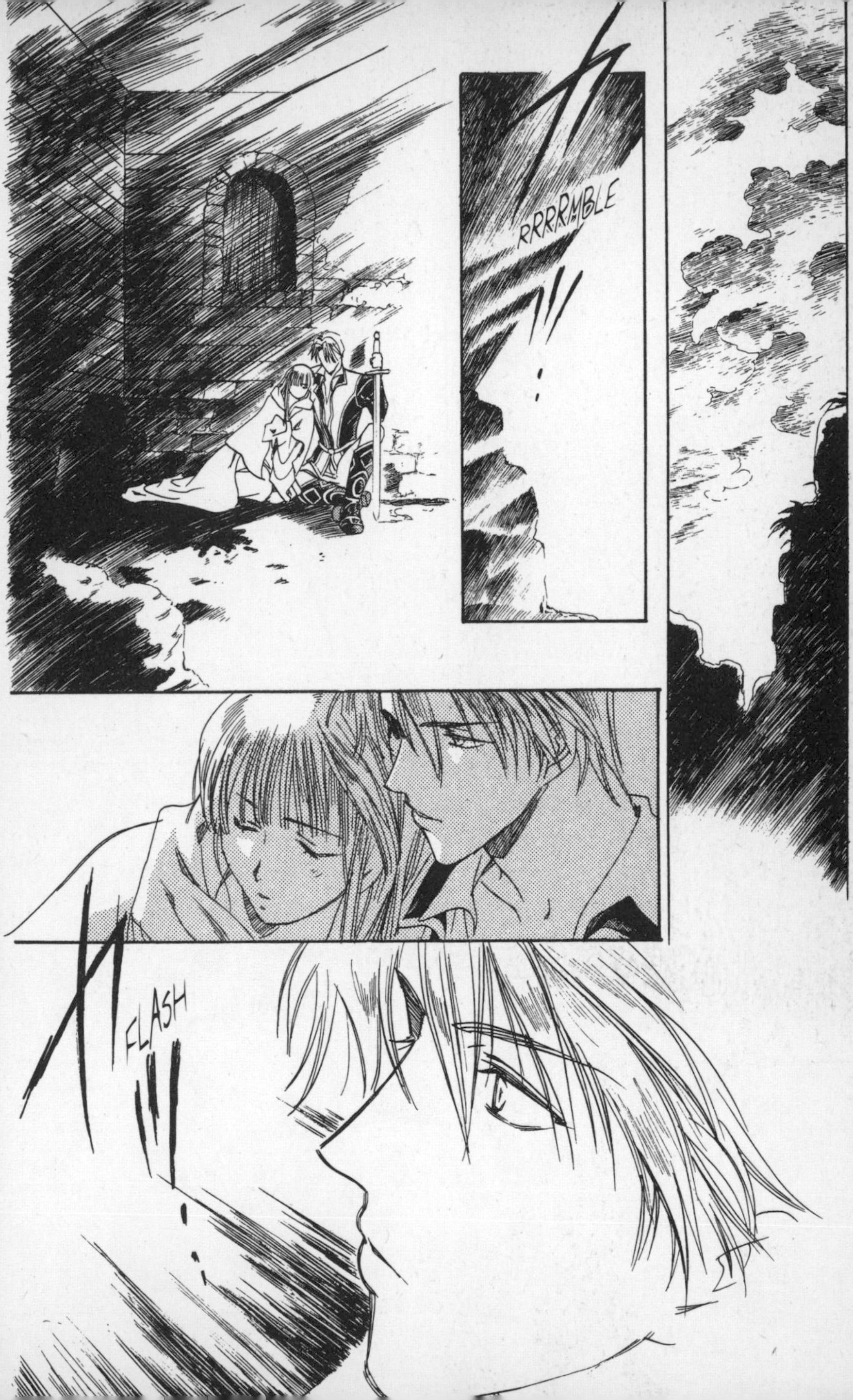
RRRRUMBLE
FLASH

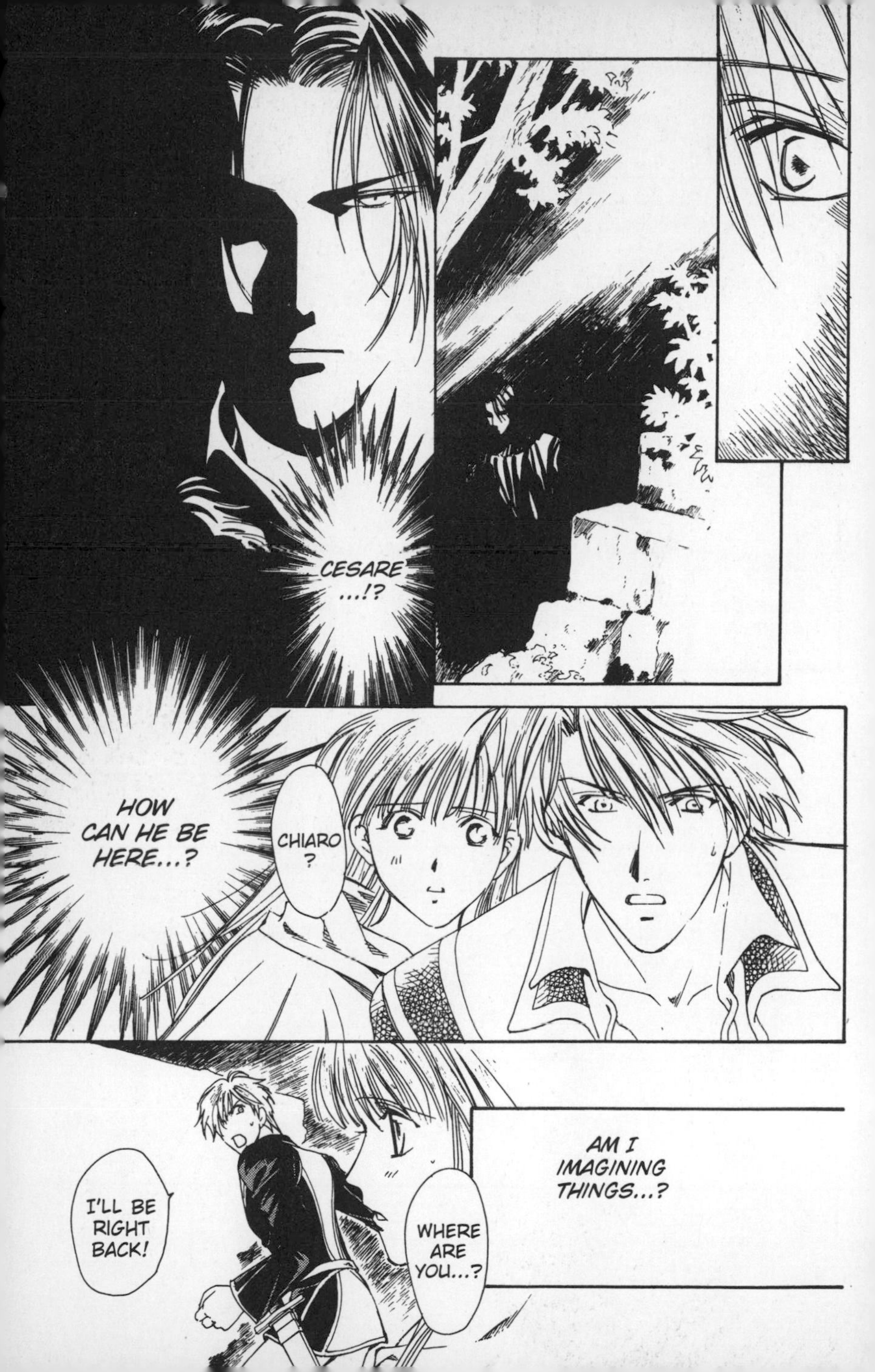
CESARE ...!?
CHIARO ?
HOW CAN HE BE HERE...?
AM I IMAGINING THINGS...?
WHERE ARE YOU...?
I'LL BE RIGHT BACK!

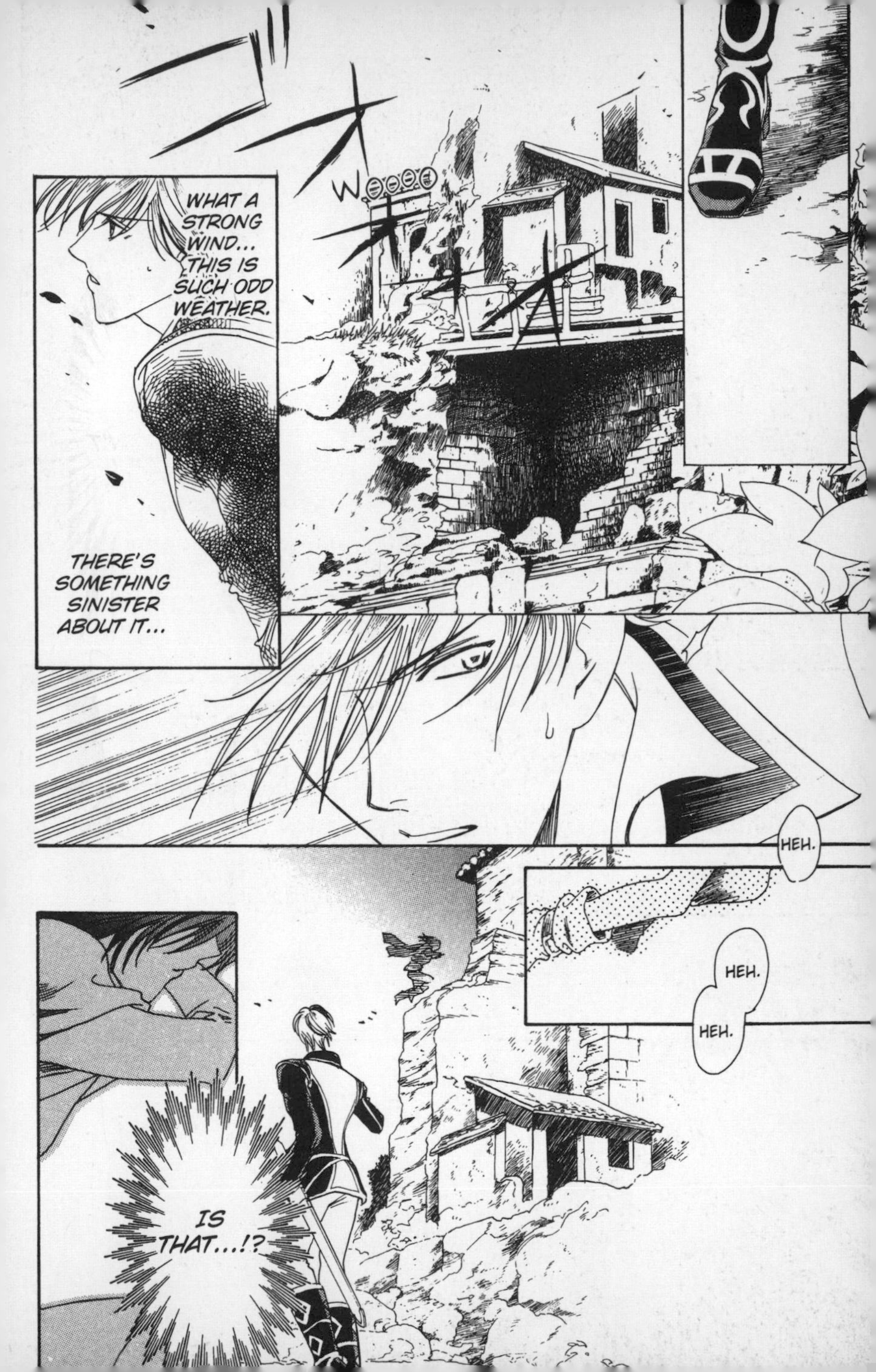
WOOOO
WHAT A STRONG WIND... THIS IS SUCH ODD WEATHER.
THERE'S SOMETHING SINISTER ABOUT IT...
HEH.
HEH.
HEH.
IS THAT...!?

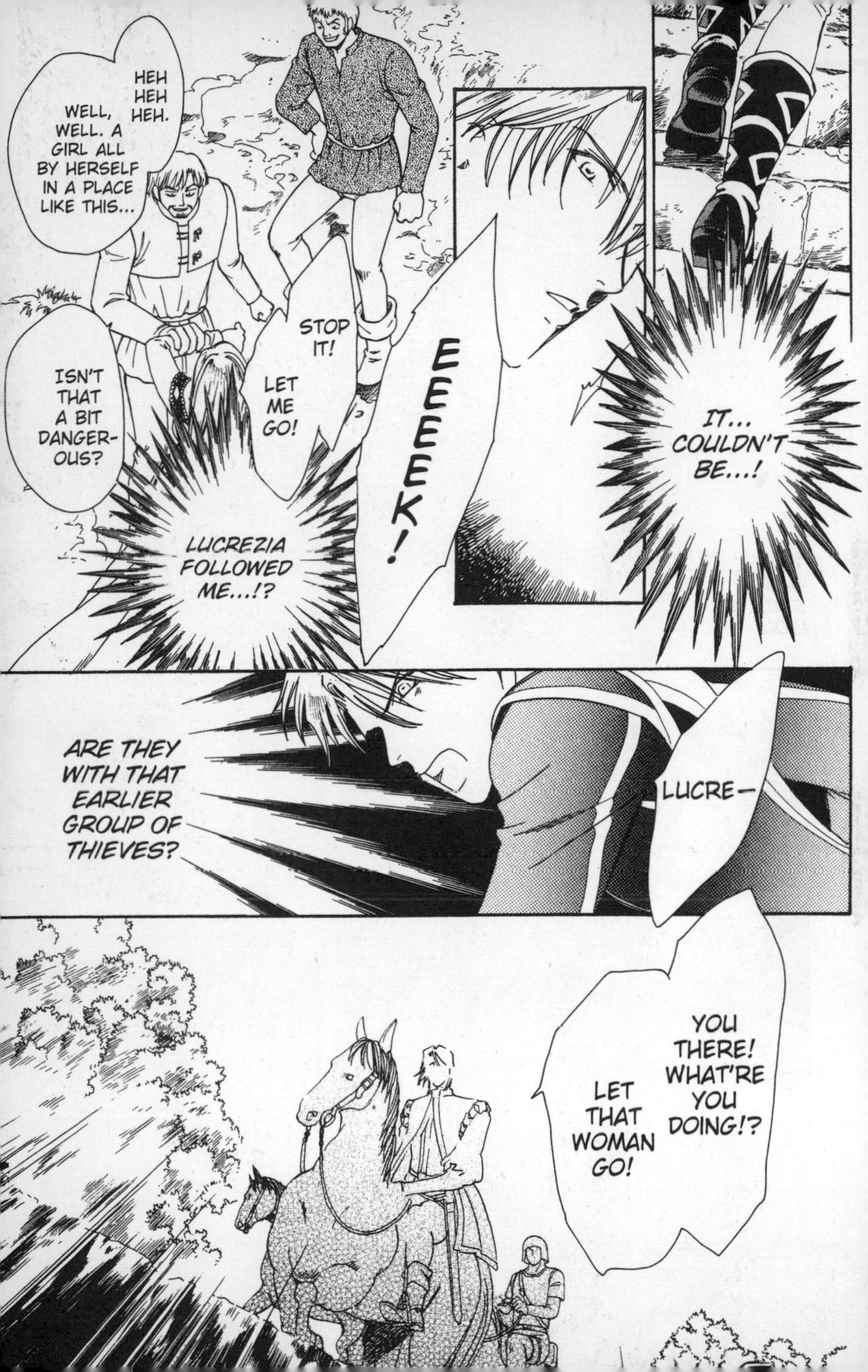
IT... COULDN'T BE...!
HEH HEH HEH.
WELL, WELL. A GIRL ALL BY HERSELF IN A PLACE LIKE THIS...
ISN'T THAT A BIT DANGEROUS?
STOP IT! LET ME GO!
EEEEK!
LUCREZIA FOLLOWED ME...!?
LUCRE—
ARE THEY WITH THAT EARLIER GROUP OF THIEVES?
YOU THERE! WHAT'RE YOU DOING!?
LET THAT WOMAN GO!

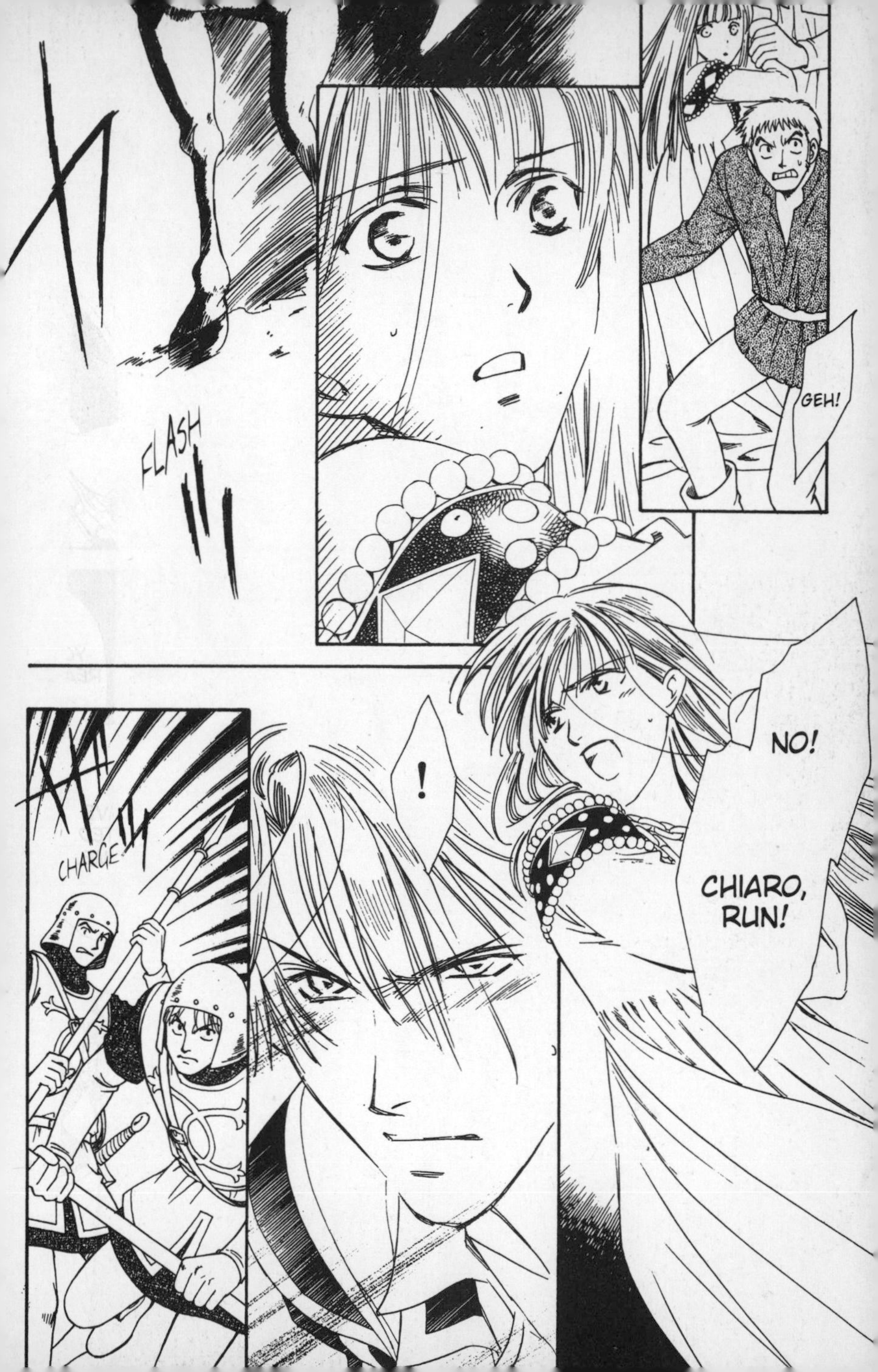
GEH!
FLASH
NO!
CHIARO, RUN!
!
CHARGE

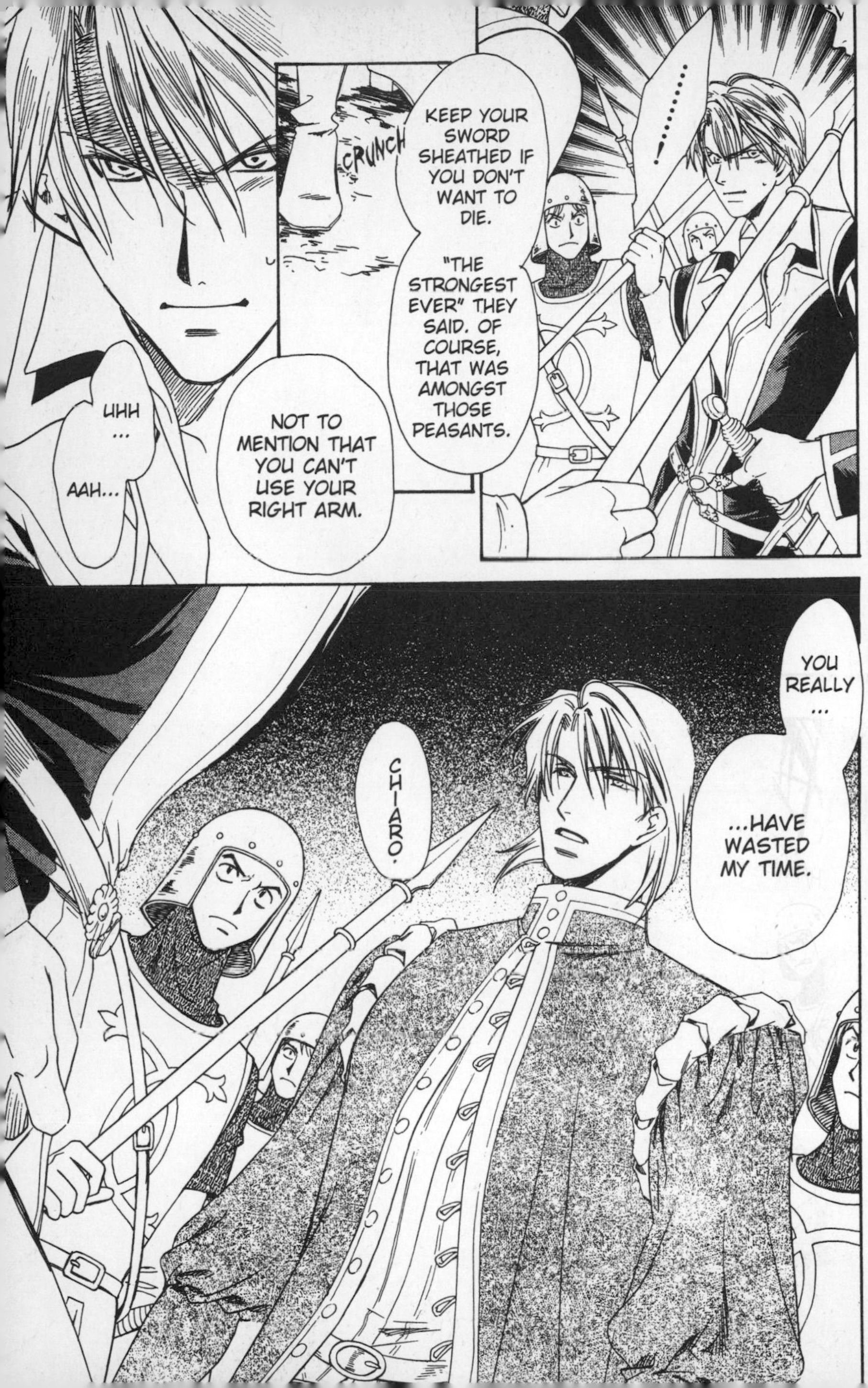
......
KEEP YOUR SWORD SHEATHED IF YOU DON'T WANT TO DIE.
"THE STRONGEST EVER" THEY SAID. OF COURSE, THAT WAS AMONGST THOSE PEASANTS.
CRUNCH
NOT TO MENTION THAT YOU CAN'T USE YOUR RIGHT ARM.
UHH ... AAH...
YOU REALLY ...
...HAVE WASTED MY TIME.
CHIARO.

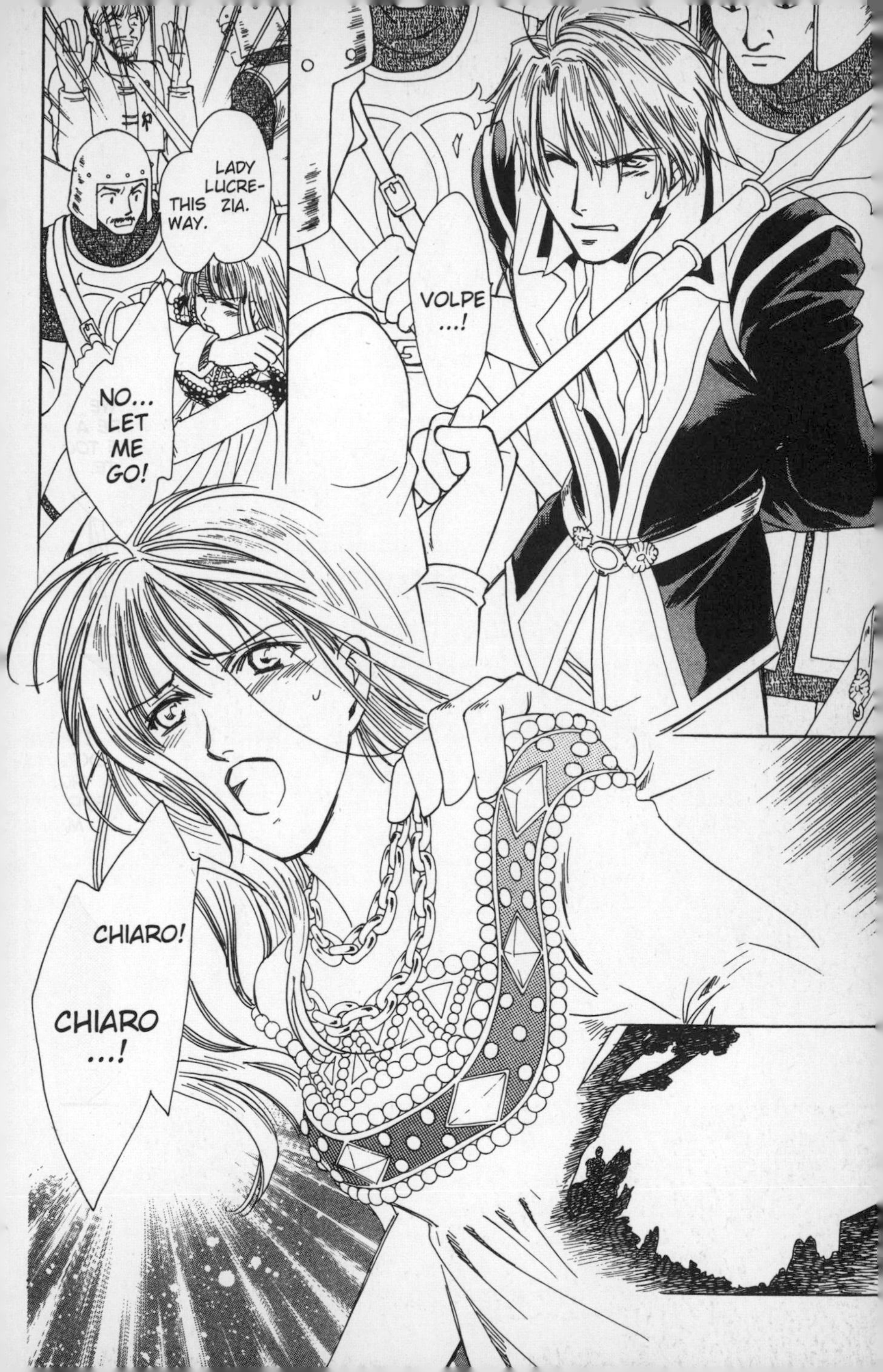
VOLPE ...!
LADY LUCREZIA. THIS WAY.
NO... LET ME GO!
CHIARO!
CHIARO ...!

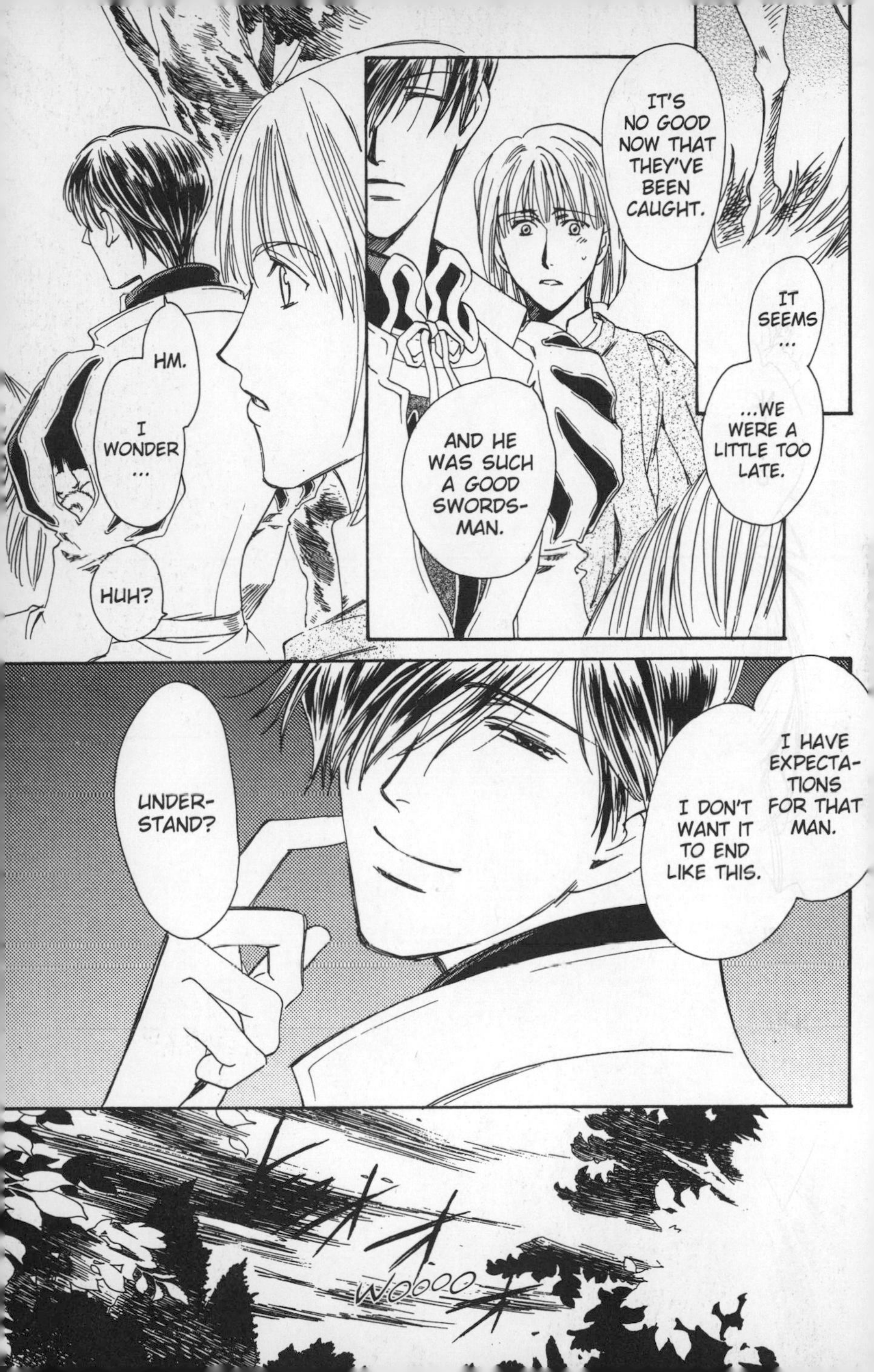
IT SEEMS...
...WE WERE A LITTLE TOO LATE.
IT'S NO GOOD NOW THAT THEY'VE BEEN CAUGHT.
AND HE WAS SUCH A GOOD SWORDS-MAN.
HM.
I WONDER...
HUH?
I HAVE EXPECTA-TIONS FOR THAT MAN.
I DON'T WANT IT TO END LIKE THIS.
UNDER-STAND?
WOOOO

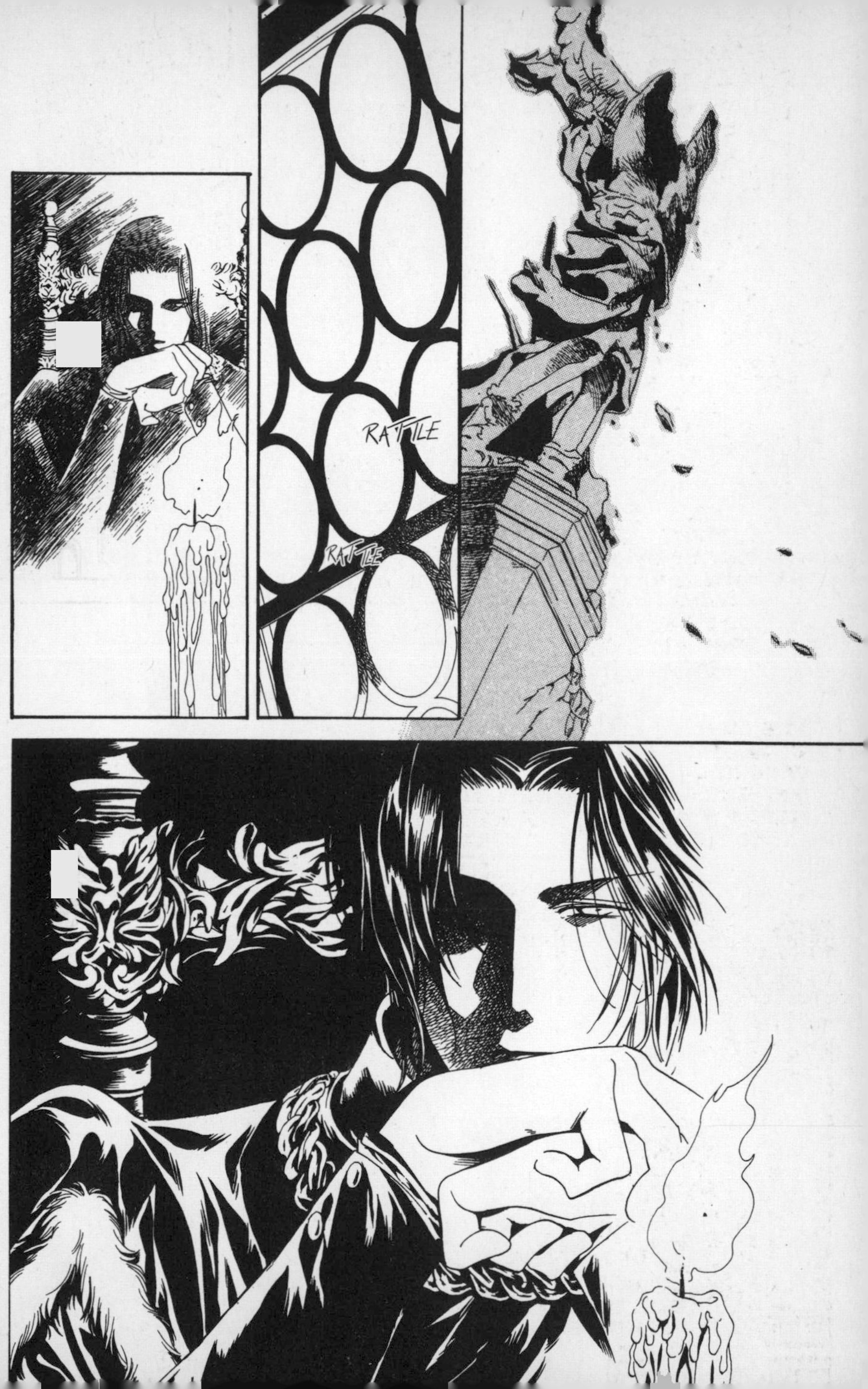
RATTLE
RATTLE

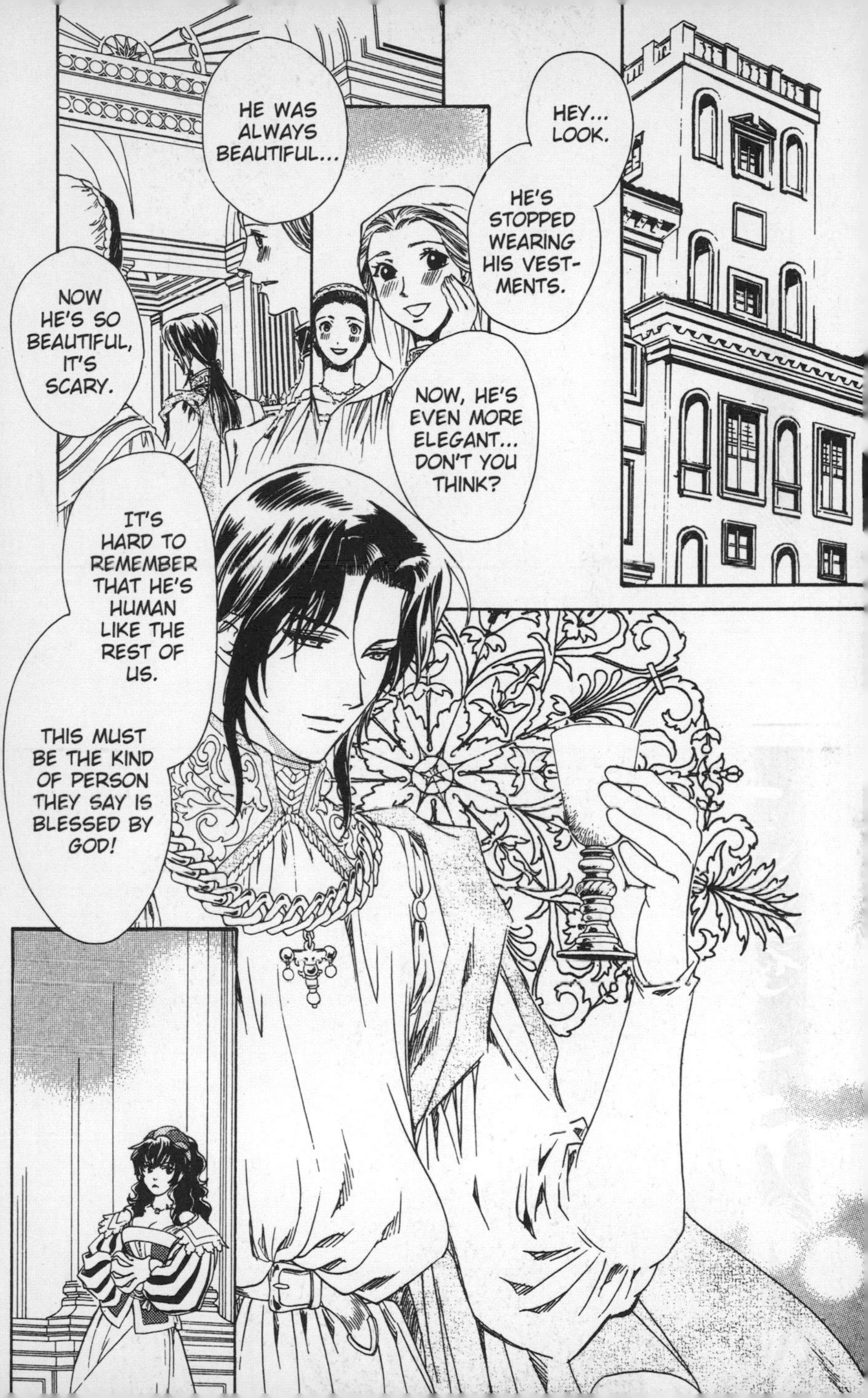
HEY... LOOK.
HE'S STOPPED WEARING HIS VEST-MENTS.
HE WAS ALWAYS BEAUTIFUL...
NOW, HE'S EVEN MORE ELEGANT... DON'T YOU THINK?
NOW HE'S SO BEAUTIFUL, IT'S SCARY.
IT'S HARD TO REMEMBER THAT HE'S HUMAN LIKE THE REST OF US.
THIS MUST BE THE KIND OF PERSON THEY SAY IS BLESSED BY GOD!

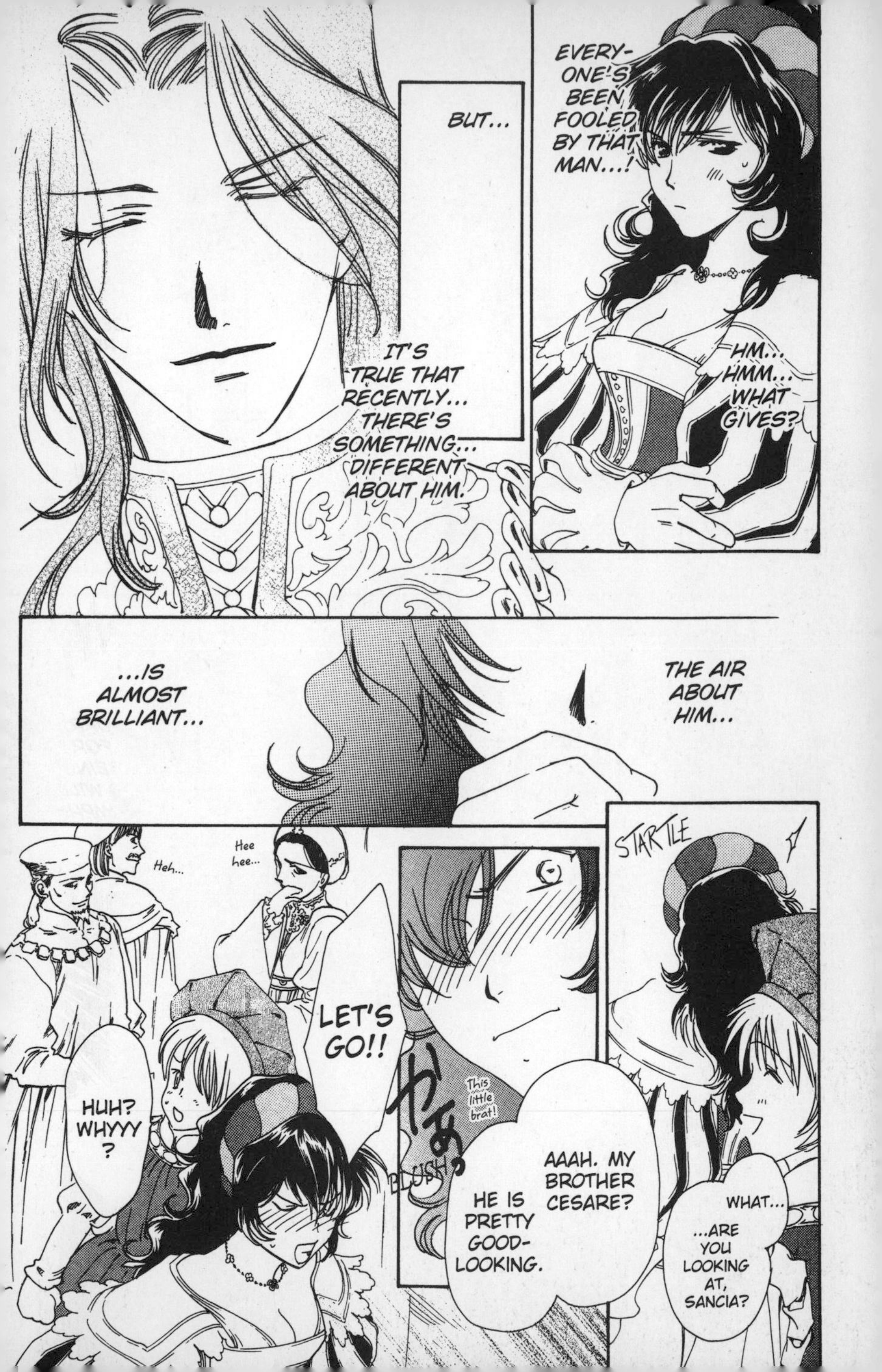
EVERY-ONE'S BEEN FOOLED BY THAT MAN...!
HM... HMM... WHAT GIVES?
BUT...
IT'S TRUE THAT RECENTLY... THERE'S SOMETHING... DIFFERENT ABOUT HIM.
THE AIR ABOUT HIM...
...IS ALMOST BRILLIANT...
STARTLE
WHAT...
...ARE YOU LOOKING AT, SANCIA?
...
AAAH. MY BROTHER CESARE?
HE IS PRETTY GOOD-LOOKING.
This little brat!
BLUSH
LET'S GO!!
Hee hee...
Heh...
HUH? WHYYY?

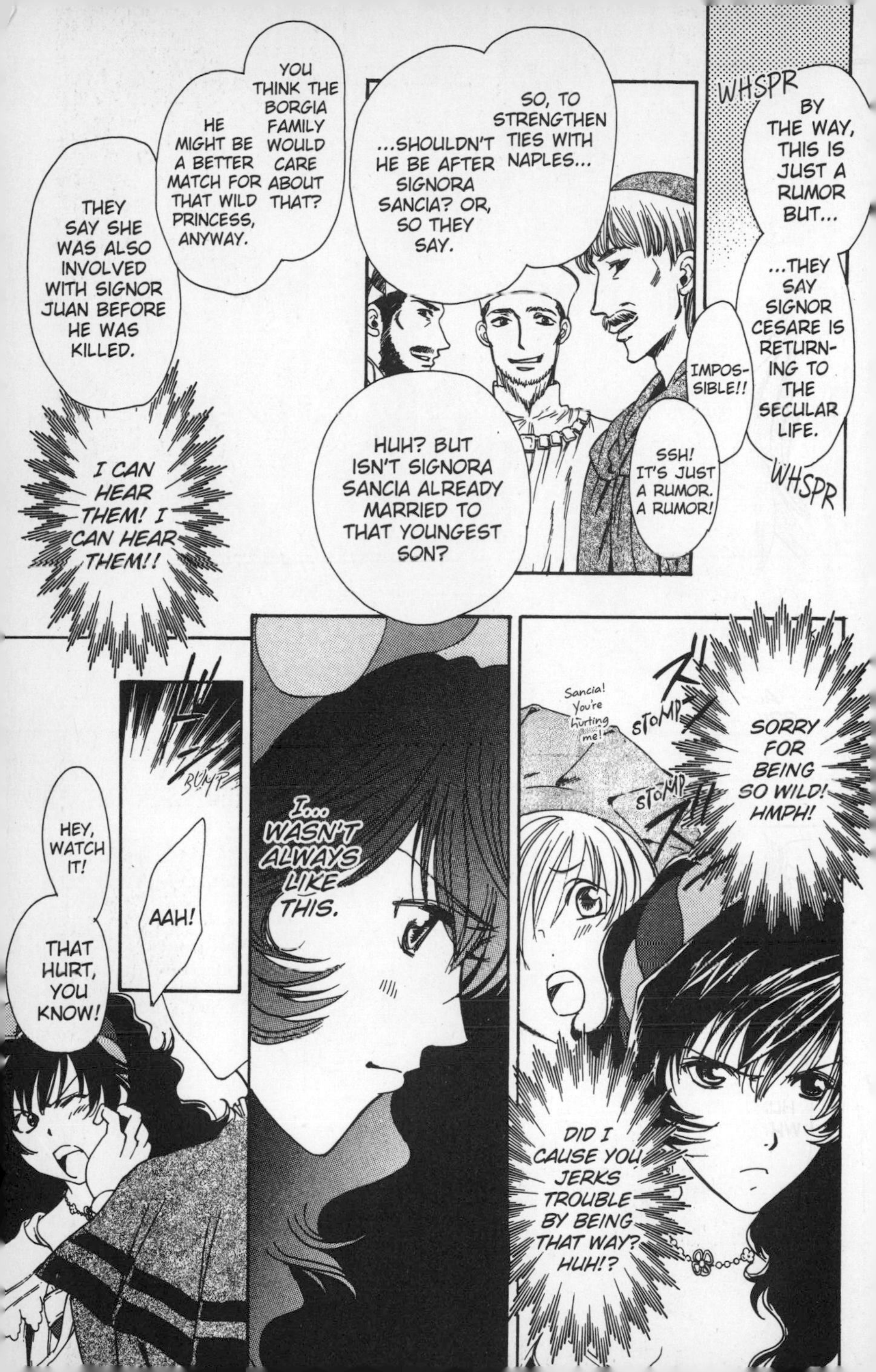
WHSPR
BY THE WAY, THIS IS JUST A RUMOR BUT...
...THEY SAY SIGNOR CESARE IS RETURNING TO THE SECULAR LIFE.
WHSPR
IMPOSSIBLE!!
SSH! IT'S JUST A RUMOR. A RUMOR!
SO, TO STRENGTHEN TIES WITH NAPLES...
...SHOULDN'T HE BE AFTER SIGNORA SANCIA? OR, SO THEY SAY.
HUH? BUT ISN'T SIGNORA SANCIA ALREADY MARRIED TO THAT YOUNGEST SON?
YOU THINK THE BORGIA FAMILY WOULD CARE ABOUT THAT?
HE MIGHT BE A BETTER MATCH FOR THAT WILD PRINCESS, ANYWAY.
THEY SAY SHE WAS ALSO INVOLVED WITH SIGNOR JUAN BEFORE HE WAS KILLED.
I CAN HEAR THEM! I CAN HEAR THEM!!
SORRY FOR BEING SO WILD! HMPH!
STOMP
Sancia! You're hurting me!
STOMP
DID I CAUSE YOU JERKS TROUBLE BY BEING THAT WAY? HUH!?
I... WASN'T ALWAYS LIKE THIS.
BUMP
AAH!
HEY, WATCH IT!
THAT HURT, YOU KNOW!

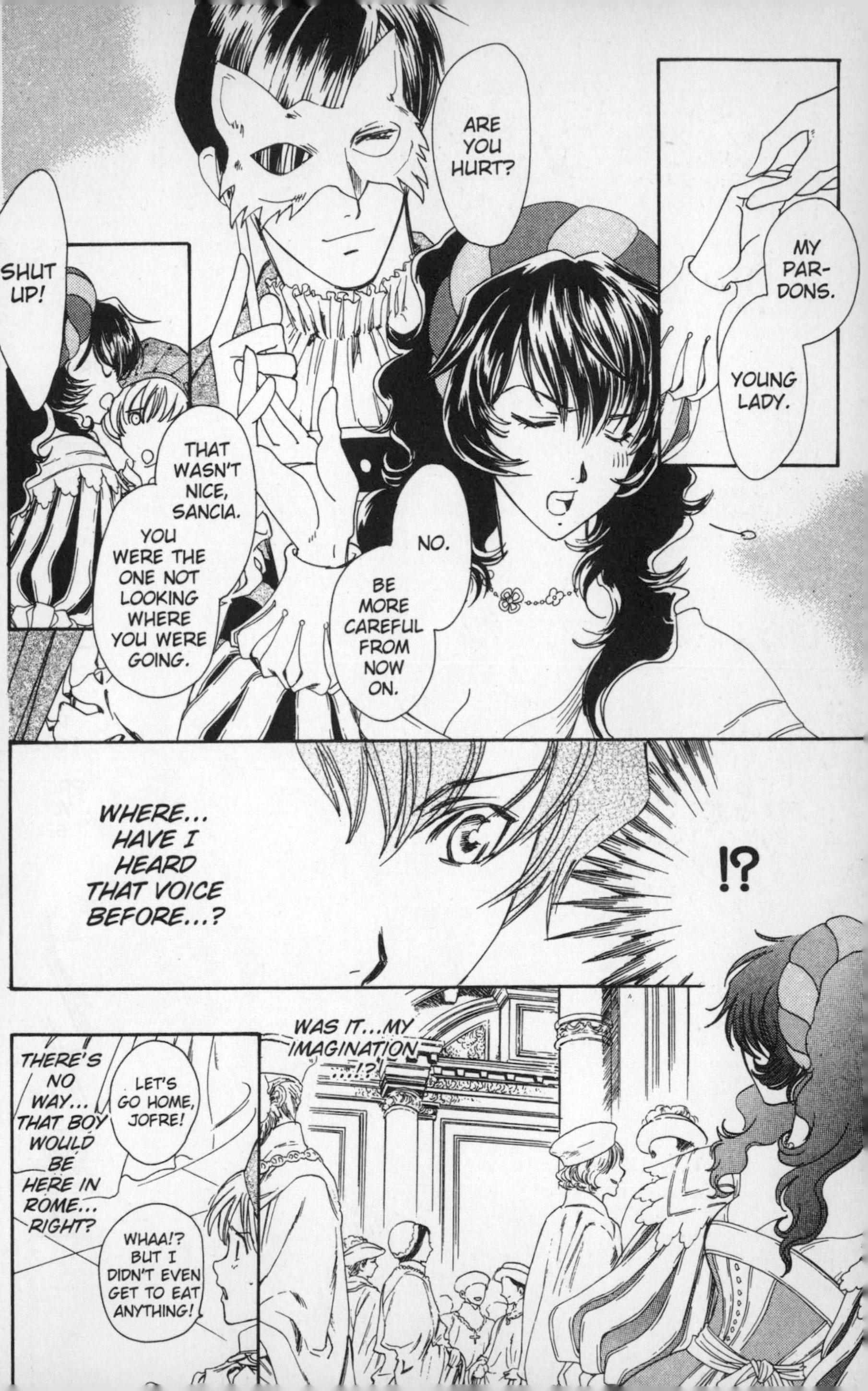
MY PARDONS.
YOUNG LADY.
ARE YOU HURT?
NO.
BE MORE CAREFUL FROM NOW ON.
SHUT UP!
THAT WASN'T NICE, SANCIA.
YOU WERE THE ONE NOT LOOKING WHERE YOU WERE GOING.
!?
WHERE... HAVE I HEARD THAT VOICE BEFORE...?
WAS IT...MY IMAGINATION...!?
LET'S GO HOME, JOFRE!
WHAA!? BUT I DIDN'T EVEN GET TO EAT ANYTHING!
THERE'S NO WAY... THAT BOY WOULD BE HERE IN ROME... RIGHT?

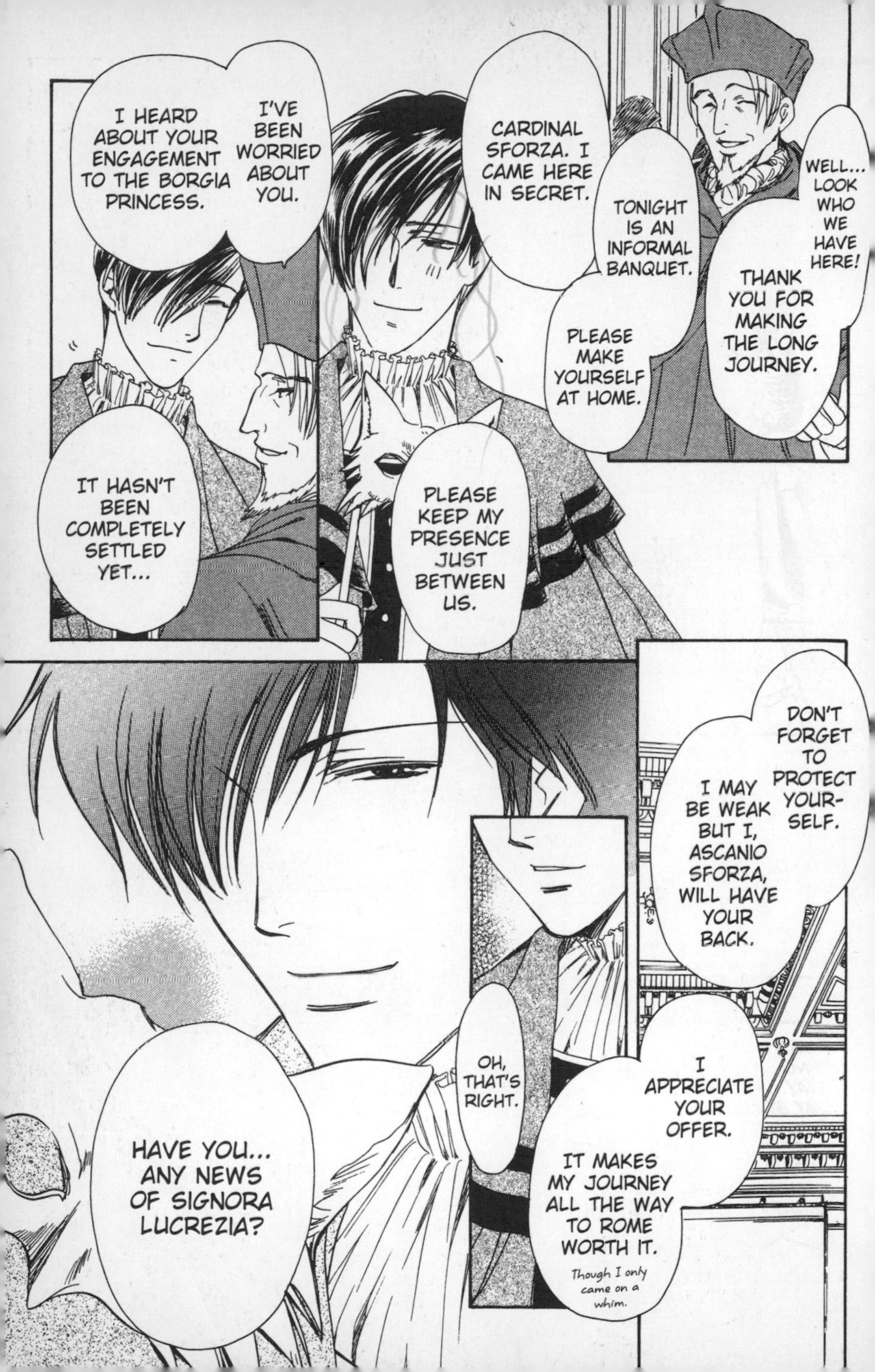
WELL... LOOK WHO WE HAVE HERE!
THANK YOU FOR MAKING THE LONG JOURNEY.
TONIGHT IS AN INFORMAL BANQUET.
PLEASE MAKE YOURSELF AT HOME.
CARDINAL SFORZA. I CAME HERE IN SECRET.
PLEASE KEEP MY PRESENCE JUST BETWEEN US.
I'VE BEEN WORRIED ABOUT YOU.
I HEARD ABOUT YOUR ENGAGEMENT TO THE BORGIA PRINCESS.
IT HASN'T BEEN COMPLETELY SETTLED YET...
DON'T FORGET TO PROTECT YOURSELF.
I MAY BE WEAK BUT I, ASCANIO SFORZA, WILL HAVE YOUR BACK.
I APPRECIATE YOUR OFFER.
IT MAKES MY JOURNEY ALL THE WAY TO ROME WORTH IT.
Though I only came on a whim.
OH, THAT'S RIGHT.
HAVE YOU... ANY NEWS OF SIGNORA LUCREZIA?

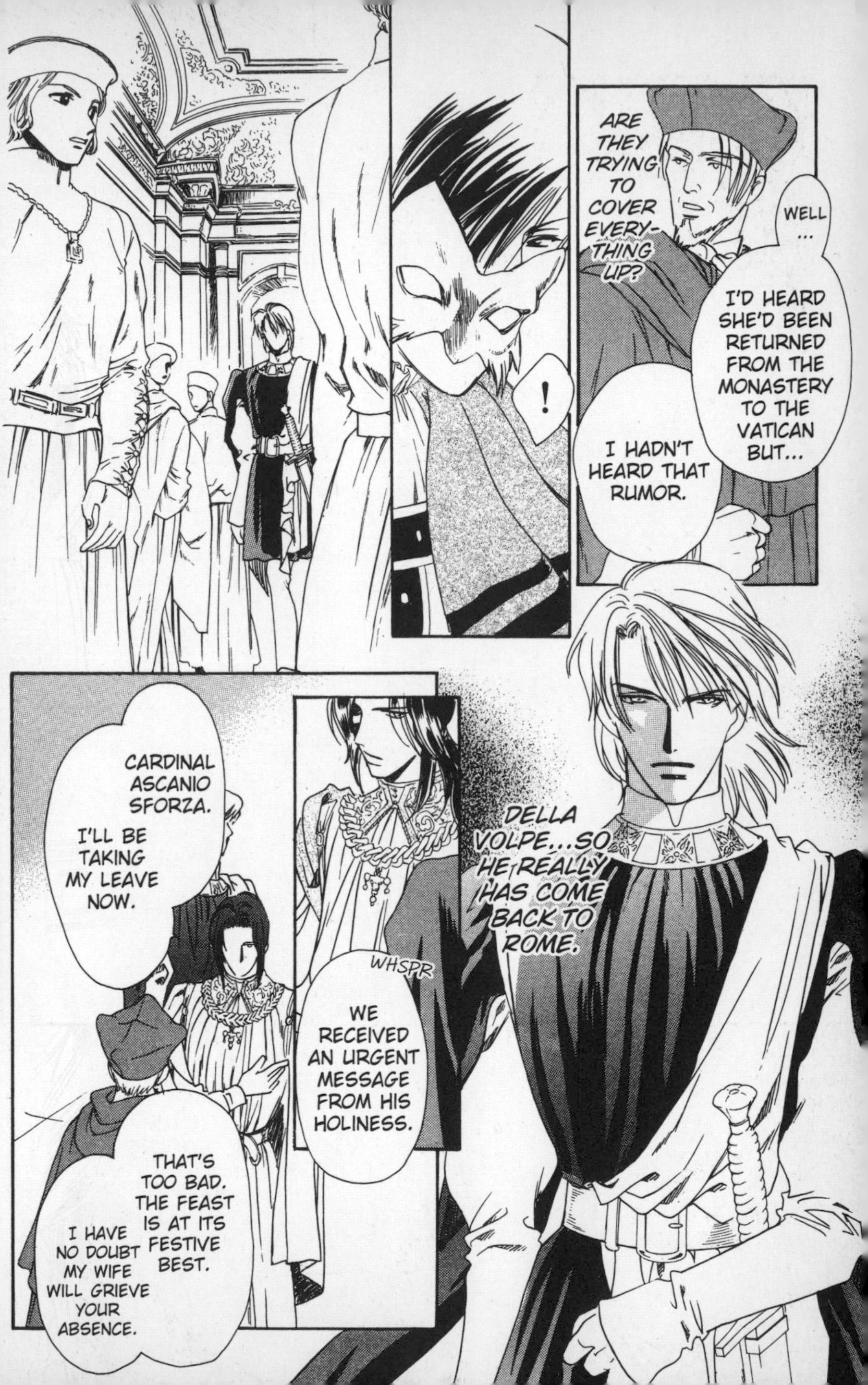
WELL ...
I'D HEARD SHE'D BEEN RETURNED FROM THE MONASTERY TO THE VATICAN BUT...
I HADN'T HEARD THAT RUMOR.
ARE THEY TRYING TO COVER EVERY-THING UP?
!
DELLA VOLPE...SO HE REALLY HAS COME BACK TO ROME.
WHSPR
WE RECEIVED AN URGENT MESSAGE FROM HIS HOLINESS.
CARDINAL ASCANIO SFORZA.
I'LL BE TAKING MY LEAVE NOW.
THAT'S TOO BAD. THE FEAST IS AT ITS FESTIVE BEST.
I HAVE NO DOUBT MY WIFE WILL GRIEVE YOUR ABSENCE.

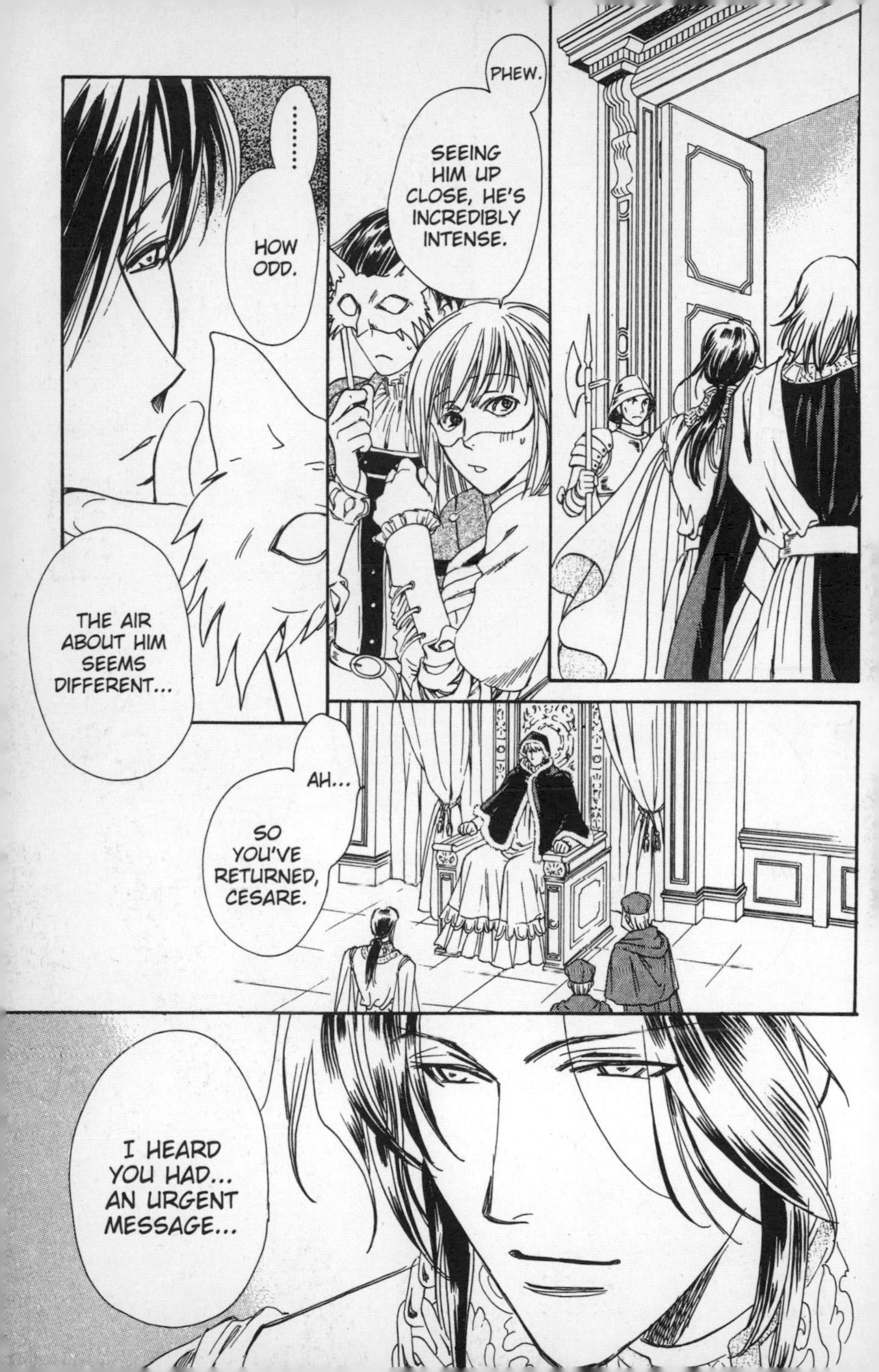
PHEW.
SEEING HIM UP CLOSE, HE'S INCREDIBLY INTENSE.
......
HOW ODD.
THE AIR ABOUT HIM SEEMS DIFFERENT...
AH...
SO YOU'VE RETURNED, CESARE.
I HEARD YOU HAD... AN URGENT MESSAGE...

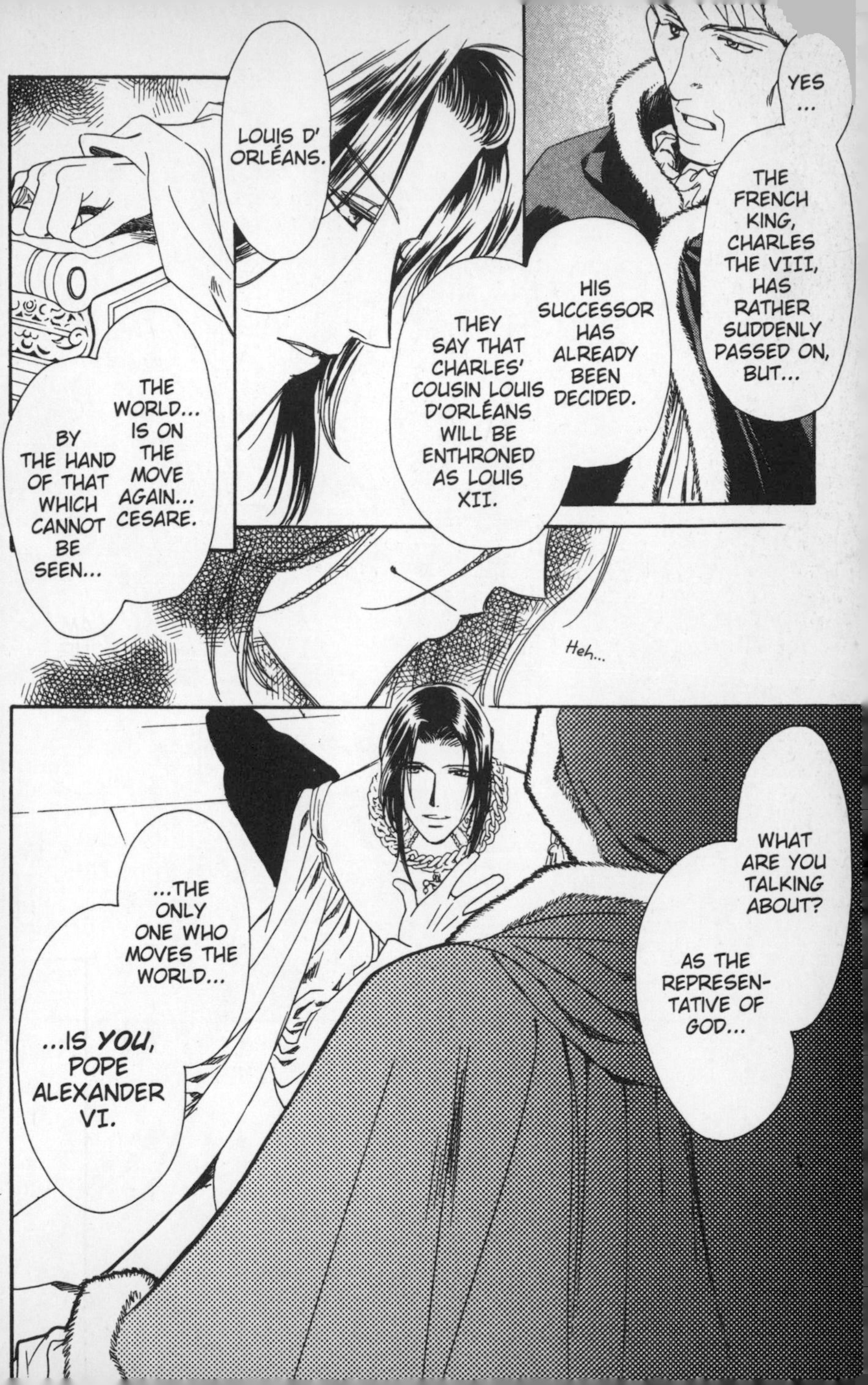
YES ...
THE FRENCH KING, CHARLES THE VIII, HAS RATHER SUDDENLY PASSED ON, BUT...
HIS SUCCESSOR HAS ALREADY BEEN DECIDED.
THEY SAY THAT CHARLES' COUSIN LOUIS D'ORLÉANS WILL BE ENTHRONED AS LOUIS XII.
LOUIS D' ORLÉANS.
Heh...
THE WORLD... IS ON THE MOVE AGAIN... CESARE.
BY THE HAND OF THAT WHICH CANNOT BE SEEN...
WHAT ARE YOU TALKING ABOUT?
AS THE REPRESEN- TATIVE OF GOD...
...THE ONLY ONE WHO MOVES THE WORLD...
...IS *YOU*, POPE ALEXANDER VI.

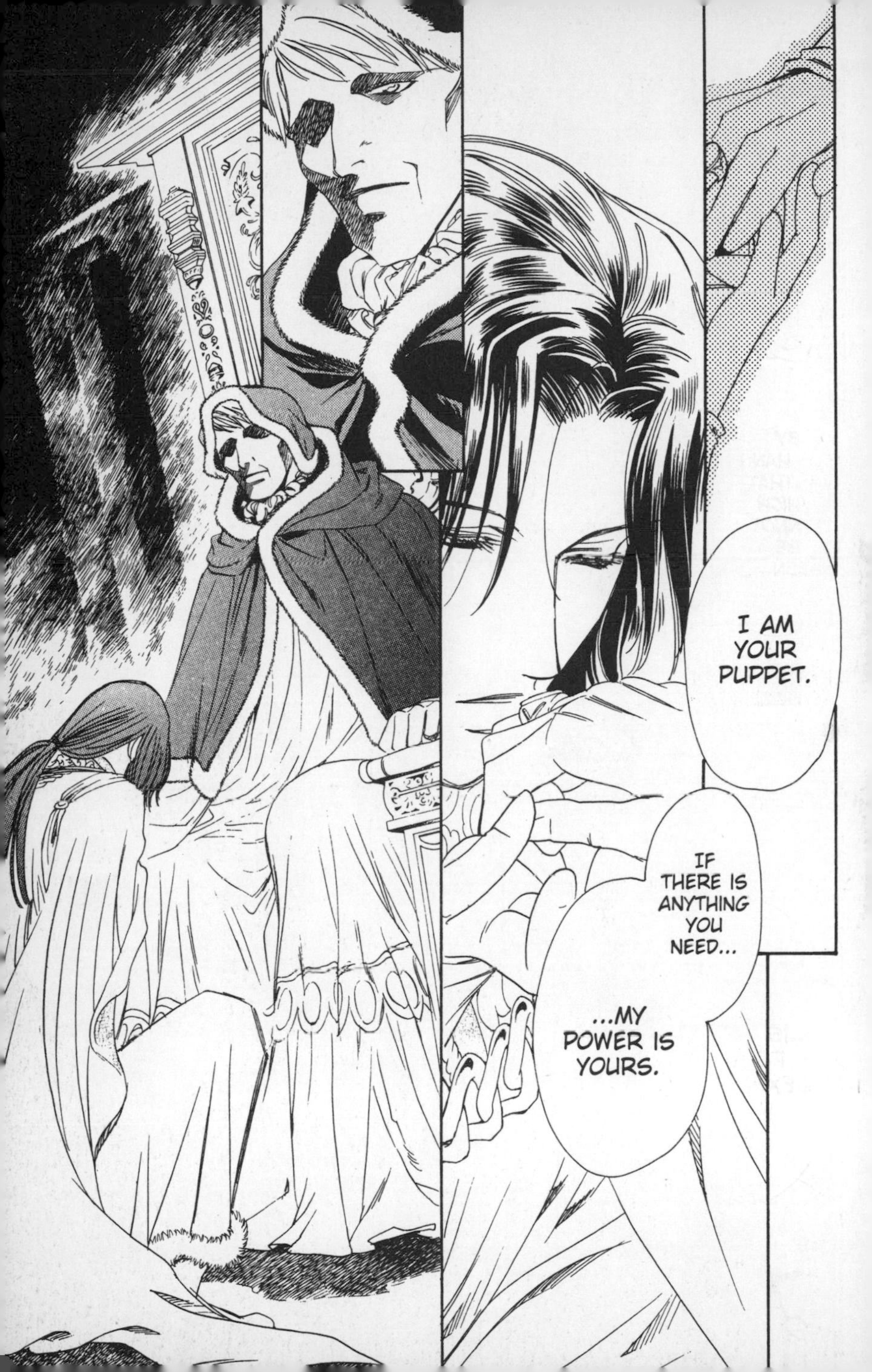
I AM YOUR PUPPET.
IF THERE IS ANYTHING YOU NEED...
...MY POWER IS YOURS.

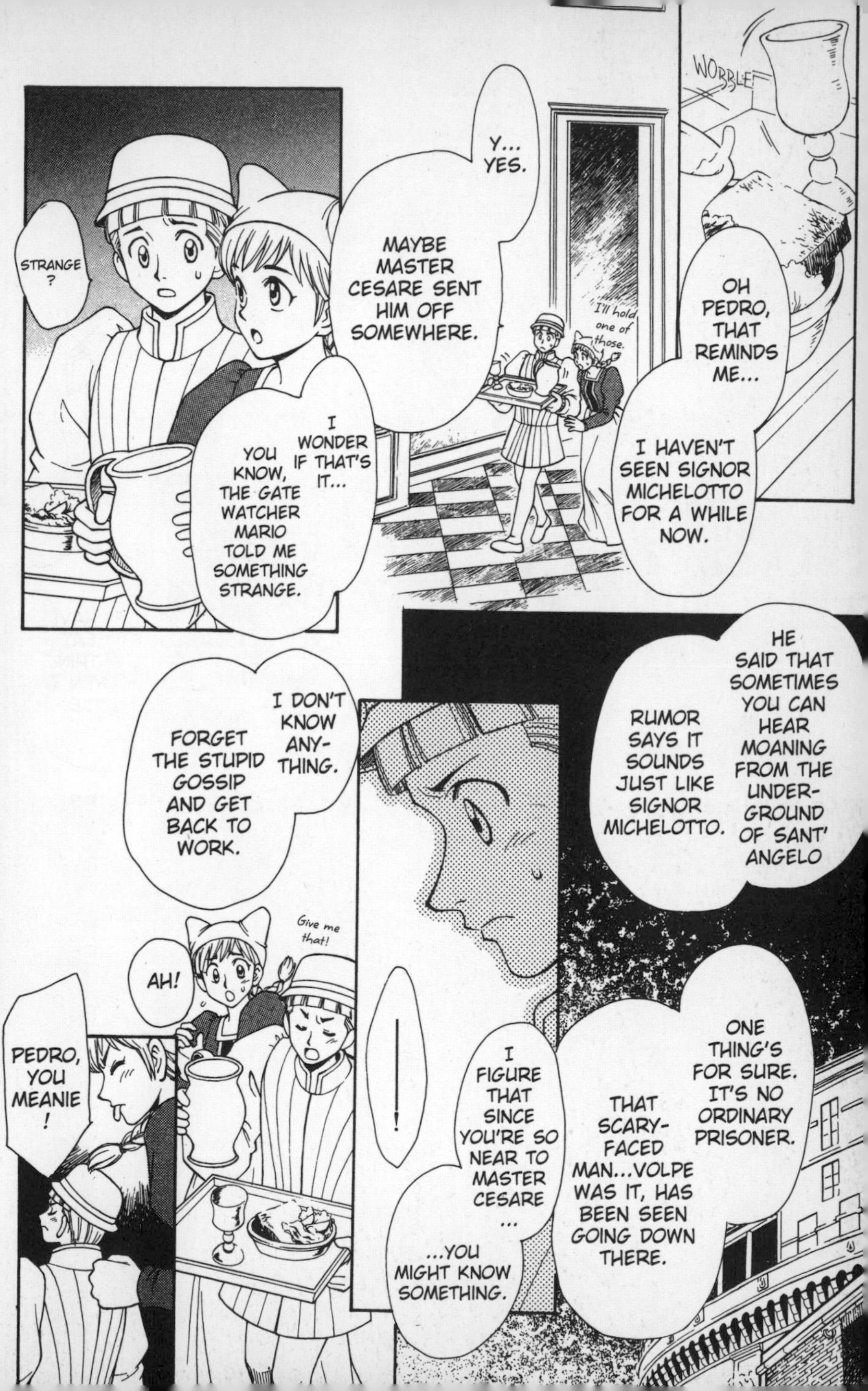
WOBBLE
OH PEDRO, THAT REMINDS ME...
I HAVEN'T SEEN SIGNOR MICHELOTTO FOR A WHILE NOW.
Y... YES.
MAYBE MASTER CESARE SENT HIM OFF SOMEWHERE.
I'll hold one of those.
I WONDER IF THAT'S IT...
YOU KNOW, THE GATE WATCHER MARIO TOLD ME SOMETHING STRANGE.
STRANGE?
HE SAID THAT SOMETIMES YOU CAN HEAR MOANING FROM THE UNDER-GROUND OF SANT' ANGELO
RUMOR SAYS IT SOUNDS JUST LIKE SIGNOR MICHELOTTO.
ONE THING'S FOR SURE. IT'S NO ORDINARY PRISONER.
THAT SCARY-FACED MAN...VOLPE WAS IT, HAS BEEN SEEN GOING DOWN THERE.
I FIGURE THAT SINCE YOU'RE SO NEAR TO MASTER CESARE ...
...YOU MIGHT KNOW SOMETHING.
!
I DON'T KNOW ANY-THING.
FORGET THE STUPID GOSSIP AND GET BACK TO WORK.
Give me that!
AH!
PEDRO, YOU MEANIE!

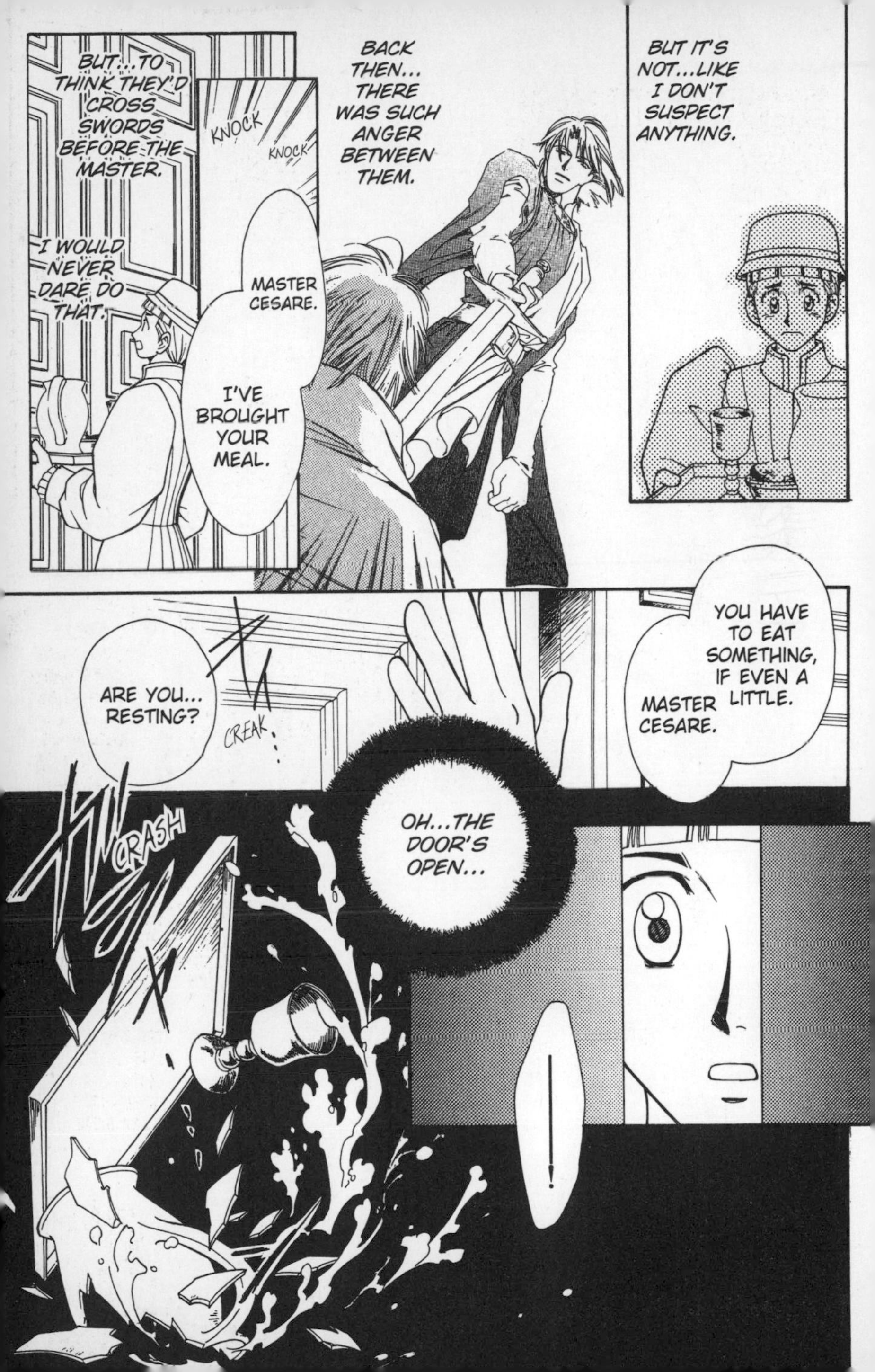
BUT IT'S NOT...LIKE I DON'T SUSPECT ANYTHING.
BACK THEN... THERE WAS SUCH ANGER BETWEEN THEM.
BUT...TO THINK THEY'D CROSS SWORDS BEFORE THE MASTER.
I WOULD NEVER DARE DO THAT.
KNOCK
KNOCK
MASTER CESARE.
I'VE BROUGHT YOUR MEAL.
YOU HAVE TO EAT SOMETHING, IF EVEN A LITTLE.
MASTER CESARE.
ARE YOU... RESTING?
CREAK
OH...THE DOOR'S OPEN...
!
CRASH

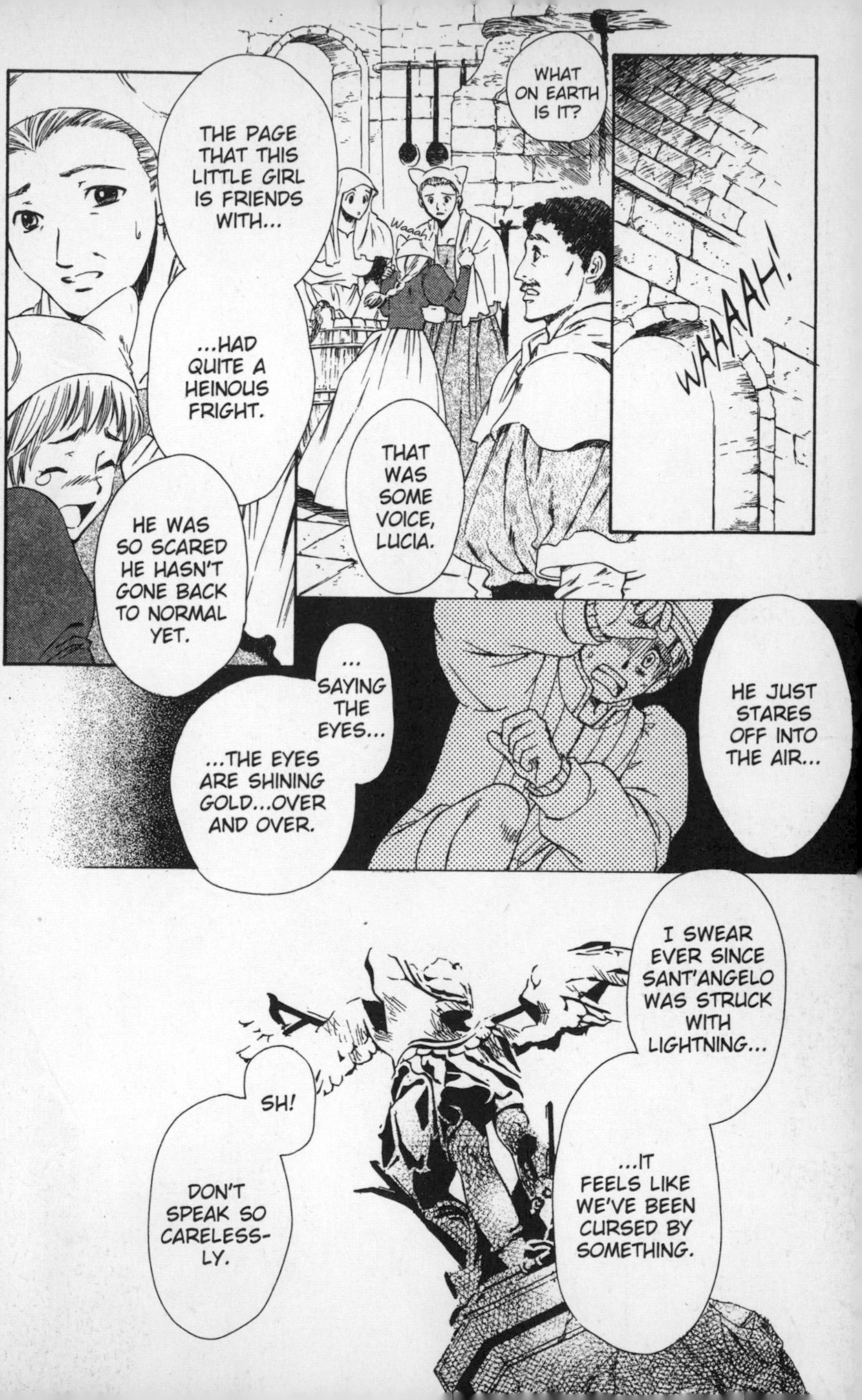
WAAAAH!
WHAT ON EARTH IS IT?
Waaah!
THAT WAS SOME VOICE, LUCIA.
THE PAGE THAT THIS LITTLE GIRL IS FRIENDS WITH...
...HAD QUITE A HEINOUS FRIGHT.
HE WAS SO SCARED HE HASN'T GONE BACK TO NORMAL YET.
HE JUST STARES OFF INTO THE AIR...
... SAYING THE EYES...
...THE EYES ARE SHINING GOLD...OVER AND OVER.
I SWEAR EVER SINCE SANT'ANGELO WAS STRUCK WITH LIGHTNING...
...IT FEELS LIKE WE'VE BEEN CURSED BY SOMETHING.
SH!
DON'T SPEAK SO CARELESS-LY.

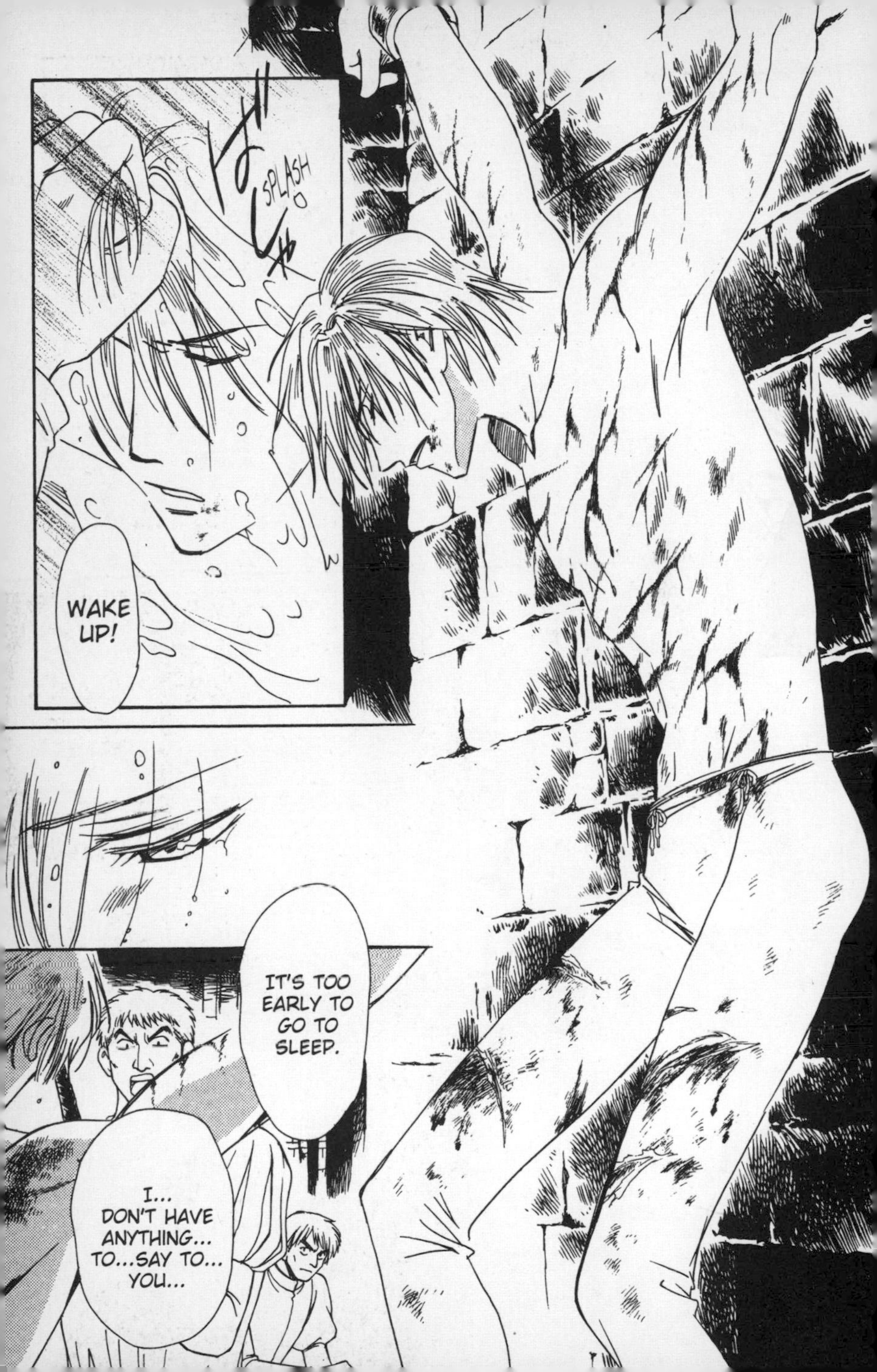
SPLASH
WAKE UP!
IT'S TOO EARLY TO GO TO SLEEP.
I... DON'T HAVE ANYTHING... TO...SAY TO... YOU...

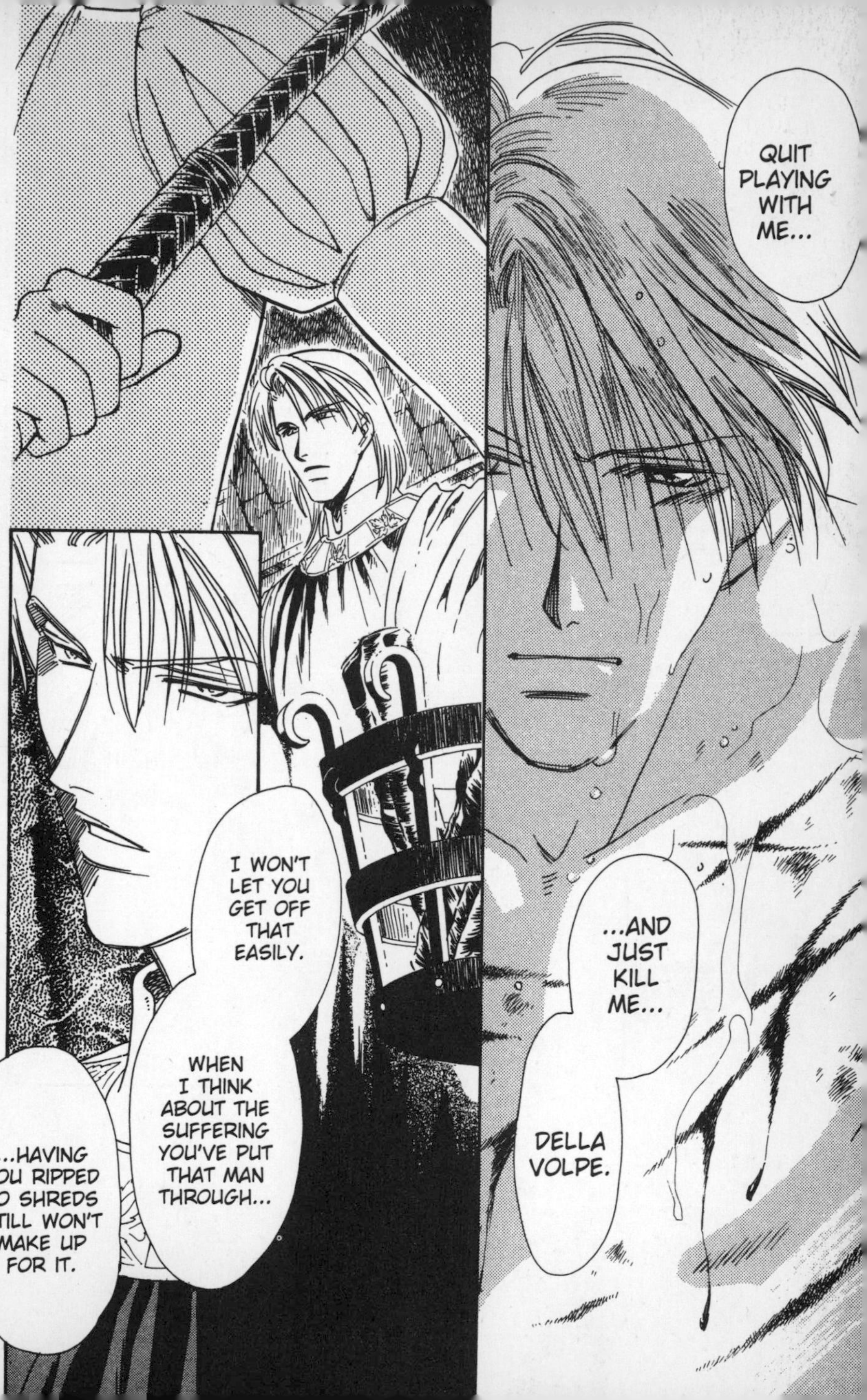
QUIT PLAYING WITH ME...
...AND JUST KILL ME...
DELLA VOLPE.
I WON'T LET YOU GET OFF THAT EASILY.
WHEN I THINK ABOUT THE SUFFERING YOU'VE PUT THAT MAN THROUGH...
...HAVING YOU RIPPED TO SHREDS STILL WON'T MAKE UP FOR IT.

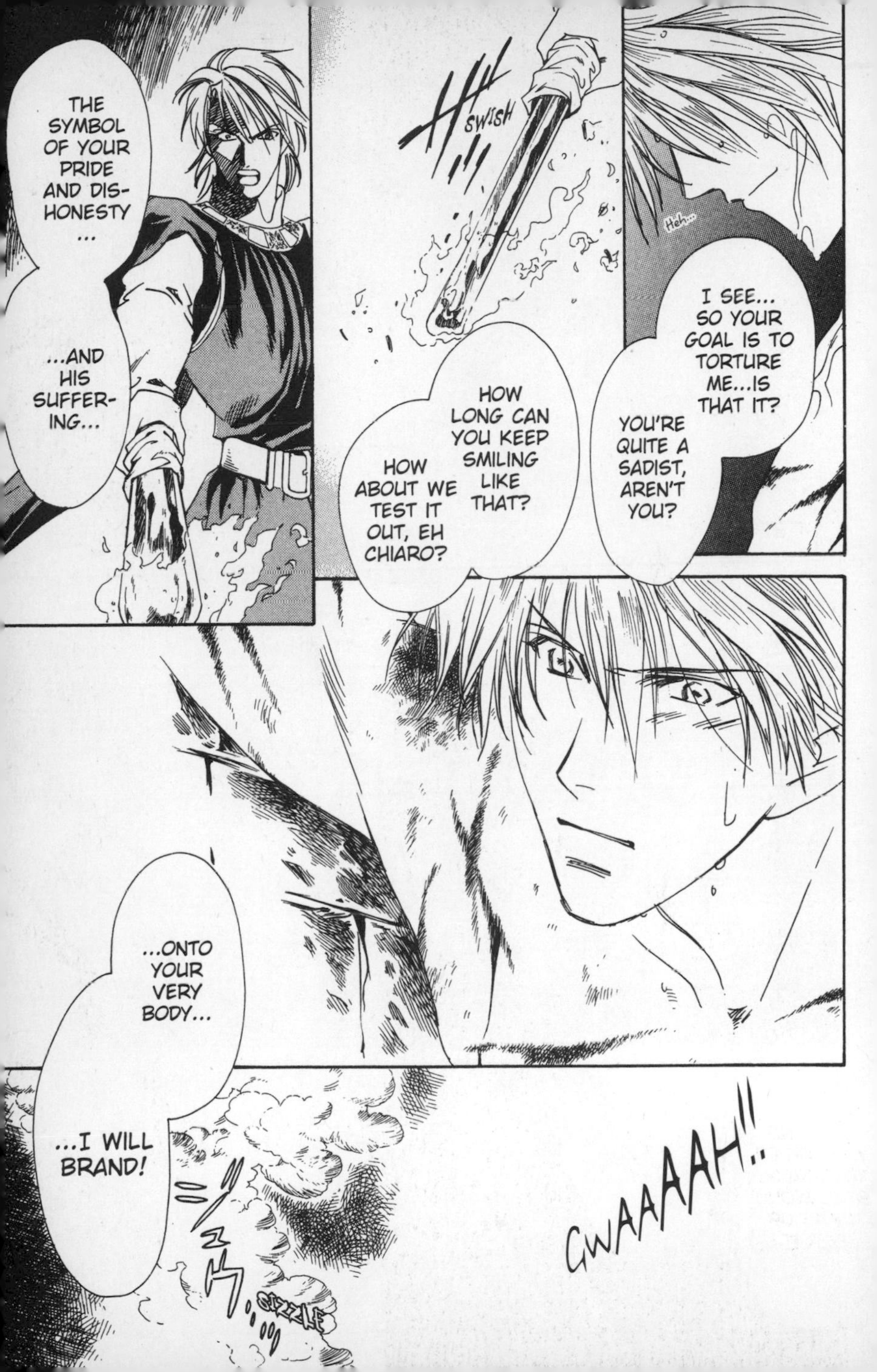
Heh...
I SEE... SO YOUR GOAL IS TO TORTURE ME...IS THAT IT?
YOU'RE QUITE A SADIST, AREN'T YOU?
SWISH
HOW LONG CAN YOU KEEP SMILING LIKE THAT?
HOW ABOUT WE TEST IT OUT, EH CHIARO?
THE SYMBOL OF YOUR PRIDE AND DIS-HONESTY ...
...AND HIS SUFFER-ING...
...ONTO YOUR VERY BODY...
...I WILL BRAND!
SIZZLE
GWAAAAH!!

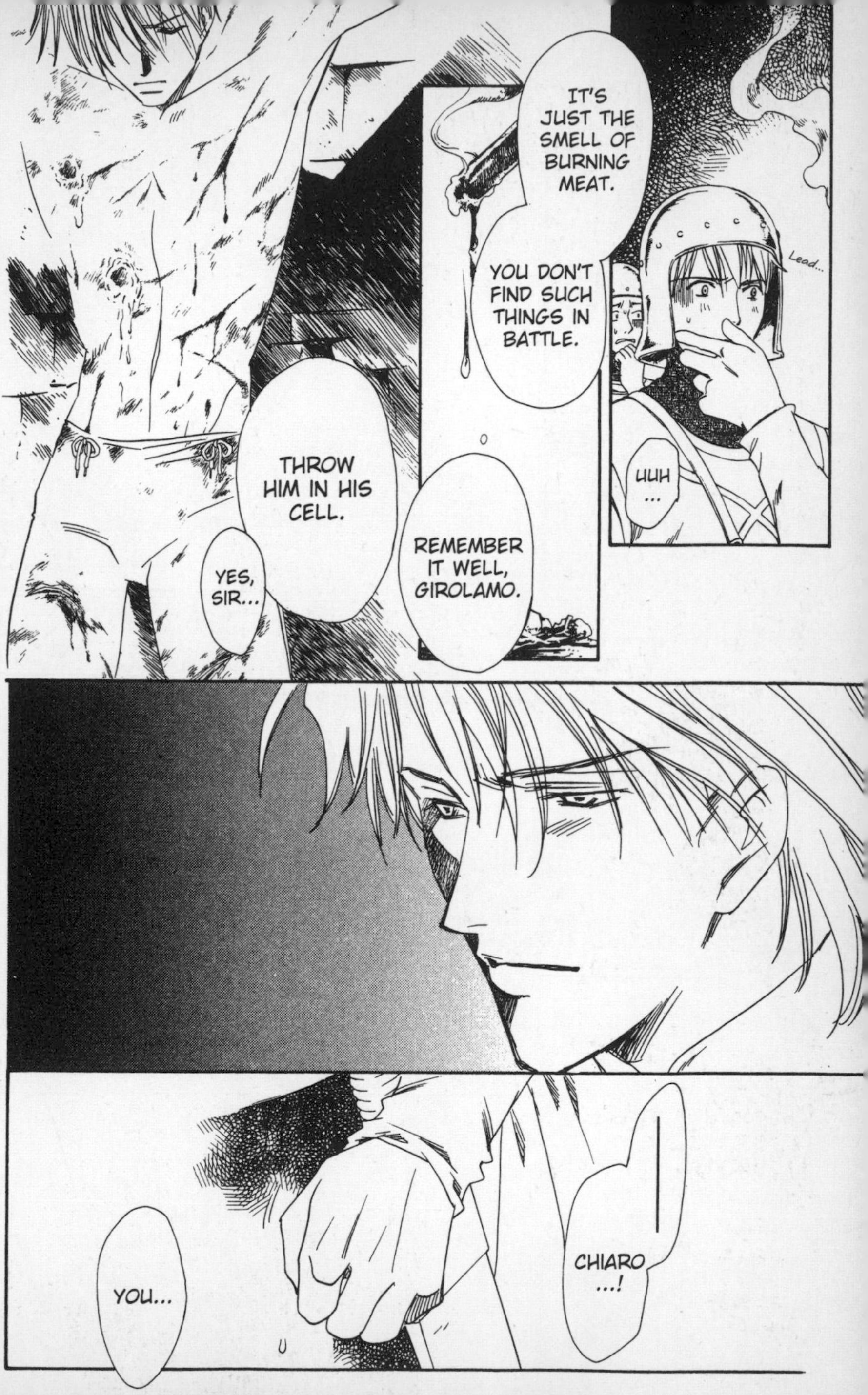
IT'S JUST THE SMELL OF BURNING MEAT.
YOU DON'T FIND SUCH THINGS IN BATTLE.
Lead...
UUH...
REMEMBER IT WELL, GIROLAMO.
THROW HIM IN HIS CELL.
YES, SIR...
CHIARO...!
YOU...

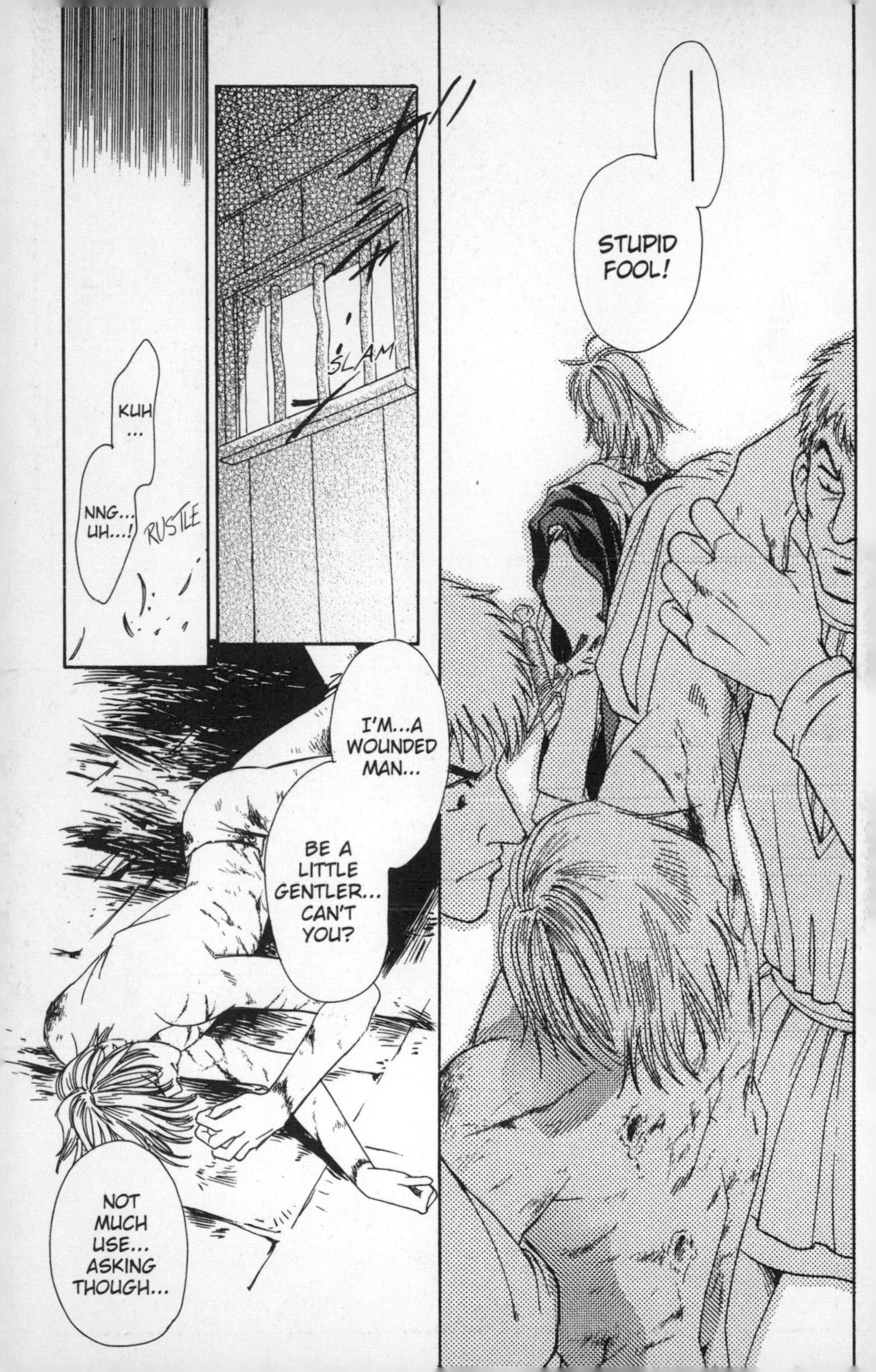
—
STUPID FOOL!
SLAM
KUH...
NNG... UH...!
RUSTLE
I'M...A WOUNDED MAN...
BE A LITTLE GENTLER... CAN'T YOU?
NOT MUCH USE... ASKING THOUGH...

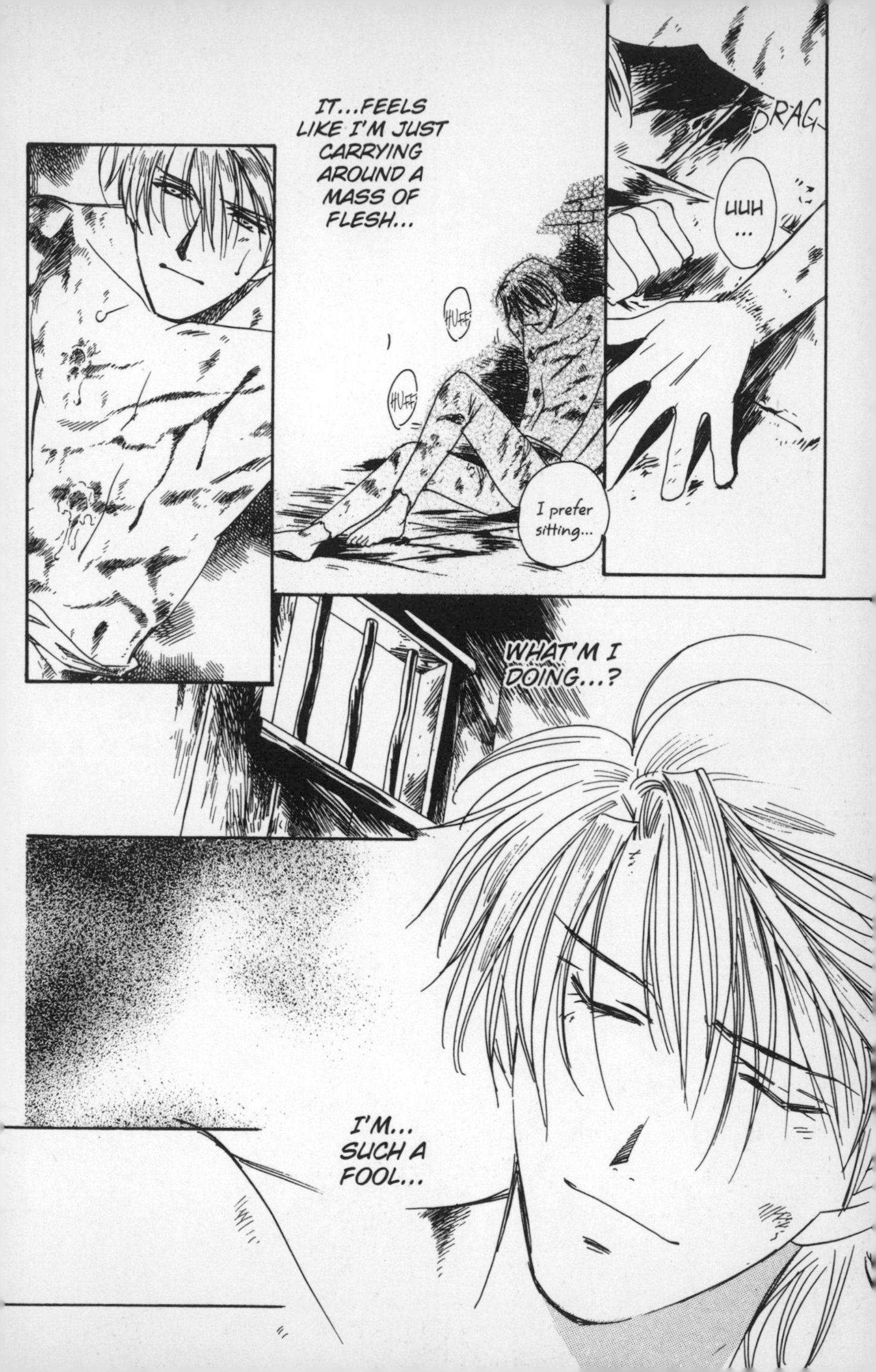
DRAG
UUH...
IT...FEELS LIKE I'M JUST CARRYING AROUND A MASS OF FLESH...
HUFF
HUFF
I prefer sitting...
WHAT'M I DOING...?
I'M... SUCH A FOOL...

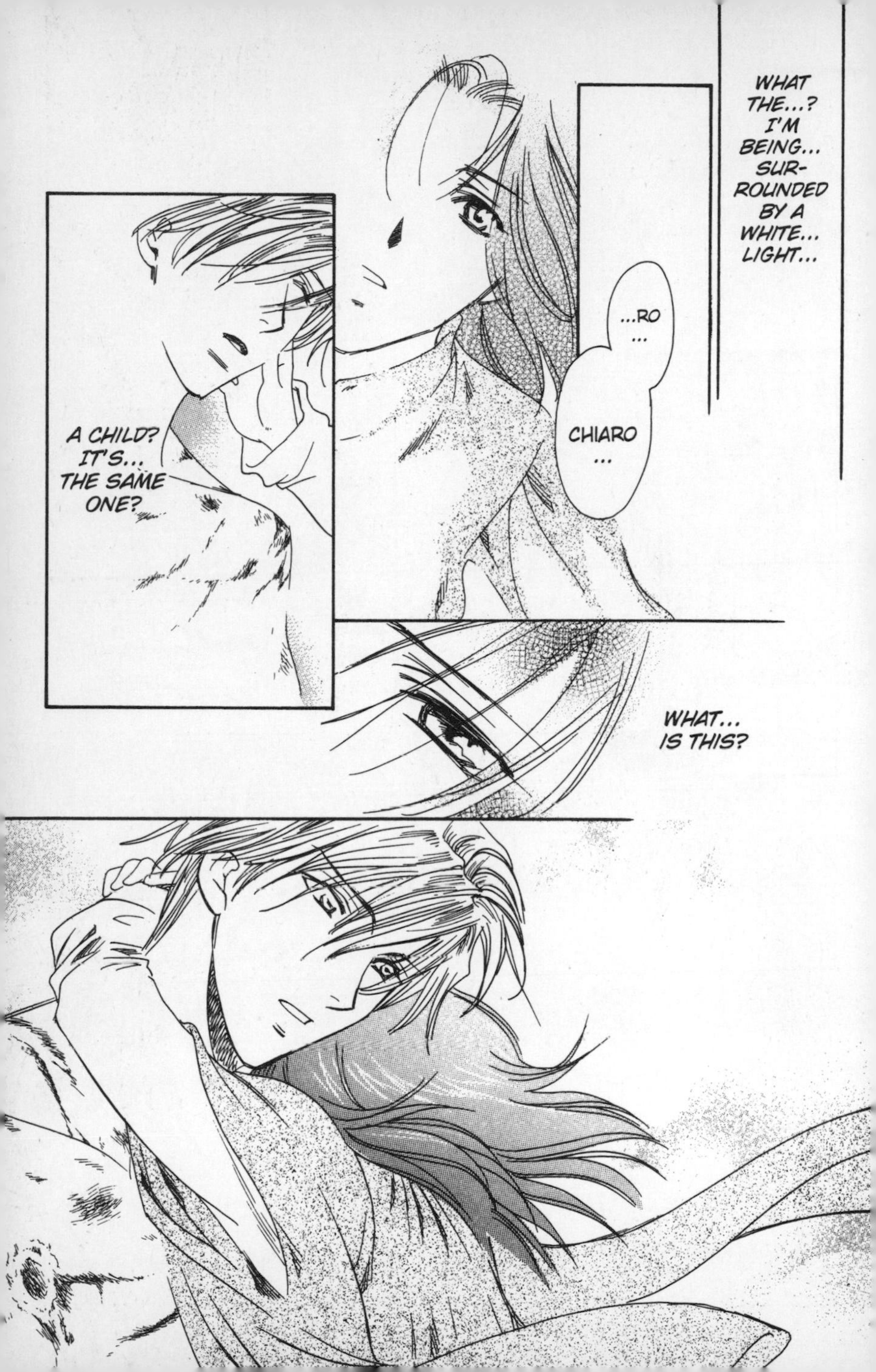
WHAT THE...? I'M BEING... SUR-ROUNDED BY A WHITE... LIGHT...
...RO ...
CHIARO ...
A CHILD? IT'S... THE SAME ONE?
WHAT... IS THIS?

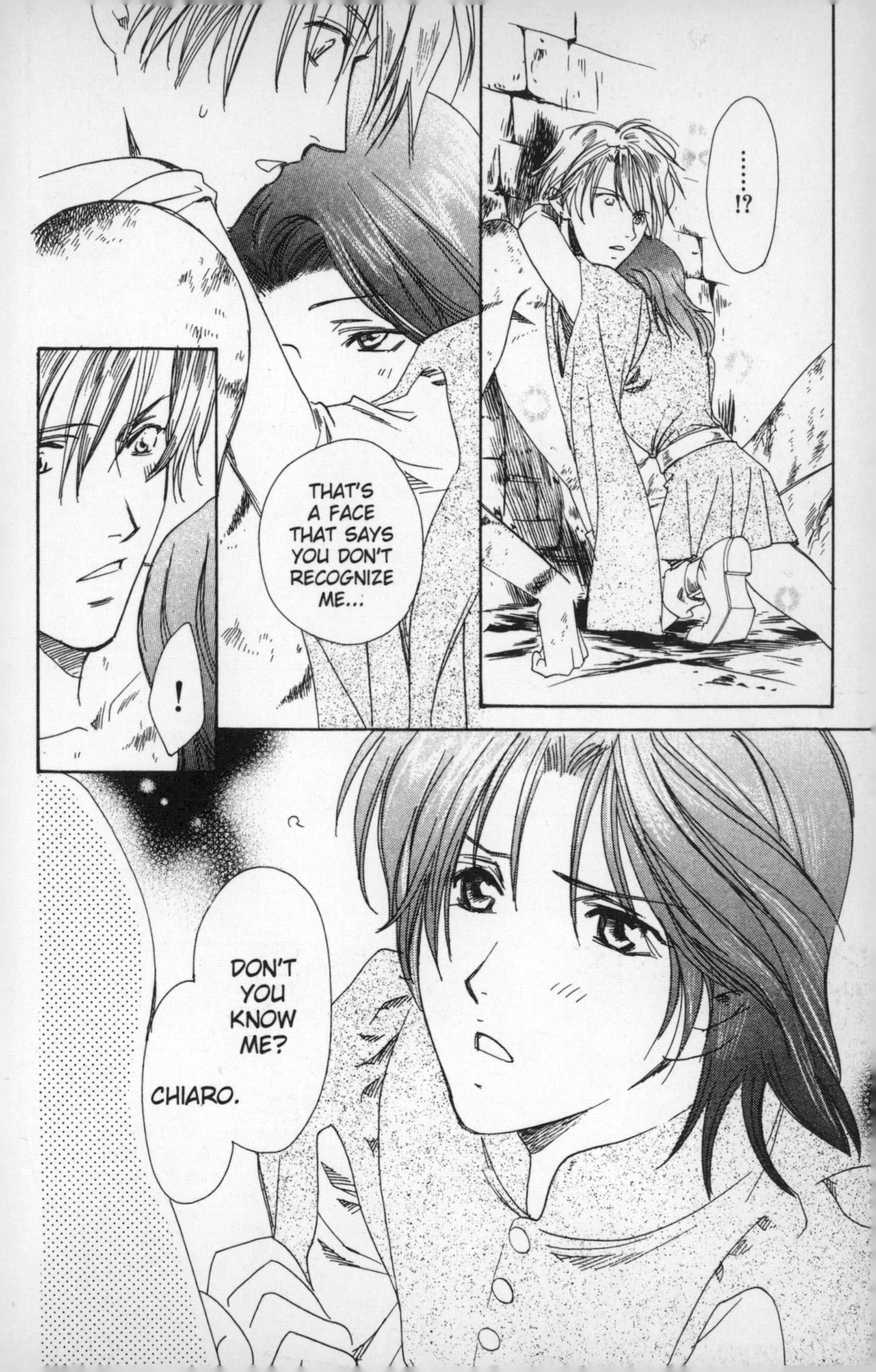
……!?
THAT'S A FACE THAT SAYS YOU DON'T RECOGNIZE ME…
!
DON'T YOU KNOW ME?
CHIARO.

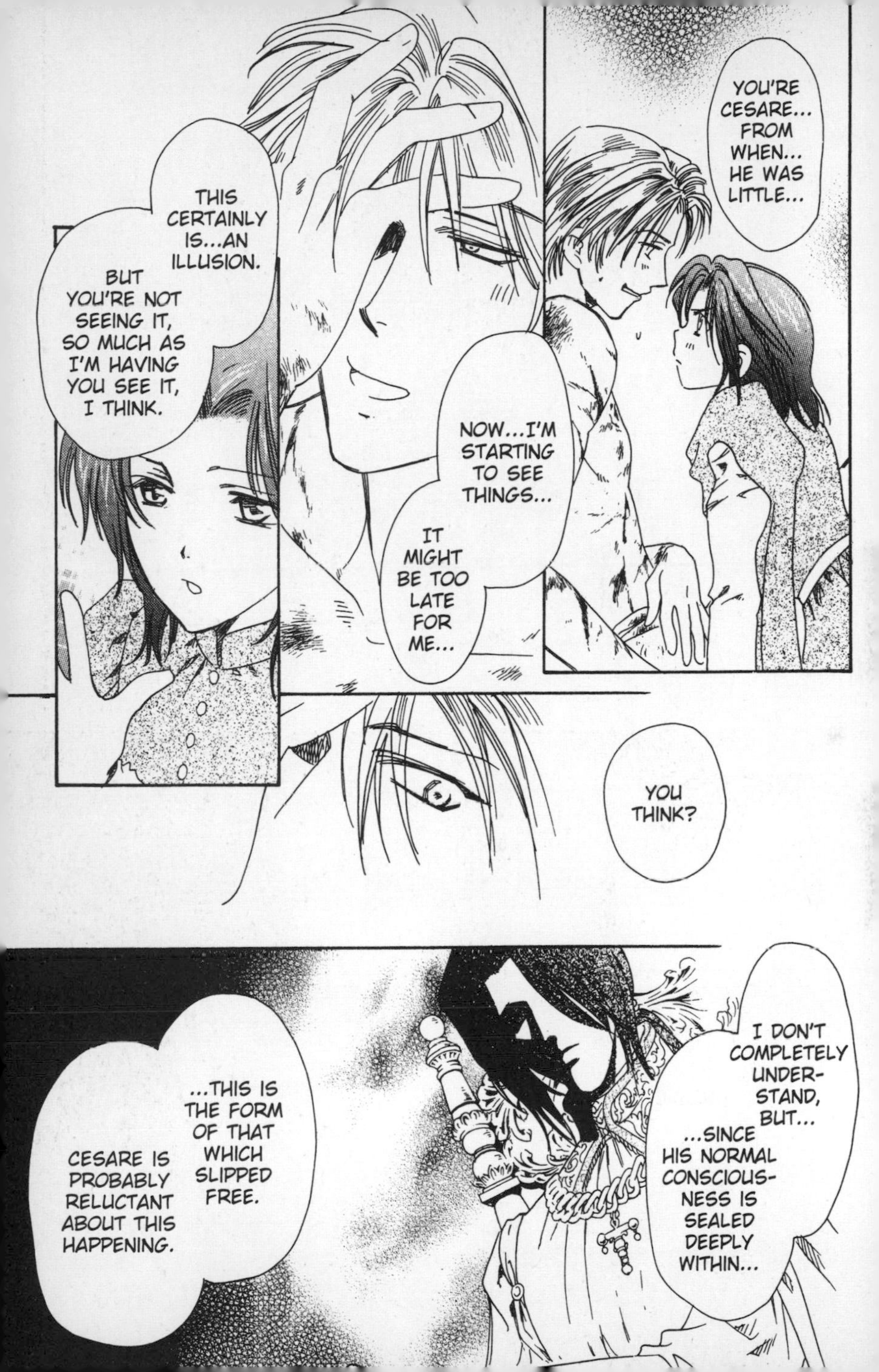
YOU'RE CESARE... FROM WHEN... HE WAS LITTLE...
NOW...I'M STARTING TO SEE THINGS...
IT MIGHT BE TOO LATE FOR ME...
THIS CERTAINLY IS...AN ILLUSION.
BUT YOU'RE NOT SEEING IT, SO MUCH AS I'M HAVING YOU SEE IT, I THINK.
YOU THINK?
I DON'T COMPLETELY UNDER-STAND, BUT...
...SINCE HIS NORMAL CONSCIOUS-NESS IS SEALED DEEPLY WITHIN...
...THIS IS THE FORM OF THAT WHICH SLIPPED FREE.
CESARE IS PROBABLY RELUCTANT ABOUT THIS HAPPENING.

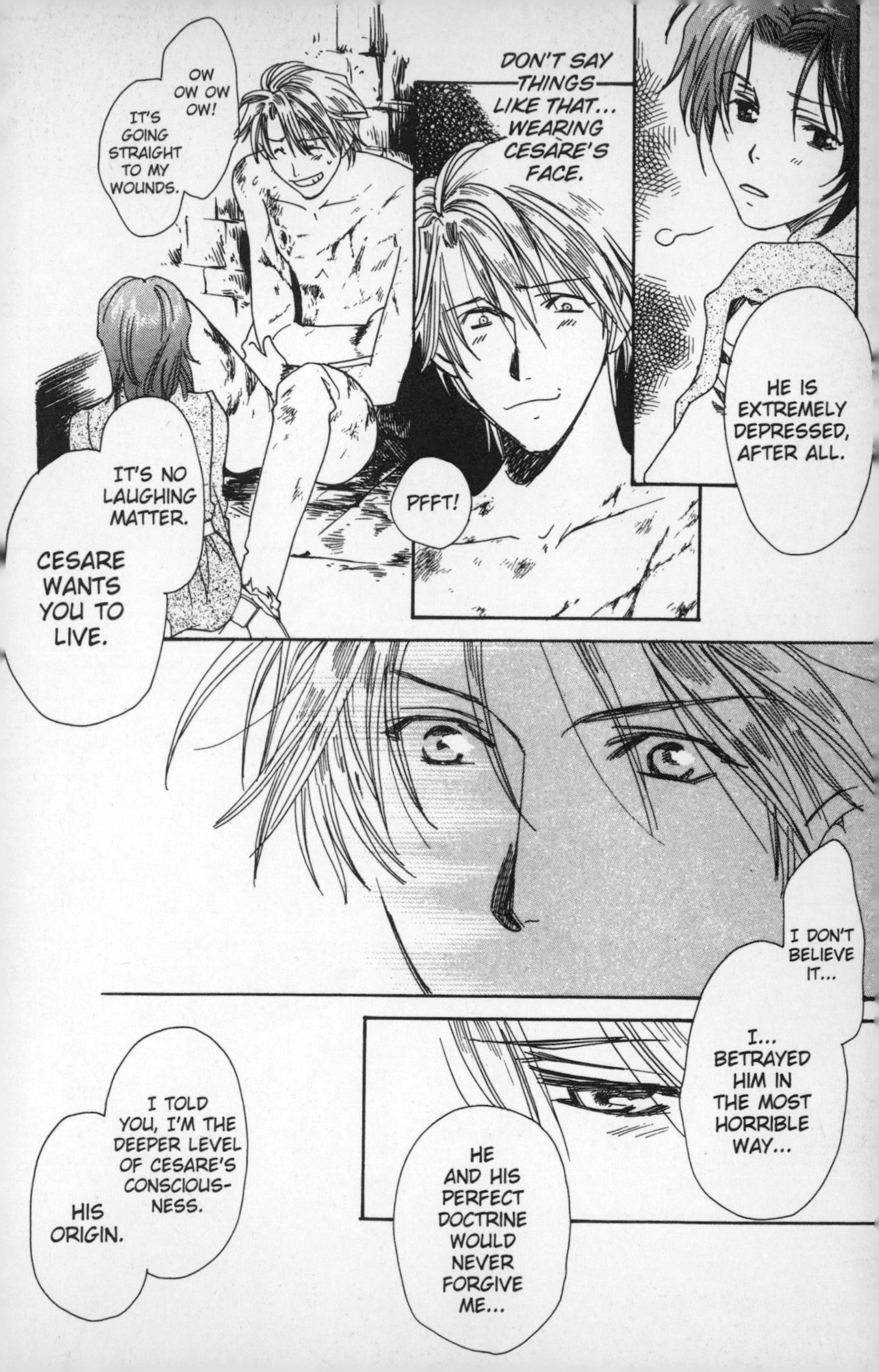
HE IS EXTREMELY DEPRESSED, AFTER ALL.
DON'T SAY THINGS LIKE THAT... WEARING CESARE'S FACE.
PFFT!
OW OW OW OW!
IT'S GOING STRAIGHT TO MY WOUNDS.
IT'S NO LAUGHING MATTER.
CESARE WANTS YOU TO LIVE.
I DON'T BELIEVE IT...
I... BETRAYED HIM IN THE MOST HORRIBLE WAY...
HE AND HIS PERFECT DOCTRINE WOULD NEVER FORGIVE ME...
I TOLD YOU, I'M THE DEEPER LEVEL OF CESARE'S CONSCIOUS-NESS.
HIS ORIGIN.

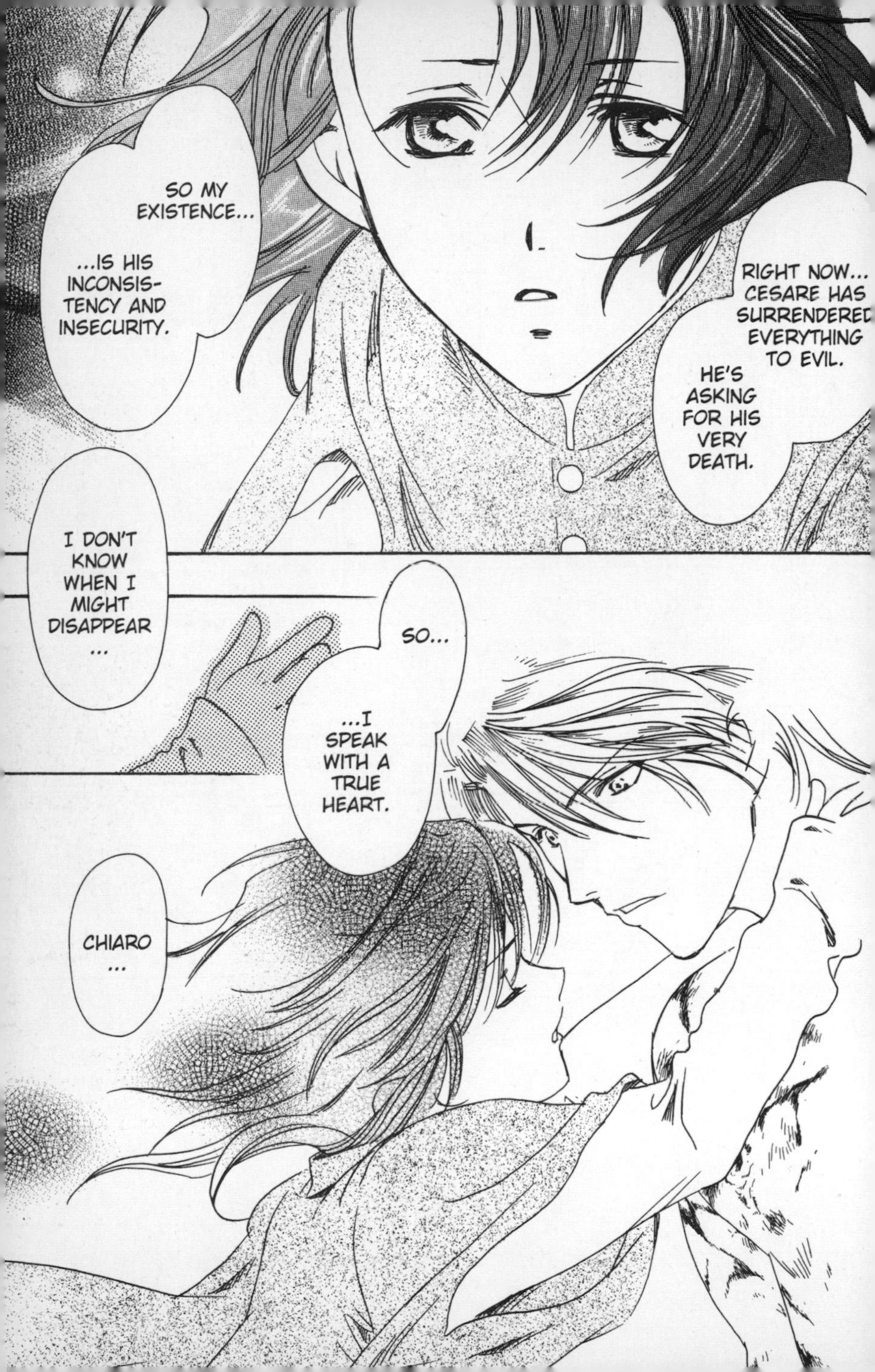
RIGHT NOW... CESARE HAS SURRENDERED EVERYTHING TO EVIL.
HE'S ASKING FOR HIS VERY DEATH.
SO MY EXISTENCE...
...IS HIS INCONSISTENCY AND INSECURITY.
I DON'T KNOW WHEN I MIGHT DISAPPEAR...
SO...
...I SPEAK WITH A TRUE HEART.
CHIARO...

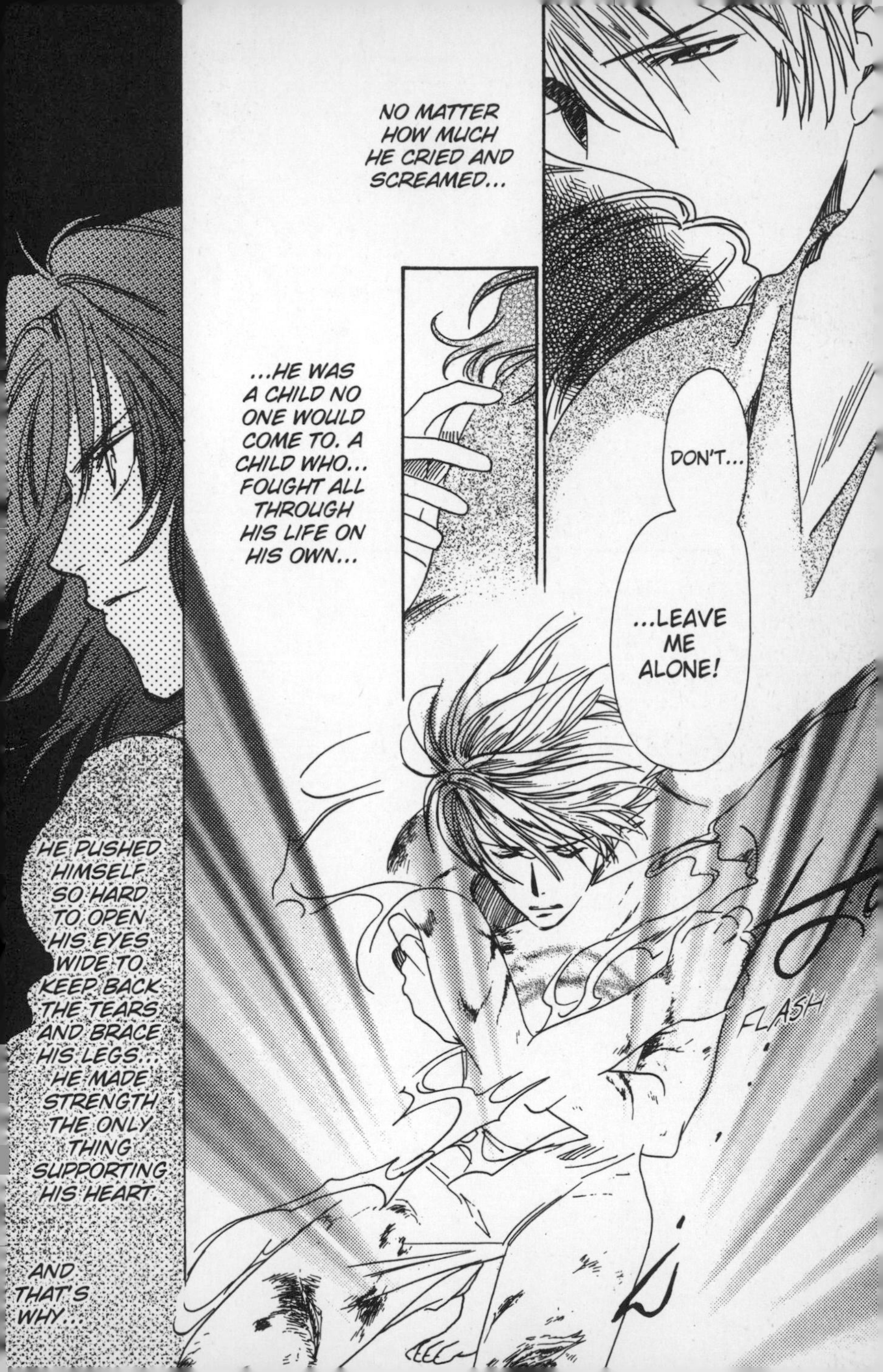
NO MATTER HOW MUCH HE CRIED AND SCREAMED...
...HE WAS A CHILD NO ONE WOULD COME TO. A CHILD WHO... FOUGHT ALL THROUGH HIS LIFE ON HIS OWN...
DON'T... ...LEAVE ME ALONE!
FLASH
HE PUSHED HIMSELF SO HARD TO OPEN HIS EYES WIDE TO KEEP BACK THE TEARS AND BRACE HIS LEGS. HE MADE STRENGTH THE ONLY THING SUPPORTING HIS HEART.
AND THAT'S WHY...

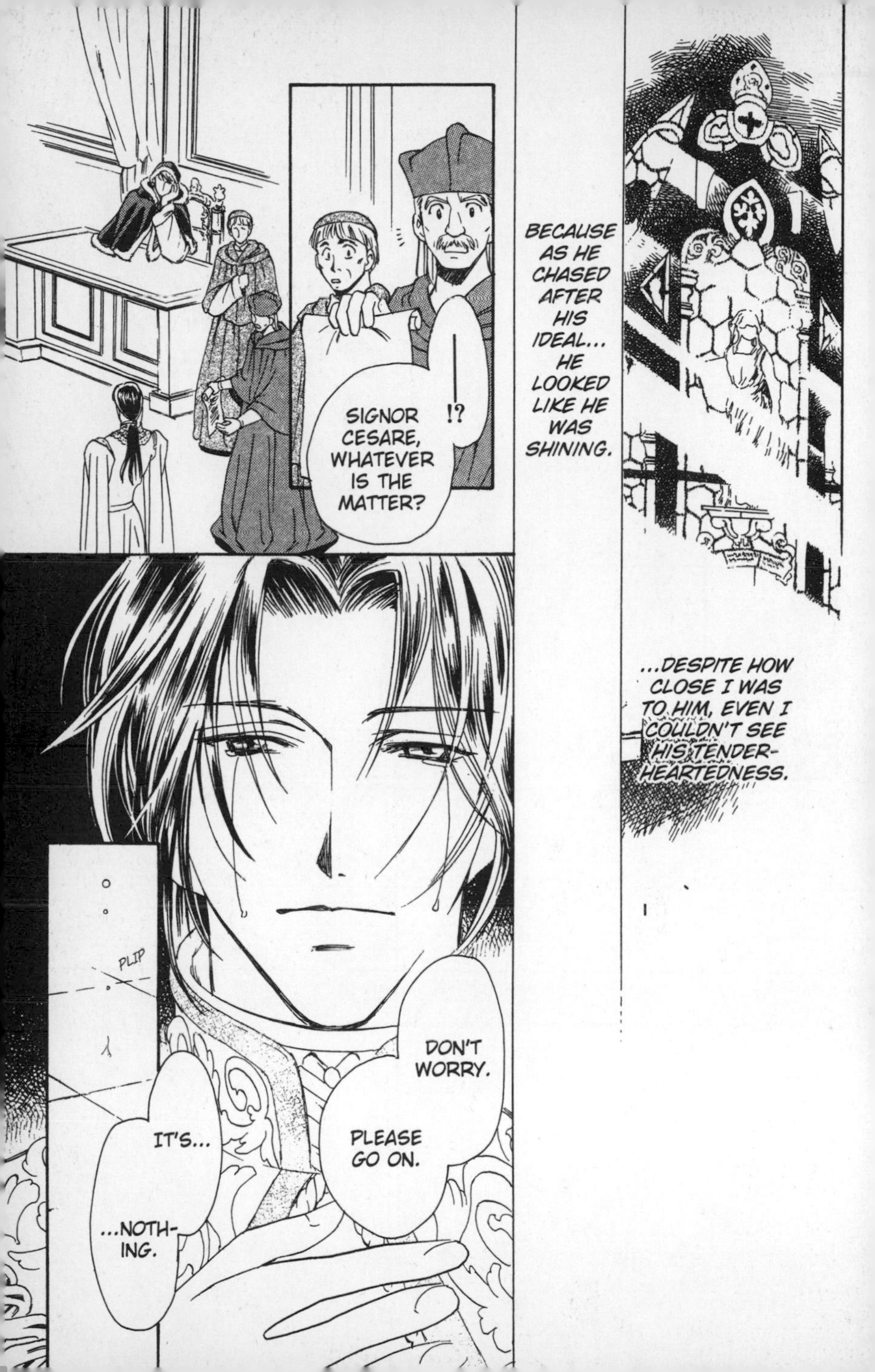
BECAUSE AS HE CHASED AFTER HIS IDEAL... HE LOOKED LIKE HE WAS SHINING.
...DESPITE HOW CLOSE I WAS TO HIM, EVEN I COULDN'T SEE HIS TENDER-HEARTEDNESS.
!?
SIGNOR CESARE, WHATEVER IS THE MATTER?
DON'T WORRY.
PLEASE GO ON.
IT'S...
...NOTH-ING.
PLIP

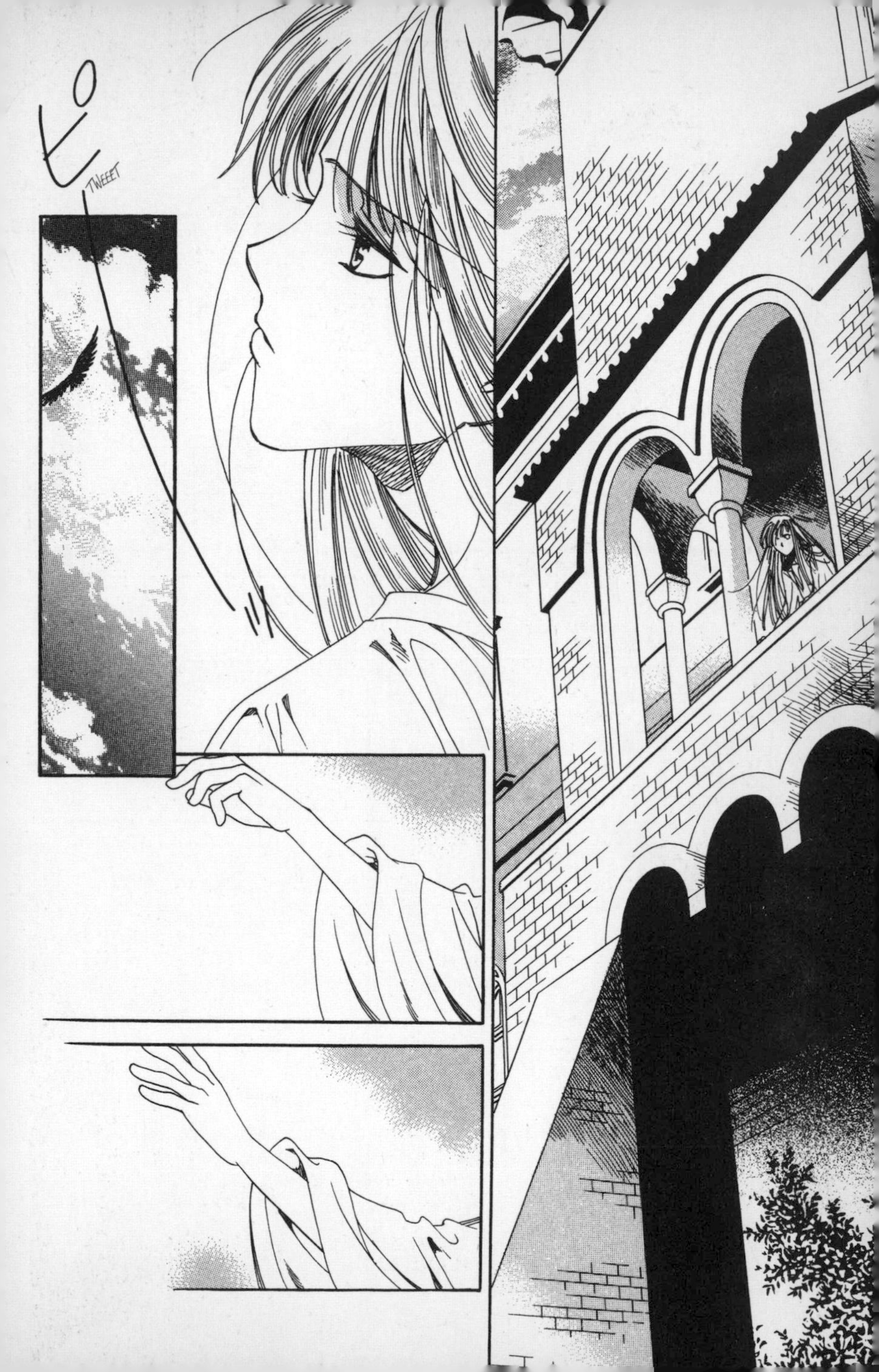
ピー
TWEEET

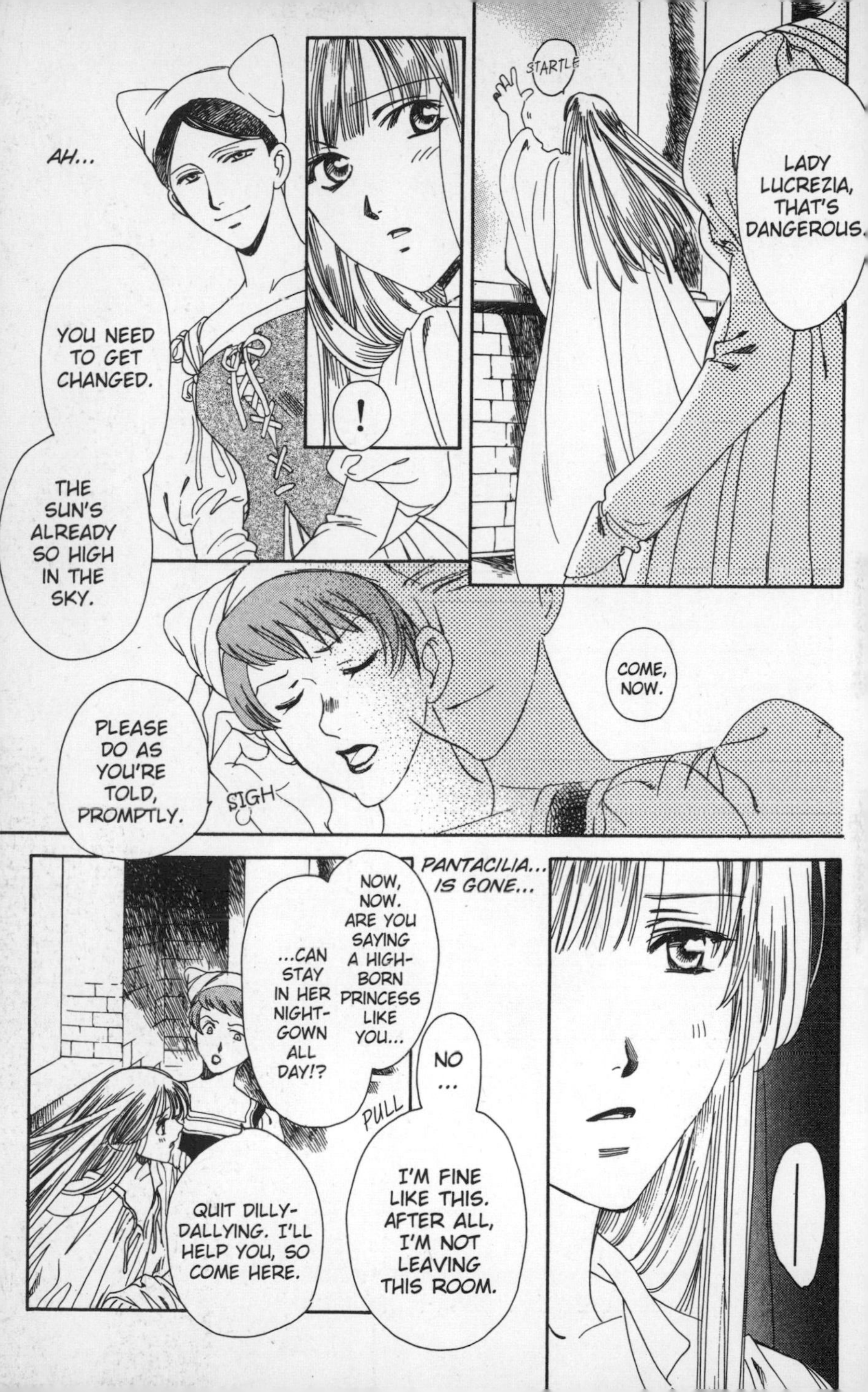
LADY LUCREZIA, THAT'S DANGEROUS.
STARTLE
!
AH...
YOU NEED TO GET CHANGED.
THE SUN'S ALREADY SO HIGH IN THE SKY.
COME, NOW.
PLEASE DO AS YOU'RE TOLD, PROMPTLY.
SIGH
PANTACILIA... IS GONE...
NOW, NOW. ARE YOU SAYING A HIGH-BORN PRINCESS LIKE YOU...
...CAN STAY IN HER NIGHTGOWN ALL DAY!?
NO...
I'M FINE LIKE THIS. AFTER ALL, I'M NOT LEAVING THIS ROOM.
PULL
QUIT DILLY-DALLYING. I'LL HELP YOU, SO COME HERE.

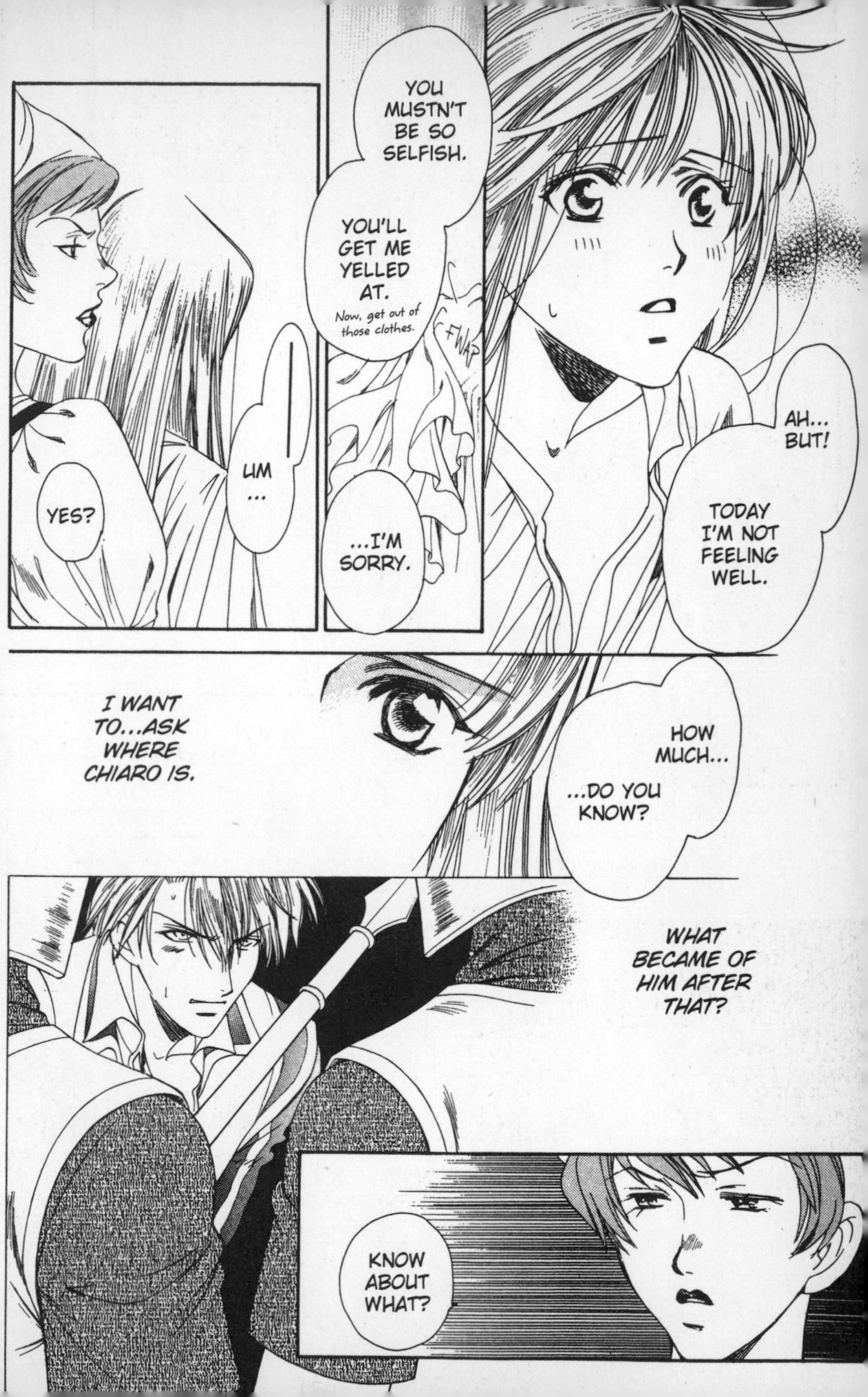
AH... BUT!
TODAY I'M NOT FEELING WELL.
YOU MUSTN'T BE SO SELFISH.
YOU'LL GET ME YELLED AT.
Now, get out of those clothes.
FWAP
...I'M SORRY.
UM ...
YES?
HOW MUCH...
...DO YOU KNOW?
I WANT TO...ASK WHERE CHIARO IS.
WHAT BECAME OF HIM AFTER THAT?
KNOW ABOUT WHAT?

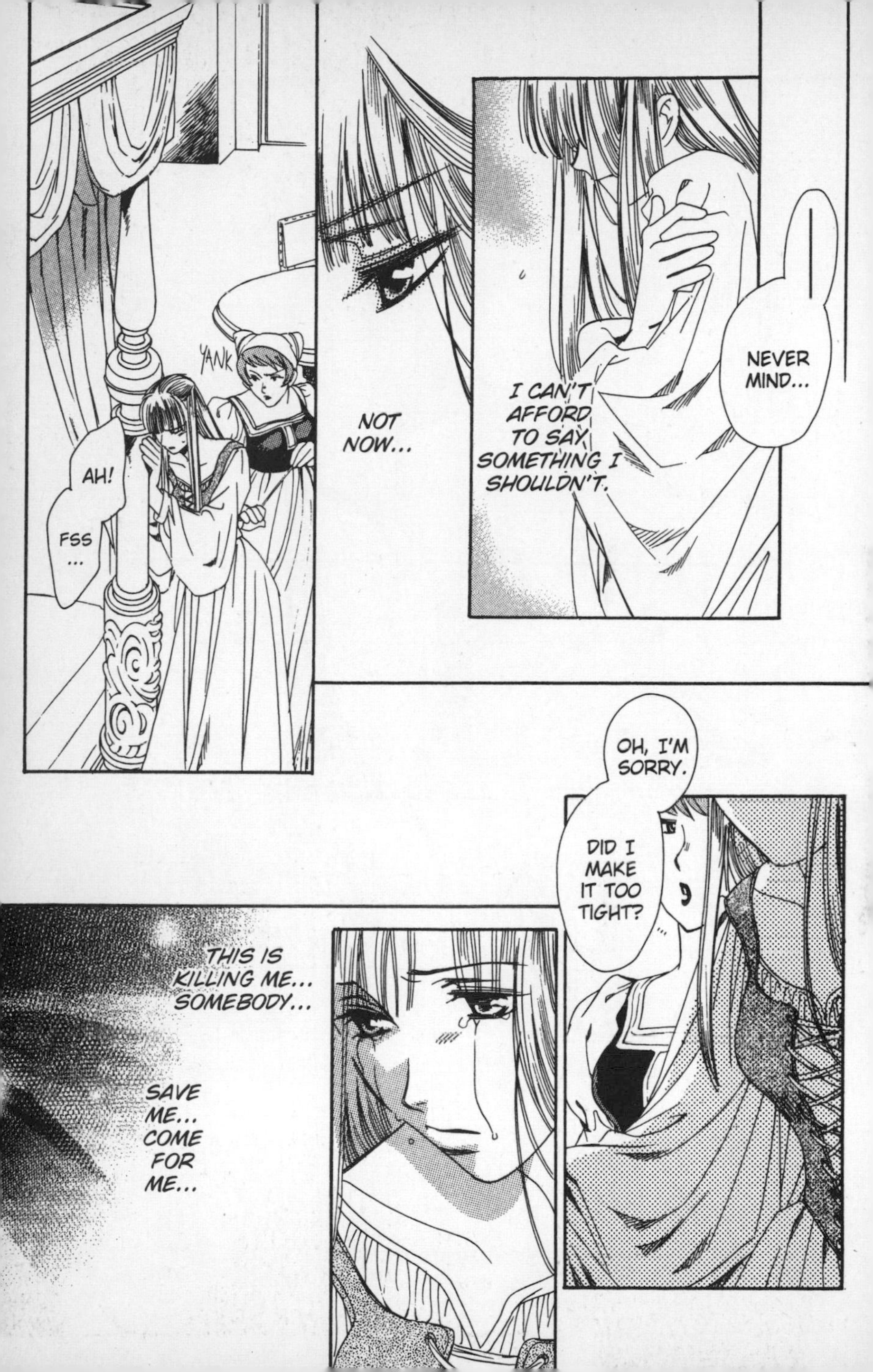
NEVER MIND...
I CAN'T AFFORD TO SAY SOMETHING I SHOULDN'T.
NOT NOW...
YANK
AH!
FSS...
OH, I'M SORRY.
DID I MAKE IT TOO TIGHT?
THIS IS KILLING ME... SOMEBODY...
SAVE ME... COME FOR ME...

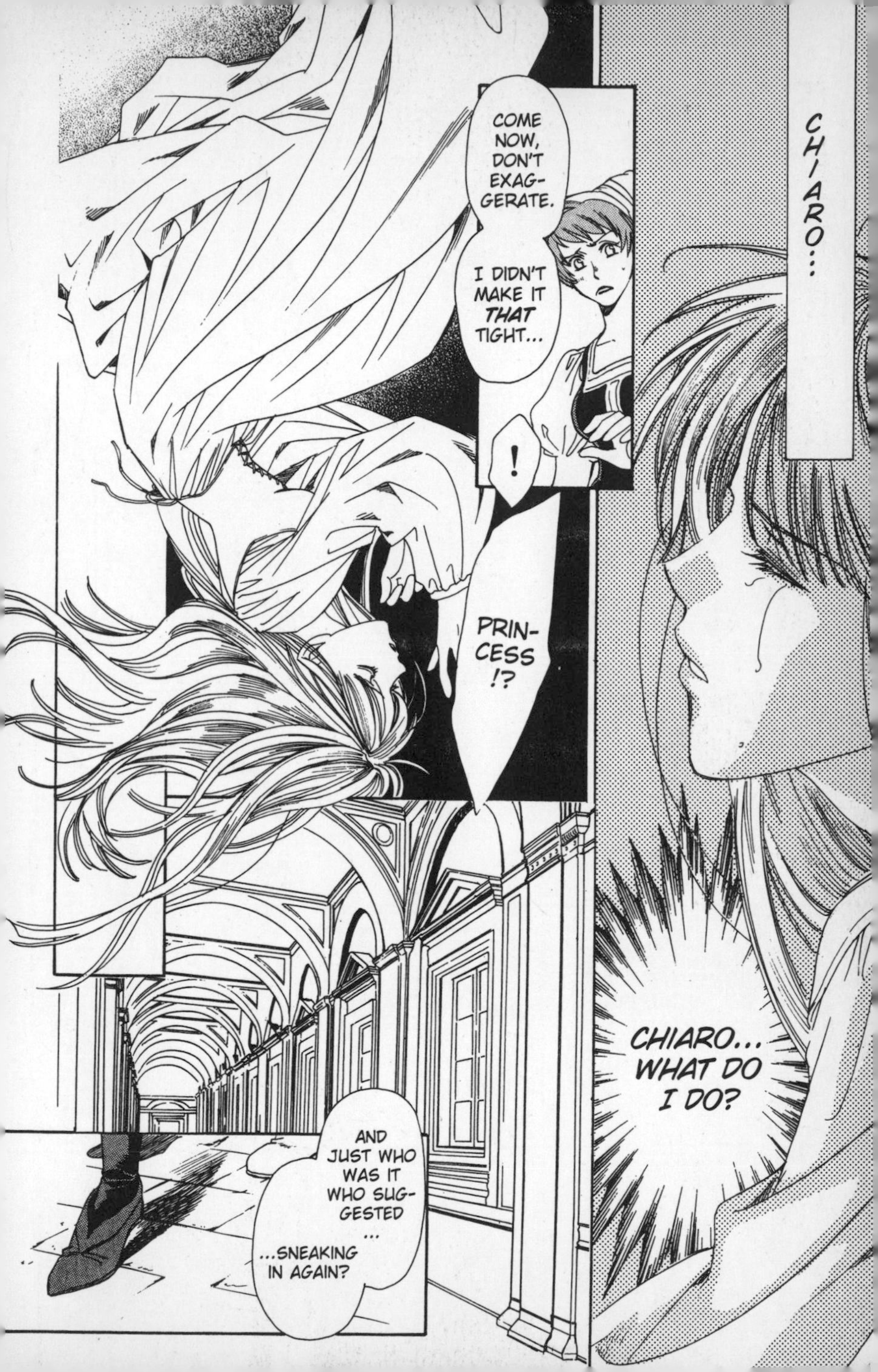

CHIARO...
CHIARO... WHAT DO I DO?
COME NOW, DON'T EXAGGERATE.
I DIDN'T MAKE IT *THAT* TIGHT...
!
PRINCESS!?
AND JUST WHO WAS IT WHO SUGGESTED...
...SNEAKING IN AGAIN?

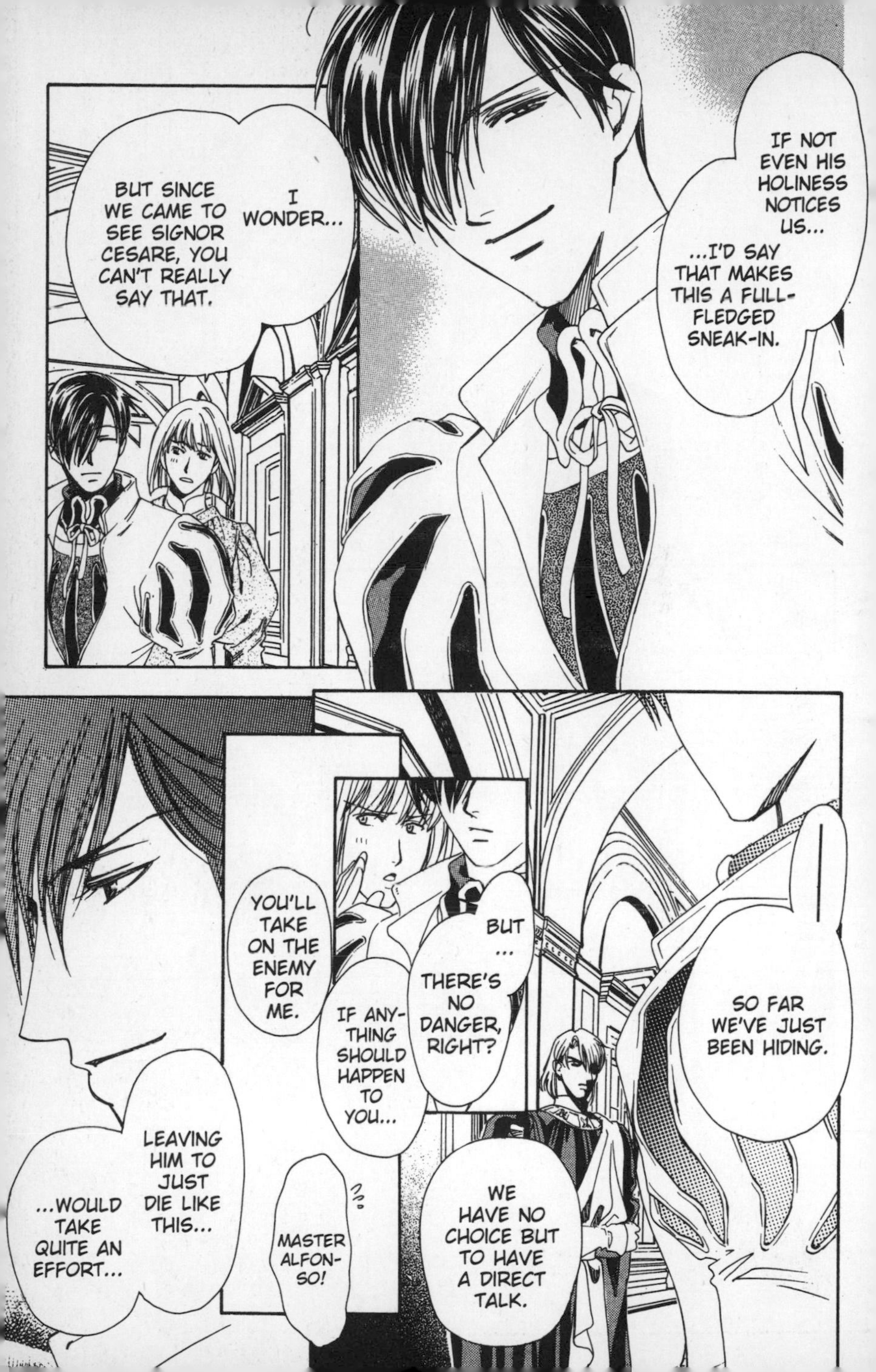
IF NOT EVEN HIS HOLINESS NOTICES US...
...I'D SAY THAT MAKES THIS A FULL-FLEDGED SNEAK-IN.
I WONDER...
BUT SINCE WE CAME TO SEE SIGNOR CESARE, YOU CAN'T REALLY SAY THAT.
SO FAR WE'VE JUST BEEN HIDING.
WE HAVE NO CHOICE BUT TO HAVE A DIRECT TALK.
BUT...
THERE'S NO DANGER, RIGHT?
YOU'LL TAKE ON THE ENEMY FOR ME.
IF ANY-THING SHOULD HAPPEN TO YOU...
MASTER ALFON-SO!
LEAVING HIM TO JUST DIE LIKE THIS...
...WOULD TAKE QUITE AN EFFORT...

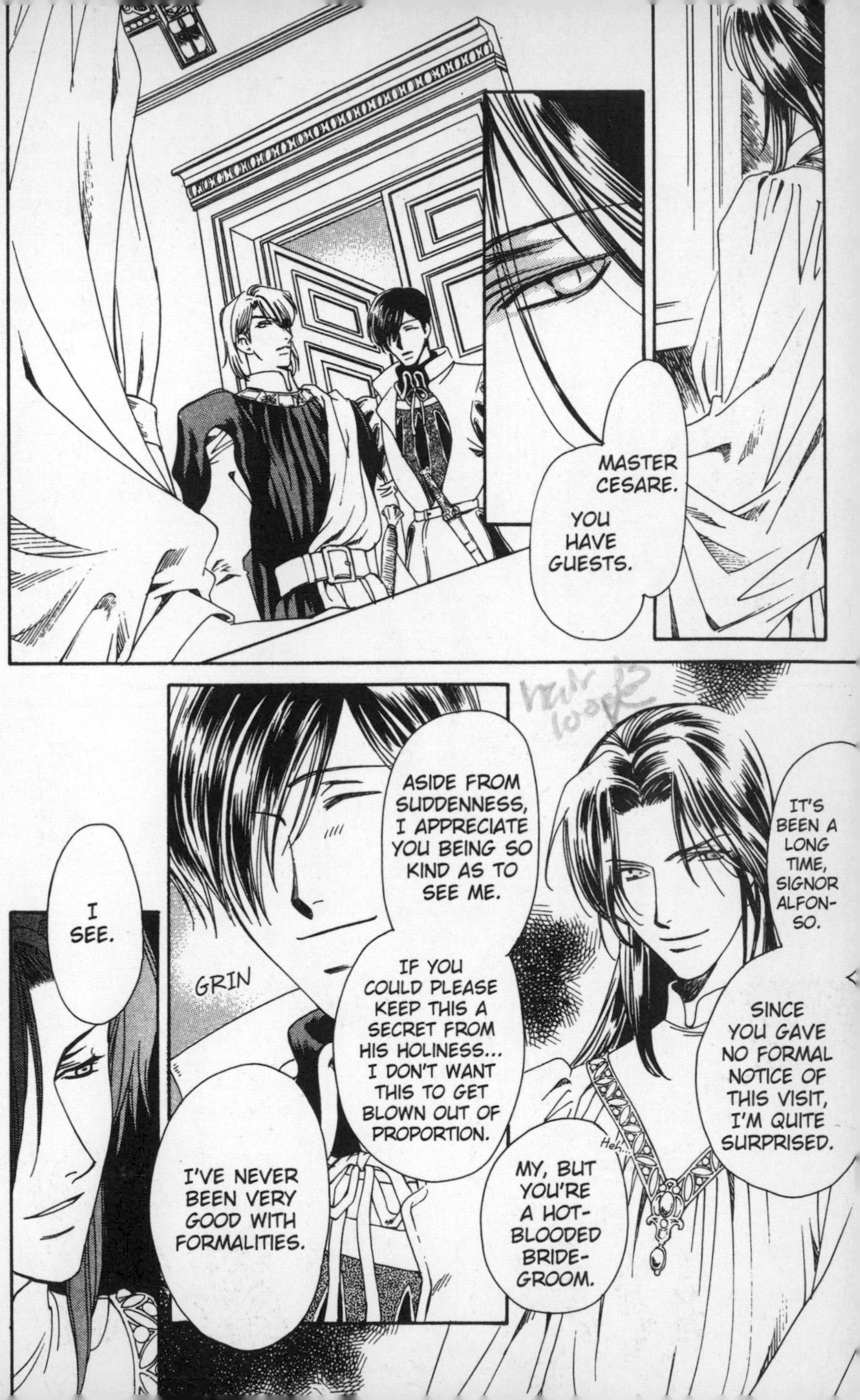
MASTER CESARE.
YOU HAVE GUESTS.
IT'S BEEN A LONG TIME, SIGNOR ALFONSO.
SINCE YOU GAVE NO FORMAL NOTICE OF THIS VISIT, I'M QUITE SURPRISED.
I'VE NEVER BEEN VERY GOOD WITH FORMALITIES.
Heh...
MY, BUT YOU'RE A HOT-BLOODED BRIDEGROOM.
ASIDE FROM SUDDENNESS, I APPRECIATE YOU BEING SO KIND AS TO SEE ME.
IF YOU COULD PLEASE KEEP THIS A SECRET FROM HIS HOLINESS... I DON'T WANT THIS TO GET BLOWN OUT OF PROPORTION.
GRIN
I SEE.

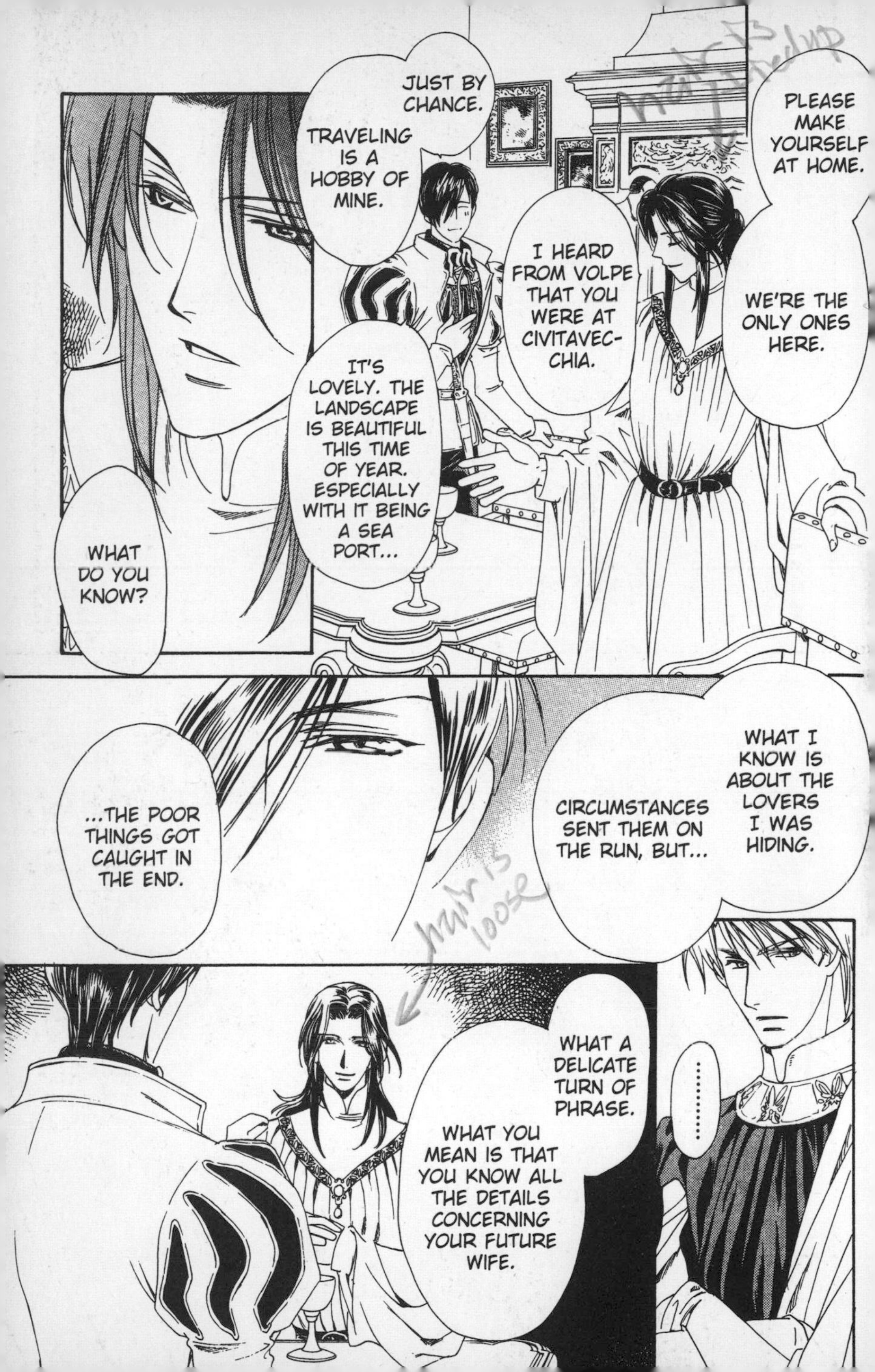
PLEASE MAKE YOURSELF AT HOME.
WE'RE THE ONLY ONES HERE.
I HEARD FROM VOLPE THAT YOU WERE AT CIVITAVECCHIA.
JUST BY CHANCE.
TRAVELING IS A HOBBY OF MINE.
IT'S LOVELY. THE LANDSCAPE IS BEAUTIFUL THIS TIME OF YEAR. ESPECIALLY WITH IT BEING A SEA PORT...
WHAT DO YOU KNOW?
WHAT I KNOW IS ABOUT THE LOVERS I WAS HIDING.
CIRCUMSTANCES SENT THEM ON THE RUN, BUT...
...THE POOR THINGS GOT CAUGHT IN THE END.
......
WHAT A DELICATE TURN OF PHRASE.
WHAT YOU MEAN IS THAT YOU KNOW ALL THE DETAILS CONCERNING YOUR FUTURE WIFE.

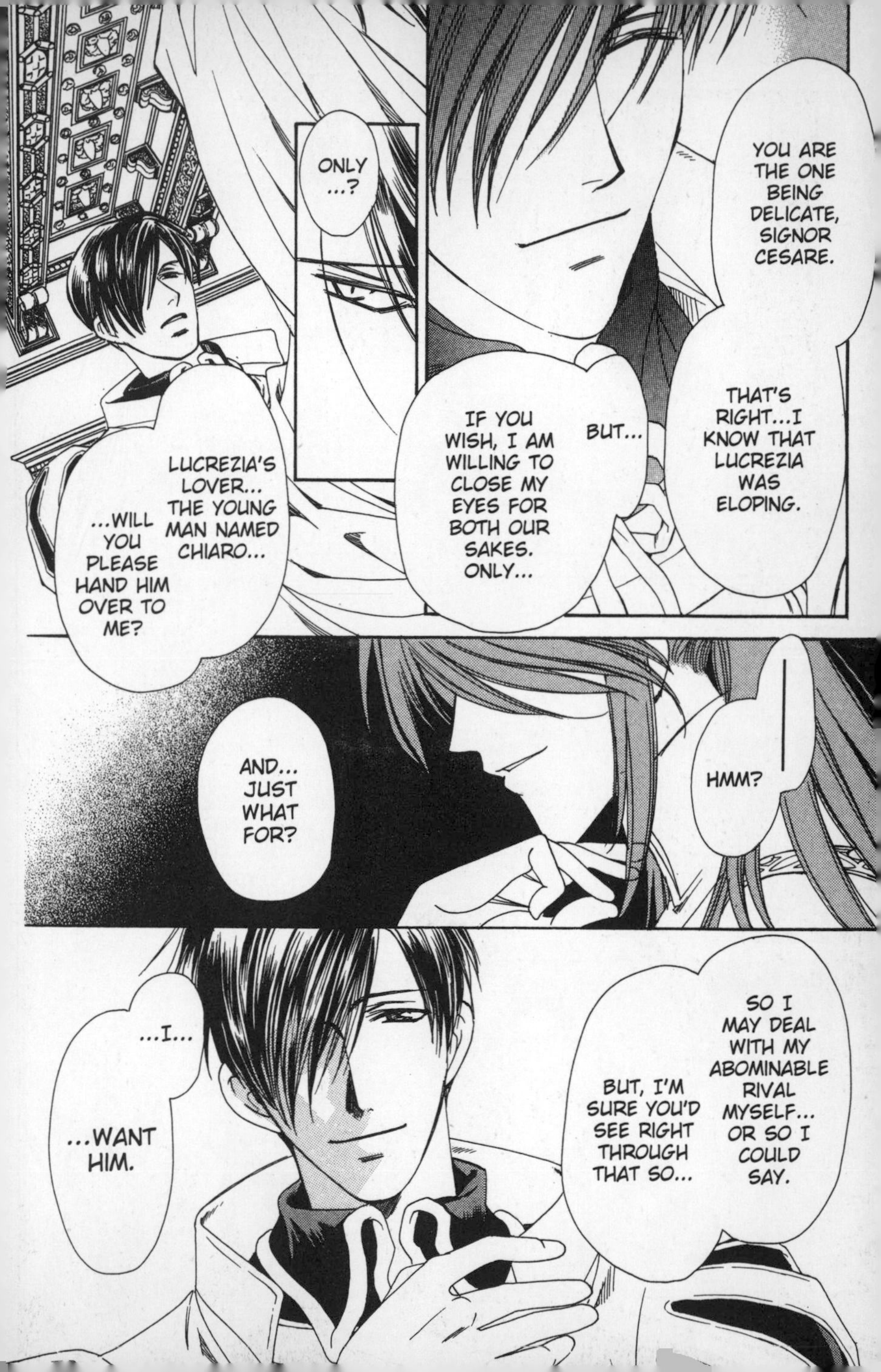
YOU ARE THE ONE BEING DELICATE, SIGNOR CESARE.
THAT'S RIGHT...I KNOW THAT LUCREZIA WAS ELOPING.
BUT...
IF YOU WISH, I AM WILLING TO CLOSE MY EYES FOR BOTH OUR SAKES. ONLY...
ONLY ...?
LUCREZIA'S LOVER... THE YOUNG MAN NAMED CHIARO...
...WILL YOU PLEASE HAND HIM OVER TO ME?
HMM?
AND... JUST WHAT FOR?
SO I MAY DEAL WITH MY ABOMINABLE RIVAL MYSELF... OR SO I COULD SAY.
BUT, I'M SURE YOU'D SEE RIGHT THROUGH THAT SO...
...I...
...WANT HIM.

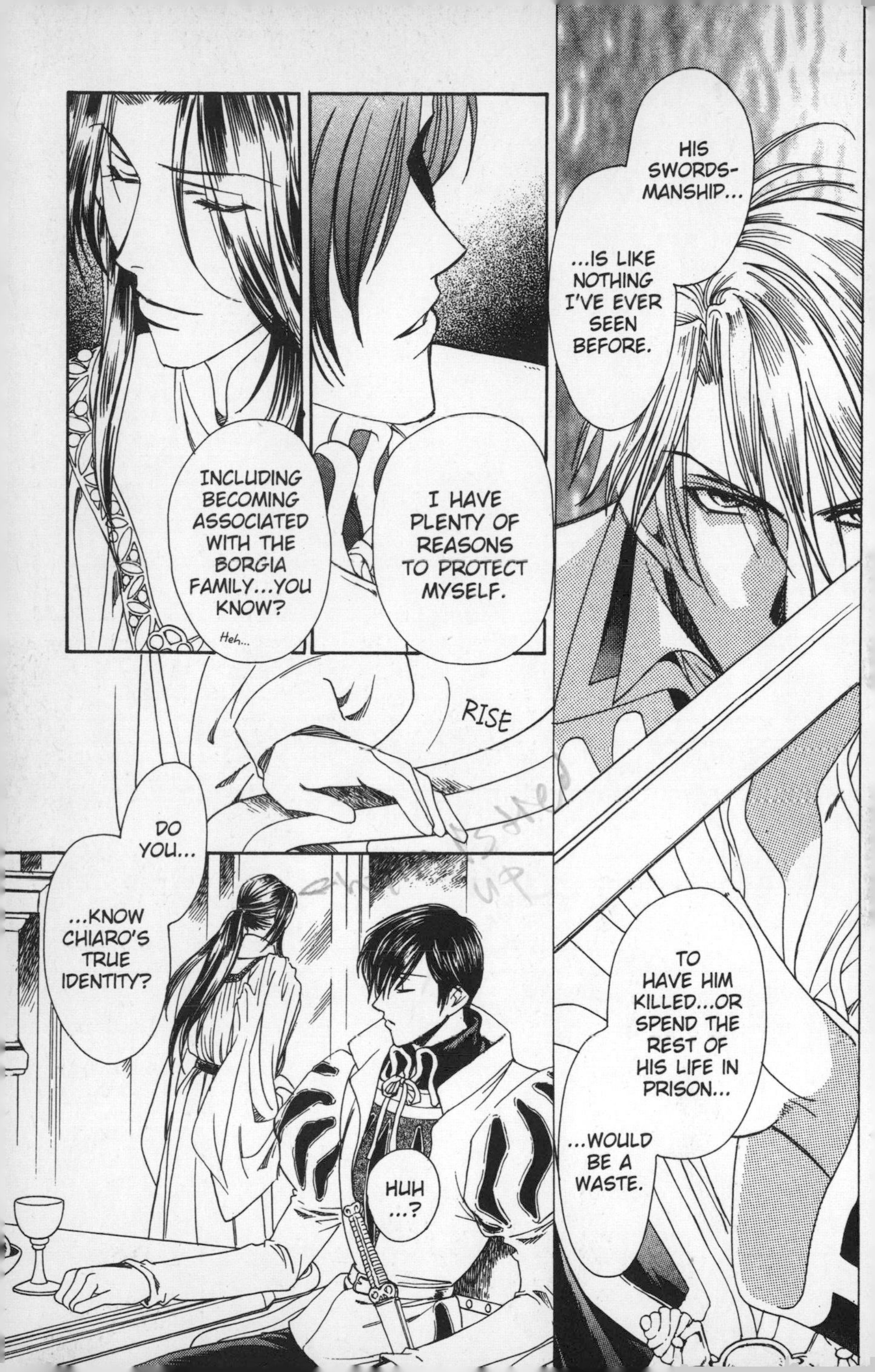
HIS SWORDS-MANSHIP...
...IS LIKE NOTHING I'VE EVER SEEN BEFORE.
TO HAVE HIM KILLED...OR SPEND THE REST OF HIS LIFE IN PRISON...
...WOULD BE A WASTE.
I HAVE PLENTY OF REASONS TO PROTECT MYSELF.
INCLUDING BECOMING ASSOCIATED WITH THE BORGIA FAMILY...YOU KNOW?
Heh...
RISE
DO YOU...
...KNOW CHIARO'S TRUE IDENTITY?
HUH ...?

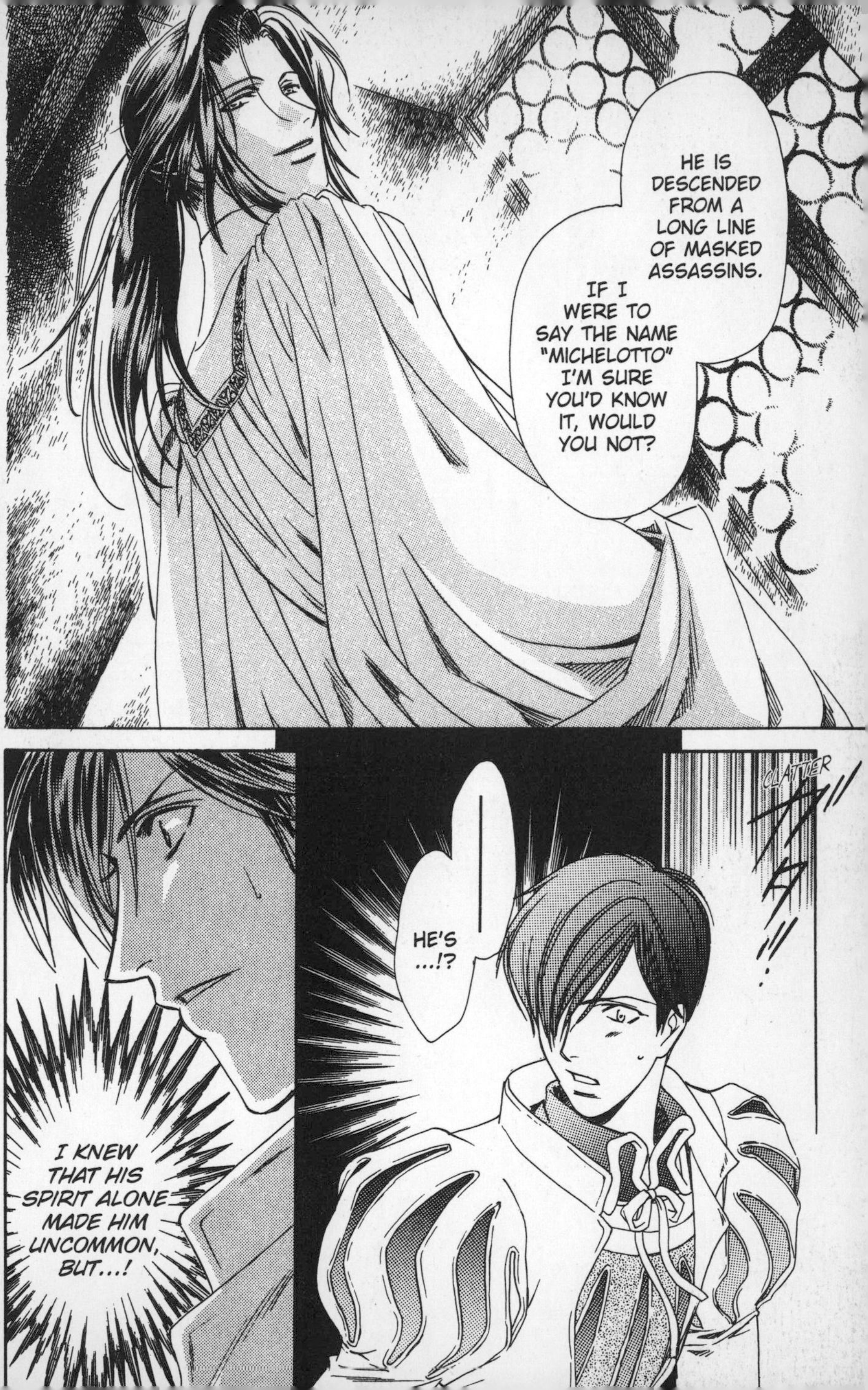
HE IS DESCENDED FROM A LONG LINE OF MASKED ASSASSINS.
IF I WERE TO SAY THE NAME "MICHELOTTO" I'M SURE YOU'D KNOW IT, WOULD YOU NOT?
CLATTER
HE'S ...!?
I KNEW THAT HIS SPIRIT ALONE MADE HIM UNCOMMON, BUT...!

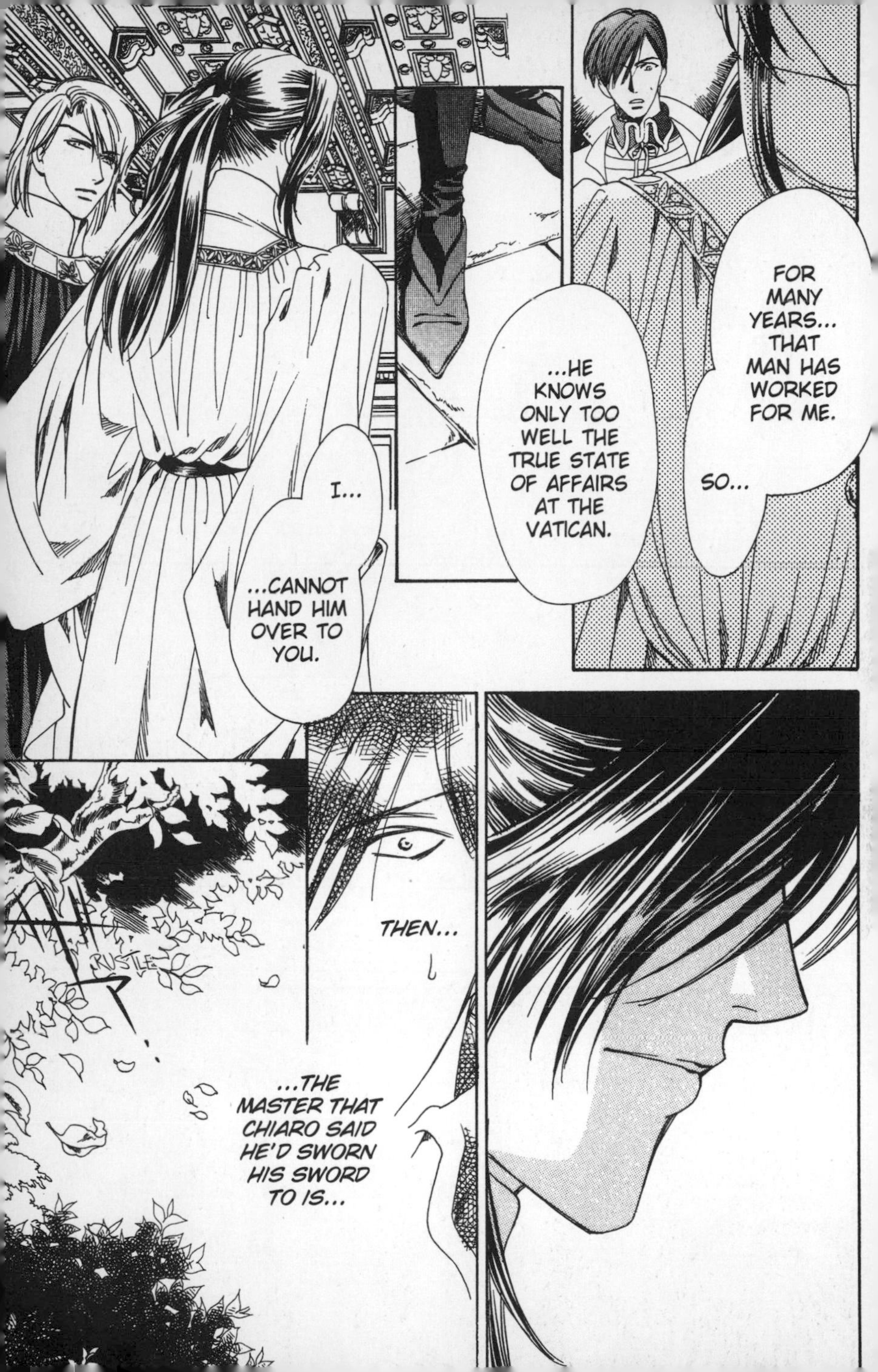
FOR MANY YEARS... THAT MAN HAS WORKED FOR ME.
SO...
...HE KNOWS ONLY TOO WELL THE TRUE STATE OF AFFAIRS AT THE VATICAN.
I...
...CANNOT HAND HIM OVER TO YOU.
THEN...
RUSTLE
...THE MASTER THAT CHIARO SAID HE'D SWORN HIS SWORD TO IS...

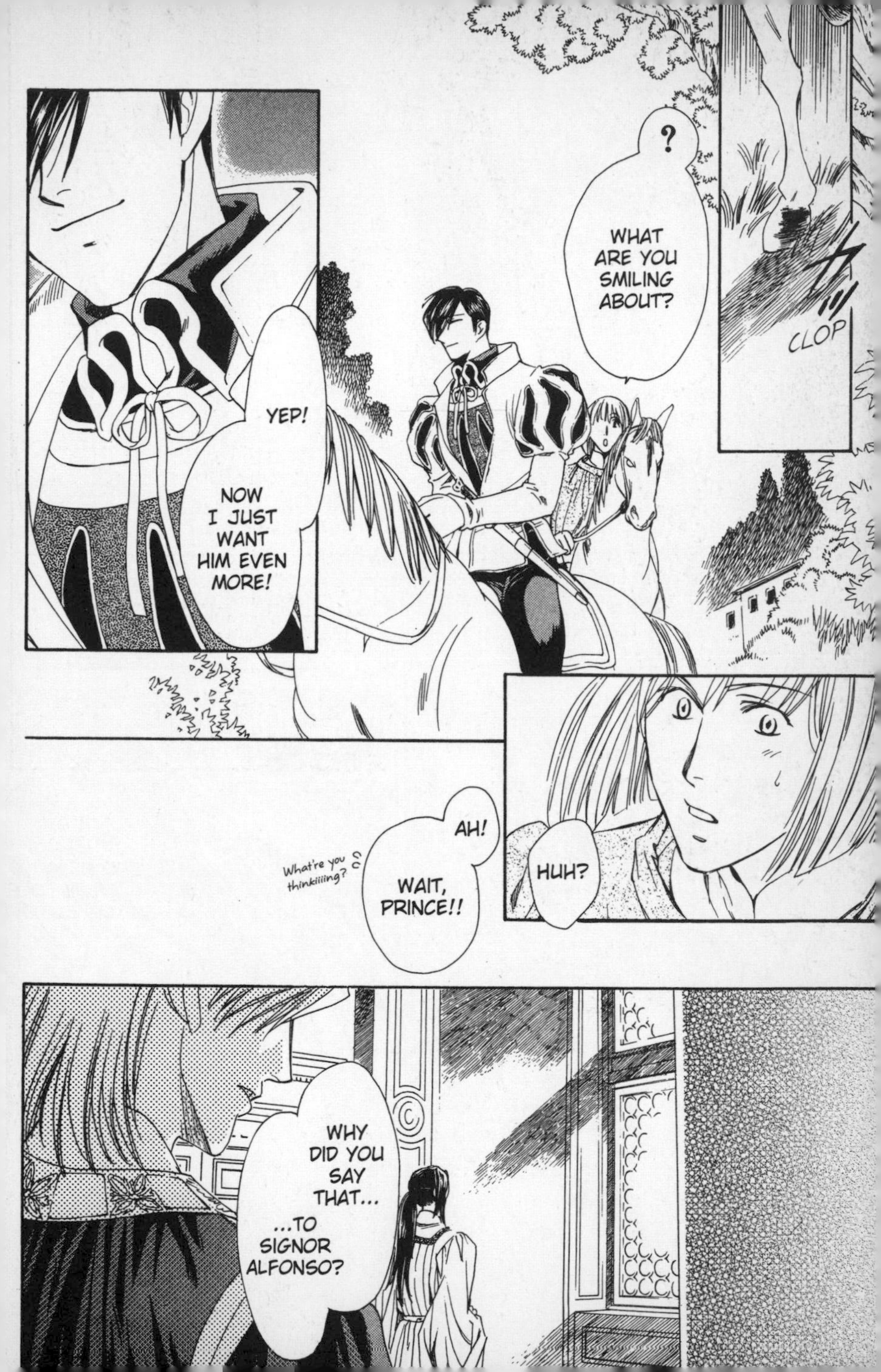
CLOP
?
WHAT ARE YOU SMILING ABOUT?
YEP!
NOW I JUST WANT HIM EVEN MORE!
HUH?
AH!
WAIT, PRINCE!!
What're you thinkiiiing?
WHY DID YOU SAY THAT...
...TO SIGNOR ALFONSO?

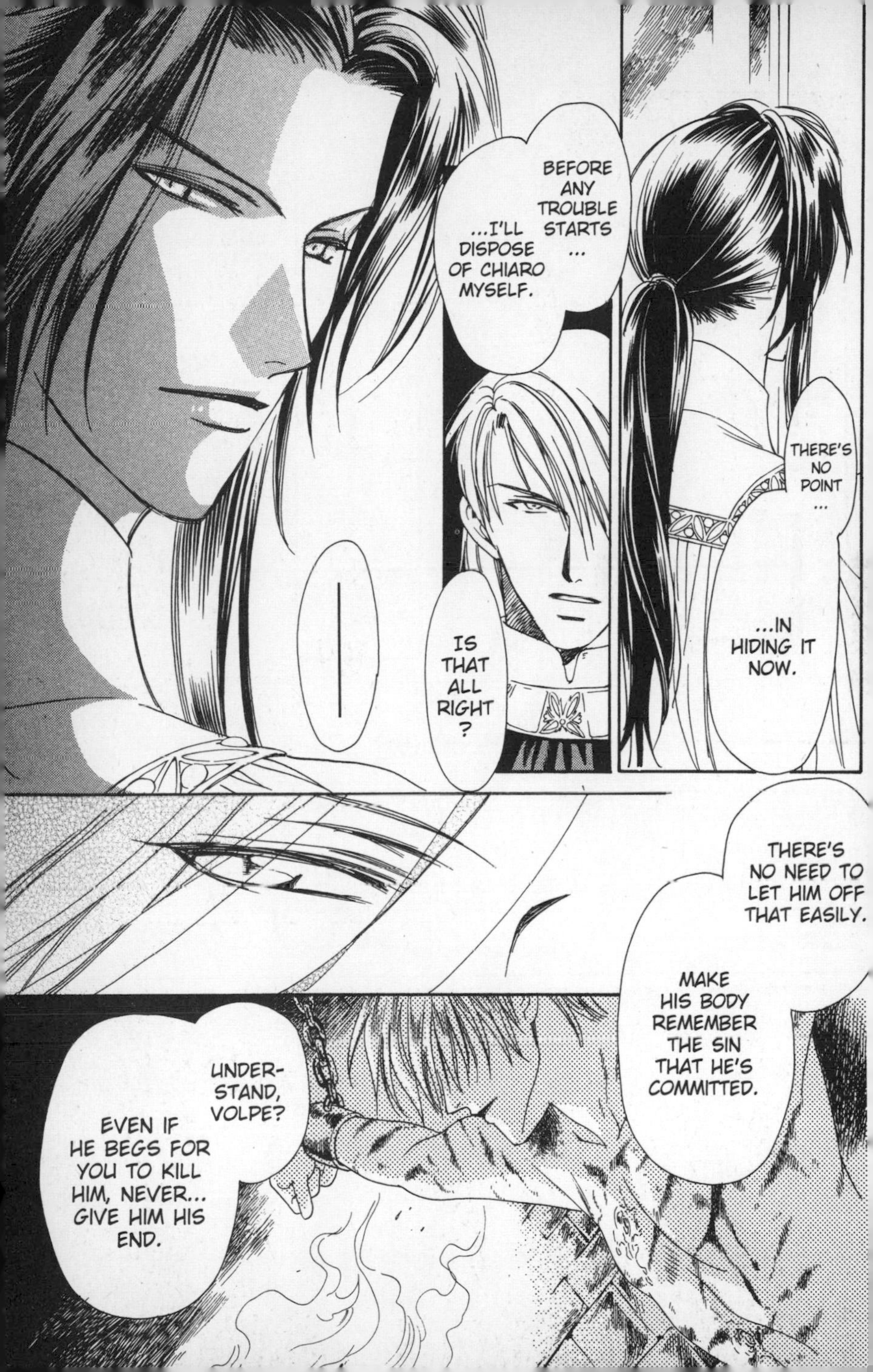
THERE'S NO POINT ...
...IN HIDING IT NOW.
BEFORE ANY TROUBLE STARTS ...
...I'LL DISPOSE OF CHIARO MYSELF.
IS THAT ALL RIGHT?
THERE'S NO NEED TO LET HIM OFF THAT EASILY.
MAKE HIS BODY REMEMBER THE SIN THAT HE'S COMMITTED.
UNDER-STAND, VOLPE?
EVEN IF HE BEGS FOR YOU TO KILL HIM, NEVER... GIVE HIM HIS END.

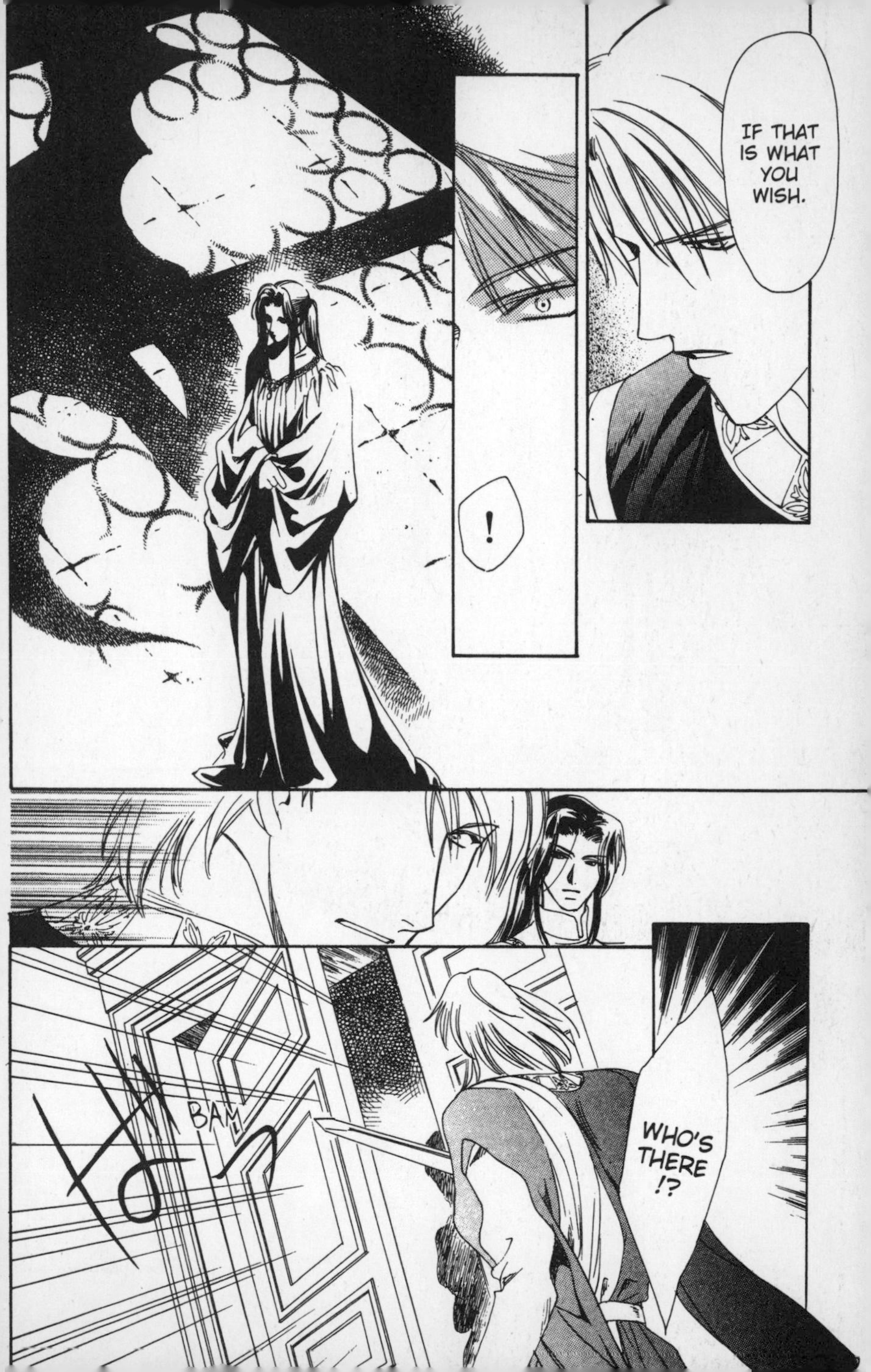
IF THAT IS WHAT YOU WISH.
!
WHO'S THERE !?
BAM

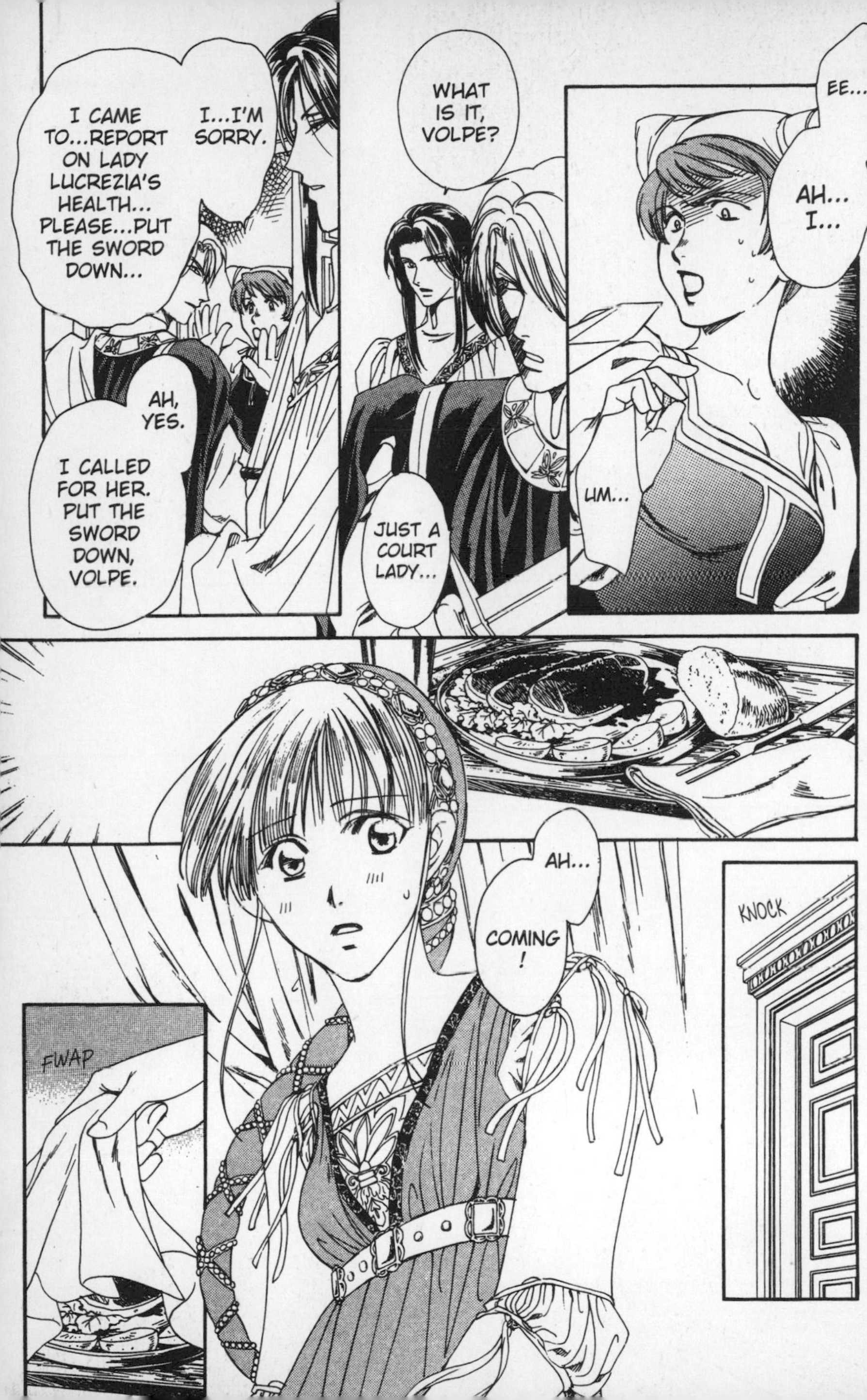
EE...!
AH... I...
UM...
WHAT IS IT, VOLPE?
JUST A COURT LADY...
I...I'M SORRY.
I CAME TO...REPORT ON LADY LUCREZIA'S HEALTH... PLEASE...PUT THE SWORD DOWN...
AH, YES.
I CALLED FOR HER. PUT THE SWORD DOWN, VOLPE.
KNOCK
AH...
COMING!
FWAP

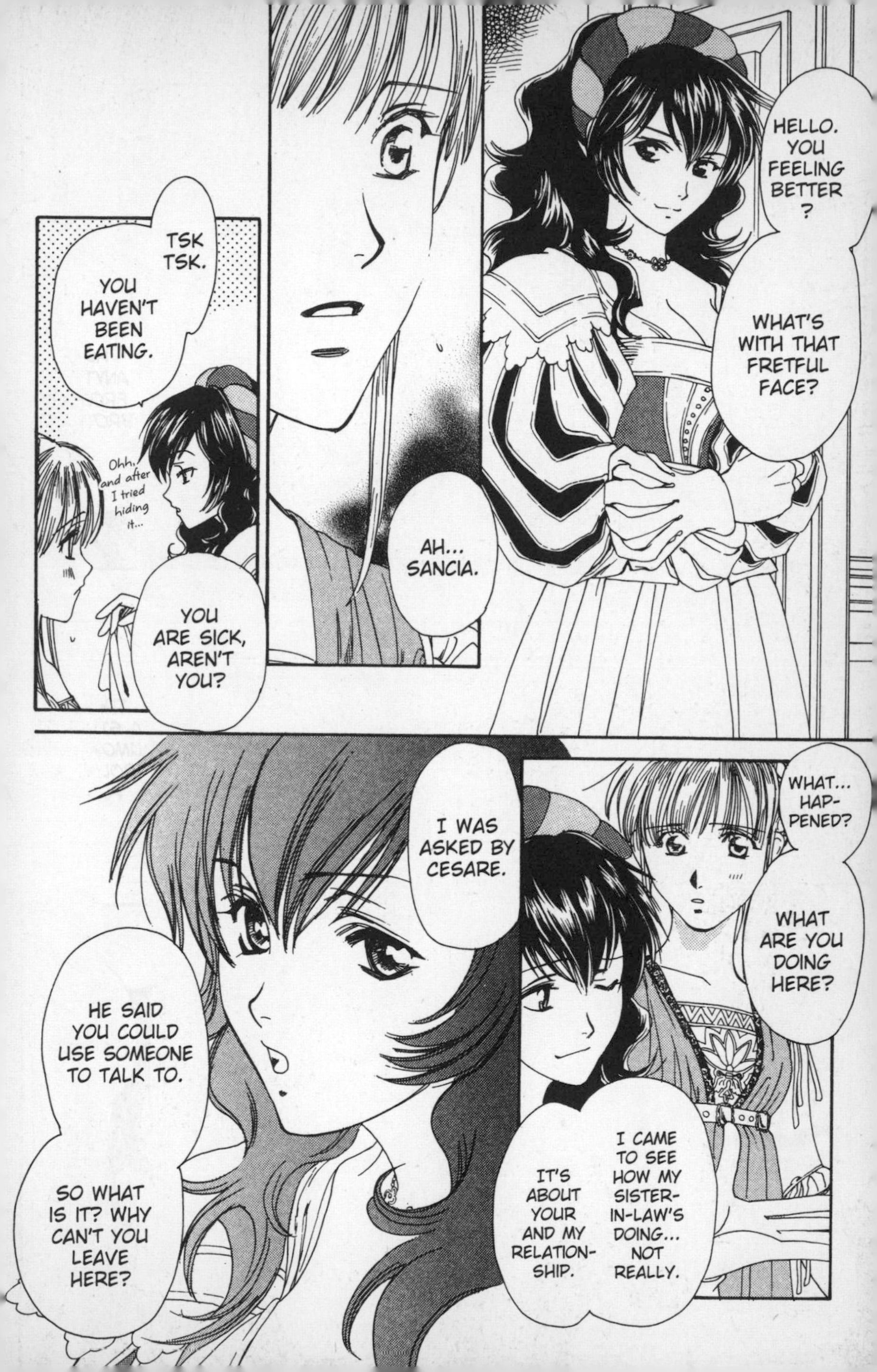
HELLO. YOU FEELING BETTER?
WHAT'S WITH THAT FRETFUL FACE?
AH... SANCIA.
TSK TSK.
YOU HAVEN'T BEEN EATING.
Ohh, and after I tried hiding it...
YOU ARE SICK, AREN'T YOU?
WHAT... HAP-PENED?
WHAT ARE YOU DOING HERE?
I CAME TO SEE HOW MY SISTER-IN-LAW'S DOING... NOT REALLY.
IT'S ABOUT YOUR AND MY RELATION-SHIP.
I WAS ASKED BY CESARE.
HE SAID YOU COULD USE SOMEONE TO TALK TO.
SO WHAT IS IT? WHY CAN'T YOU LEAVE HERE?

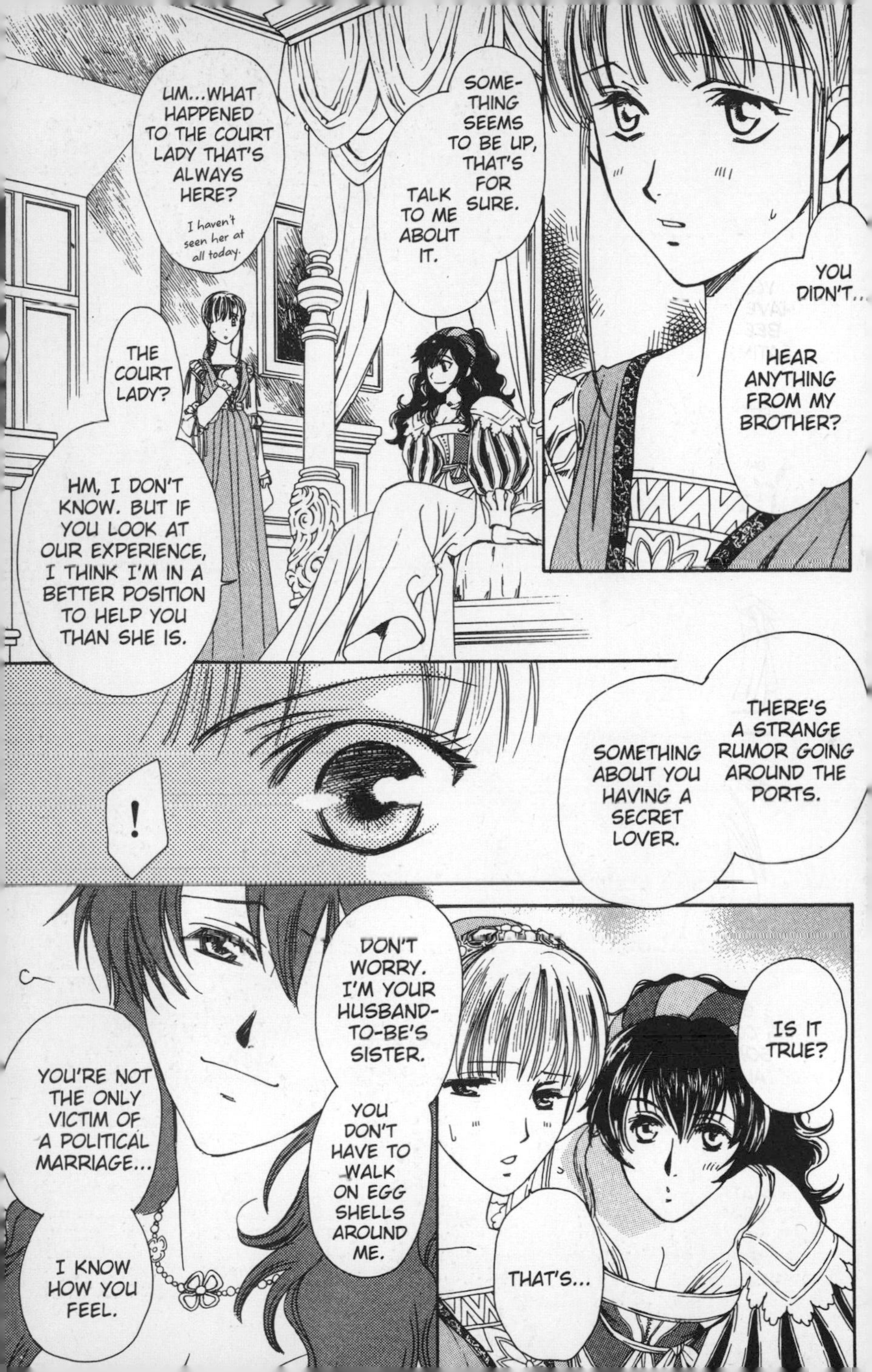
YOU DIDN'T...
HEAR ANYTHING FROM MY BROTHER?
SOME-THING SEEMS TO BE UP, THAT'S FOR SURE.
TALK TO ME ABOUT IT.
UM...WHAT HAPPENED TO THE COURT LADY THAT'S ALWAYS HERE?
I haven't seen her at all today.
THE COURT LADY?
HM, I DON'T KNOW. BUT IF YOU LOOK AT OUR EXPERIENCE, I THINK I'M IN A BETTER POSITION TO HELP YOU THAN SHE IS.
THERE'S A STRANGE RUMOR GOING AROUND THE PORTS.
SOMETHING ABOUT YOU HAVING A SECRET LOVER.
!
IS IT TRUE?
THAT'S...
DON'T WORRY. I'M YOUR HUSBAND-TO-BE'S SISTER.
YOU DON'T HAVE TO WALK ON EGG SHELLS AROUND ME.
YOU'RE NOT THE ONLY VICTIM OF A POLITICAL MARRIAGE...
I KNOW HOW YOU FEEL.

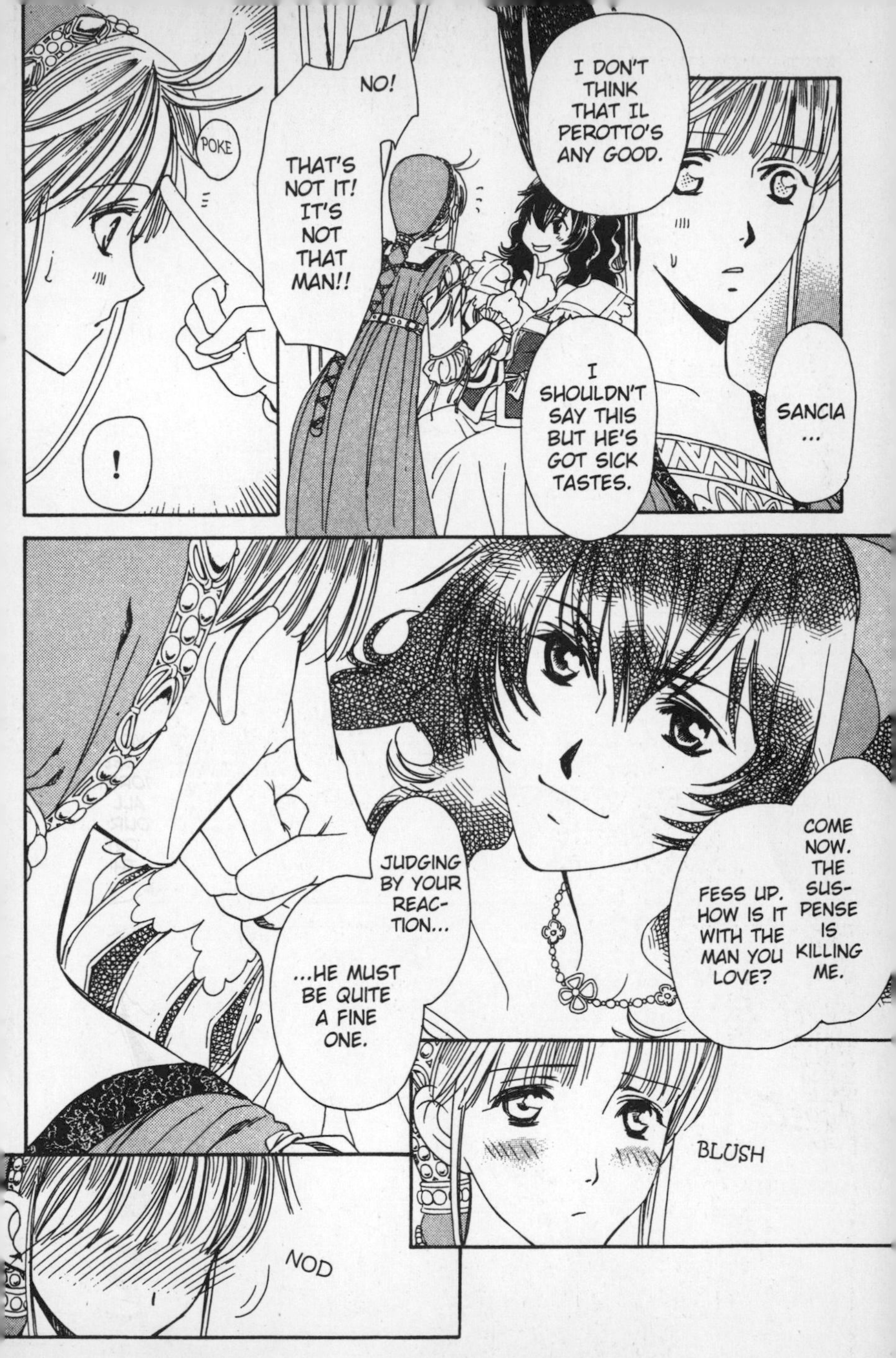
I DON'T THINK THAT IL PEROTTO'S ANY GOOD.
I SHOULDN'T SAY THIS BUT HE'S GOT SICK TASTES.
SANCIA ...
NO!
THAT'S NOT IT! IT'S NOT THAT MAN!!
POKE
!
COME NOW. THE SUS-PENSE IS KILLING ME.
FESS UP. HOW IS IT WITH THE MAN YOU LOVE?
JUDGING BY YOUR REAC-TION...
...HE MUST BE QUITE A FINE ONE.
BLUSH
NOD

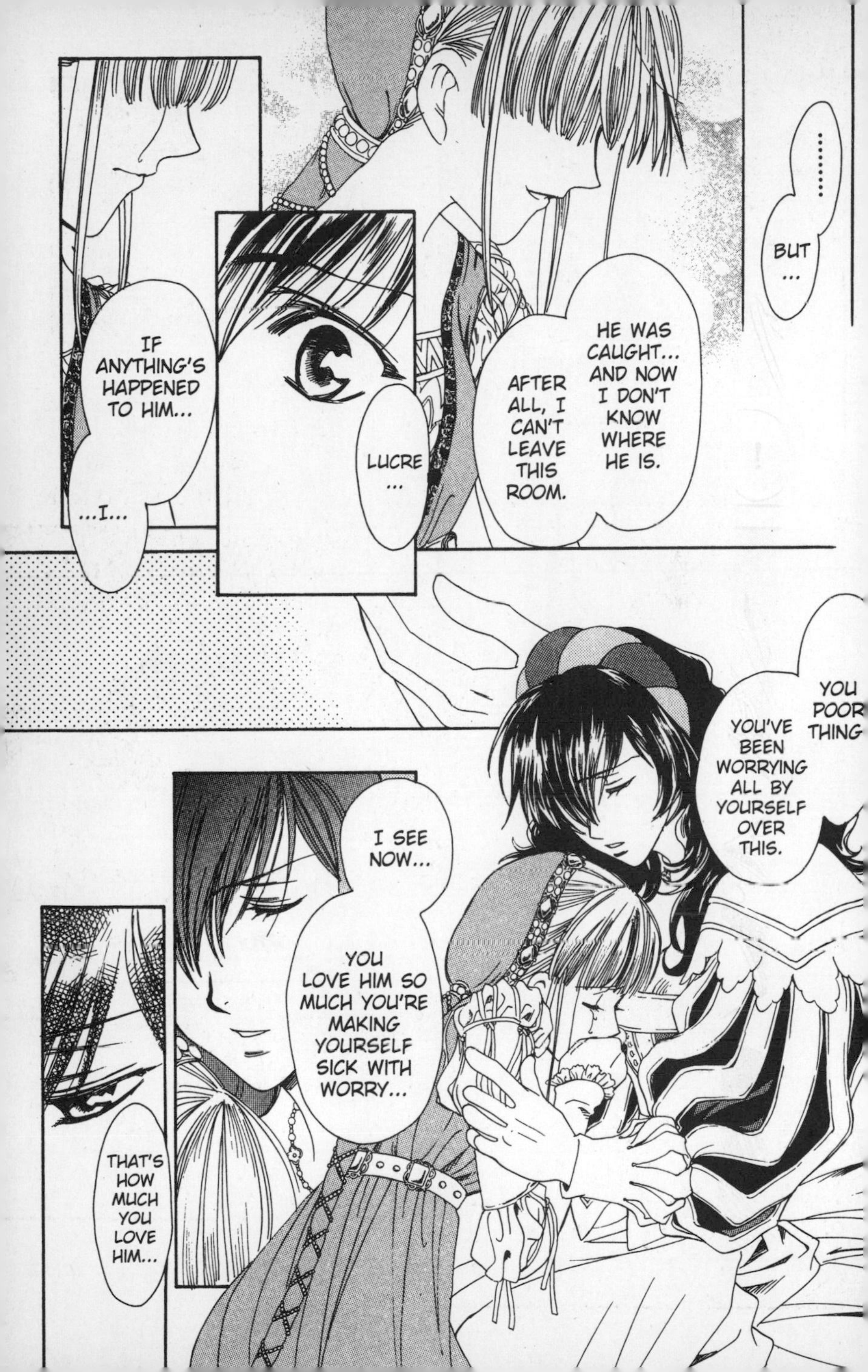
......
BUT ...
HE WAS CAUGHT... AND NOW I DON'T KNOW WHERE HE IS.
AFTER ALL, I CAN'T LEAVE THIS ROOM.
LUCRE ...
IF ANYTHING'S HAPPENED TO HIM...
...I...
YOU POOR THING
YOU'VE BEEN WORRYING ALL BY YOURSELF OVER THIS.
I SEE NOW...
YOU LOVE HIM SO MUCH YOU'RE MAKING YOURSELF SICK WITH WORRY...
THAT'S HOW MUCH YOU LOVE HIM...

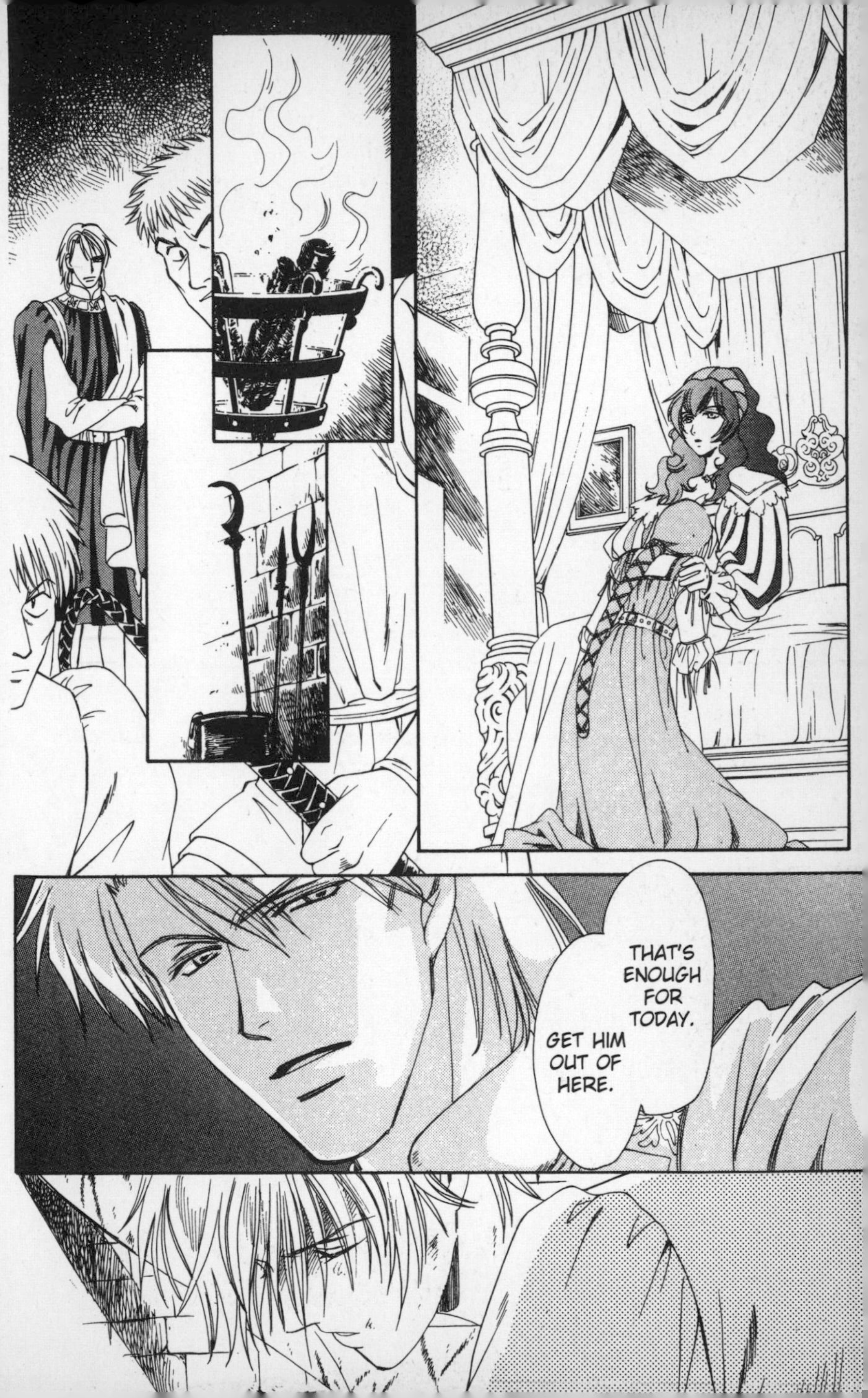
THAT'S ENOUGH FOR TODAY.
GET HIM OUT OF HERE.

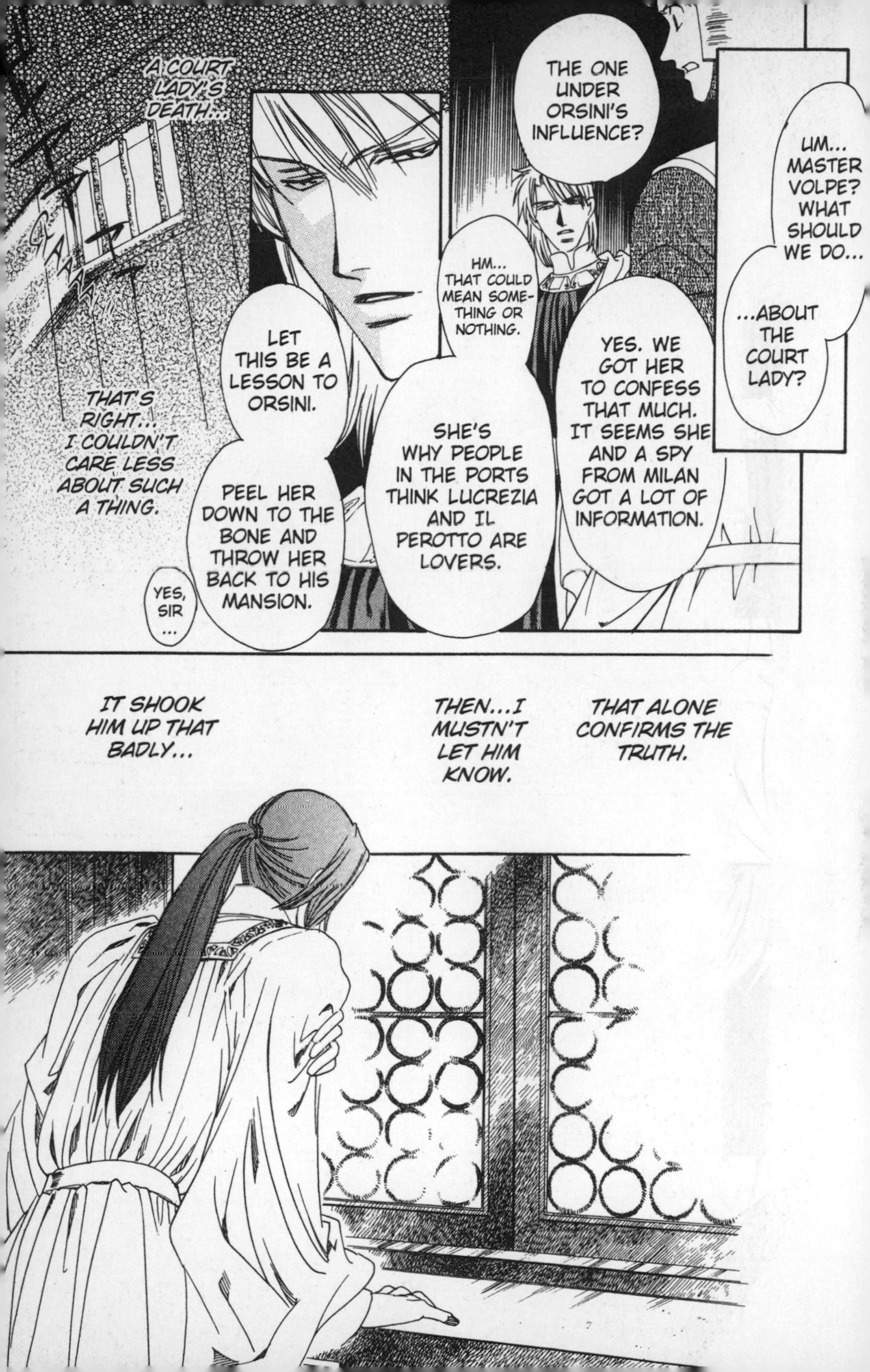
UM... MASTER VOLPE? WHAT SHOULD WE DO...
...ABOUT THE COURT LADY?
THE ONE UNDER ORSINI'S INFLUENCE?
YES. WE GOT HER TO CONFESS THAT MUCH. IT SEEMS SHE AND A SPY FROM MILAN GOT A LOT OF INFORMATION.
HM... THAT COULD MEAN SOME-THING OR NOTHING.
SHE'S WHY PEOPLE IN THE PORTS THINK LUCREZIA AND IL PEROTTO ARE LOVERS.
LET THIS BE A LESSON TO ORSINI.
PEEL HER DOWN TO THE BONE AND THROW HER BACK TO HIS MANSION.
YES, SIR ...
A COURT LADY'S DEATH...
THAT'S RIGHT... I COULDN'T CARE LESS ABOUT SUCH A THING.
THAT ALONE CONFIRMS THE TRUTH.
THEN...I MUSTN'T LET HIM KNOW.
IT SHOOK HIM UP THAT BADLY...

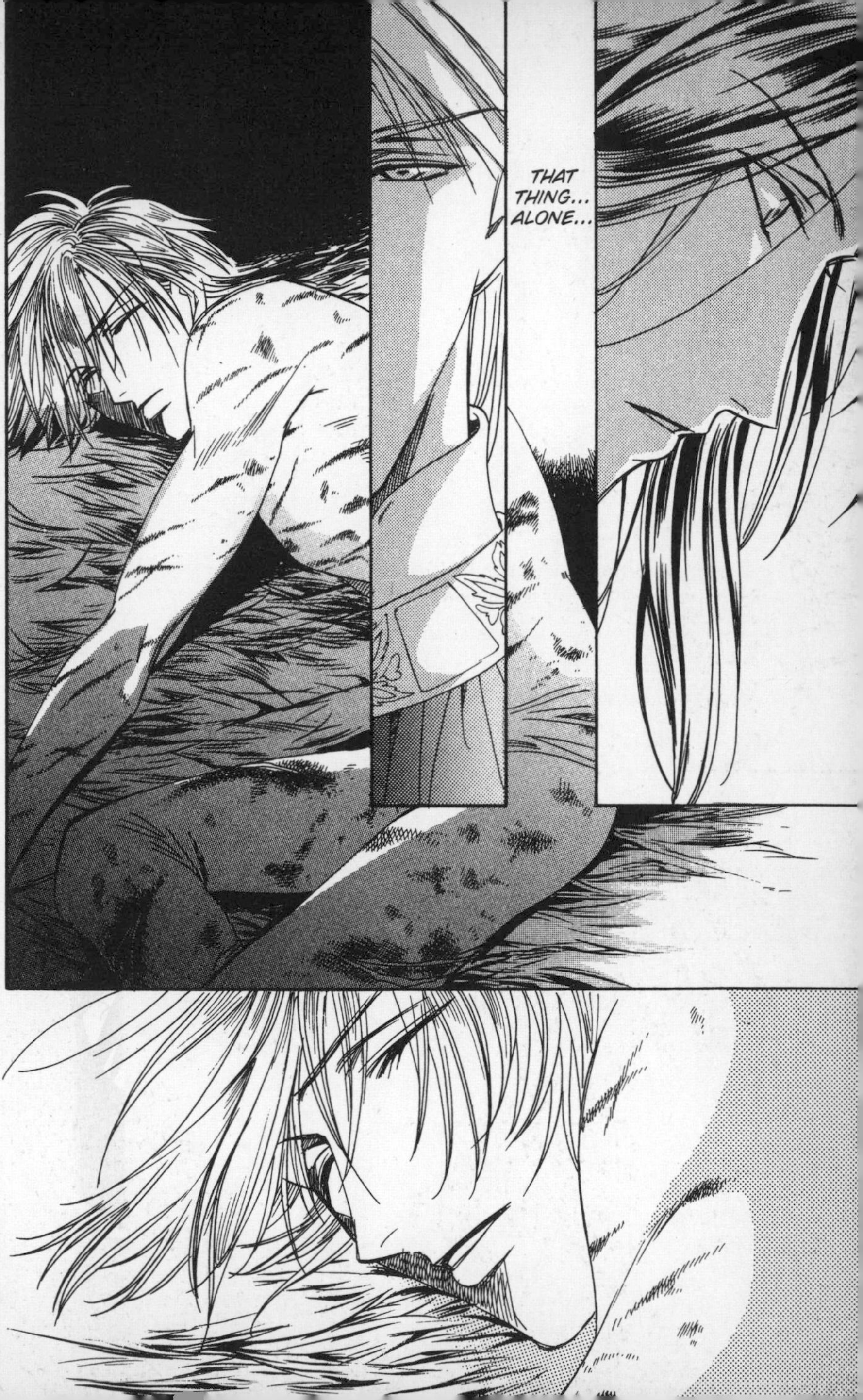
THAT THING... ALONE...

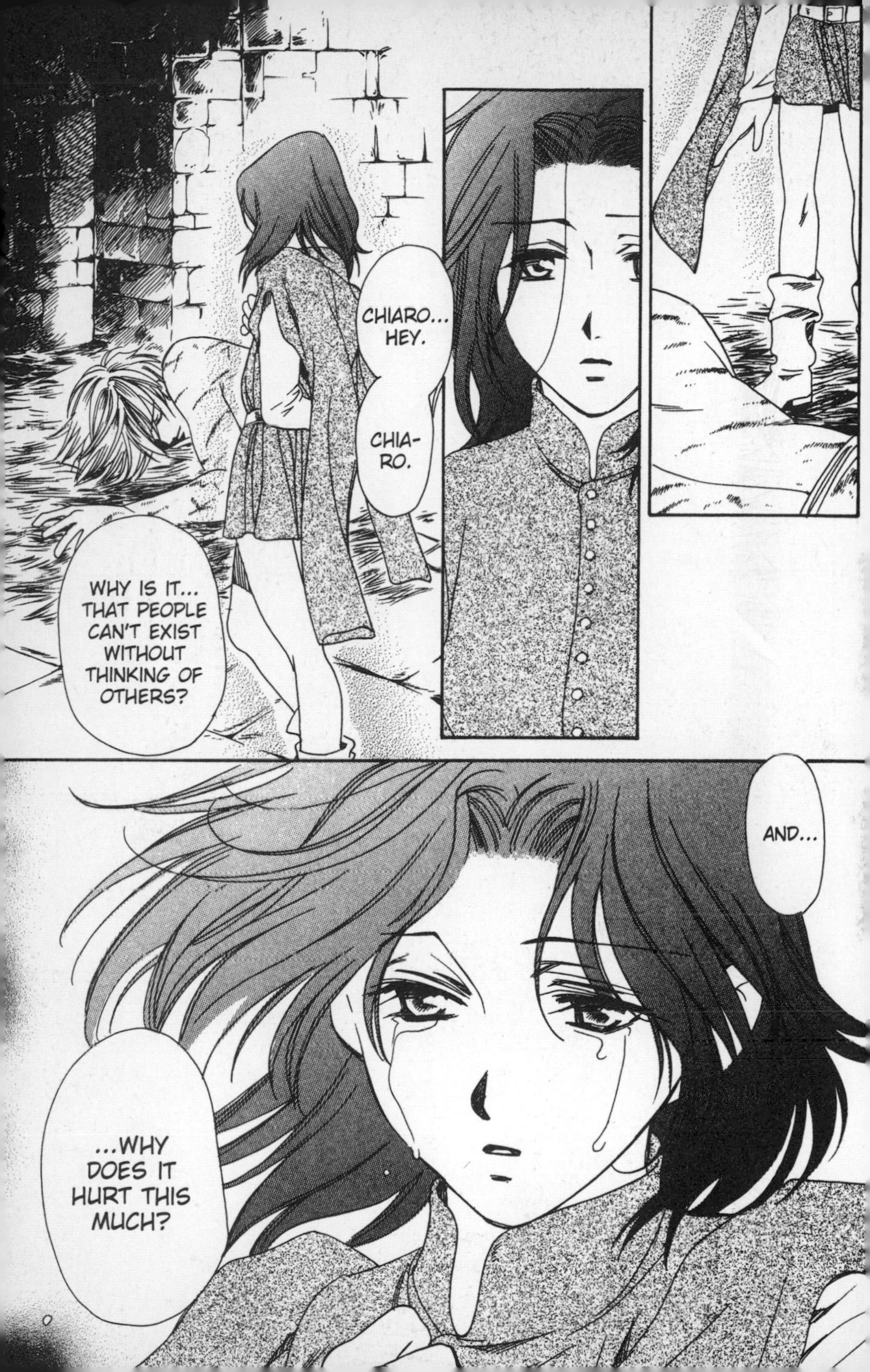
CHIARO... HEY.
CHIA-RO.
WHY IS IT... THAT PEOPLE CAN'T EXIST WITHOUT THINKING OF OTHERS?
AND...
...WHY DOES IT HURT THIS MUCH?

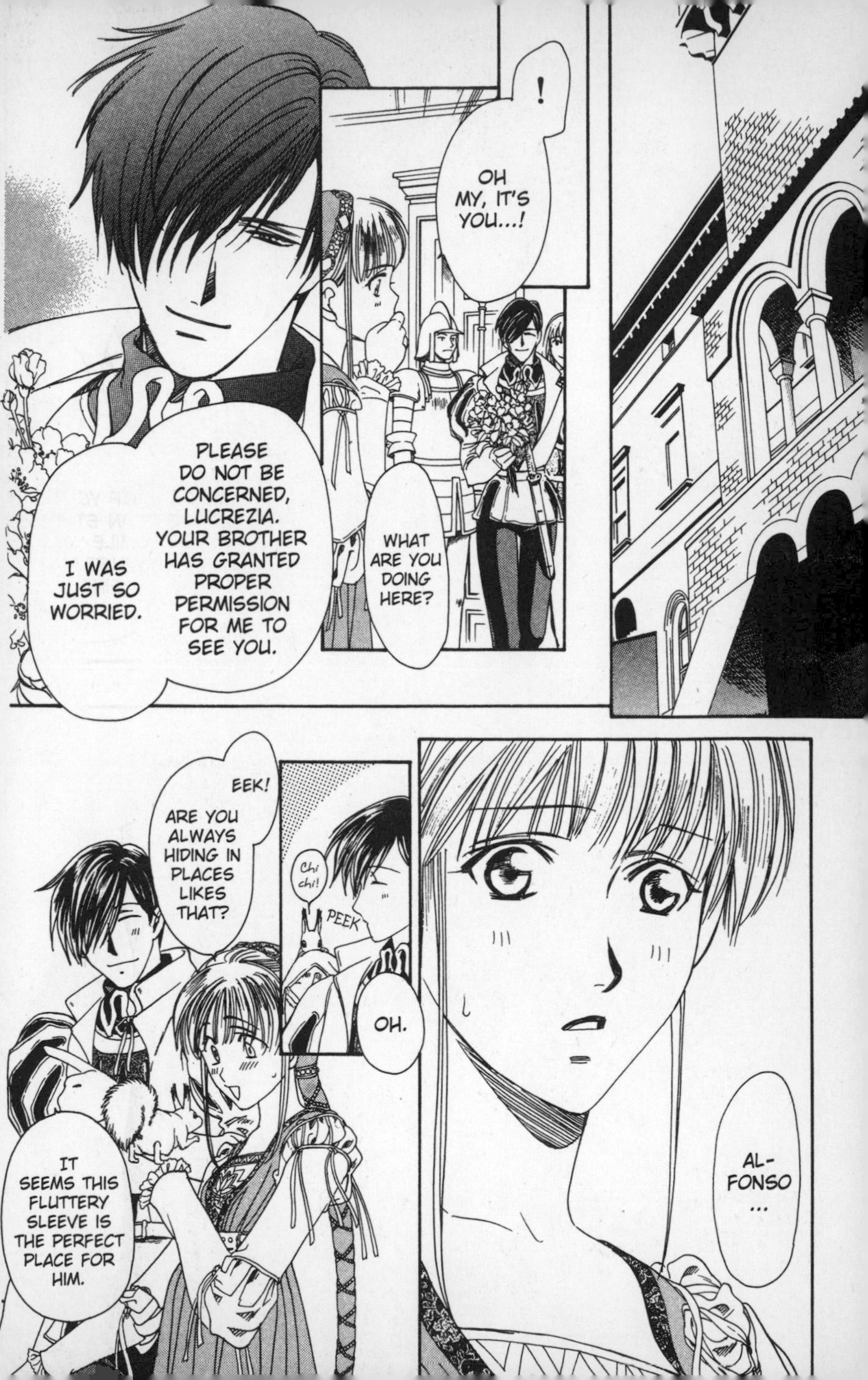
!
OH MY, IT'S YOU...!
WHAT ARE YOU DOING HERE?
PLEASE DO NOT BE CONCERNED, LUCREZIA. YOUR BROTHER HAS GRANTED PROPER PERMISSION FOR ME TO SEE YOU.
I WAS JUST SO WORRIED.
AL-FONSO...
Chi chi!
PEEK
OH.
EEK!
ARE YOU ALWAYS HIDING IN PLACES LIKES THAT?
IT SEEMS THIS FLUTTERY SLEEVE IS THE PERFECT PLACE FOR HIM.

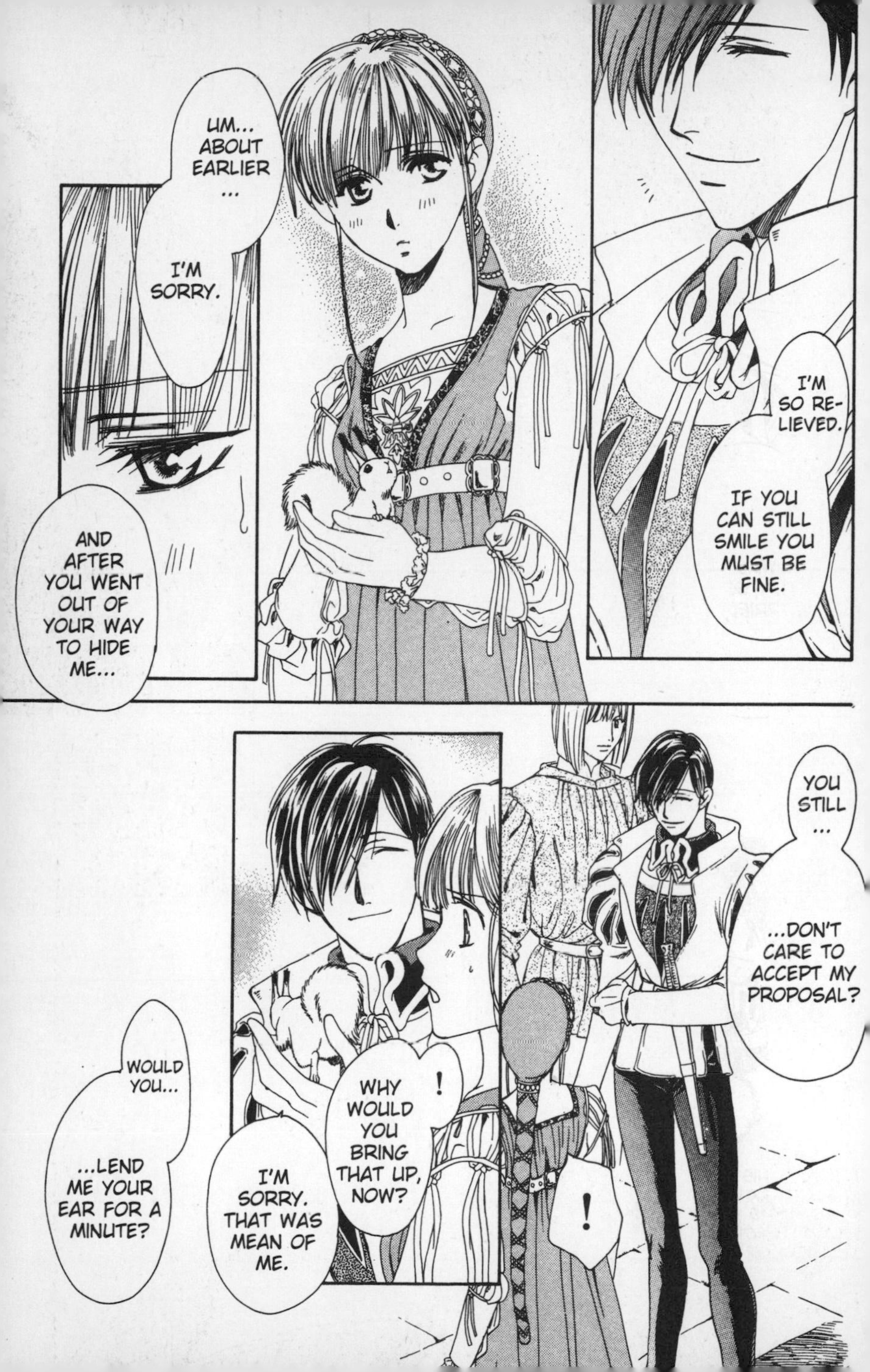
I'M SO RE-LIEVED.
IF YOU CAN STILL SMILE YOU MUST BE FINE.
UM... ABOUT EARLIER ...
I'M SORRY.
AND AFTER YOU WENT OUT OF YOUR WAY TO HIDE ME...
YOU STILL ...
...DON'T CARE TO ACCEPT MY PROPOSAL?
!
!
WHY WOULD YOU BRING THAT UP, NOW?
I'M SORRY. THAT WAS MEAN OF ME.
WOULD YOU...
...LEND ME YOUR EAR FOR A MINUTE?

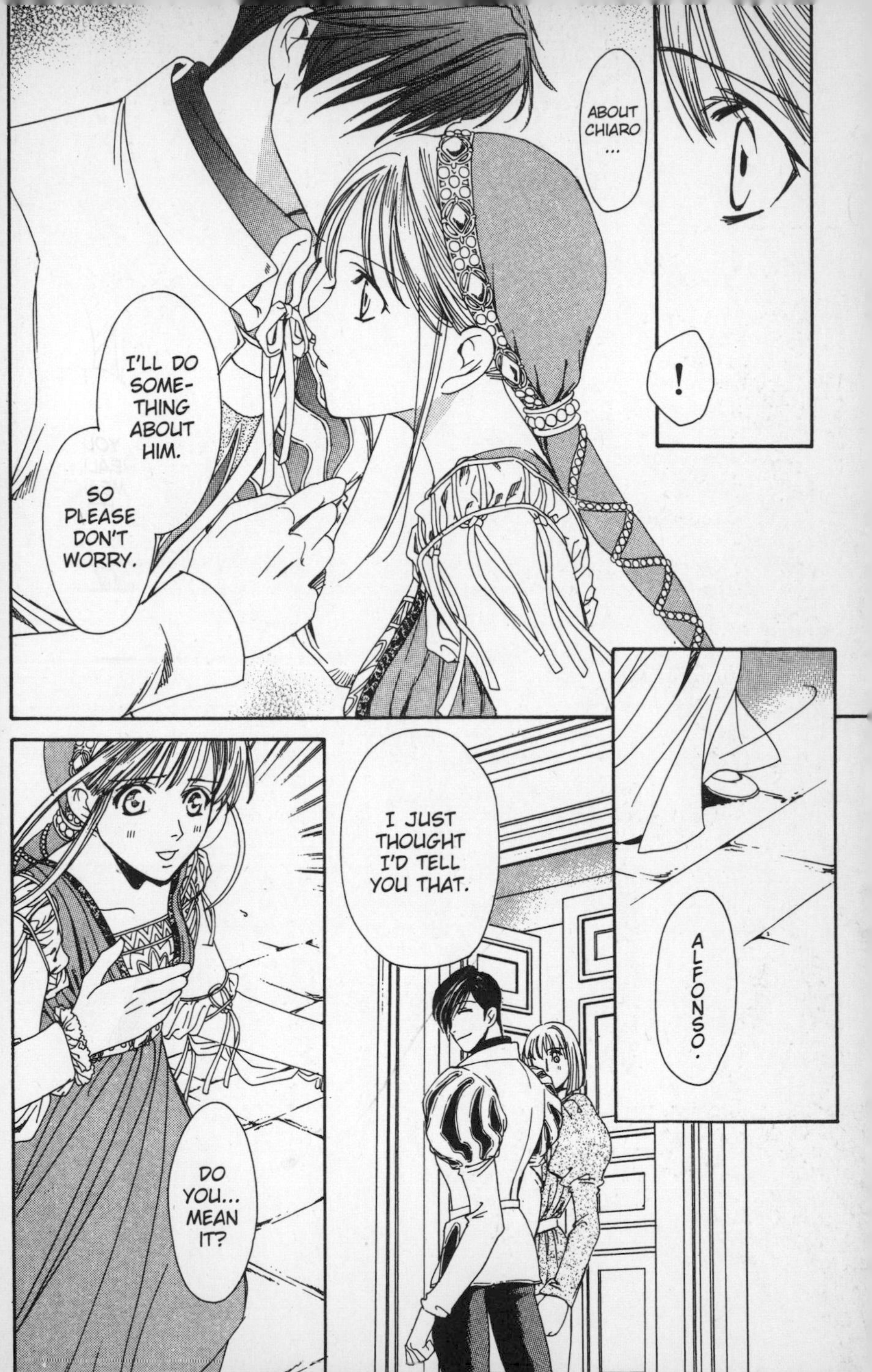
!
ABOUT CHIARO ...
I'LL DO SOME-THING ABOUT HIM.
SO PLEASE DON'T WORRY.
ALFONSO.
I JUST THOUGHT I'D TELL YOU THAT.
DO YOU... MEAN IT?

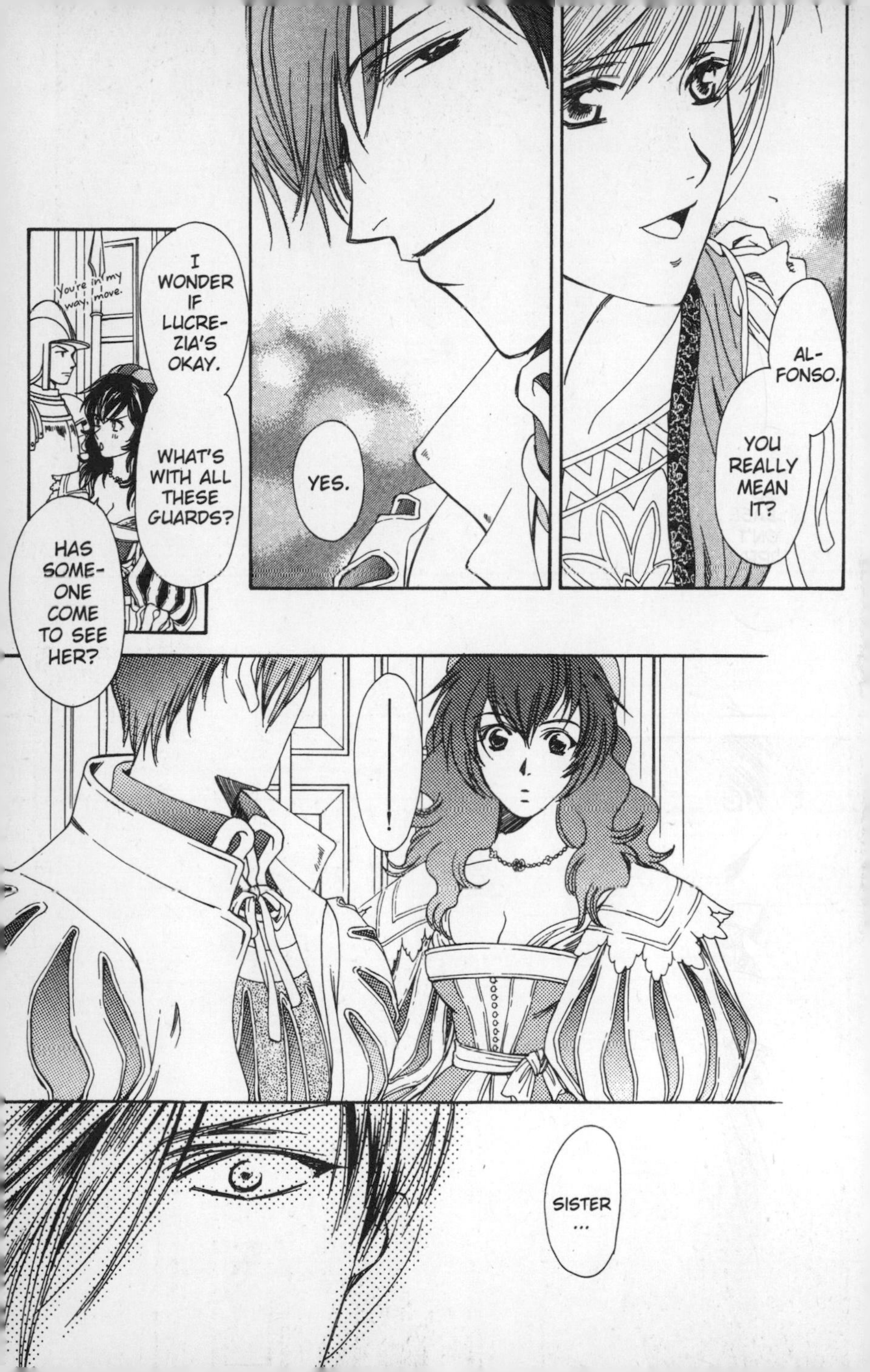
AL-FONSO.
YOU REALLY MEAN IT?
YES.
I WONDER IF LUCRE-ZIA'S OKAY.
You're in my way, move.
WHAT'S WITH ALL THESE GUARDS?
HAS SOME-ONE COME TO SEE HER?
!
SISTER ...

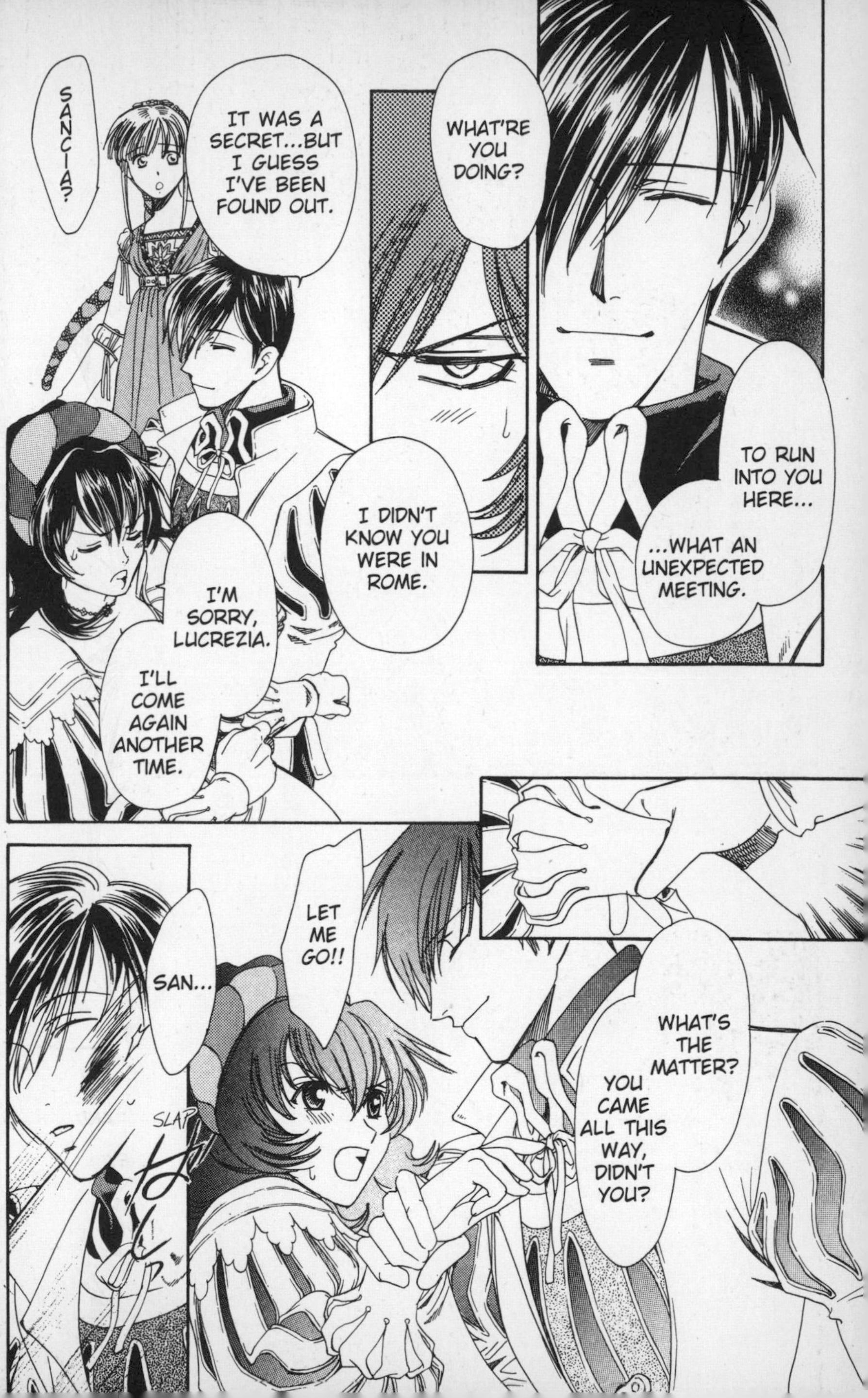
WHAT'RE YOU DOING?
TO RUN INTO YOU HERE...
...WHAT AN UNEXPECTED MEETING.
I DIDN'T KNOW YOU WERE IN ROME.
IT WAS A SECRET...BUT I GUESS I'VE BEEN FOUND OUT.
SANCIA?
I'M SORRY, LUCREZIA.
I'LL COME AGAIN ANOTHER TIME.
WHAT'S THE MATTER?
YOU CAME ALL THIS WAY, DIDN'T YOU?
LET ME GO!!
SAN...
SLAP

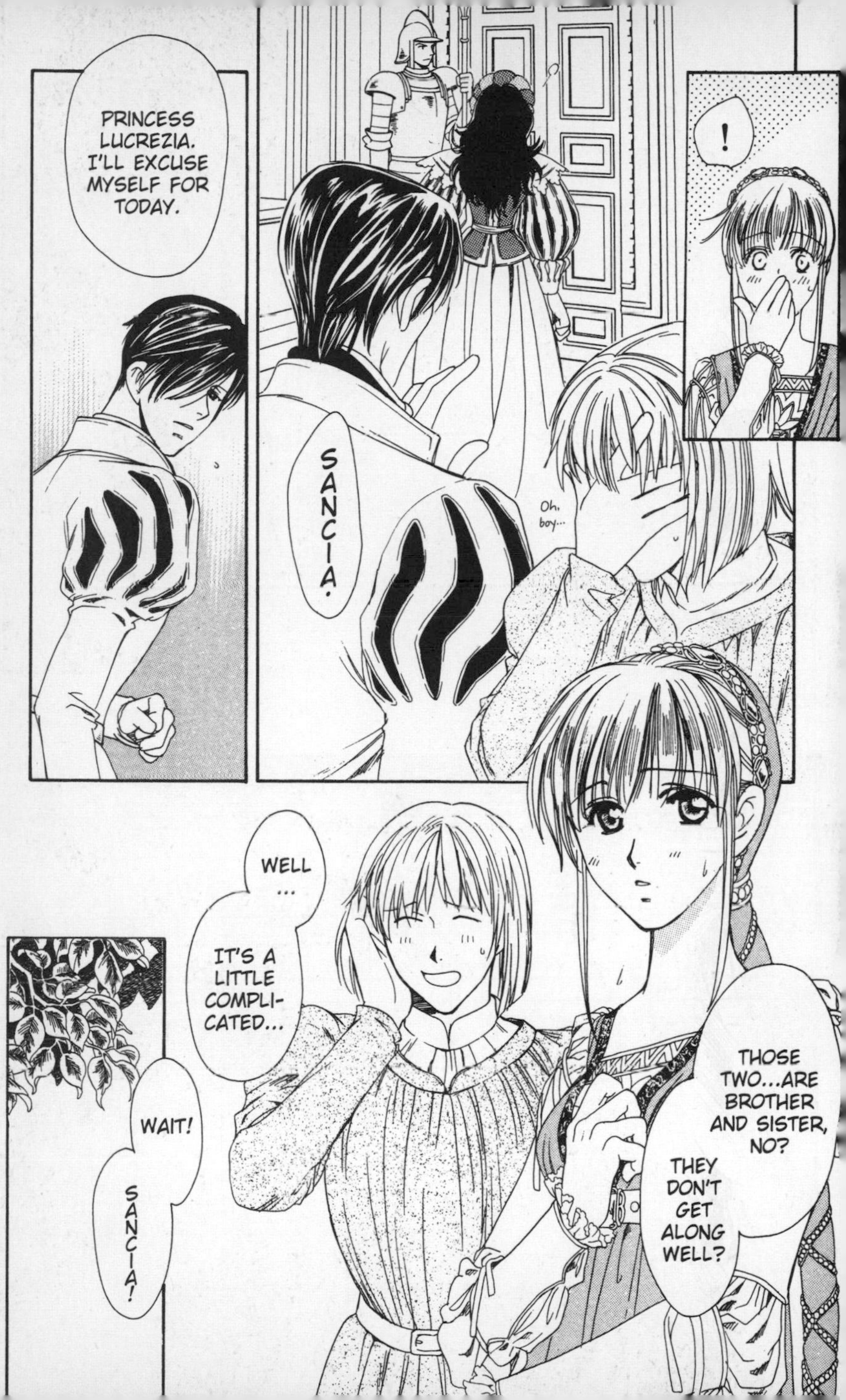
!
SANCIA.
Oh, boy...
PRINCESS LUCREZIA. I'LL EXCUSE MYSELF FOR TODAY.
THOSE TWO...ARE BROTHER AND SISTER, NO?
THEY DON'T GET ALONG WELL?
WELL ...
IT'S A LITTLE COMPLICATED...
WAIT!
SANCIA!

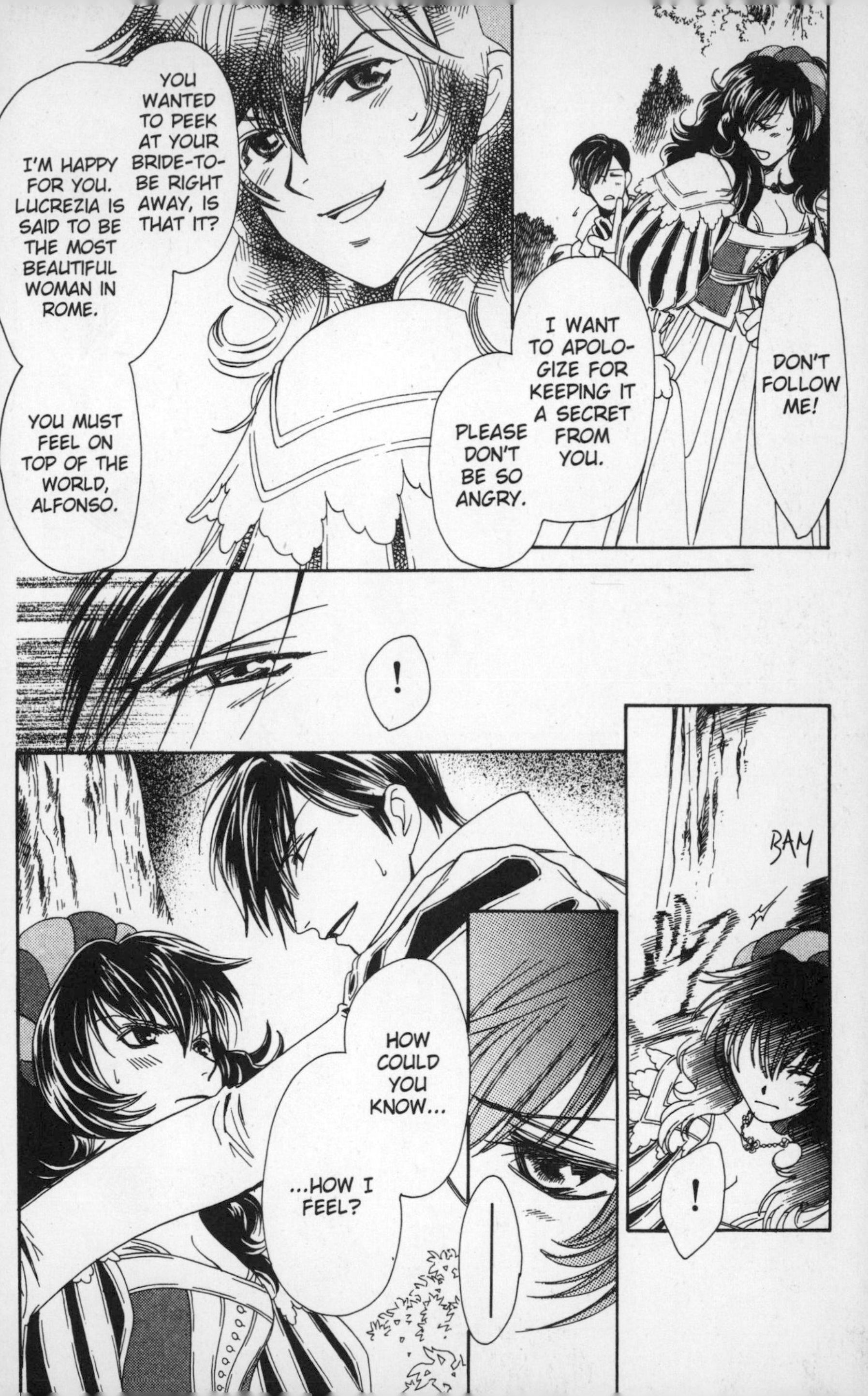
DON'T FOLLOW ME!
I WANT TO APOLOGIZE FOR KEEPING IT A SECRET FROM YOU.
PLEASE DON'T BE SO ANGRY.
YOU WANTED TO PEEK AT YOUR BRIDE-TO-BE RIGHT AWAY, IS THAT IT?
I'M HAPPY FOR YOU. LUCREZIA IS SAID TO BE THE MOST BEAUTIFUL WOMAN IN ROME.
YOU MUST FEEL ON TOP OF THE WORLD, ALFONSO.
!
BAM
!
HOW COULD YOU KNOW...
...HOW I FEEL?

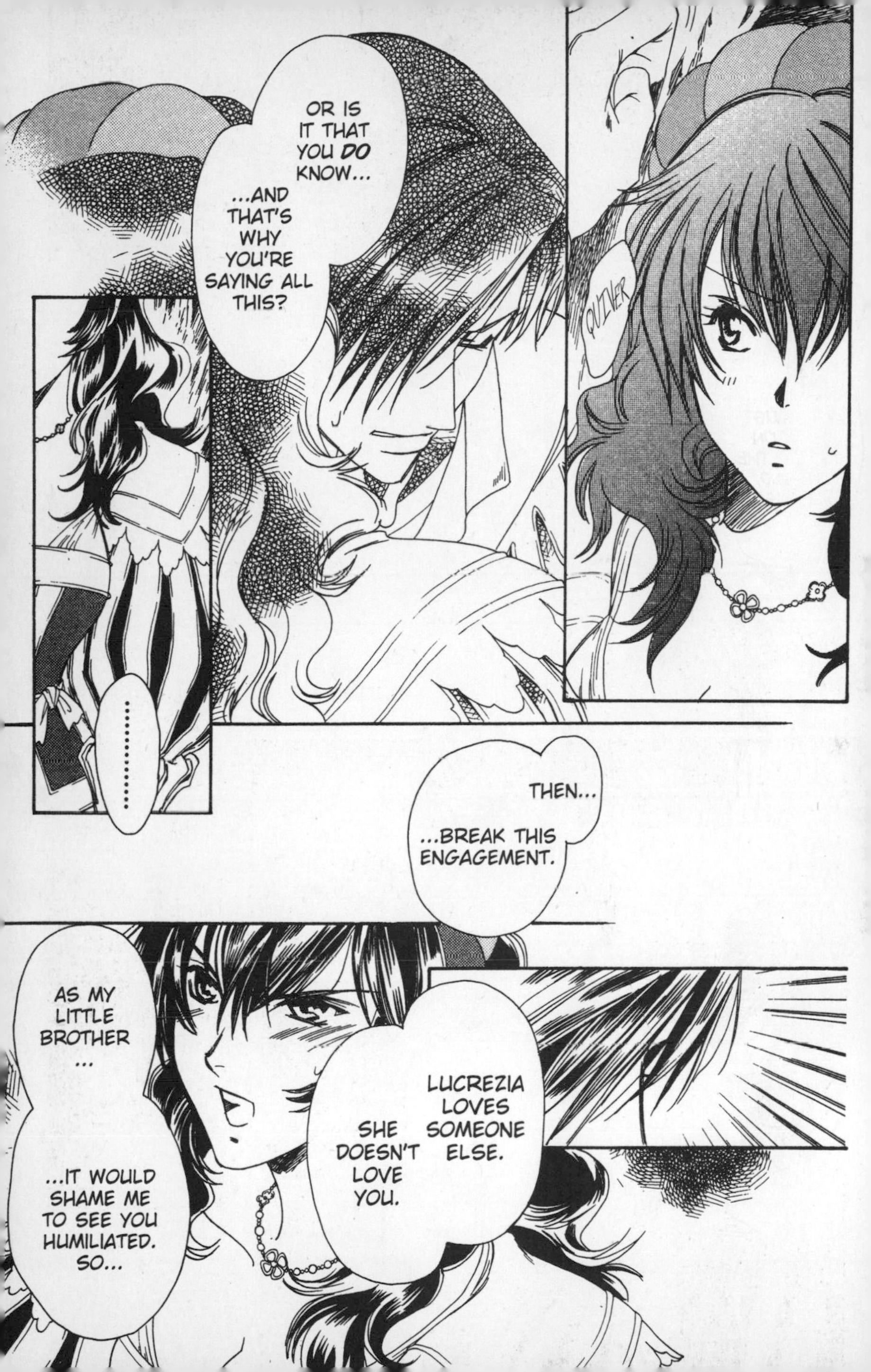

OR IS IT THAT YOU **DO** KNOW...
...AND THAT'S WHY YOU'RE SAYING ALL THIS?
QUIVER
......
THEN...
...BREAK THIS ENGAGEMENT.
LUCREZIA LOVES SOMEONE ELSE.
SHE DOESN'T LOVE YOU.
AS MY LITTLE BROTHER ...
...IT WOULD SHAME ME TO SEE YOU HUMILIATED. SO...

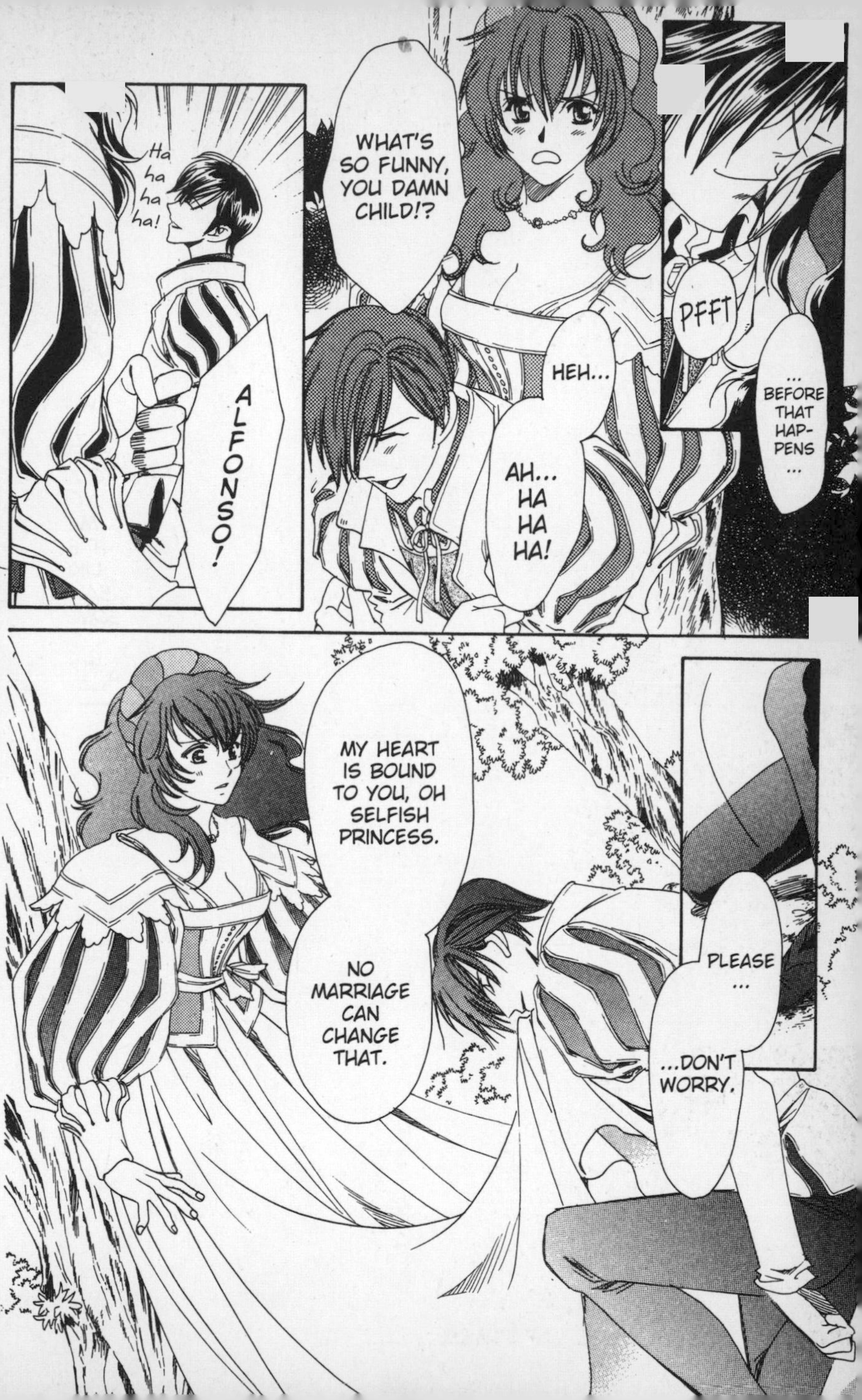
PFFT
...BEFORE THAT HAPPENS...
WHAT'S SO FUNNY, YOU DAMN CHILD!?
HEH...
AH... HA HA HA!
Ha ha ha ha!
ALFONSO!
PLEASE...
...DON'T WORRY.
MY HEART IS BOUND TO YOU, OH SELFISH PRINCESS.
NO MARRIAGE CAN CHANGE THAT.

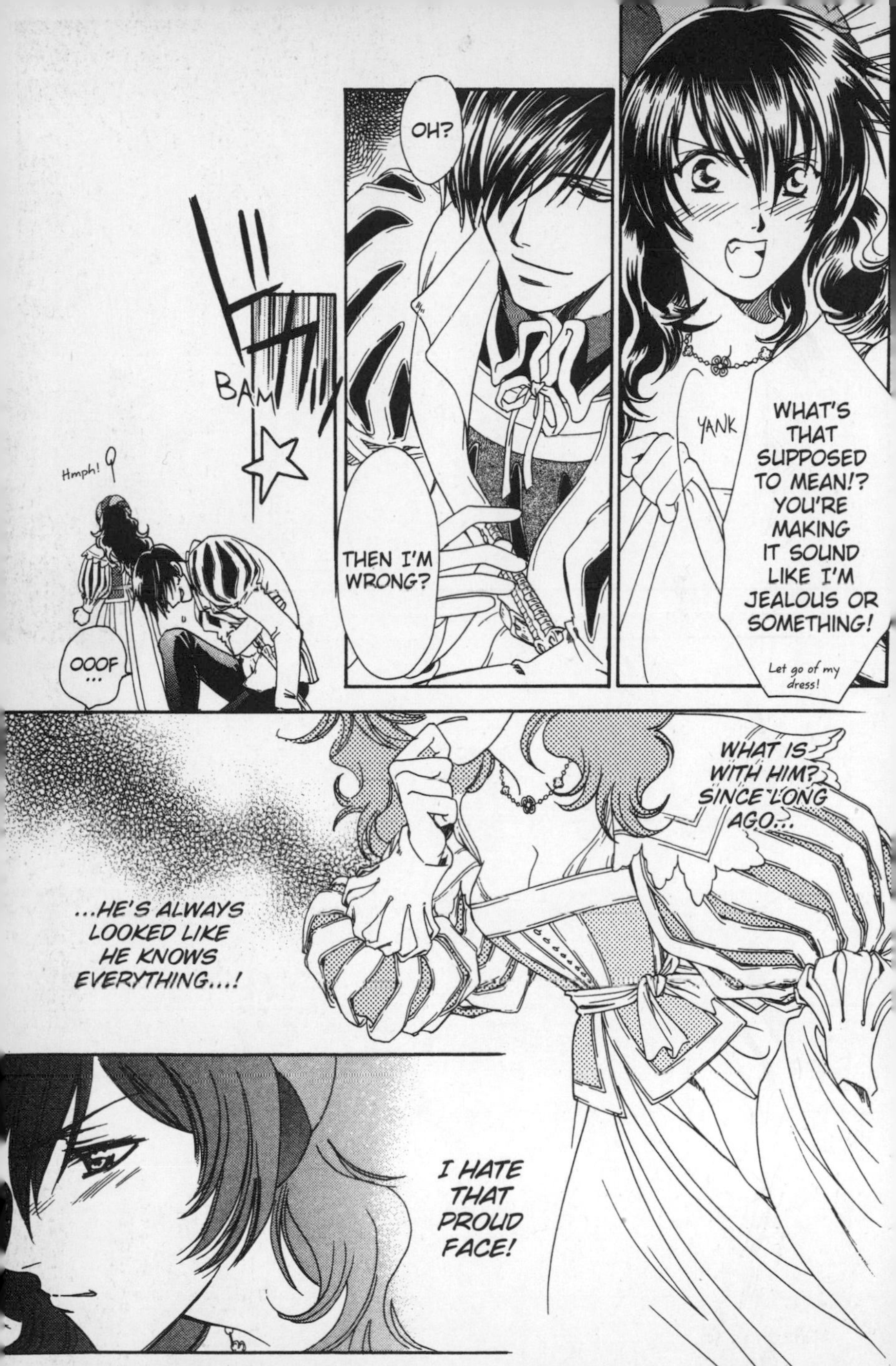
WHAT'S THAT SUPPOSED TO MEAN!? YOU'RE MAKING IT SOUND LIKE I'M JEALOUS OR SOMETHING!
YANK
Let go of my dress!
OH?
THEN I'M WRONG?
BAM
Hmph!
OOOF ...
WHAT IS WITH HIM? SINCE LONG AGO...
...HE'S ALWAYS LOOKED LIKE HE KNOWS EVERYTHING...!
I HATE THAT PROUD FACE!

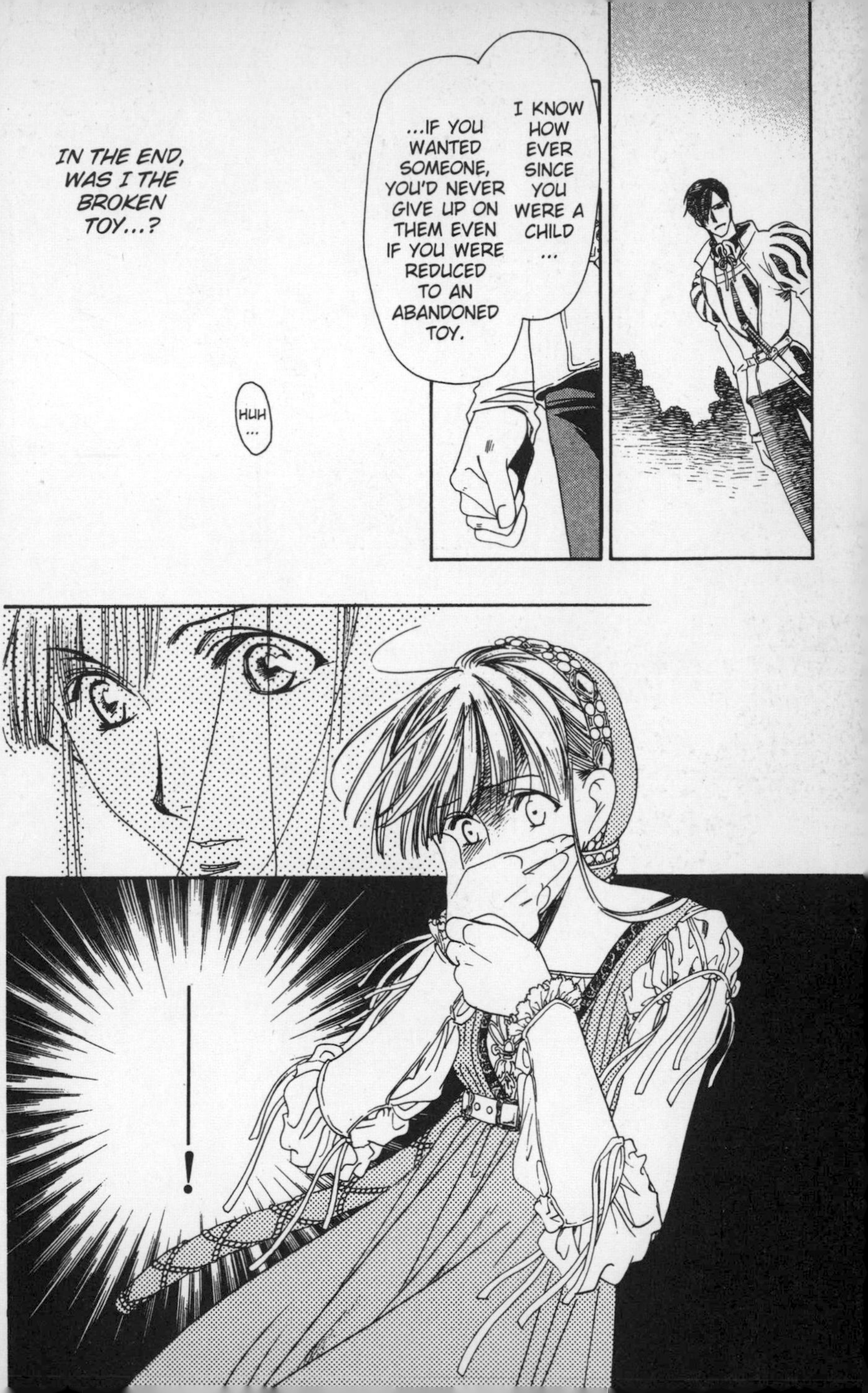

I KNOW HOW EVER SINCE YOU WERE A CHILD ...
...IF YOU WANTED SOMEONE, YOU'D NEVER GIVE UP ON THEM EVEN IF YOU WERE REDUCED TO AN ABANDONED TOY.
HUH ...
IN THE END, WAS I THE BROKEN TOY...?
!

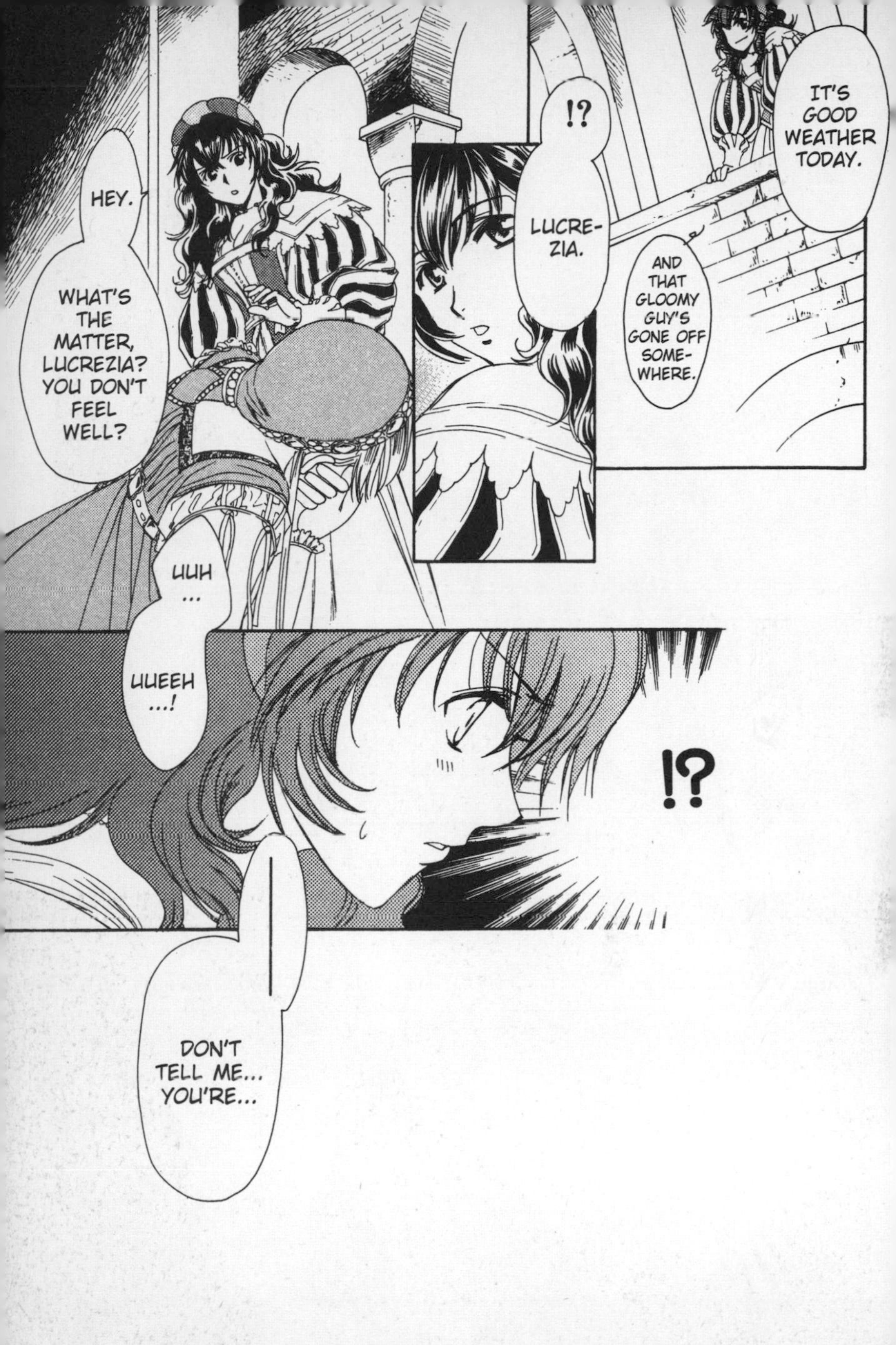
IT'S GOOD WEATHER TODAY.
AND THAT GLOOMY GUY'S GONE OFF SOME-WHERE.
!?
LUCRE-ZIA.
HEY.
WHAT'S THE MATTER, LUCREZIA? YOU DON'T FEEL WELL?
UUH...
UUEEH...!
!?
DON'T TELL ME... YOU'RE...

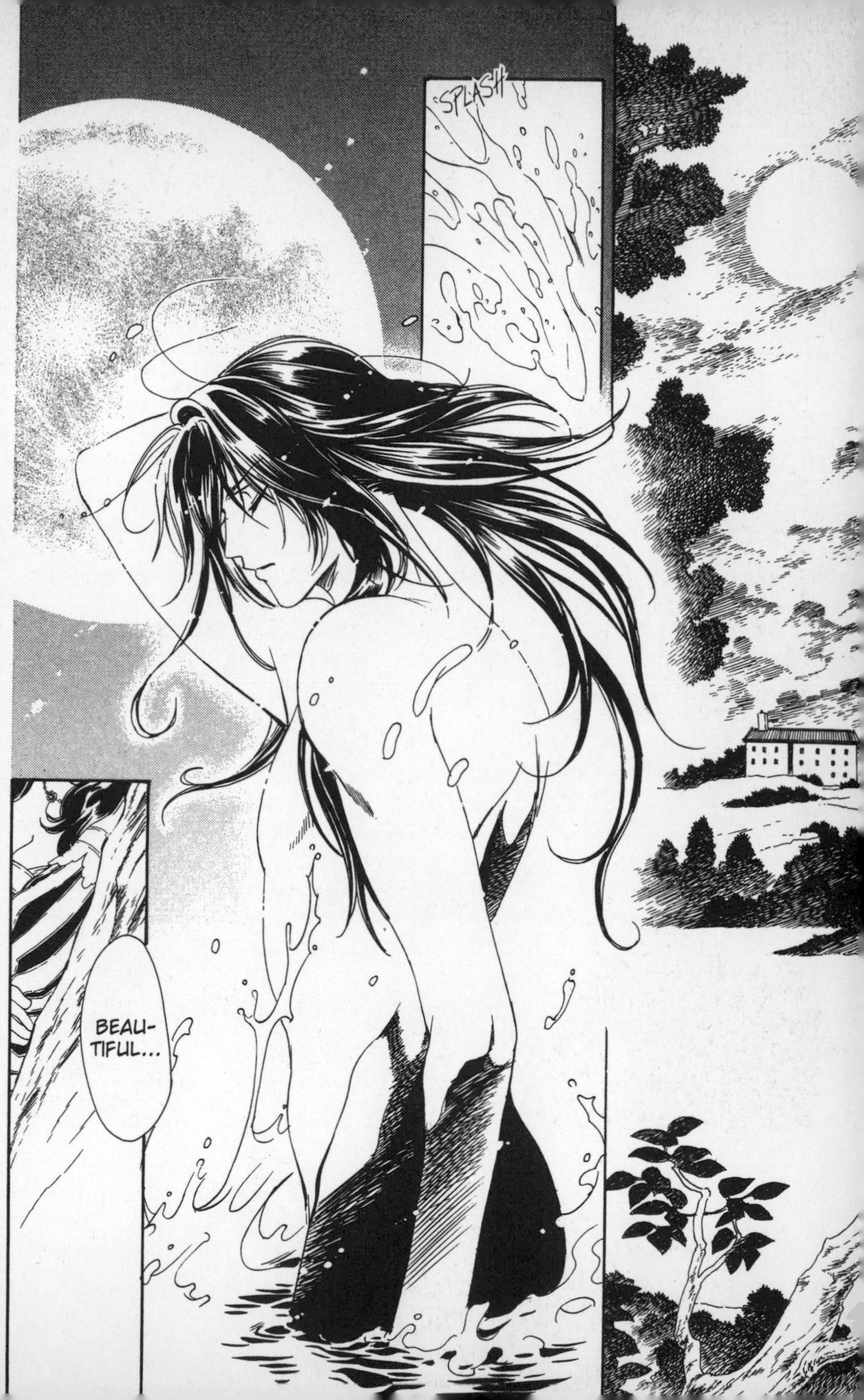
SPLASH
BEAU-TIFUL...

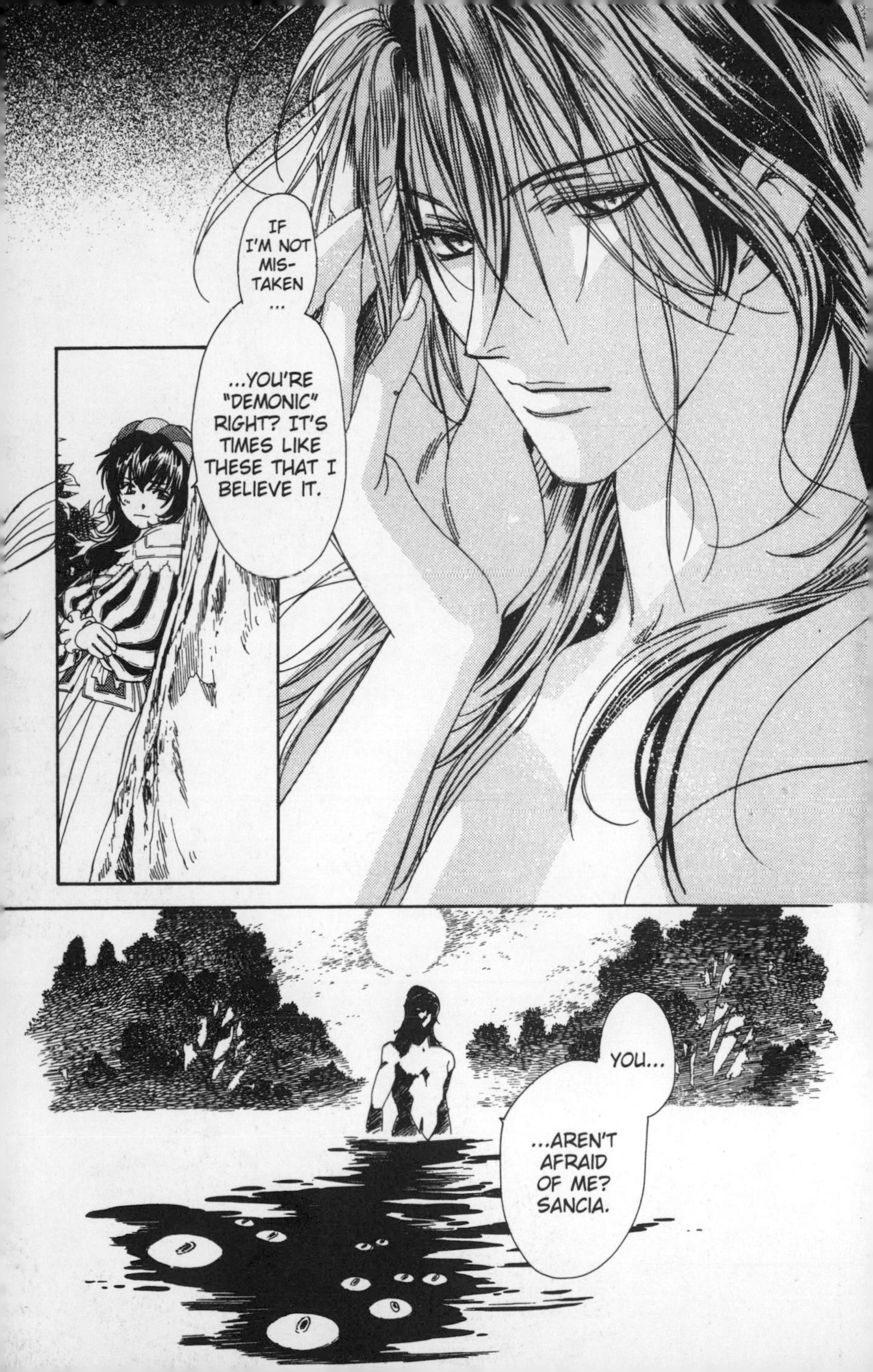
IF I'M NOT MIS-TAKEN ...
...YOU'RE "DEMONIC" RIGHT? IT'S TIMES LIKE THESE THAT I BELIEVE IT.
YOU...
...AREN'T AFRAID OF ME? SANCIA.

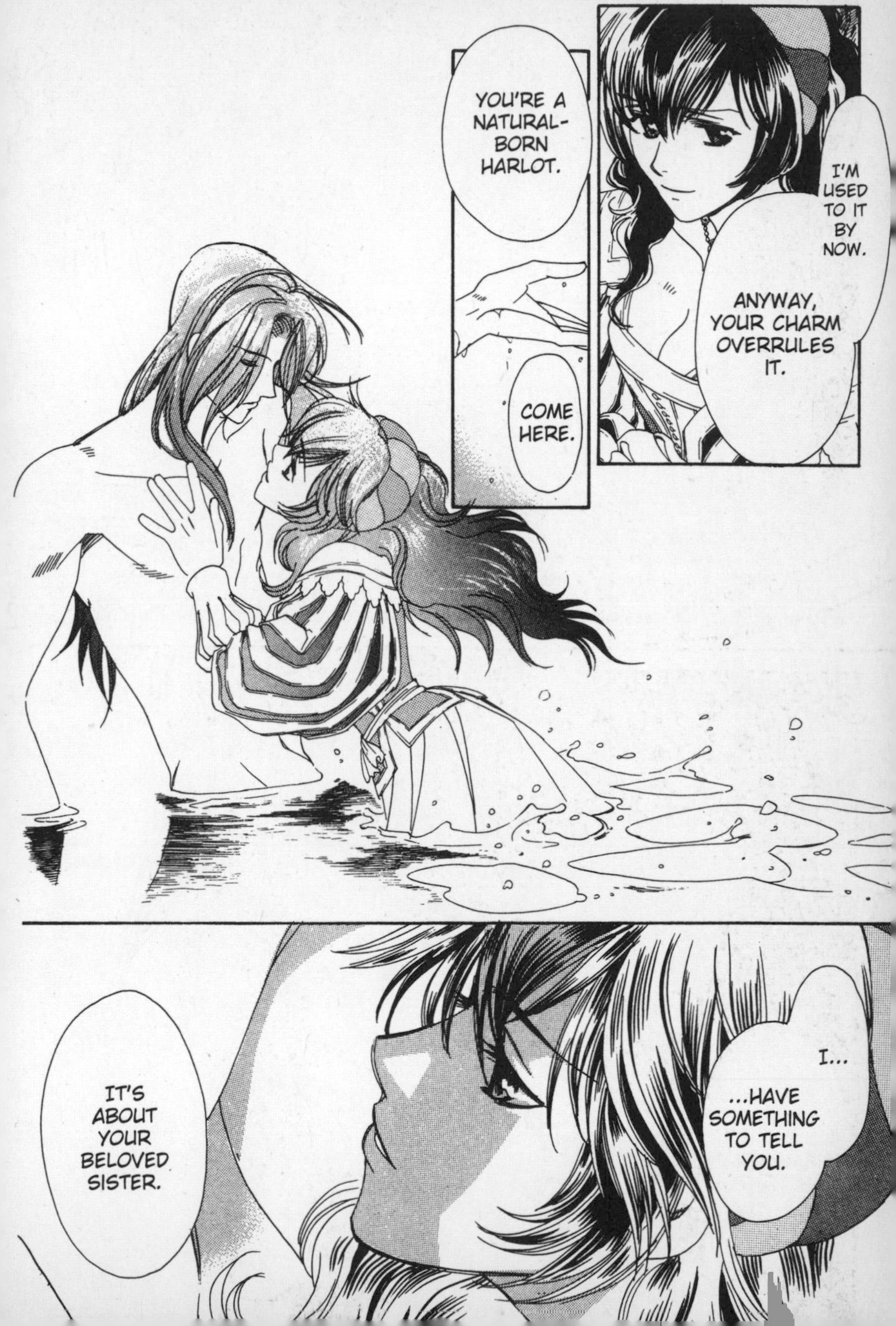
I'M USED TO IT BY NOW.
ANYWAY, YOUR CHARM OVERRULES IT.
YOU'RE A NATURAL-BORN HARLOT.
COME HERE.
I...
...HAVE SOMETHING TO TELL YOU.
IT'S ABOUT YOUR BELOVED SISTER.

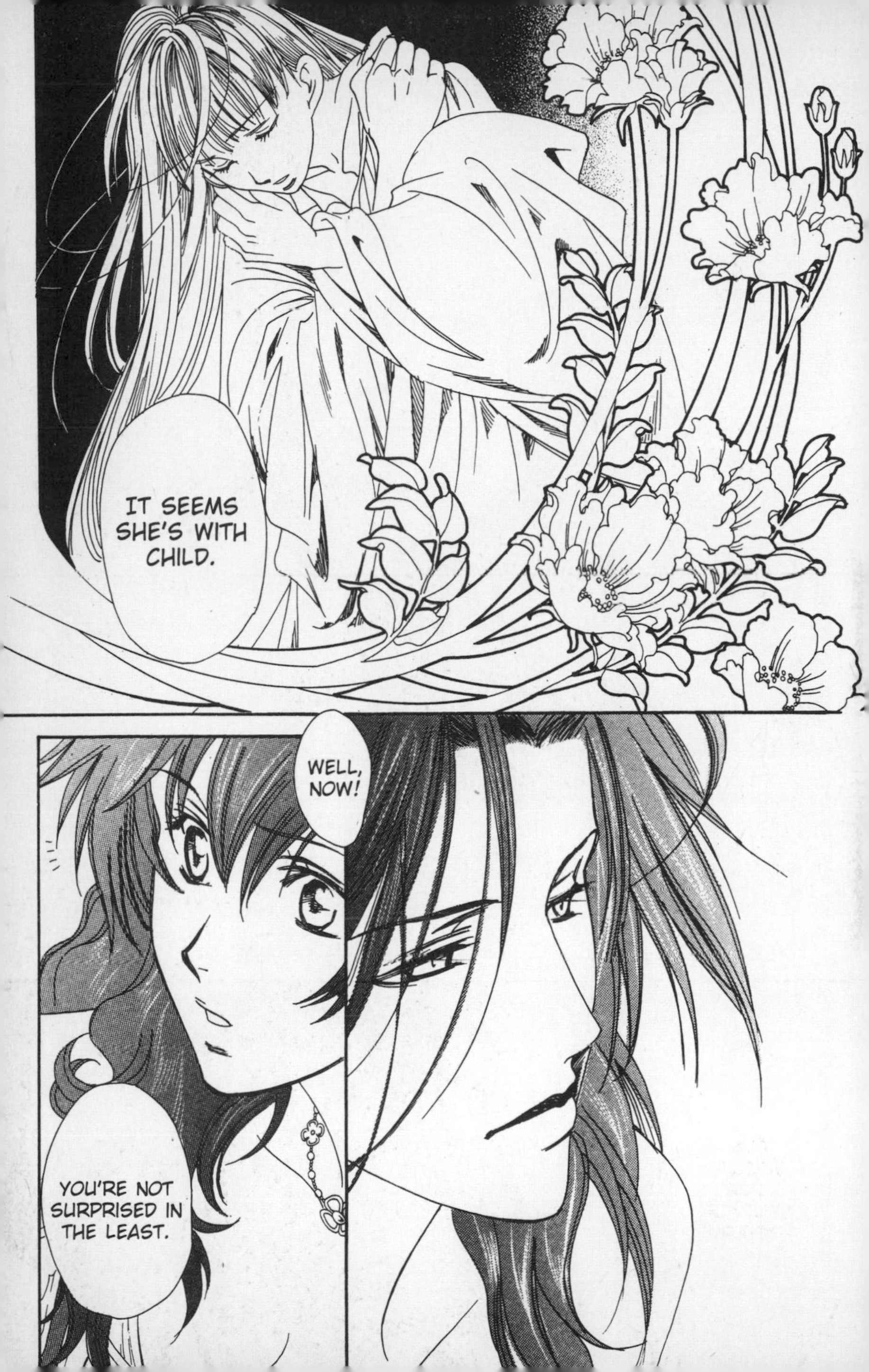
IT SEEMS SHE'S WITH CHILD.
WELL, NOW!
YOU'RE NOT SURPRISED IN THE LEAST.

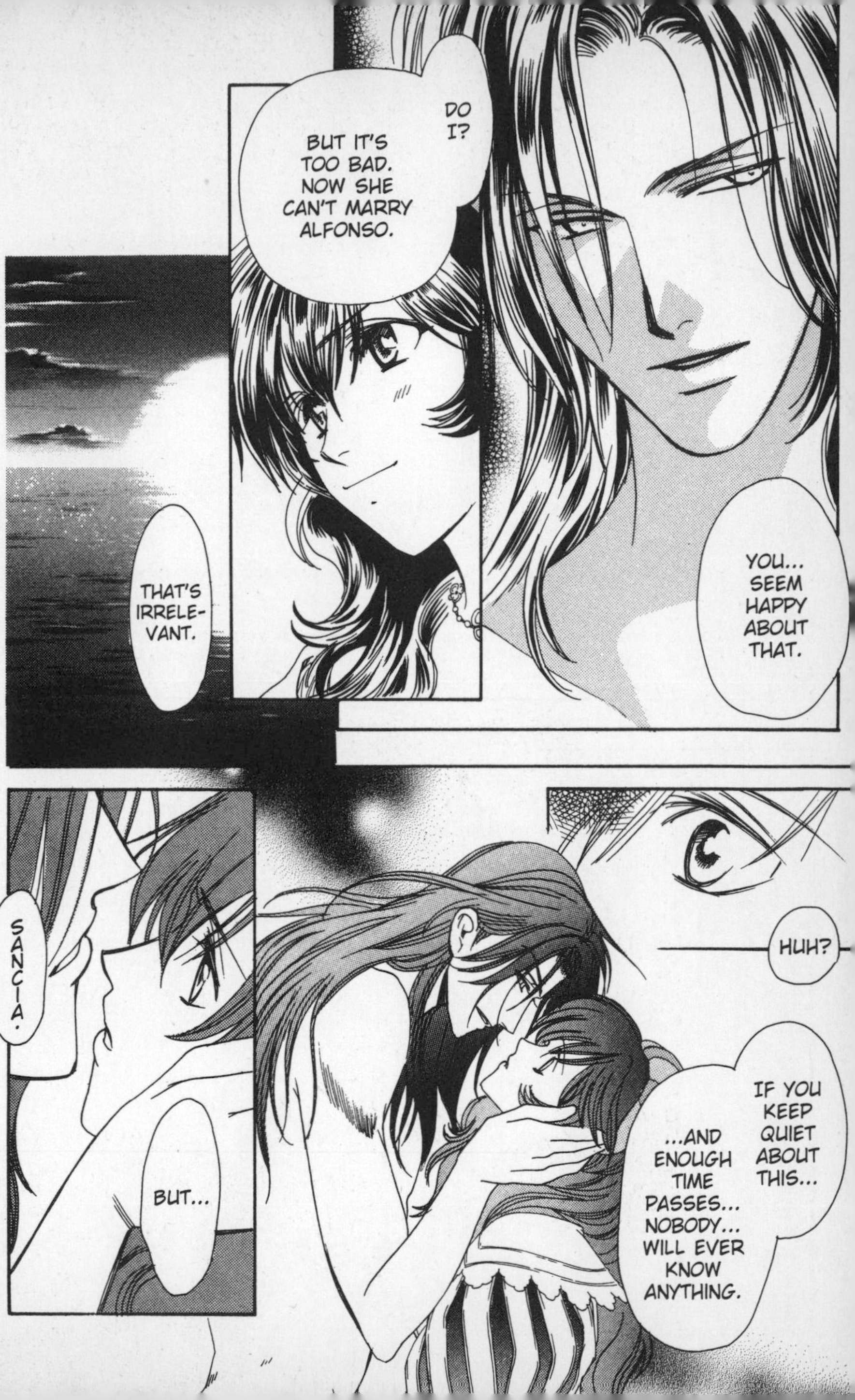
YOU... SEEM HAPPY ABOUT THAT.
DO I?
BUT IT'S TOO BAD. NOW SHE CAN'T MARRY ALFONSO.
THAT'S IRRELE-VANT.
HUH?
IF YOU KEEP QUIET ABOUT THIS...
...AND ENOUGH TIME PASSES... NOBODY... WILL EVER KNOW ANYTHING.
SANCIA.
BUT...

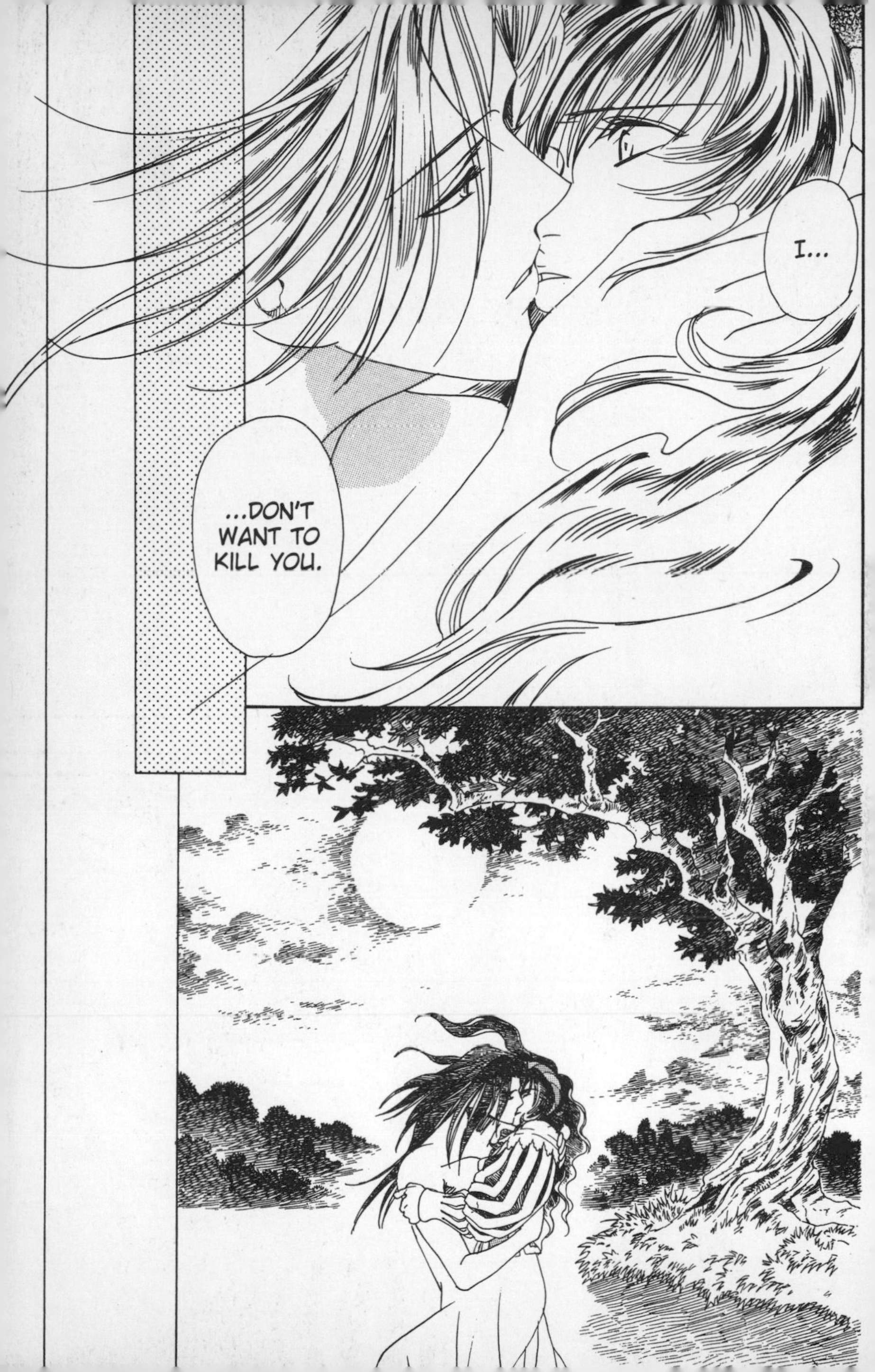
I...
...DON'T WANT TO KILL YOU.

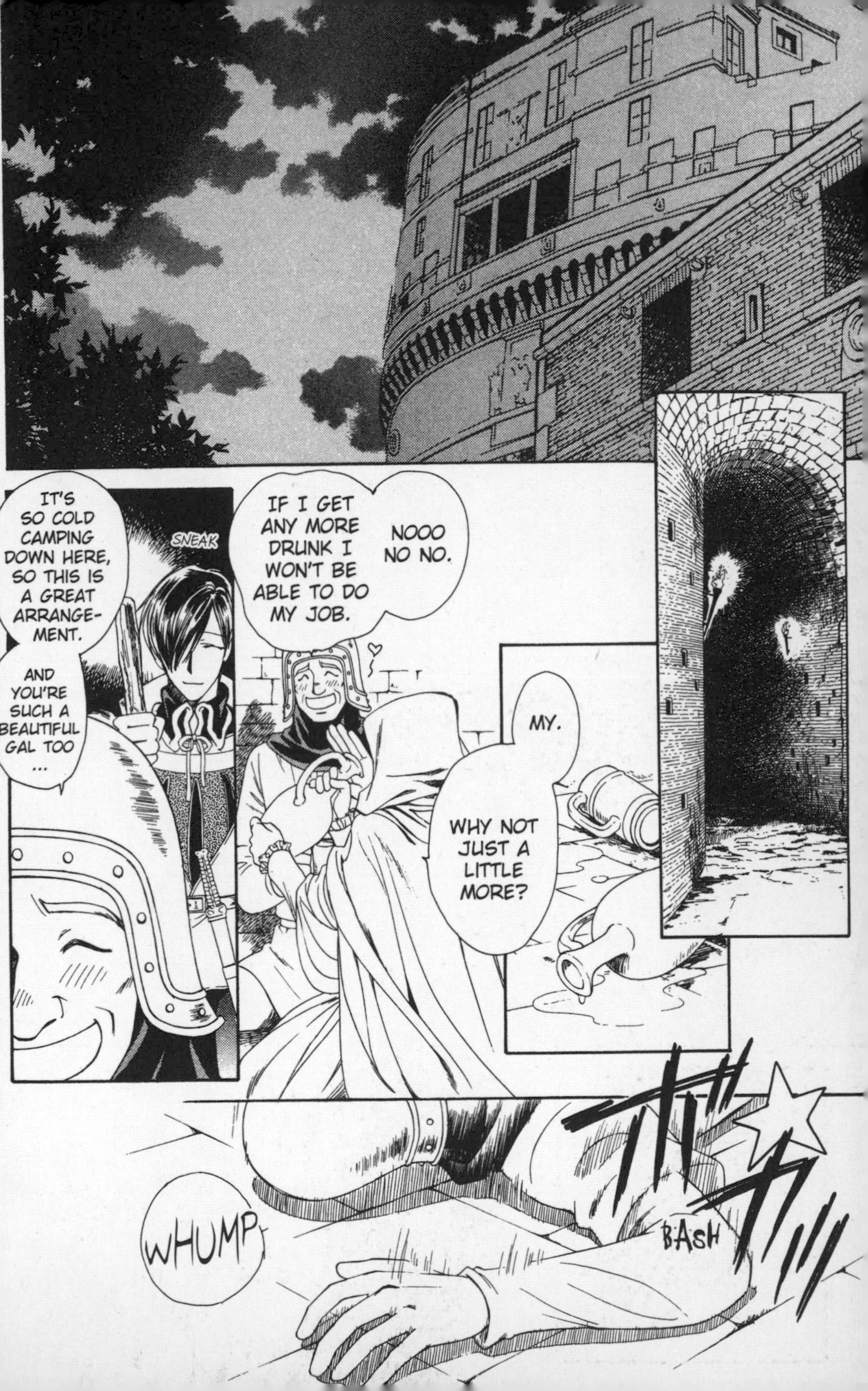
MY.
WHY NOT JUST A LITTLE MORE?
NOOO NO NO.
IF I GET ANY MORE DRUNK I WON'T BE ABLE TO DO MY JOB.
SNEAK
IT'S SO COLD CAMPING DOWN HERE, SO THIS IS A GREAT ARRANGE-MENT.
AND YOU'RE SUCH A BEAUTIFUL GAL TOO ...
BASH
WHUMP

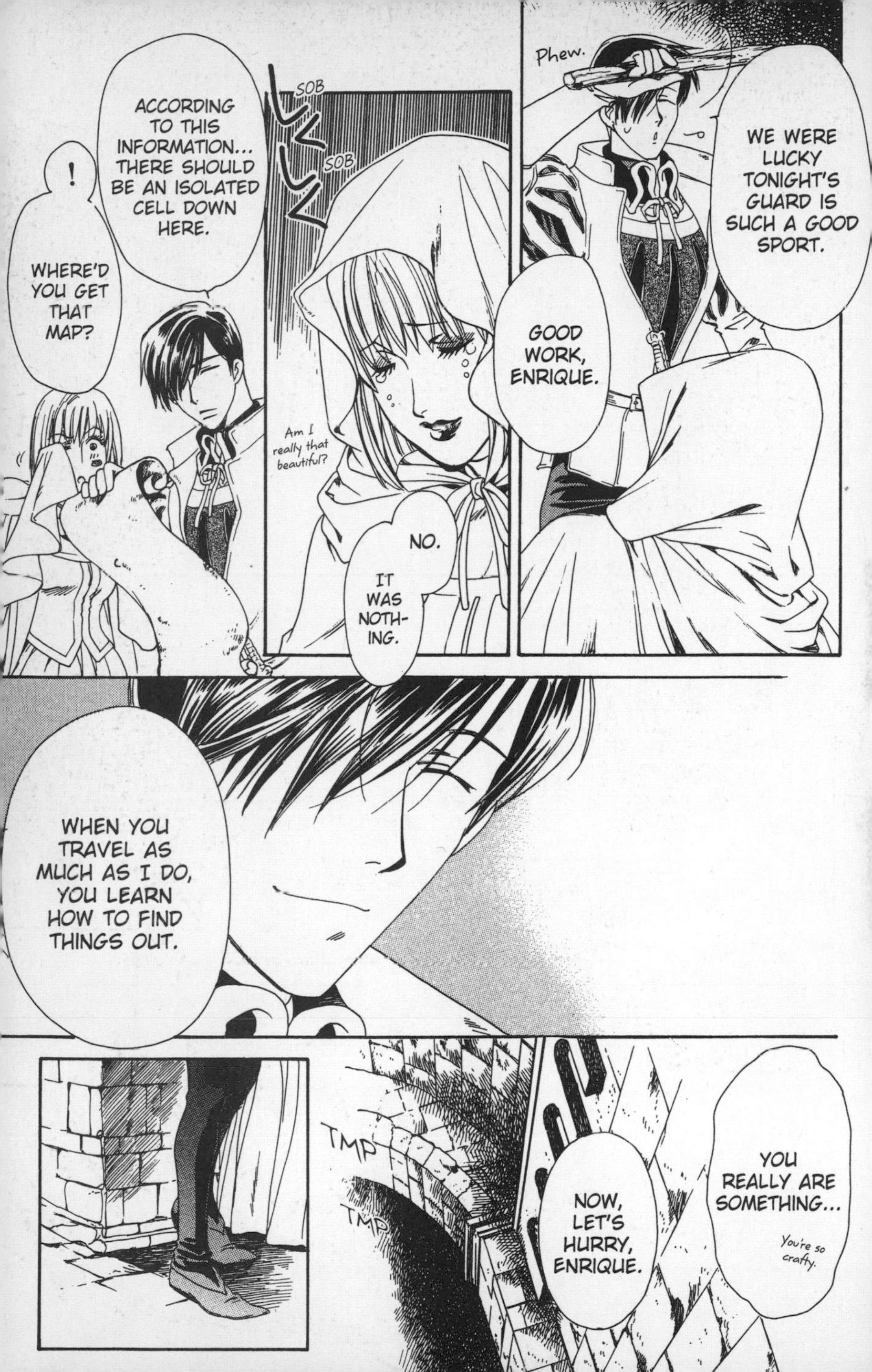

Phew.
WE WERE LUCKY TONIGHT'S GUARD IS SUCH A GOOD SPORT.
GOOD WORK, ENRIQUE.
SOB
SOB
Am I really that beautiful?
NO.
IT WAS NOTHING.
ACCORDING TO THIS INFORMATION... THERE SHOULD BE AN ISOLATED CELL DOWN HERE.
!
WHERE'D YOU GET THAT MAP?
WHEN YOU TRAVEL AS MUCH AS I DO, YOU LEARN HOW TO FIND THINGS OUT.
YOU REALLY ARE SOMETHING...
You're so crafty.
NOW, LET'S HURRY, ENRIQUE.
TMP
TMP

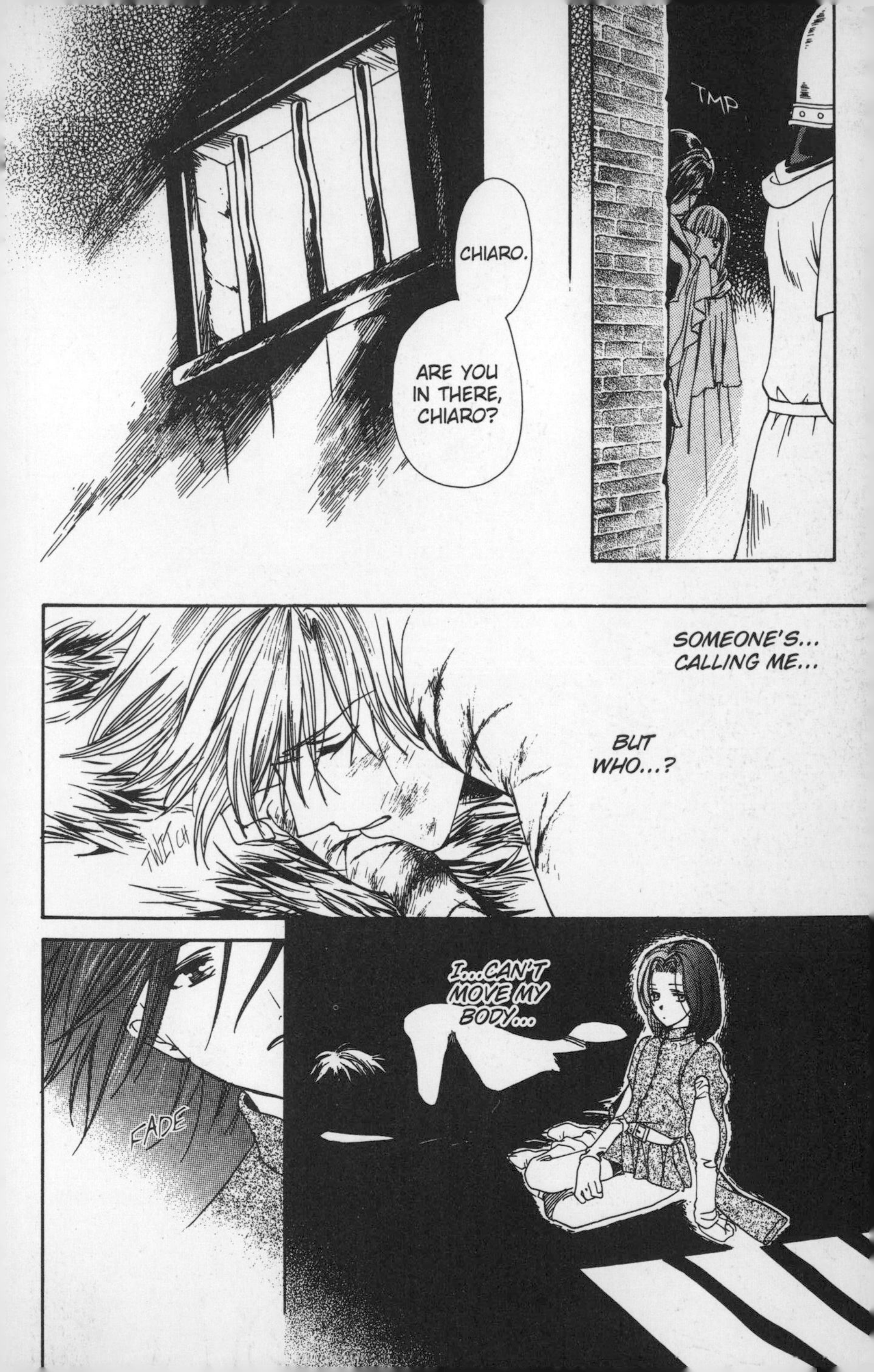
TMP
CHIARO.
ARE YOU IN THERE, CHIARO?
SOMEONE'S... CALLING ME...
BUT WHO...?
TWITCH
I...CAN'T MOVE MY BODY...
FADE

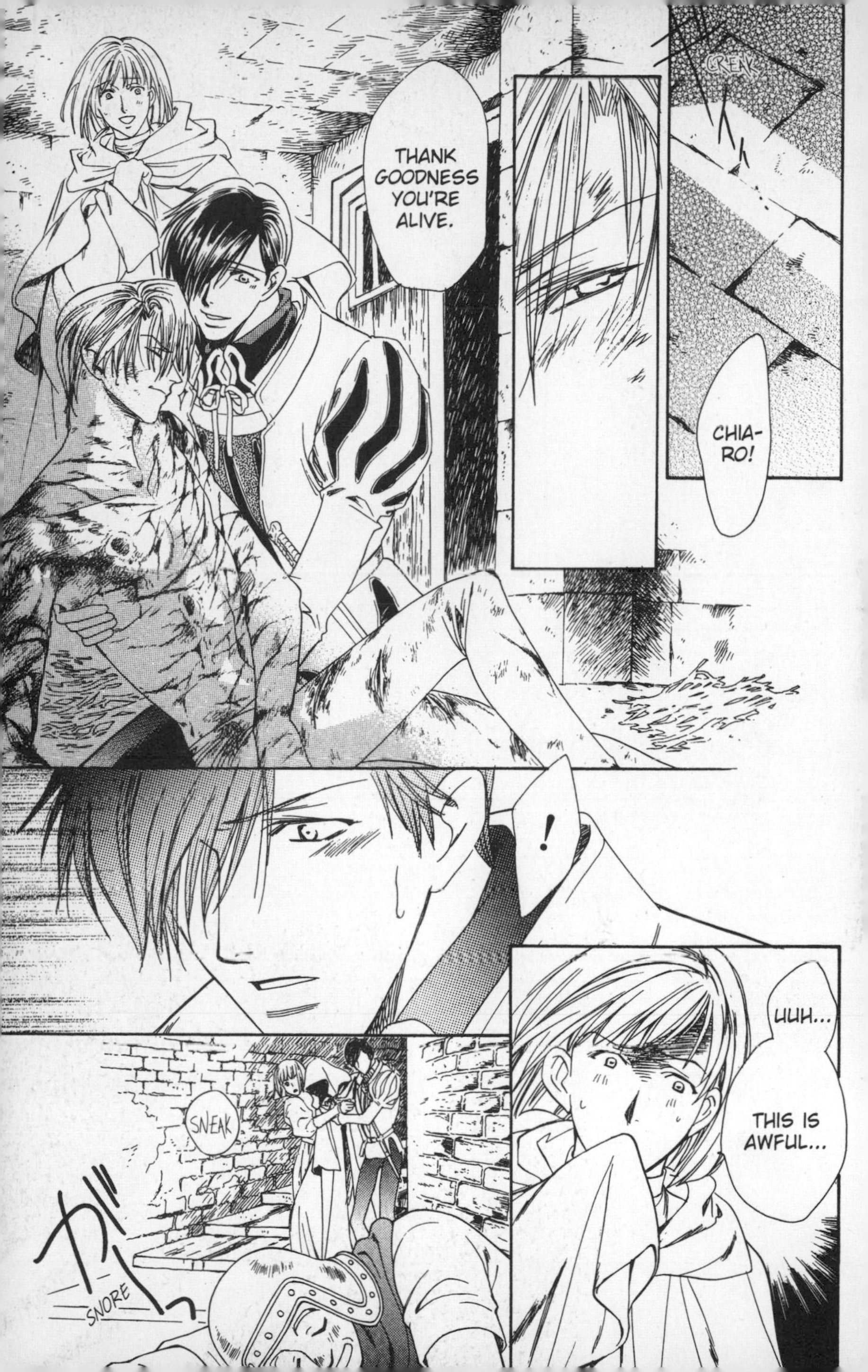
CREAK
CHIA-RO!
THANK GOODNESS YOU'RE ALIVE.
!
UUH...
THIS IS AWFUL...
SNEAK
SNORE

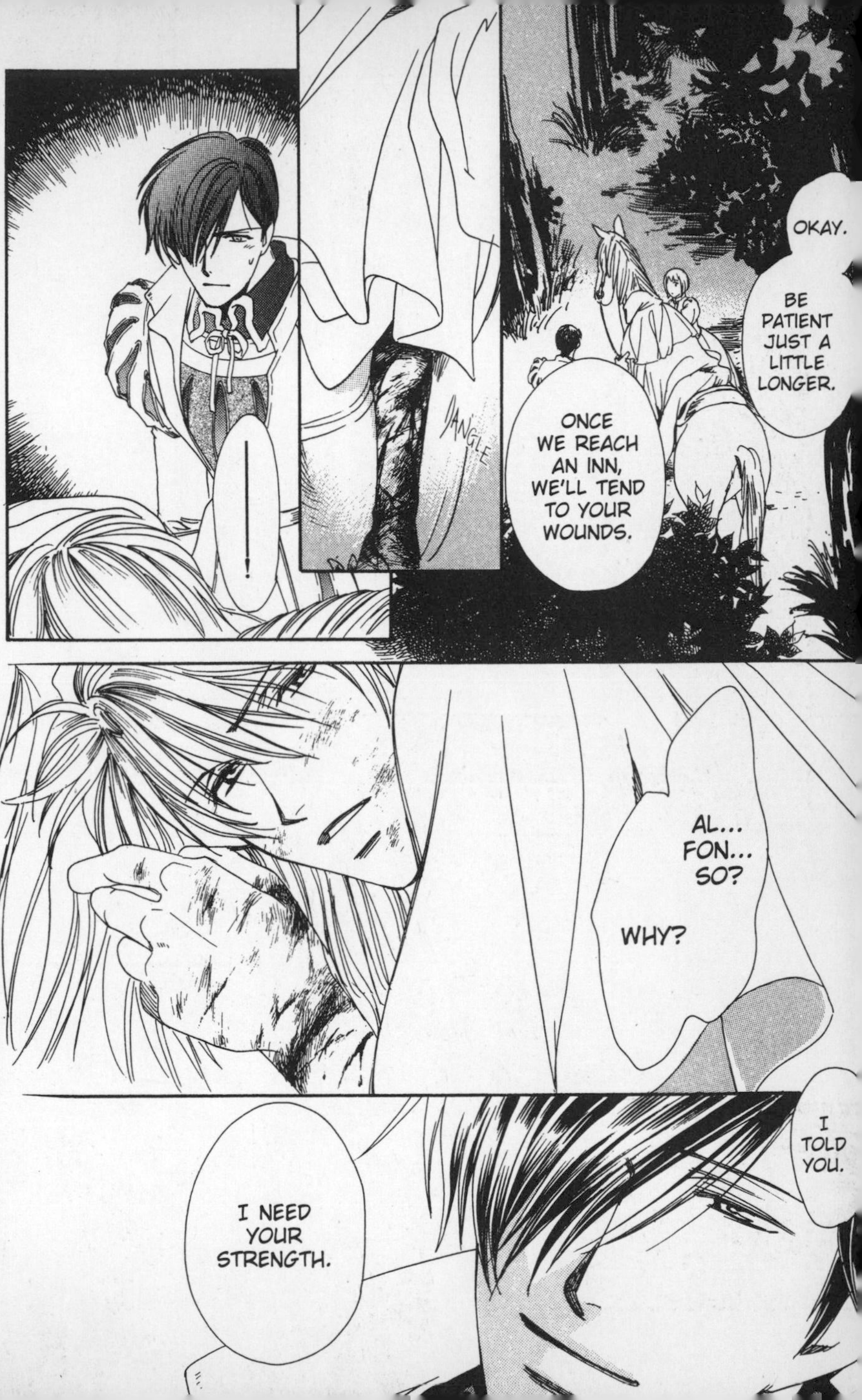
OKAY.
BE PATIENT JUST A LITTLE LONGER.
ONCE WE REACH AN INN, WE'LL TEND TO YOUR WOUNDS.
DANGLE
...!
AL... FON... SO?
WHY?
I TOLD YOU.
I NEED YOUR STRENGTH.

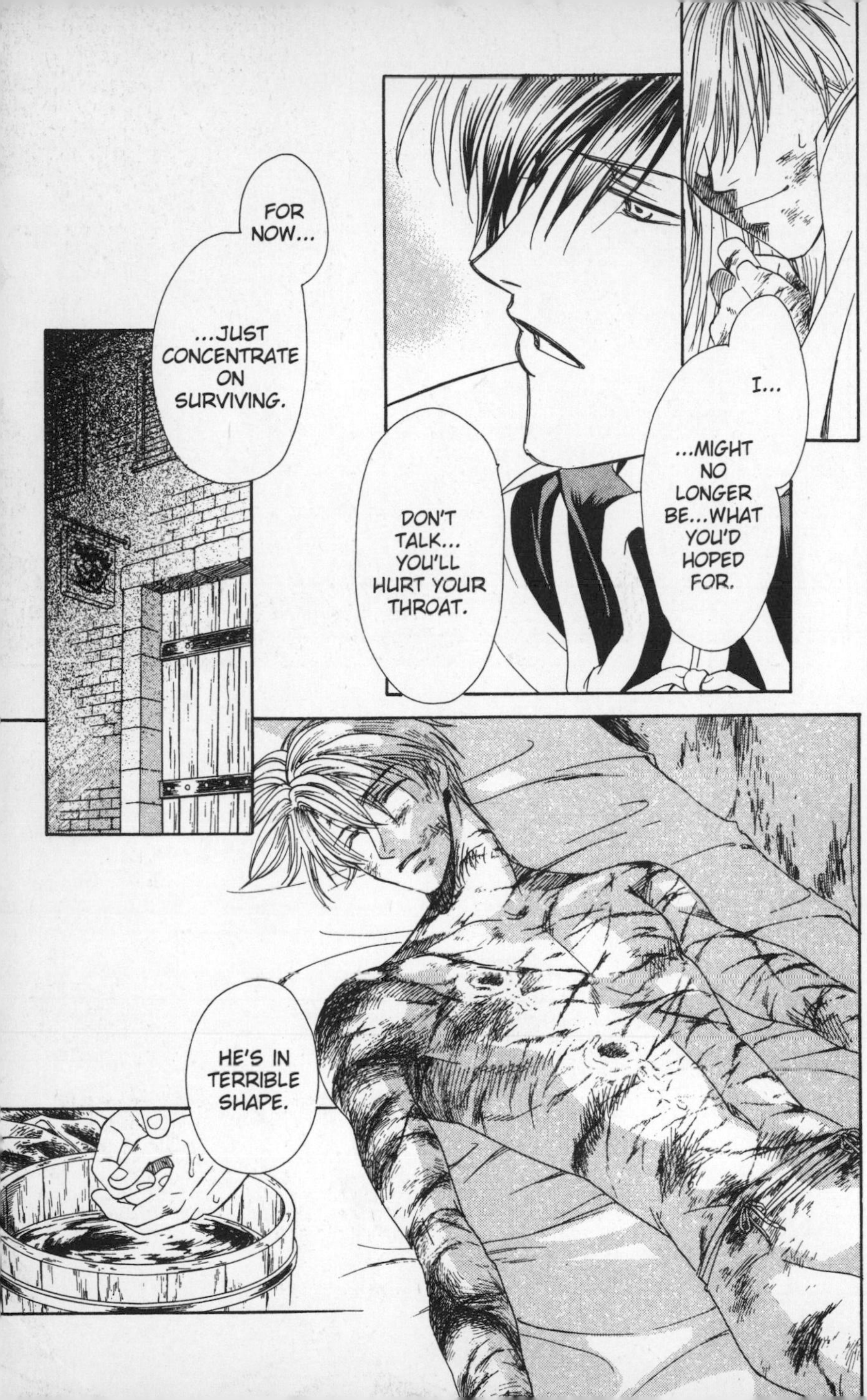
I...
...MIGHT NO LONGER BE...WHAT YOU'D HOPED FOR.
DON'T TALK... YOU'LL HURT YOUR THROAT.
FOR NOW...
...JUST CONCENTRATE ON SURVIVING.
HE'S IN TERRIBLE SHAPE.

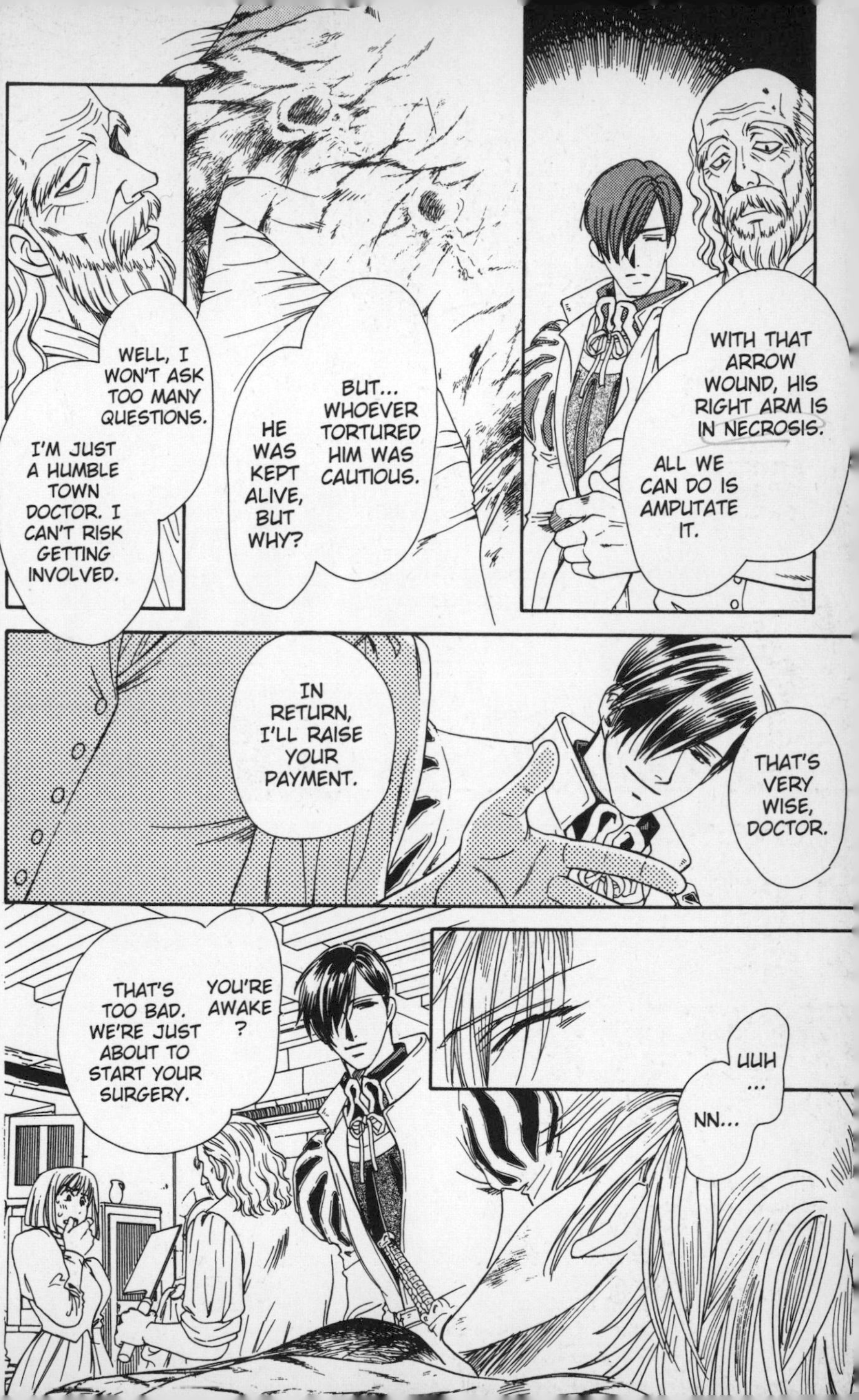
WITH THAT ARROW WOUND, HIS RIGHT ARM IS IN NECROSIS.
ALL WE CAN DO IS AMPUTATE IT.
BUT... WHOEVER TORTURED HIM WAS CAUTIOUS.
HE WAS KEPT ALIVE, BUT WHY?
WELL, I WON'T ASK TOO MANY QUESTIONS.
I'M JUST A HUMBLE TOWN DOCTOR. I CAN'T RISK GETTING INVOLVED.
THAT'S VERY WISE, DOCTOR.
IN RETURN, I'LL RAISE YOUR PAYMENT.
UUH ...
NN...
YOU'RE AWAKE?
THAT'S TOO BAD. WE'RE JUST ABOUT TO START YOUR SURGERY.

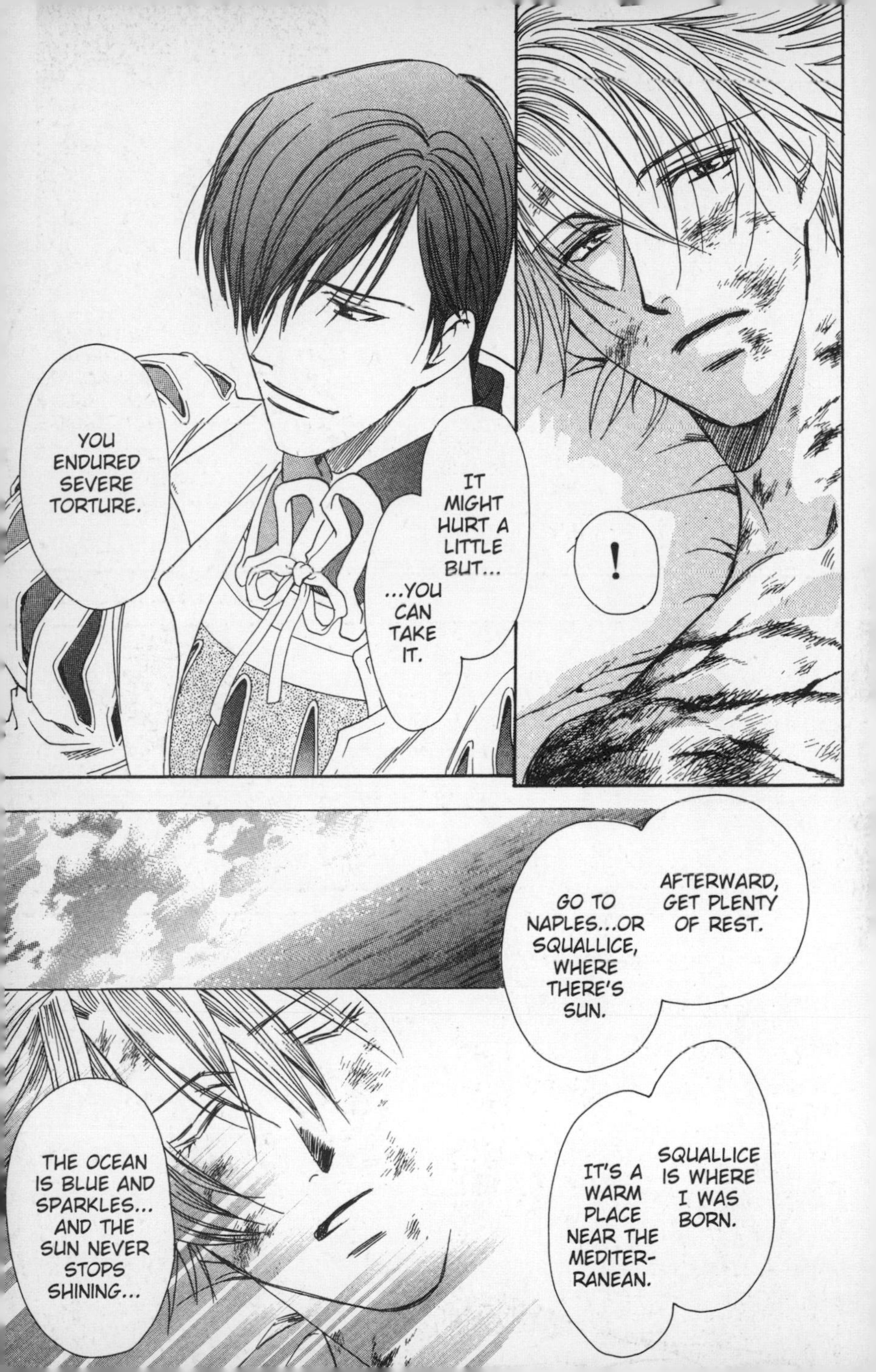
!
IT MIGHT HURT A LITTLE BUT...
...YOU CAN TAKE IT.
YOU ENDURED SEVERE TORTURE.
AFTERWARD, GET PLENTY OF REST.
GO TO NAPLES...OR SQUALLICE, WHERE THERE'S SUN.
SQUALLICE IS WHERE I WAS BORN.
IT'S A WARM PLACE NEAR THE MEDITER-RANEAN.
THE OCEAN IS BLUE AND SPARKLES... AND THE SUN NEVER STOPS SHINING...

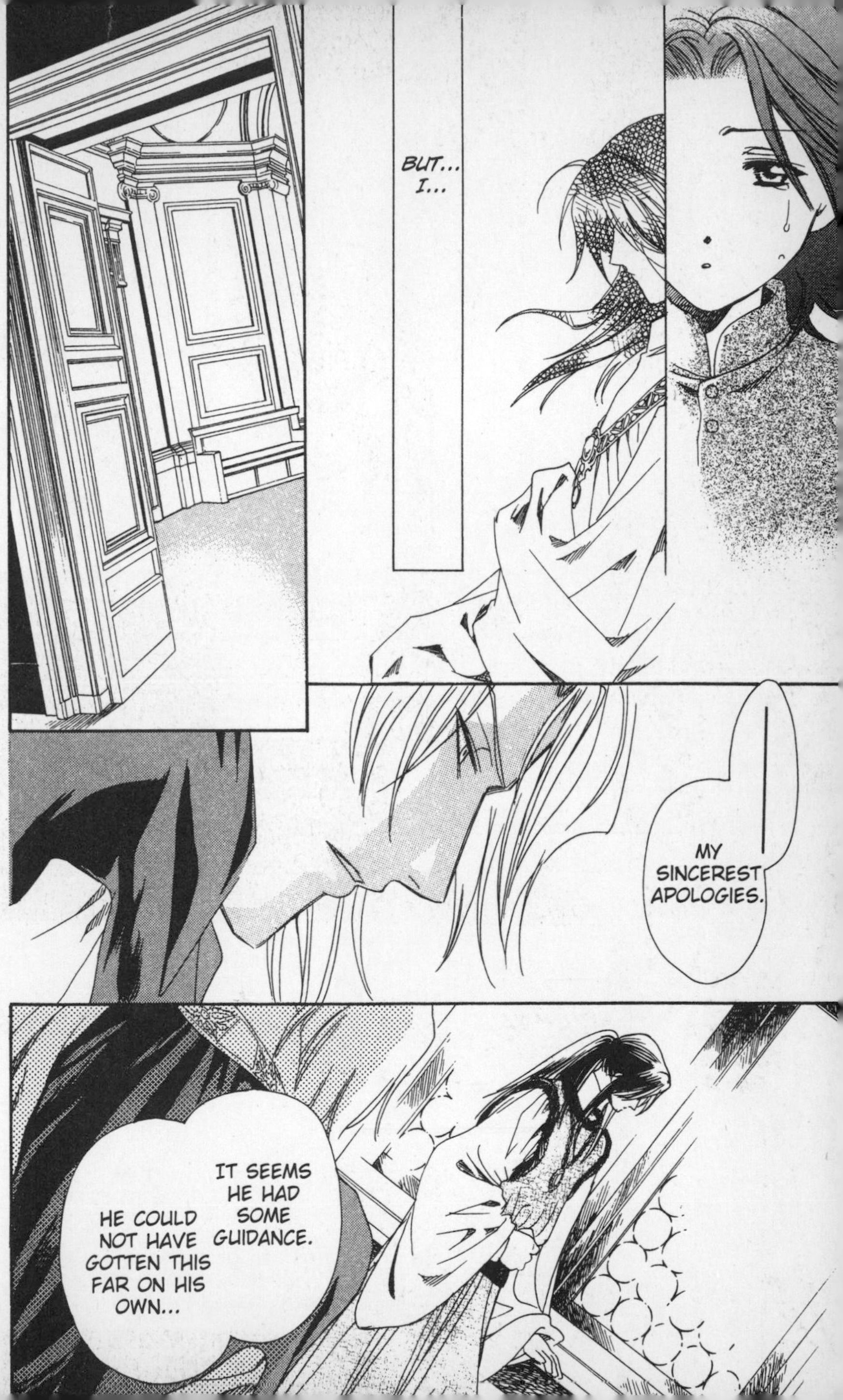
BUT... I...
MY SINCEREST APOLOGIES.
IT SEEMS HE HAD SOME GUIDANCE.
HE COULD NOT HAVE GOTTEN THIS FAR ON HIS OWN...

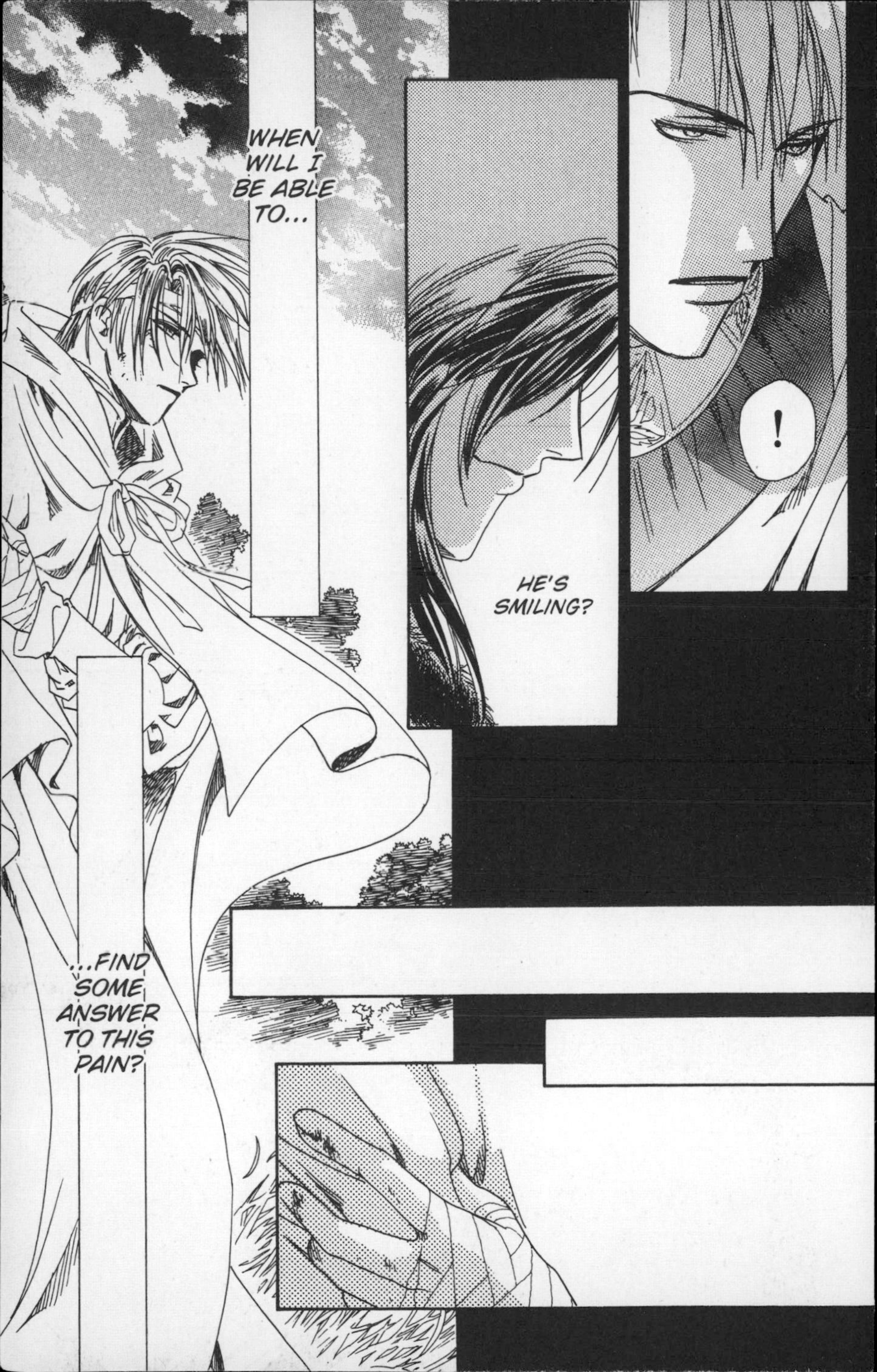
!
HE'S SMILING?
WHEN WILL I BE ABLE TO...
...FIND SOME ANSWER TO THIS PAIN?

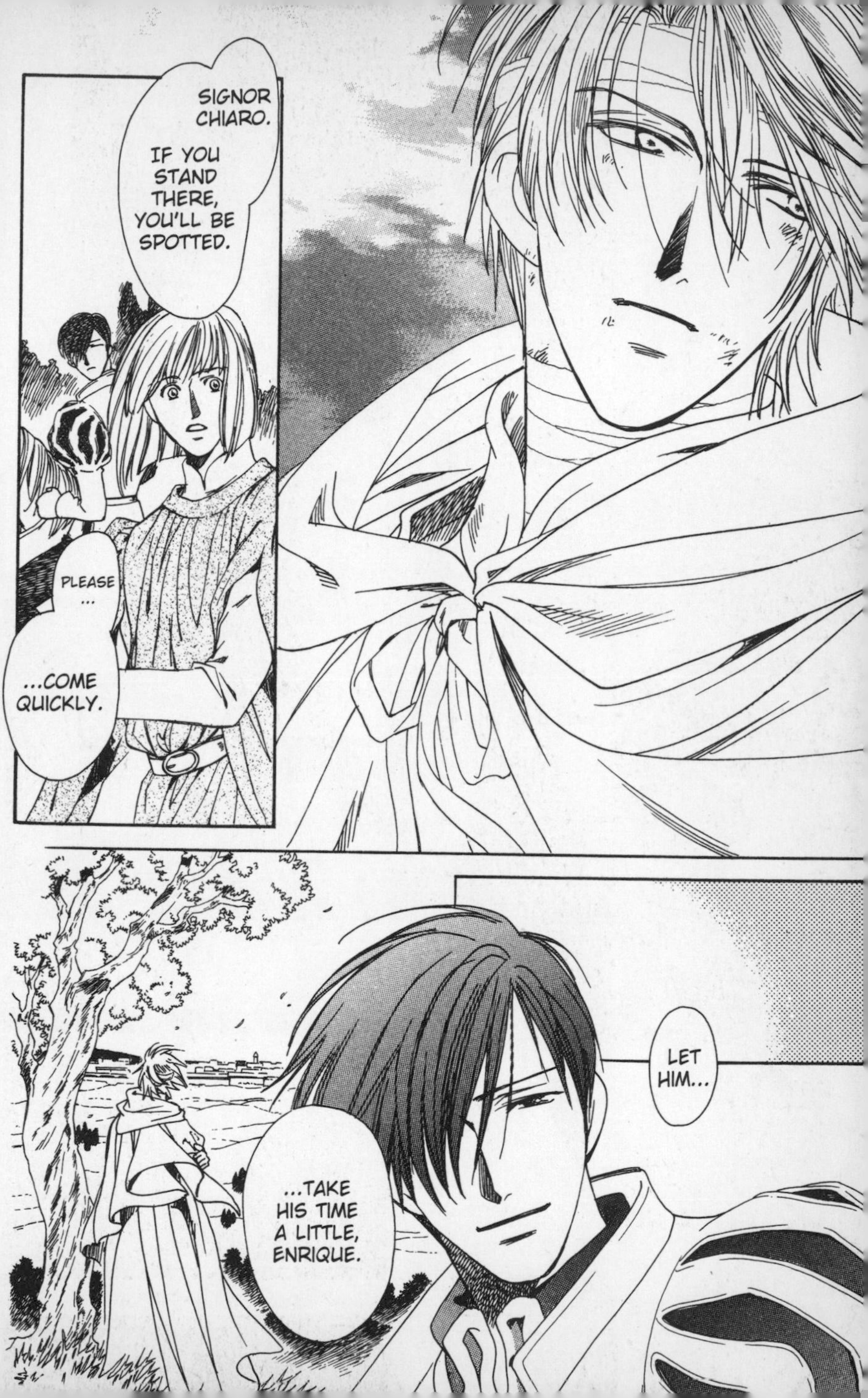
SIGNOR CHIARO.
IF YOU STAND THERE, YOU'LL BE SPOTTED.
PLEASE ...
...COME QUICKLY.
LET HIM...
...TAKE HIS TIME A LITTLE, ENRIQUE.

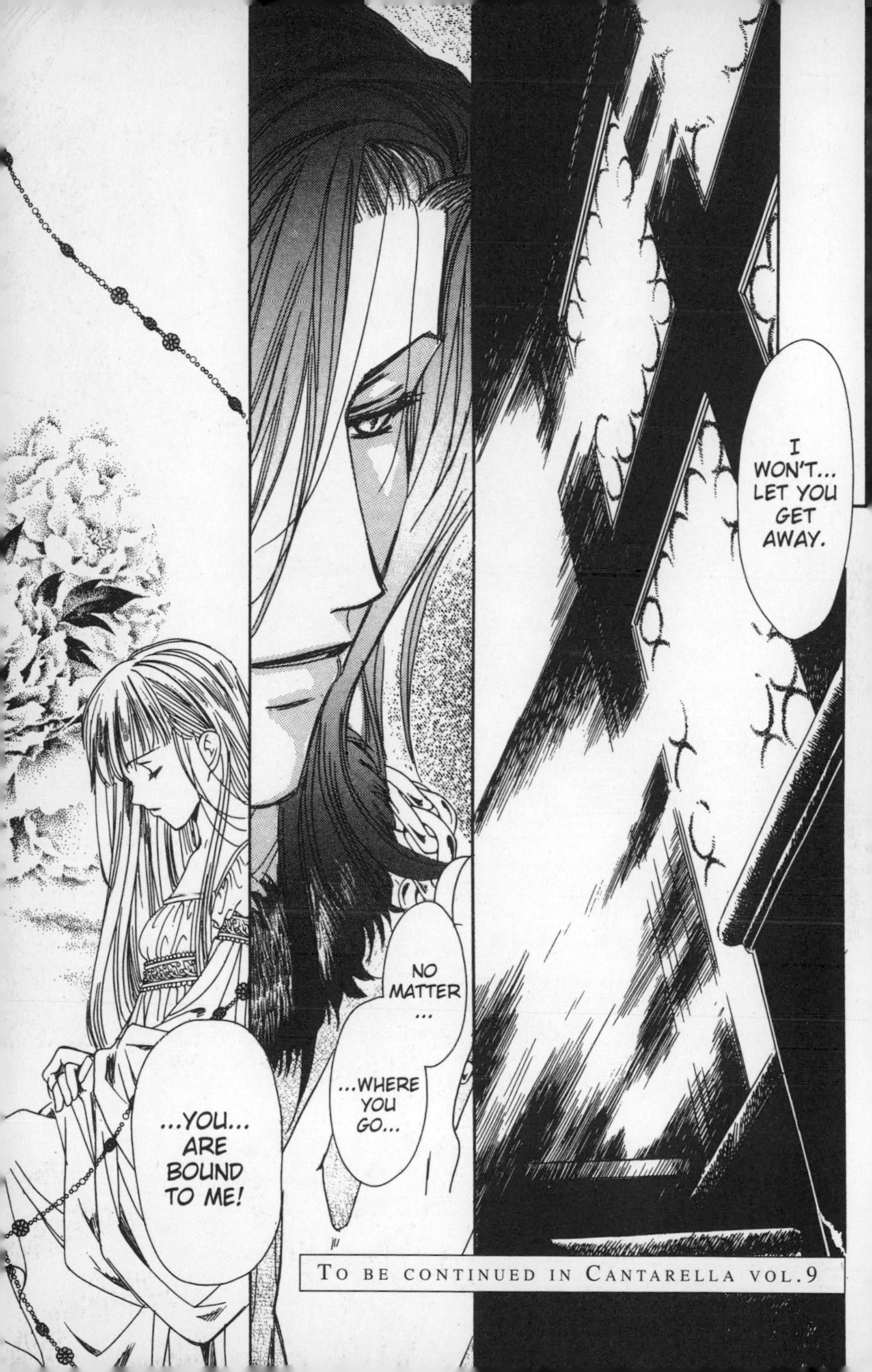
I WON'T... LET YOU GET AWAY.
NO MATTER ...
...WHERE YOU GO...
...YOU... ARE BOUND TO ME!
TO BE CONTINUED IN CANTARELLA VOL. 9

Special Thanks

Naoko Nakatsuji-san, Izumi Hijiri-san, Wakusa
Miyakoshi-san, Mitsuru Fuyutsuki-san, Akiyoshi-san,
Asakura-san, Yuki Koryu-san, Akito Aizawa-san,
Kana Kitahara-san, my chief Oda, my manager
Y-sama, and the Princess editorial staff.

Address for letters ♥:

YOU HIGURI
c/o Audry Taylor
Go! Media Entertainment, LLC
5737 Kanan Rd. #591
Agoura Hills CA 91301

Or visit her official website in English at:
http://www.youhiguri.com

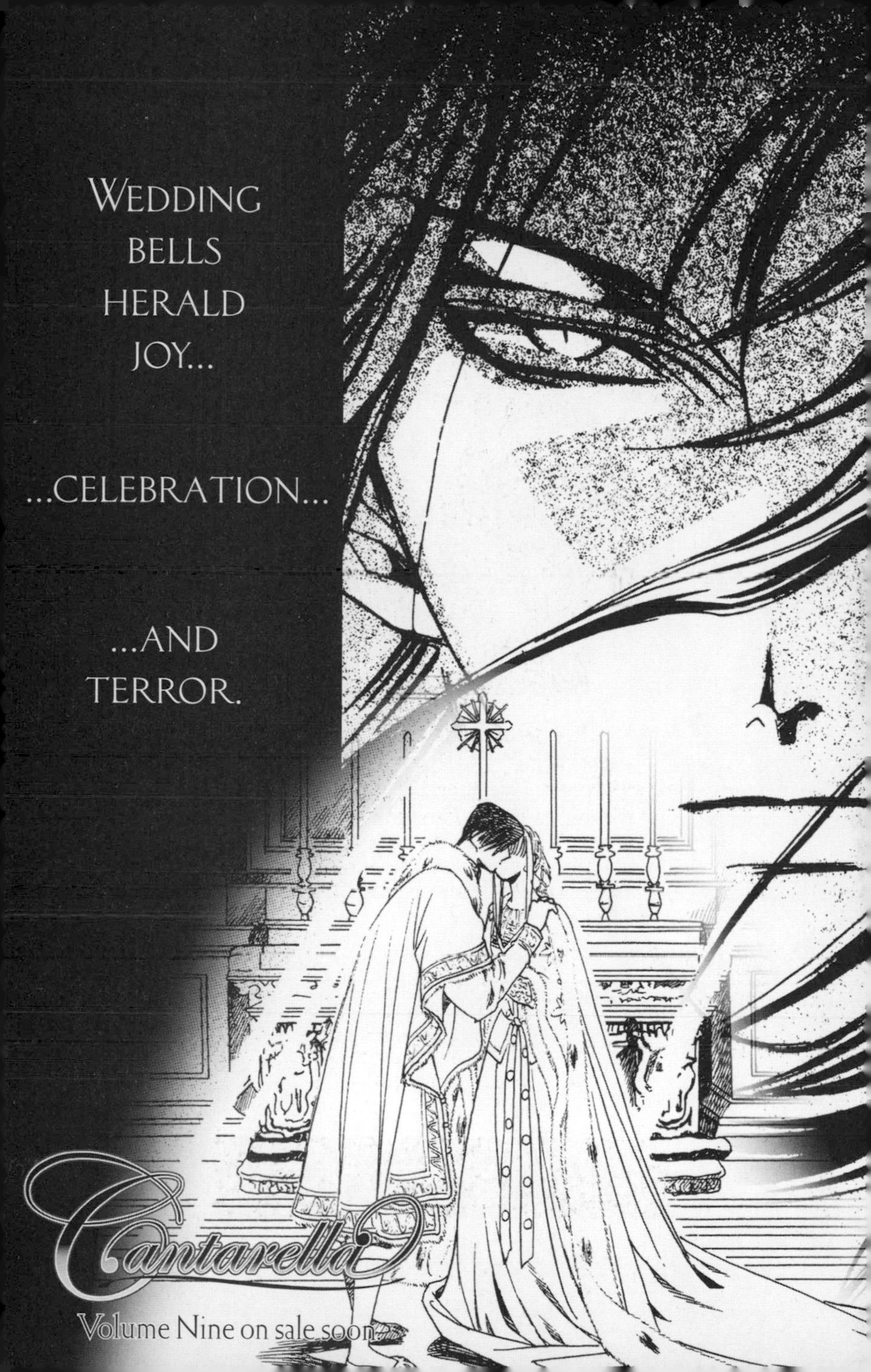
WEDDING BELLS HERALD JOY...
...CELEBRATION...
...AND TERROR.
Cantarella
Volume Nine on sale soon!

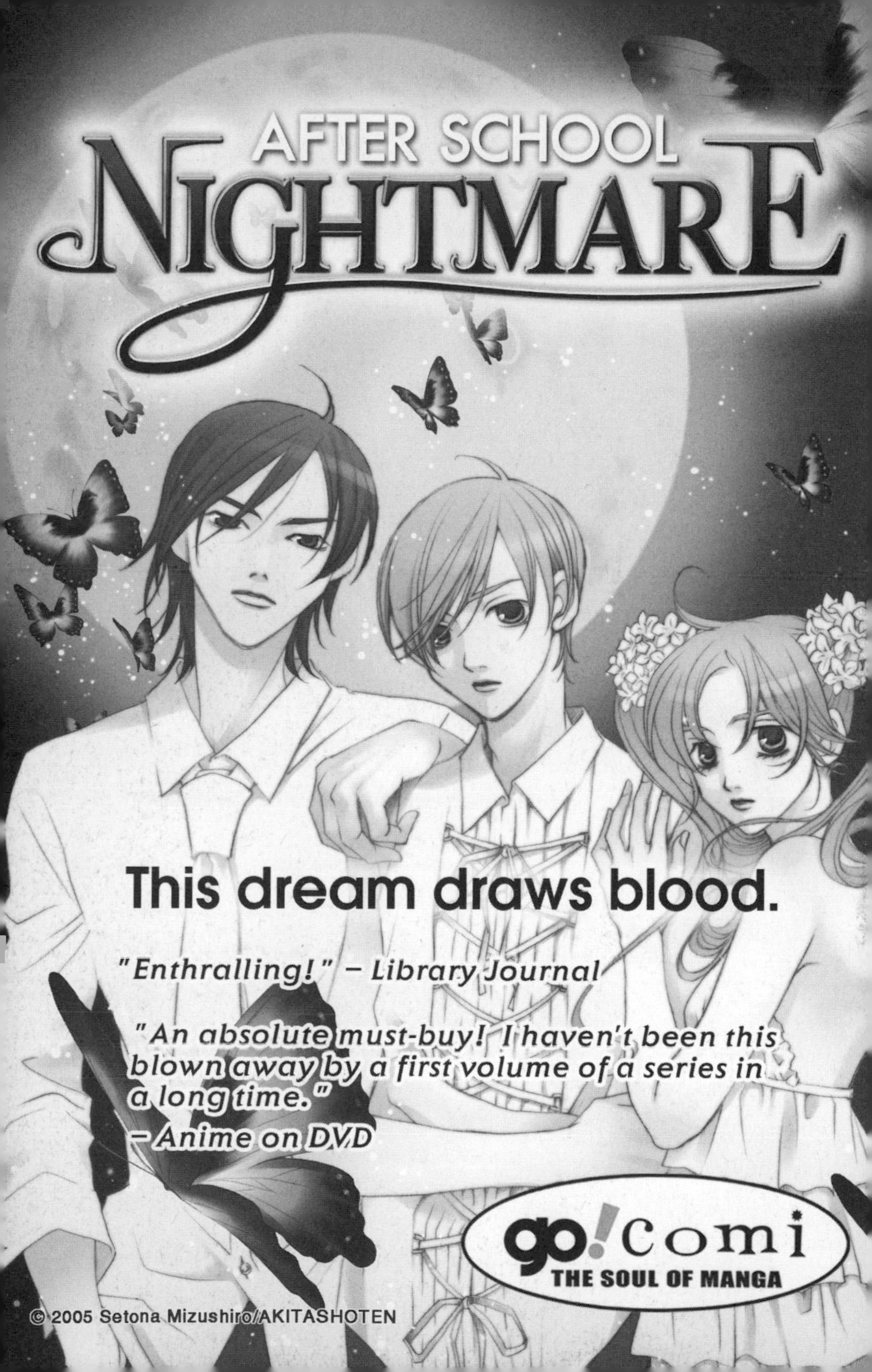
AFTER SCHOOL
NIGHTMARE
This dream draws blood.
"Enthralling!" – Library Journal
"An absolute must-buy! I haven't been this blown away by a first volume of a series in a long time."
– Anime on DVD
go!comi
THE SOUL OF MANGA
© 2005 Setona Mizushiro/AKITASHOTEN

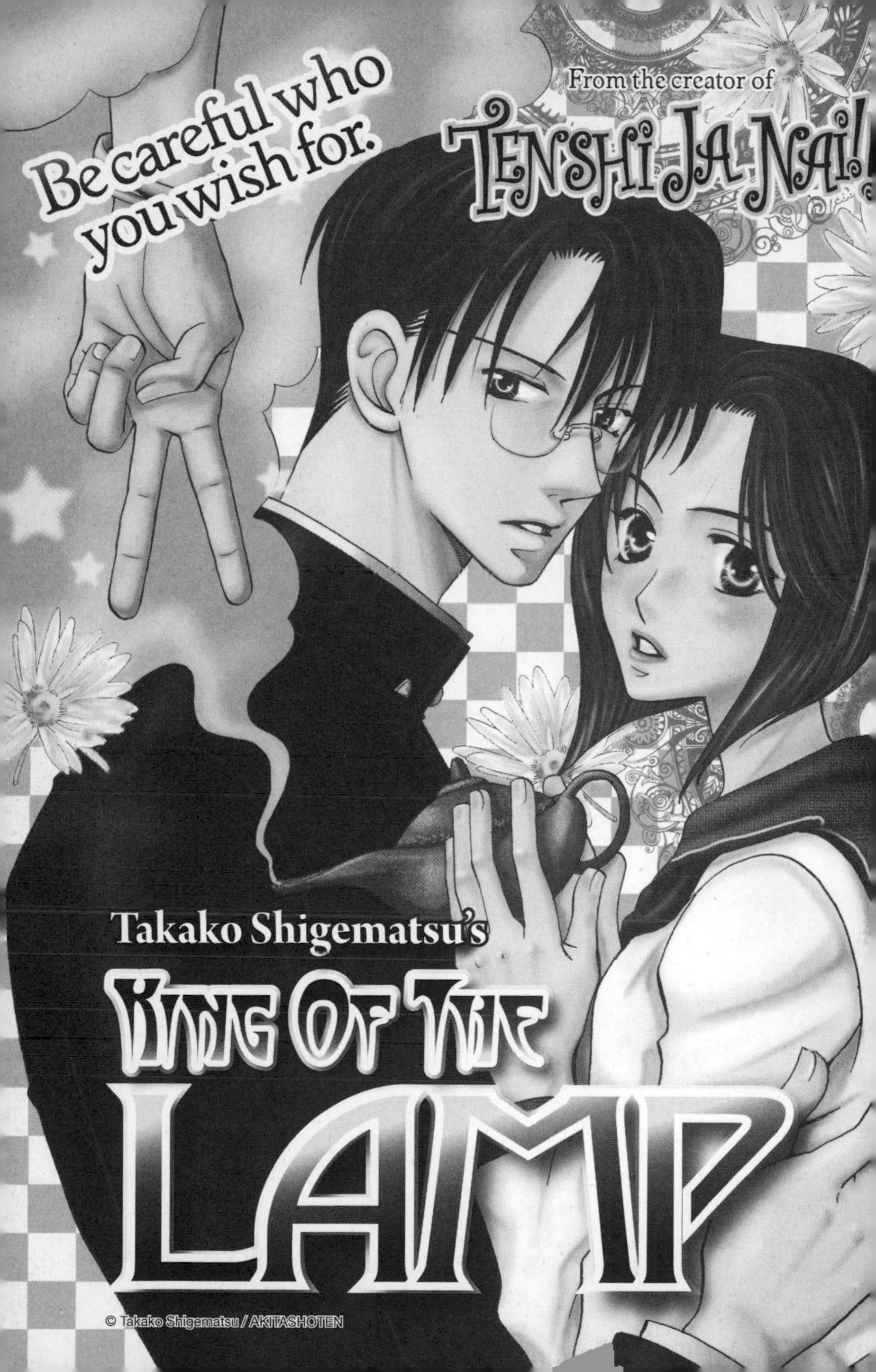
Be careful who you wish for.
From the creator of
TENSHI JA NAI!
Takako Shigematsu's
KING OF THE LAMP
© Takako Shigematsu / AKITASHOTEN

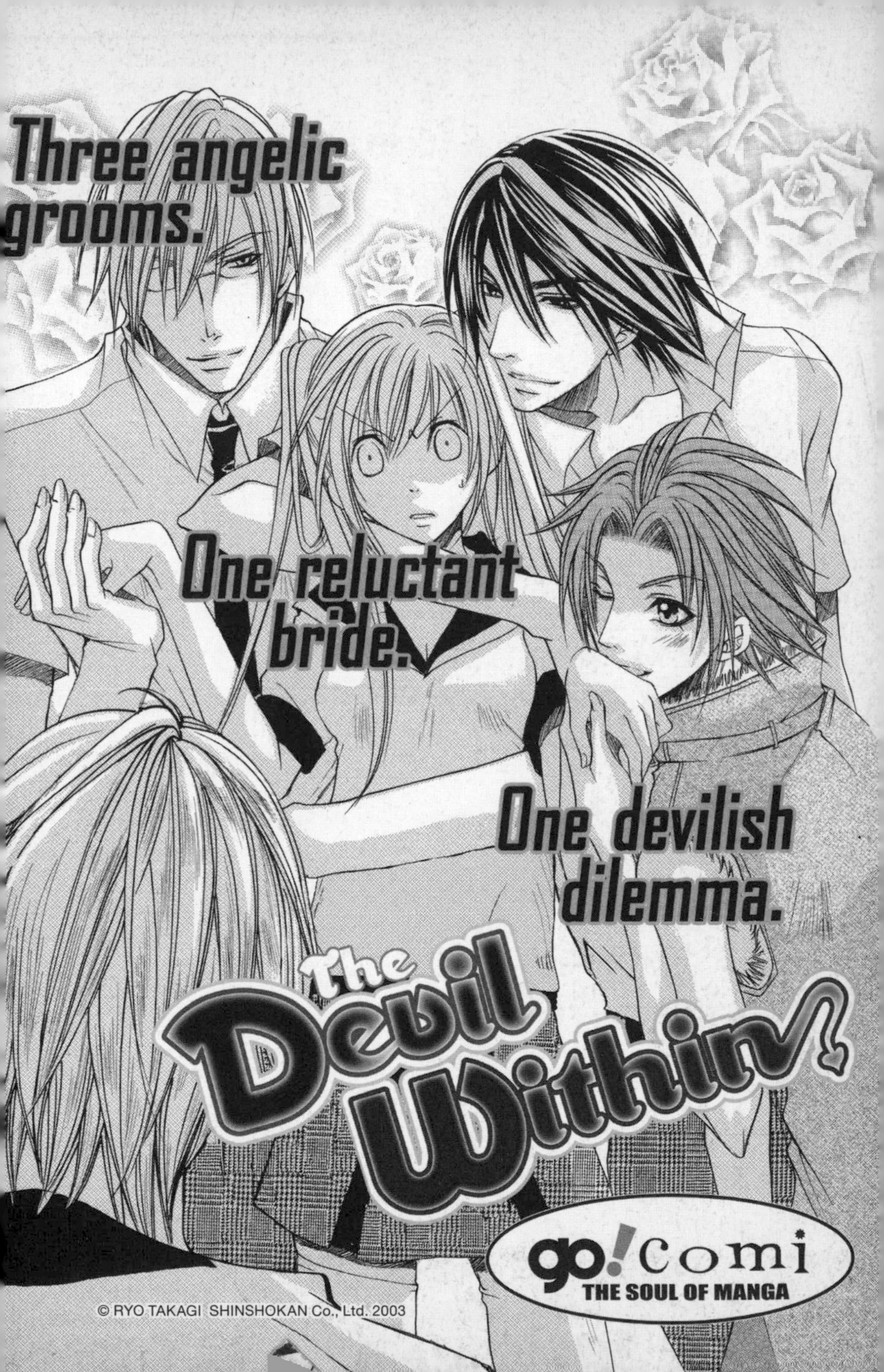

Three angelic grooms.
One reluctant bride.
One devilish dilemma.
The Devil Within!
go!comi
THE SOUL OF MANGA

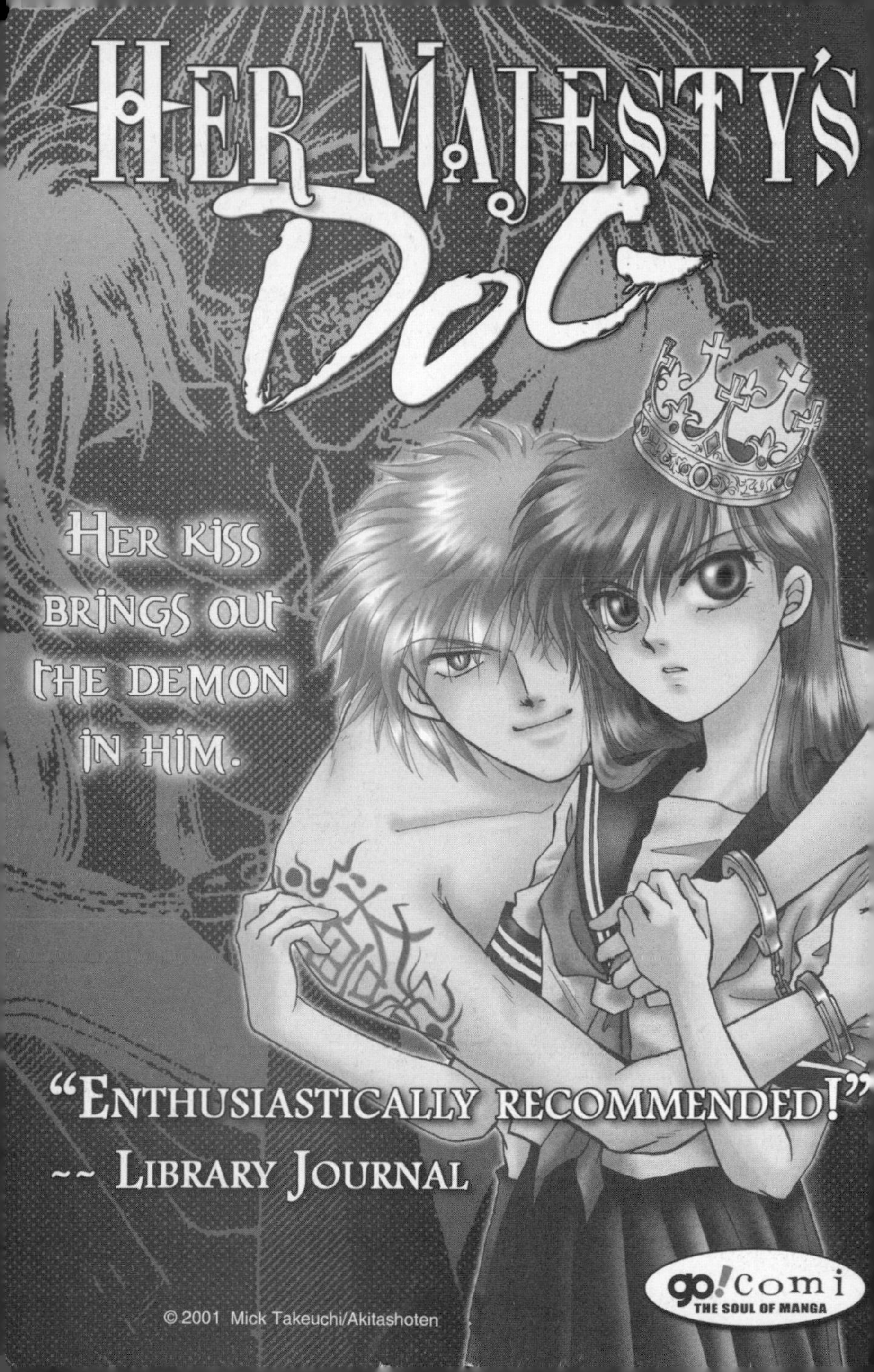

AUTHOR'S NOTE

The other day I went to an Italian restau-
rant and looked at the map of Italy they
had inside. I found myself muttering,
"Here's Calabria, and here's Umbria..."
I was saying the names of the
nation-states. Does this count as
an occupational disease!?

Visit You Higuri online at
www.youhiguri.com